Environmental, Social, and Governance (ESG) Investing

A Balanced Analysis of the Theory and Practice of a Sustainable Portfolio

Environmental, Social, and Governance (ESG) Investing

A Balanced Analysis of the Theory and Practice of a Sustainable Portfolio

John Hill
President and CEO of Derivatives Strategy Group, Rye, NY, United States

ACADEMIC PRESS

An imprint of Elsevier

Academic Press is an imprint of Elsevier
125 London Wall, London EC2Y 5AS, United Kingdom
525 B Street, Suite 1650, San Diego, CA 92101, United States
50 Hampshire Street, 5th Floor, Cambridge, MA 02139, United States
The Boulevard, Langford Lane, Kidlington, Oxford OX5 1GB, United Kingdom

British Library Cataloguing-in-Publication Data
A catalogue record for this book is available from the British Library

Library of Congress Cataloging-in-Publication Data
A catalog record for this book is available from the Library of Congress

ISBN: 978-0-12-818692-3

For Information on all Academic Press publications
visit our website at https://www.elsevier.com/books-and-journals

Publisher: Candice Janco
Acquisitions Editor: Scott J. Bentley
Editorial Project Manager: Redding Morse
Production Project Manager: Surya Narayanan
Cover Designer: Mark Rogers

Typeset by MPS Limited, Chennai, India

Working together
to grow libraries in
developing countries

www.elsevier.com • www.bookaid.org

Contents

1.	Introduction	1
	Principles for responsible investing	5
	Sustainable development goals	6
	The scope of this book	7
	Chapter 2: ESG, SRI, and impact investing	8
	Chapter 3: Theories of the firm	8
	Chapter 4: Fiduciary duty in investment management	9
	Chapter 5: Overview of financial institutions	9
	Chapter 6: Financial markets: equities	10
	Chapter 7: Financial markets: bonds	10
	Chapter 8: Shareholder engagement	10
	Chapter 9: Defining and measuring ESG performance	10
	Chapter 10: ESG in managing institutional investor funds	11
	Chapter 11: ESG in managing college and university endowments	11
	Chapter 12: ESG in managing sovereign wealth and government sponsored funds	11
	Chapter 13: ESG in managing family foundations and family offices	11
	Chapter 14: Faith-based investing	11
	Chapter 15: ESG investing-organizations having direct impact	12
	Chapter 16: What's next for ESG investing	12
2.	ESG, SRI, and impact investing	13
	Environmental, social, and governance investing	13
	Socially responsible investment	14
	Divestment: South Africa	14
	Divestment: sin stocks	15
	Impact investing	18
	The Rise Fund	19
	Mission investing	22
	United Nations principles for responsible investing	23
	United Nations sustainable development goals	25
	Financial returns versus social and environmental returns	25
	Global sustainable investment	26

3. Theory of the firm 29

The social responsibility of business is to increase its profits 29
Maximize shareholder welfare, not market value 32
Maximizing welfare 34
Shareholder rights 36
Summary 39
Appendix 39

4. Fiduciary duty in investment management 45

Addressing the Agency Problem 46
Fiduciary duty 48
Fiduciary obligations 48
"Prudent Man" rule 49
Uniform Prudent Investor Act 51
Uniform Prudent Management of Institutional Funds Act 53
Freshfields Report 54
Fiduciary II 56
United Nations Principles for Responsible Investing 57
Organization for Economic Cooperation and Development 58
Summary 58

5. Overview of financial institutions 59

Information asymmetries, moral hazard, and adverse selection 60
Commercial banks 63
Credit unions 64
Investment banks 66
Trading and research 68
Asset securitization 70
Mergers and acquisitions 71
Prime brokerage 71
Central banks 71
Conventional monetary tools 73
Unconventional monetary policy 74
Other central banks 75
Shadow banking: other financial intermediaries 76
Insurance companies 78
Categories of insurance 78
Prudential Financial Inc 83
MetLife Inc 84
Zurich Insurance Group 86
Pension funds 86
Largest pension funds 89
CalPERS 90
Florida State Board of Administration 92
Asset managers 92

	Hedge funds	94
	Private equity	94

6.	**Financial markets: equities**	97
	Risk, return, and diversification	98
	Capital asset pricing model	100
	Efficient market hypothesis	101
	Random walk	101
	Types of orders	101
	Equity trading venues	103
	Regulation	105
	Investing in equities	106
	Collective investment vehicles: mutual funds and exchange-traded funds	107
	Equity indexes	108
	ESG indexes	109
	MSCI	110
	FTSE Russell	111
	Morningstar	113
	Robo-advisors	115

7.	**Financial markets: bonds**	117
	Future value and present value	118
	Internal rate of return	120
	Credit instruments	121
	Fisher's law	122
	Term structure and yield curve	122
	Types of debt instruments: money market instruments	124
	Types of debt instruments: US Treasury securities	127
	Types of debt instruments: agency securities	129
	Types of debt instruments: corporate bonds	129
	Types of debt instruments: municipal securities	132
	Types of debt instruments: sovereign debt	133
	Fixed income trading	133
	Fixed income indexes and funds	136
	ESG bond funds	136
	ESG bond fund managers	139
	Green bonds	141

8.	**Shareholder engagement**	145
	Using engagement to create value for both investors and companies	146
	Shareholder activism	147
	Shareholder voting by proxy	149
	Key corporate governance and shareholder voting trends	150
	Recent shareholder proposals	152

Examples of shareholder engagement policies   155
Blackrock   156
CalPERS   157
T. Rowe Price   158
The New York City Comptroller's Office   159
Vanguard   159
Institutional investors acting together   161
The Investor Stewardship Group   163
The 30% Club   164
Sustainability Accounting Standards Board   165

9.   Defining and measuring ESG performance   167

ESG factors in portfolio construction   167
Standards for companies to report their ESG impacts   168
Global Reporting Initiative   169
Sustainability Accounting Standards Board   173
United Nations Global Compact   174
The United Nations Guiding Principles   175
Quality issues in ESG reporting   175
Corporate ESG reporting: findings   176
Services providing an assessment of corporate ESG   177
Sustainalytics   177
MSCI   177
RepRisk ESG Business Intelligence   178
Ceres   178
JUST Capital   179
How do mutual funds and ETFs rate ESG performance
    of portfolio companies?   180
Does ESG investing require lower returns?   180
Conceptual critiques of ESG investing   180
Empirical studies   181

10.   ESG in managing institutional investor funds   185

BlackRock   188
Sustainable investment choices   188
Fidelity   193
PIMCO   194
Goldman Sachs   198
J.P. Morgan   200
Betterment   201
JUST Capital   203

11.   ESG in managing college and university endowments   205

Hampshire College   209
Yale University   212

University of California   214
Brown University   215
Harvard   217
Columbia University   220
ESG investing in other schools   221
Organizations providing analysis, support, consulting, and
   investing services for endowment management   222
Commonfund   222
The Intentional Endowments Network   222
National Association of College and University Business
   Officers   223
The Forum for Sustainable and Responsible Investment   224

12. ESG in managing sovereign wealth and government sponsored funds

                                                                     227

Transparency issues and concerns   229
Linaburg—Maduell Transparency Index   232
ESG investing by SWFs   232
ESG investing policy in selected sovereign wealth funds   235
Norway's Government Pension Fund-Global   235
The French Pension Reserve Fund   238
Temasek Holdings Private Limited   239
China Investment Corporation   240
New Zealand Superannuation Fund   241
Future Fund, Australia's Sovereign Wealth Fund   242
Middle East Sovereign Wealth Funds   243
Mubadala Investment Company (Abu Dhabi)   243
Public Investment Fund of Saudi Arabia   244
Other sovereign wealth fund activities   245

13. ESG in managing family foundations and family offices

                                                                     247

The family office   248
Chan Zuckerberg Initiative   250
The Giving Pledge   253
Bill & Melinda Gates Foundation   253
Lilly Endowment Inc   257
Day One Fund   257
Open Society Foundations   258
The Robert Wood Johnson Foundation   260
The Rockefeller Foundation   261
Bloomberg Family Foundation (Bloomberg Philanthropies)   262
The Ford Foundation   265
Carnegie Corporation of New York   267

Providing Services to the Foundation Community   269
Council on Foundations   269
The Foundation Center   270

14. Faith-based investing   273

Common features   273
Christian values investing   274
GuideStone   275
New Covenant Funds   275
The Interfaith Center on Corporate Responsibility   276
Christian Super   277
Timothy Plan Funds   281
Eventide Funds   282
Catholic values investing: socially responsible investment
  guidelines   284
USCCB investment policies   287
Catholic values mutual funds   289
Ave Maria Mutual Funds   289
LKCM Aquinas Catholic Equity Fund   291
Catholic values ETF   291
Islamic values investing   291
Green sukuk bonds   293
Islamic values indexes, mutual funds, and ETFs   294
MSCI Islamic index series   296
FTSE Shariah indexes   296
Amana Mutual Funds   297
The Iman Fund   298
Shariah compliant ETFs   299
Jewish values investing   299
Jewish values indexes, mutual funds, and ETFs   300

15. ESG investing-organizations having direct impact 303

Women's Sports Foundation   305
USA for UNHCR   308
Michael J. Fox Foundation for Parkinson's Research   309
Elton John AIDS Foundation   310
Water.org   310
Ocean Conservancy   312
Project AWARE   313
Sea Shepherd Conservation Society   313
UNICEF and UNESCO   315
UNICEF   315
UNESCO   317
Red Cross and Red Crescent Societies   319
The Salvation Army   322

Meals on Wheels   327
Habitat for Humanity   327

16. **What's next for ESG investing?**   329

Empirical studies of environmental, social, and governance
  investment performance   331
The future of environmental, social, and governance investing   332
Environmental, social, and governance investment concerns
  to be addressed   333

References   337
Index   341

Chapter 1

Introduction

Chapter Outline

Principles for responsible investing 5
Sustainable development goals 6
The scope of this book 7
Chapter 2: ESG, SRI, and impact investing 8
Chapter 3: Theories of the firm 8
Chapter 4: Fiduciary duty in investment management 9
Chapter 5: Overview of financial institutions 9
Chapter 6: Financial markets: equities 10
Chapter 7: Financial markets: bonds 10
Chapter 8: Shareholder engagement 10
Chapter 9: Defining and measuring ESG performance 10
Chapter 10: ESG in managing institutional investor funds 11
Chapter 11: ESG in managing college and university endowments 11
Chapter 12: ESG in managing sovereign wealth and government sponsored funds 11
Chapter 13: ESG in managing family foundations and family offices 11
Chapter 14: Faith-based investing 11
Chapter 15: ESG investing-organizations having direct impact 12
Chapter 16: What's next for ESG investing 12

Individuals and institutional investors alike have increasingly expressed their concerns about the environmental, social, and governance (ESG) practices of companies they invest in. In annual surveys asking institutional investors to rate the characteristics of a company that they most respect, "ethical business practices" has risen to the top, over other categories such as "strong management." In the last decade, the amount of assets being invested in socially responsible investment products has increased dramatically, and with the growing importance of the Millennial generation and the emergence of Generation Z, this trend is likely to accelerate. Roughly one-quarter of all global assets under management (AUM) are now being invested with a consideration of ESG factors (GSIA, 2017). It's estimated that ESG AUM global totals are over $23 trillion. In the United States, ESG-focused AUM were estimated to be $12 trillion at the start of 2018. This is about 26% of total assets under professional management. As impressive as these totals are, interest in ESG seems even more widespread. One Wall Street firm found that 75% of individual investors sought to include ESG considerations into their investment choices. These trends are not going unnoticed. All the large

Environmental, Social, and Governance (ESG) Investing. DOI: https://doi.org/10.1016/B978-0-12-818692-3.00001-3

investment managers have developed funds oriented to investors concerned with ESG issues. Undoubtedly, some of these offerings have more to do with marketing the concept than rigorously pursuing ESG goals, but the fact that they exist points to recognition of growing investor interest.

Some key takeaways on the growth of ESG investing:

- Growth of AUM in ESG investments will continue and be even more significant in the coming years.
- ESG portfolios can have financial performance like conventional portfolios, but this requires attention to the risk and return characteristics of the portfolio components. Simply divesting "sin" stocks is likely to result in portfolio underperformance, which can have substantial risks, including insufficient returns to support retiree and other beneficiary income requirements, and may result in employment risks to fund managers.
- Significant issues remain in defining ESG factors, measurement of impacts and reporting.
- While ESG is growing, it is still the focus of a minority of investors; 75% of US investing is in conventional portfolios and 80% of university and college endowments similarly follow conventional investing prescriptions.

One of the world's largest fixed income investment managers identified the following factors as drivers of the increased focus on ESG investment (PIMCO, 2017):

- Good governance is systemically important.
   The global financial crisis of 2008 brought a renewed awareness of the importance of improved corporate governance.
- Public−private partnerships are expanding.
   Public−private collaboration has grown to tackle broader social and environmental issues.
- Growing recognition that climate change is a reality.
   Climate change is now (almost) universally acknowledged. Public and private initiatives include sustainable investment portfolios and more disclosure of climate-related financial risks.
- Energy sources are shifting.
   Natural gas usage is increasing and renewable energy sources are becoming cheaper and scalable.
- Technology is changing what we demand and how we consume.
   Technology is driving widespread change, and most sectors of the economy are seeing paradigm shifts in the way business is conducted. Companies unwilling or unable to change are falling behind and are likely to put investors at risk.
- Social media is influencing social norms.

With its borderless nature, and dominance by Millennials and Gen Xers, social media has been effective in communicating new values and norms in responsible consumption and investing.

- We are living longer.

  By 2050, there will be 2.3 billion people in the world over age 65. Sustainability issues will directly affect financial security of these retirees.

- Demographics are changing.

  Millennials have become the largest population cohort and are increasingly changing business, financial, and political landscapes. For example, younger generations are driving the fast growth of the "green bond" market and the field of sustainable finance in general.

- Regulation is providing tailwinds.

  ESG considerations have driven new regulations in a growing list of countries. Examples include the shutdown of nuclear power in Germany, the Supervisory Review and Evaluation Process (SREP) in Europe, which governs subordinated financial debt, and France's mandatory reporting of climate risk, which raises the bar for financial institutions. In the United States, regulatory support is not as aggressive, but may be growing.

- Value chains are global.

  Large corporations' value chains are increasingly global. Global investors can be quick to punish companies for child labor practices, human rights issues, environmental impact and poor governance.

While ESG investing is growing in importance, it is also clear that most investing today is done with little if any concern about ESG factors. In the quarterly earnings calls that companies hold with investors ESG issues rarely if ever are brought up. If 25% of global AUM are invested with at least some reference to ESG factors, then 75%, a very large majority, still do not consider these factors. In many academic communities, ESG issues are strongly and fervently supported. Yet university endowment ESG investments are estimated at less than 20% of total AUM, leaving 80% of endowments to be invested using more traditional criteria. It would be naïve and counterproductive to think that all these investors are ill informed, or unconcerned about ESG issues. An important perspective of this book is to fairly consider the point of view of those investors who are not yet convinced of the relevance of ESG factors to their investment decision-making.

Until recently, the popular wisdom has been that ESG investors would have to accept a lower return from their "virtuous" portfolios. This assumption is no longer universally accepted and empirical evidence, although mixed, seems in most cases to support the contention that ESG investing does not have to underperform traditional portfolios. Early studies looking at simple divestment strategies found that those funds often underperformed.

But more nuanced strategies are seen to support the conclusion that ESG investments need not result in subpar financial performance.

Morningstar, the highly respected rater of investment funds, in its review of ESG fund performance in 2017 concluded that "sustainable funds are competitive on price and performance" and "performance skews positive over both the short term and the long term."

There have also been several thorough reviews of meta-studies of ESG performance. These reviews support the conclusion that companies with strong ESG performance also score highly on traditional financial metrics (Morningstar, 2018).

There is an increasing belief that sustainability and profitability are two complementary sides of the same coin. But there are several challenges to investing both profitably and responsibly, or "doing well while doing good." There are difficulties in identifying ESG goals, and there is an equally challenging task of understanding if specific actions will be efficient in effecting those goals. And how do we measure companies' progress?

"Arguably, the first waves of socially responsible investing were implemented too soon, were at times too politically focused, and attempted to use poor to non-existent data, which often resulted in somewhat poorly constructed, ineffective negative screens. Is it any wonder more sophisticated investors looked the other way?" (Krosinsky and Purdom, 2017)

There will always be differences of opinion on both goals and means, but there is growing consensus on at least some of these factors and the lack of perfection should be no excuse for not doing the best that we can. Now, investors and investment managers are able to find more politically balanced investments, have much better (although still not perfect) data, and are able to construct better and better screens. A study of fund flows in US open-end equity mutual funds from March 2016 to June 2018 (Kleeman and Sargis, 2018) supports the perception that ESG considerations are increasingly important. Some findings:

- Investors focus on excluding funds with poor Morningstar Sustainability Ratings-Funds which received the lowest sustainability ratings experienced a -3.7% growth rate, while funds in the two highest categories of sustainability ratings saw $+1.4\%$ to $+1.5\%$ higher inflows.
- Investors avoid funds with high negative Controversy scores.
   Newsworthy incidents are seen to have an impact on stakeholders. Investors were found to react strongly to the extreme ends of the Controversy score range: pulling more money out of funds with the greatest (negative) controversy.
- Within the group of funds rated in the lowest category of the Morningstar Sustainability Rating, a fund with a higher ESG score performed better than funds with lower scores.

While funds in this category still did poorly in terms of fund flow growth rates as compared to funds with higher Sustainability Ratings, there was a relative differentiation in that investors were seen to be less likely to sell out of funds with higher ESG scores as compared to funds with lower ESG scores.

"Doing well while doing good." While some activists may place a higher value on ESG factors than on financial returns, a broader range of investors want to have it all: investing in companies that earn a decent return and contribute positive environmental and social value. One path to achieving this duality is to focus on the longer term, as opposed to managing only for the next quarter.

From a speech by Mark Carney, Governor of the Bank of England (Carney, 2018): "There are two paradoxes in managing the financial risks from climate change. The first is that the future will be past. Climate change is a tragedy of the horizon which will impose major costs on future generations that the current one has no direct incentive to fix. The catastrophic impacts of climate change will be felt beyond the horizons of most actors. Once climate change becomes a clear and present danger to financial stability it may already be too late to stabilize the atmosphere. The second paradox is that success is failure. Too rapid a move towards a low-carbon economy could materially damage financial stability. A wholesale reassessment of prospects could destabilize markets, spark a pro-cyclical crystallization of losses and lead to a persistent tightening of financial conditions: a climate Minsky moment. The Prudential Regulation Authority (PRA) recognizes these paradoxes could have implications for the financial system. The first implies a need to adjust time horizons for the long term, and to consider actions today in light of how the financial risks from climate change may evolve in the future. The second implies the need to find the right balance; it is foreseeable financial risks will be realized in some form, the challenge is minimizing their impact while firms and society maximize the opportunities."

Modern Portfolio Theory has given us the twin concepts of risk and return in evaluating investment portfolios. The advent of ESG investing adds a third leg. An efficient portfolio frontier can now be conceptualized as a three-dimensional surface, optimizing risk, return, and social impact.

The large asset managers have all developed policies for implementing ESG investment strategies. Underlying many of them are the United Nations Principles for Responsible Investment and Sustainable Development Goals.

Principles for responsible investing

Principles for responsible investing (PRI) is an independent nonprofit organization supported by, but not part of the United Nations. It has developed a set of six voluntary and aspirational investment principles which have attracted a large group of global investment professionals. As of 2018, there were approximately 2000 signatories, with almost $90 trillion in AUM. More than half of the firms were located in Europe and 456 were North American.

The six principles are as follows:

- Principle 1: We will incorporate ESG issues into investment analysis and decision-making processes.
- Principle 2: We will be active owners and incorporate ESG issues into our ownership policies and practices.
- Principle 3: We will seek appropriate disclosure on ESG issues by the entities in which we invest.
- Principle 4: We will promote acceptance and implementation of the Principles within the investment industry.
- Principle 5: We will work together to enhance our effectiveness in implementing the Principles.
- Principle 6: We will each report on our activities and progress towards implementing the Principles.

Sustainable development goals

In September 2015, the United Nations General Assembly adopted the 2030 Agenda for sustainable development that includes 17 sustainable development goals (SDGs). The SDGs address global challenges including those related to poverty, inequality, climate, environmental degradation, prosperity, and peace and justice. They are as follows:

- Goal 1: No poverty
- Goal 2: Zero hunger
- Goal 3: Good health and well-being
- Goal 4: Quality education
- Goal 5: Gender equality
- Goal 6: Clean water and sanitation
- Goal 7: Affordable and clean energy
- Goal 8: Decent work and economic growth
- Goal 9: Industry, innovation, and infrastructure
- Goal 10: Reduced inequality
- Goal 11: Sustainable cities and communities
- Goal 12: Responsible consumption and production
- Goal 13: Climate action
- Goal 14: Life below water
- Goal 15: Life on land
- Goal 16: Peace and justice strong institutions
- Goal 17: Partnerships to achieve the goal

For many organizations and investors, the SDGs are an aspirational blueprint for action.

Companies today are approaching social responsibility from many different directions. They are minimizing their carbon footprint; creating a workplace where all employees can feel valued and empowered; working with customers, suppliers, and all stakeholders to ensure ESG goals are understood and acted upon, while recognizing that there is a continuing diversity of opinions and stages of development. All these activities are important in today's world and the world we will leave to our children.

The scope of this book

ESG investing is a controversial topic, to say the least, at every step of the way. There are alternative beliefs in the appropriate weight ESG factors should receive in investing, and in managing individual firms themselves. There are challenges in defining ESG goals and means, difficulties in defining, measuring and reporting company ESG performance, and alternative often conflicting studies of the relative performance of sustainable investments. Heightening the controversy is the passion with which advocates for each side hold their opinions. Each side is convinced that they are right and not only that the other side is wrong, but that they must be evil to hold such opposing opinions. Most books and articles on this topic are written with a preexisting tilt to one side or the other on this topic. This book takes the radical approach of attempting to present each side fairly. Undoubtedly, this will prove to irritate both proponents and opponents of ESG investing. To paraphrase former New York City Mayor Ed Koch: if both sides are mad at me, I know I am doing my job. But this author also believes that ESG investments are here to stay and will likely continue to grow, especially as the Millennial generation becomes a greater investment force. Individuals are increasingly understood as not just income maximizing shareholders, or profit maximizing corporate managers, but are also concerned citizens who value clean air, clean water, and good governance principles. The objectives of this book are twofold: first, provide an overview of the competing theories and empirical evidence underlying ESG investment and second, summarize some of the most interesting forms of ESG investment vehicles and modalities themselves. The book is focused on ESG considerations in investment decisions, with an emphasis on portfolio construction. But there are several additional modalities for investors to give effect to their ESG sensitivities. Consequently, topics such as shareholder activism, impact and mission investing, family foundations, and faith-based investing are also discussed.

In Chapter 2, ESG, SRI, and impact investing, we define and contrast commonly used terms such as socially responsible investing, ESG investing, and mission investing. Chapter 3, Theories of the firm, summarizes the theoretical arguments for and against ESG activities by individual firms. In

Chapter 4, Fiduciary duty in investment management, we discuss the obligations of fiduciaries, those who manage money on behalf of beneficiaries. To what extent are they permitted to consider factors other than simple short-term financial maximization? To lay the foundation to understand ESG investment concepts, Chapters 5−7 present an overview of financial institutions and the equity and bond markets. An important means of "nudging" or influencing companies to adopt ESG friendly behavior is for investors to be active shareholders, engaging with company management and voting on shareholder resolutions. These activities are covered in Chapter 8, Shareholder engagement. Chapters 10−15 look at ESG investment activity in different kinds of organizations. But before we do that, we need to understand how ESG factors are defined, measured and reported. These important topics are covered in Chapter 9, Defining and measuring ESG performance. Then we can go on to look at ESG investment by institutional investment managers (Chapter 10: ESG in managing institutional investor funds), university endowments (Chapter 11: ESG in managing college and university endowments), sovereign and government sponsored funds (Chapter 12: ESG in managing sovereign wealth and government sponsored funds), family foundations and family offices (Chapter 13: ESG in managing family foundations and family offices), and faith-based investing (Chapter 14: Faith-based investing). In Chapter 15, ESG investing-organizations having direct impact, we look at impact investing in some charitable organizations.

Here are brief descriptions of each of the chapters to follow.

Chapter 2: ESG, SRI, and impact investing

The various terms used to describe investing with a social purpose are often used interchangeably and in a somewhat confusing manner. In this chapter, we describe the differences among the various styles and give a brief historical context.

Chapter 3: Theories of the firm

Desired ESG outcomes can be addressed not only by structuring investment portfolios but also by more direct means such as corporate social actions. Are a firm's board of directors and management free to use corporate resources for the betterment of society? Or are they required only to focus on maximizing financial return to shareholders? This chapter looks at both sides of this argument. Some of the sources to be covered are as follows:

- Milton Friedman makes the argument to maximize shareholder value. Social issues are reserved for actions by elected government.
- Zingales et al. says the firm should maximize shareholder welfare, including monetary and nonmonetary issues.

- The question for Zingales: how to identify and measure nonmonetary values?
- If there are long-run business risks from ESG issues, shouldn't even a narrow focus on financial return require addressing these issues?
- Contrary to popular belief, there is no legal obligation for corporations to maximize shareholder value. This is the argument put forth in Lynn Stout "The shareholder value myth: how putting shareholders first harms investors, corporations, and the public." The theory of what a firm's managers should and shouldn't do is presented in some depth in this chapter.

In August 2019, the Business Roundtable issued a statement asserting that short-term profit maximization is not enough. The statement, signed by 181 CEOs of America's largest corporations, affirmed the need to manage their businesses in a way that supports the long-term interests of all stakeholders: employees, customers, suppliers, the local community, as well as shareholders.

Chapter 4: Fiduciary duty in investment management

Fiduciaries manage assets on behalf of beneficiaries. They have several obligations of duty to protect those beneficiaries who in most cases do not have the information or expertise that the asset managers have. The fiduciary relationship is analyzed in the context of the Agency-Principal problem.

A nuanced argument for including ESG factors is made in the United Nations Environmental Programmes' Finance Initiative "Freshfields Report":

> ... *prudence of any investment will only be assessed within the context of the overall investment strategy ... no reason why investment strategies should not include investments with positive ESG characteristics ... No investment should be made purely to give effect to the personal views of the decision maker ... In short, there appears to be no bar to integrating ESG considerations into the day-to-day process of fund management, provided the focus is always on the beneficiaries/purposes of the fund and not on unrelated objectives.*

Chapter 5: Overview of financial institutions

This chapter lays the groundwork for understanding the financial participants, products, and services which are prominent in later chapters. It starts with the underlying economic functions of banks, outlines what it is that commercial and investment banks do, and covers the basics of banking regulation.

Chapter 6: Financial markets: equities

Much of ESG investing is in equities markets. This chapter presents the theoretical background including modern portfolio theory, describes the markets for equity distribution and trading, and explores modern products such as mutual funds and exchange traded funds.

Chapter 7: Financial markets: bonds

Fixed income markets are hugely important to funding corporate, government, and the financial sector's capital requirements and instruments such as "green bonds" are increasingly playing a significant role in ESG finance. Theoretical background for interest rates and debt markets are covered here.

Chapter 8: Shareholder engagement

There is a growing importance of shareholders engaging in active dialogue with investee company management. There is also much more care given to voting on corporate resolutions. These topics and the detailed characteristics of recent shareholder resolutions and voting behavior are explored in this chapter.

Chapter 9: Defining and measuring ESG performance

As we have seen, the amount of funds invested with consideration of ESG factors has grown dramatically. But how do investors and investment managers know which companies are performing well on ESG issues? What are the sources of guidance and principles for corporate self-reporting on ESG criteria? In this chapter, we will delve into the specifics of how ESG factors are defined and measured, and how corporate performance against these factors is reported.

Much of the work covered in this chapter is done to help construct portfolios that have positive ESG characteristics but also have expected financial returns that are consistent with conventional portfolios. The second half of this chapter summarizes reviews of empirical research that on the whole confirm that ESG portfolios can be constructed to have the expectation of earning market rates of return.

With these chapters providing a solid foundation, we then move on to the second half of the book, where we investigate how a broad range of different categories of investors are incorporating ESG factors into their decision-making.

Chapter 10: ESG in managing institutional investor funds

The dramatic increase in ESG investments has led to the creation and popularity of ESG offerings at every large investment management firm. This chapter looks at what some of the largest institutional asset managers are doing in ESG investment.

Chapter 11: ESG in managing college and university endowments

While ESG issues have received a lot of attention on college campuses, only about 20% of college and university endowments include investments ranking high on ESG criteria in their portfolios. What are the issues, metrics, and operational details of the investments of the endowments which are active in ESG? A Bloomberg Opinion article was headlined: "Yale Champions Social Investing (Whatever That Is) ... The broad sustainable movement has garnered a lot of attention but done a poor job of explaining what it is and what it wants to do" (Kaissar, 2018). Hopefully, this book and this chapter in particular will help lift the veil on university ESG investing.

Chapter 12: ESG in managing sovereign wealth and government sponsored funds

Norway, Saudi Arabia, Singapore, and other nations have sovereign wealth and government sponsored funds which have been active investors in global markets. More recently, some have become leaders in developing alternative investment strategies. This chapter looks more closely at their activities.

Chapter 13: ESG in managing family foundations and family offices

Multiinvestor funds must address potential disagreements among their beneficiaries with respect to investment goals. Family foundations and family offices have the advantage of fewer beneficiaries and are (usually) able to identify investment goals with more unanimity. Accordingly, some of the most focused ESG investing has come out of family offices such as Rockefeller, Ford, and Gates.

Chapter 14: Faith-based investing

Investment funds organized according to religious principles were some of the earliest sources of socially responsible investing. In this chapter we look at investing styles based on Christian, Islamic, and Jewish values.

Chapter 15: ESG investing-organizations having direct impact

The previous chapters looked at several different sources of ESG investing. In this chapter, we consider some examples of charities, organizations which are the recipients of those investments. They are the "tip of the spear" in "making a difference." These are enterprises that generate direct social or environmental benefits and can have the most focused impact on ESG issues. Donations or other gifts to these organizations are made with the intention of generating positive, measurable social and environmental impact. Generating a financial return, if any, is a secondary objective at best.

Chapter 16: What's next for ESG investing

The final chapter summarizes some thoughts for the future of ESG investing.

Chapter 2

ESG, SRI, and impact investing

Chapter Outline

Environmental, social, and
governance investing   13
Socially responsible investment   14
Divestment: South Africa   14
Divestment: sin stocks   15
Impact investing   18
   The Rise Fund   19
Mission investing   22

United Nations principles for
responsible investing   23
United Nations sustainable
development goals   25
Financial returns versus social and
environmental returns   25
Global sustainable investment   26

There is no universal agreement on definitions for the various styles of investment which seek a positive social or environmental outcome in addition to earning at least some financial return. There is significant overlap in these styles and many practitioners use similar names interchangeably to identify them. In this chapter, we will present some of these investment styles while recognizing that usage can be arbitrary and ambiguous.

Environmental, social, and governance investing

The term "environmental, social, and governance (ESG) investing" is attributed to a 2004 report (The Global Compact, 2004) which reported the conviction of more than 20 of the world's largest financial institutions that positively addressing ESG issues is important to the overall quality of companies' management. They further stated that: "Companies that perform better with regard to these issues can increase shareholder value by, for example, properly managing risks, anticipating regulatory action or accessing new markets, while at the same time contributing to the sustainable development of the societies in which they operate. Moreover, these issues can have a strong impact on reputation and brands, an increasingly important part of company value."

ESG is sometimes used as a catchall label to describe any investing style which has an element of social purpose. While understanding that there is a need for a shorthand umbrella label, we prefer to reserve this term for a more sophisticated approach to portfolio investing, wherein the

Environmental, Social, and Governance (ESG) Investing. DOI: https://doi.org/10.1016/B978-0-12-818692-3.00002-5
13

investor or fund manager invests in public debt and/or equity, often via mutual funds or exchange-traded funds. The portfolio often has an objective of earning a market rate of return, while investing in assets which score favorably on ESG factors. We investigate this style of investing in detail in later chapters.

Socially responsible investment

Socially responsible investment (SRI) focuses on the impact of companies in specific areas of interest. It most commonly involves investing using a negative screen which would exclude companies engaging in activities the investor finds undesirable. For example, an SRI investment strategy could exclude companies involved in alcohol, tobacco, gambling, and/or guns. Countries with patterns of human rights abuses have also been screened out of portfolios. Historically, SRI has also excluded companies active in apartheid era South Africa and more recently companies engaged in commerce involving conflict minerals. The divestment is often made relying on indexes provided by one or more vendors or consultants. This investment style doesn't always have to be focused on exclusion of bad actors. It may instead proactively invest in companies which feature activity in social justice, or environmental solutions. It may also include investment in organizations providing services to a local community. But the most common distinction is that SRI factors result in screening out certain companies while, in contrast ESG investing gives guidance on what companies to include within an overall portfolio approach. A major concern is that a strategy of simply excluding companies may lead to portfolio returns that underperform market benchmarks. Older studies showing the historical underperformance of these funds are often cited as evidence of the poor performance of all SRI and ESG funds, whether divestment oriented or more sophisticated.

An interesting example of a divestment strategy was the focus on excluding companies active in apartheid era South Africa.

Divestment: South Africa

Divestment as an instrument of social change is most associated with the antiapartheid movement protesting conditions in South Africa. In 1962 the United Nations passed a resolution condemning apartheid, but Western companies for the most part continued with business as usual. Beginning in the 1960s, students and others sought to bring attention to western companies operating in South Africa and began a campaign to influence those companies to exit the country. In 1977 a code of conduct for ethically operating in South Africa was drafted by a Philadelphia preacher, the Reverend Doctor Leon Sullivan. These guidelines, later expanded, became known as the

Sullivan Principles, and specified what we would now consider to be basic human rights:

- nonsegregation of the races in all eating, comfort, and work facilities;
- equal and fair employment practices;
- equal pay for all employees doing equal or comparable work;
- initiation of and development of training programs for all;
- increasing the number of blacks and other nonwhites in management and supervisory positions;
- improving the quality of life for blacks and other nonwhites outside the work environment in such areas as housing, transportation, school, recreation, and health facilities; and
- working to eliminate laws and customs that impede social, economic, and political justice.

Today, this looks like a pretty basic HR policy for any modern company. At the time, however, these guidelines were in direct conflict with the policies and laws of the South African government and would make it impossible for companies to operate there. But why were they significant? They might just be a toothless statement by an American social activist. What put weight behind them, however, was that Sullivan was in fact a member of the board of General Motors and General Motors was the largest employer in South Africa. (GM would sell its South African operations in 1986. It would later reenter the country beginning in 1997, after democratic elections.) The Sullivan Principles, and support from the United Nations and others led to many shareholder resolutions calling for exiting South Africa, and pressure on institutional investors to divest holdings in companies active there.

By the late 1980s, 155 US universities had dropped or "divested" holdings of companies active in South Africa from their endowments' portfolios. States, counties, and cities across America also divested shares of companies in South Africa in their pension funds. Some argue that divestment often hurts most the people its proponents seek to help. Companies operating in South Africa were providing jobs and believed they had some leverage in seeking to weaken apartheid. If they were to exit the country, they argued, their employees would directly suffer, and the company would lose any negotiating power with the existing government. They favored a policy of "constructive engagement." While this argument has some merit, progress to end apartheid in South Africa was negligible and divestment along with sanctions, boycotts, and internal resistance is given much of the credit for bringing about the end to this policy.

Divestment: sin stocks

The so-called sin stocks are shares in companies which operate in the alcohol, tobacco, gambling, and other industries which are considered by some to represent human vices or sins. In most Western countries, however, these industries and their products and services are legally permitted by the laws of the land and are regulated by various governmental bodies. Despite being legal, some investors consider these industries to pose not only moral and ethical risks but financial risk due to potential regulatory, litigation, and supply chain uncertainties. While there is a case to be made that divestment of companies in South Africa had a major role in ending apartheid, its less clear that divestment of sin stocks has had an effect in terms of either swaying individual behavior or of changing corporate actions. And divestment may have negative financial consequences for the investor. Over various time horizons the shares of tobacco companies, gun makers, and oil and gas companies have all outperformed market indexes. Investors may agree on goals for a more sustainable society with reduced carbon emissions, but there is little evidence that divestment will accomplish those goals. Selling Exxon shares may have some symbolic value, but it is unlikely to have any influence on the demand for oil and gas.

There are several challenges to a divestment strategy:

- Difficulties in identifying companies—one may want to divest holdings in gun resellers, but what is the appropriate identifier? Walmart sells a lot of guns, but guns and ammunition account for a tiny fraction of Walmart sales.
- Effectiveness—in most cases, divestment has simply resulted in substituting one group of shareholders for another, often more enthusiastic group of shareholders.
- Collateral damage—although divesting energy company stocks is likely to have little impact, what if it did? If oil and gas prices were to rise precipitously, the poorest members of society would suffer disproportionately.
- Costs—a divestment program could be costly to the organization both in terms of expenses incurred to design, enact, and track performance and in terms of potential below market investment performance. For organizations with funding requirements, such as pension funds, this can be a significant risk.
- Employment risk—for funds with transparent reporting requirements and funding obligations, below market financial returns can be a source of employment risk for portfolio managers, executives, and board members, especially where the social goals of the divestment program are controversial and do not reflect a broad consensus of beneficiaries.
- Fiduciary duty—in many cases, investment managers have obligations to beneficiaries that would preclude sacrificing financial gains (more about this in Chapter 4: Fiduciary duty in investment management). If a simple divestment policy leads to submarket returns, these managers would be challenged to defend their strategy.

A public pension fund, then, would need to carefully balance ethical considerations with its responsibility to provide for its financial obligations. Nonetheless, investors with deep ethical commitments continue to support the divestment of sin stocks.

One such "sin" industry is tobacco. Beginning in the 1950s tobacco smoking was found to be linked to lung and other cancers. The industry was revealed to be killing their customers and causing massive public health expenditures. Lawsuits were filed against the largest companies. At first the companies prevailed in these court cases, but in the late 1990s the tide would turn, the plaintiffs started to have more success and increasingly substantial damages were awarded. There was now little debate on the damage caused by tobacco to smokers, and there was a growing recognition of the financial burden of medical care placed on individuals and society as a whole. Consequently, investors began to divest holdings of tobacco companies. But the tobacco companies produced above market returns for their continuing investors. The FTSE All World Tobacco Index, for example, showed a 988% return from 2000 to 2016 versus a 131% return for the FTSE All World index. One study estimated that CalPERS alone forfeited $3.6 billion by excluding tobacco investments. Some divestment proponents make the argument that tobacco companies are unlikely to continue their success as adverse regulations will spread across the globe to countries that have seen recent growth in cigarette consumption. But many pension funds continue to hold their tobacco investments. They reason that they owe their beneficiaries the best possible financial return, and they cannot justify excluding an industry which does not operate in violation of international and country laws. This last issue, how to think about "sin" industries or companies which deal in disfavored products or services but still operate in compliance with all laws and regulations, is a common source of confrontation. Take the case of gun makers and retailers.

In early 2018, in response to horrific shootings of American civilians, several financial institutions stated that they would stop financing gun manufacturers and retailers. Citigroup was the first bank to announce restrictions on its lending activities to firearms retailers who did not meet the bank's requirements. It said it would require all of its customers to follow several principles restricting gun sales, including banning the sale of bump stocks, limiting sales to people over the age of 21, and ensuring background checks are performed before firearms are sold. A Bank of America executive made public comments to the effect that her bank would cease providing funds for manufacturers of military style firearms for civilian use. The executive also stated that she did not believe that this action would solve the problem of gun violence and that issues of mental health and gun ownership are matters of public policy. Other financial institutions seemed to be moving more slowly, engaging with gun company managements and participating in policy initiatives. Banking is one of the most heavily regulated industries and the banks' actions did not go unnoticed by lawmakers. Mike Crapo, Republican Senator from Idaho and Chair of the Senate Banking Committee sent a letter to the CEOs of Citigroup and Bank of America criticizing them for restricting business with the firearms industry. Crapo called out the banks for using their size and reach to influence social policy and demanded to know how they collect information about consumers who purchase guns. "We should all be concerned if banks like yours seek to replace legislators and policy makers and attempt to manage social policy by limiting access to credit," wrote Crapo. Banks "should not deny financial services to customers they disfavor." While many support measures to restrict gun violence, there is concern about the danger in banks attempting to circumvent the political process. What are the risks involved in granting bank executives the ability to effectively ban the purchase of something that is legal? What if banking executives decided abortion clinics should not receive funding? Or that loans for cars running on gasoline should be denied? Could a few banking executives or regulators decide to deny credit card processing and other financial services to businesses that support gay marriage? This would set a precedent in allowing banks to settle controversial political and social disputes with none of the checks and balances inherent in our system of government. Given the importance of credit to the economy, it would seem to be a dangerous route to take.

There have also been attempts to use regulatory agencies to deny access to banking services by companies in "sin" industries. In 2018 the Chairman of the FDIC, Yelena McWilliams, stated that: "Regulatory threats, undue pressure, coercion, and intimidation designed to restrict access to financial services for lawful businesses have no place at this agency…Under my leadership, the FDIC's oversight responsibilities will be exercised based on our laws and our regulations, not personal or political beliefs."

Impact investing

The term "impact investing" was coined in 2007 by The Rockefeller Foundation which has over one hundred years' experience in charitable investing. Traditional impact investors large and small have recently been joined by dedicated funds and products from the very largest investment management firms. Consequently, the global impact investment market has ballooned to an estimated $228 billion in 2017.

In contrast to other investment styles, impact investing is typically more direct and focuses on achieving a specific influence on a social or environmental issue. Impact investments may be in financial inclusion, education, healthcare, housing, water, clean and renewable energy, agriculture, and other areas. Investments cover a wide geography: Latin America and the Caribbean, Eastern Europe and Central Asia, East Asia and the Pacific, South Asia, sub-Saharan Africa, Middle East, and North Africa. Much of our discussion in later chapters will be focused on ESG funds which invest primarily in public debt and equity markets. A distinction of impact investing is that most assets tend to be in other asset classes. Private debt (34%), real assets (22%), and private equity (19%) account for 75% of assets invested by impact investors. Investment size varies from microfinance to many millions. Investments often are made with an expectation that financial returns will be minimal or nonexistent, but this is not always the case. One review (Mudaliar and Bass, 2017) of dozens of studies of the financial performance of impact investing concluded that returns for market rate seeking impact investments were comparable to those of conventional investment portfolios. Impact investing and mission investing have many similarities and the terms are often used interchangeably. Here, we would make the differentiation that impact investing can be undertaken by any investor or organization and we reserve mission investing to be used to refer to activities undertaken by organizations whose areas of investment focus are central to their existence. There is, however, substantial overlap in usage of the two terms and the investments made in each category can be similar. Some of the most active investors in both impact and mission investing have been the large foundations and endowments. Figs. 2.1–2.3 list the assets of some of these organizations.

The data were estimated by the author from public reports. Note that the Chan Zuckerberg Initiative is structured as an LLC rather than a charitable foundation, and as of this writing, the founders were in the process of providing $10 billion, its initial targeted level of assets. The LLC or limited liability company structure allows the founders to exercise more control than the typical nonprofit structure which has several statutory requirements such as restrictions on the types of expenditures which can be made and a requirement of spending a minimum of 5% of its assets each year. As an LLC, the Chan Zuckerberg Initiative can provide funding to for-profit companies which are working in ESG areas the founders favor, and it can support policy initiatives which they support. Chan and Zuckerberg have indicated that they intend to leave the bulk of their $50 billion plus fortune to their philanthropic endeavors, so we have indicated the assets of this entity as simply $10 + billions.

There were many contenders for the last entry on Fig. 2.1 as there were between 5 and 10 foundations with assets of between $6 and $8 billion. Depending on the allocation of those assets and their market valuations, any one of those foundations might have assets valued in excess of the Bloomberg Philanthropies.

The Rise Fund

In late 2017, a new private equity fund, the Rise Fund, managed by TPG, raised $2 billion for impact investments. The managers of this fund seek to aggressively address a concern that some impact investments might be well

Bill & Melinda Gates Foundation	$52 billion
Howard Hughes Medical Institute	$20 billion
Ford Foundation	$14 billion
Lilly Endowment	$11.7 billion
Robert Wood Johnson Foundation	$11.4 billion
William and Flora Hewlett Foundation	$9.9 billion
J. Paul Getty Trust	$10.4 billion
Chan Zuckerberg Initiative LLC	$10+ billion
William and Flora Hewlett Foundation	$9.9 billion
Bloomberg Family Foundation	$7 billion

FIGURE 2.1   Largest US foundations. Source: *Data compiled by the author from various public reports.*

intentioned but argue that results are often poorly reported or even go unmeasured. To address these issues, this fund has developed a methodology to quantify the economic value of the social and environmental impact of investment candidates. The methodology, the impact multiple of money (IMM), produces a single number to value an investment, If the IMM indicates a social return of 2.5 × or $2.50 return on each $1, then Rise will invest in the company. The six steps involved in the calculation are as follows:

- Assess relevance and scale: Does the company create positive social or environmental impact, can it be measured, and does it have a large enough impact?
- Identify evidence-based outcomes: Identify social or environmental outcome targets—linked to the United Nations's sustainable development goals—and verify that the outcomes are achievable and measurable.
- Estimate the economic value of those outcomes to society: Use economic research to put a dollar value on the projected social or environmental change.

Silicon Valley Community Foundation	$13.6 billion
Tulsa Community Foundation	$4.1 billion
The Greater Kansas City Community Foundation	$3.2billion
The New York Community Trust	$2.8 billion
The Chicago Community Trust	$2.8 billion
The Cleveland Foundation	$2.5 billion
Foundation For The Carolinas	$2.5 billion
The Columbus Foundation and Affiliated Organizations	$2.3 billion
The Oregon Community Foundation	$2.3 billion
Marin Community Foundation	$2.2 billion

FIGURE 2.2 Largest US community foundations. Source: *Data compiled by the author from various public reports.*

- Adjust for risks: Discount the likelihood of achieving the projected social or environmental value.
- Estimate terminal value: Estimate the probability that the social or environmental value created will continue (and diminish) for 5 years after an investment terminates.
- Calculate the return on every dollar invested: Start with the total projected value created by the investment, calculate the investor's proportional ownership stake, and divide by the initial investment.

While this methodology provides significant guidance on expected returns, there are obviously many assumptions involved. It should be most useful in ranking investments against each other and providing investors with substantial insight into social and environmental impacts. It most likely will prove more useful with later stage projects than with early stage undertakings where implementation and other risks can be more significant.

Harvard University	$39.2 billion
University of Texas	$32.6 billion
Yale University	$29.4 billion
Stanford University	$26.5 billion
Princeton University	$25.9 billion
MIT	$16.4 billion
University of Pennsylvania	$13.8 billion
University of Michigan	$11.9 billion
Columbia University	$10.9 billion

FIGURE 2.3 Largest US university endowments. Source: *Data compiled by the author from various public reports.*

Mission investing

Closely related to impact investing, the term mission investing is often used to refer to the investing activities of charitable foundations or religious funds which have relatively specific social, environmental, or spiritual purposes. Religious values investing is another related term which we consider to be a subset of mission investing, where the investment criteria are based on the religious values of the organization. In Chapter 14, Faith-based investing, we will look at religious values investing in more detail.

Mission investments are designed to have an impact on specific philanthropic goals. Some examples would be providing improved healthcare or enhanced educational opportunities for children. These investments are expected to have a positive social impact while earning a financial return to contribute to the institution's financial stability. Program related investments have a primary focus on the social value of the investment and may earn submarket returns. Impact investments, as mentioned above, have many of the same characteristics but may be made by individuals or other institutions as opposed to mission investments originating from the charitable or religious foundation.

One relatively new philanthropy is Arnold Ventures. This group works in four areas: health, criminal justice, public, finance and education. Their methodology is to identify problems, rigorously research them, and search for solutions. Once an idea is tested, validated, and prove to be effective, they fund policy development and technical assistance with a goal to create change that outlasts their funding from several sources. Their areas of focus:

- Criminal justice
  - Policing
  - Pretrial justice
  - Community supervision
  - Prisons
  - Reintegration
- Health
  - The opioid epidemic
  - Contraceptive choice and access
  - Drug prices
  - Commercial sector prices
  - Low-value care
  - Complex care
- Education
  - K−12
  - Higher education
- Public finance
  - Retirement policy
  - Policy labs

United Nations principles for responsible investing

Started in 2005, the UN principles for responsible investing (PRI) program provides coordination for banks, companies, and researchers concerned about sustainability issues. This initial group was later joined by a key group of participants: institutional investors. There are now 2000 signatories with $80 trillion in assets under management. The goal of the PRI program is to get investors to consider and implement responsible ESG factors in their investment decisions across a panoply of investments: stocks, fixed income, private equity, hedge funds, and real assets.

The signatories commit to the following: "As institutional investors, we have a duty to act in the best long-term interests of our beneficiaries. In this fiduciary role, we believe that environmental, social, and corporate governance (ESG) issues can affect the performance of investment portfolios (to varying degrees across companies, sectors, regions, asset classes and through time)."

They go further to state that they recognize that broader objectives of society may be consistent with the Principles.

"...Therefore, where consistent with our fiduciary responsibilities, we commit to the following:

- Principle 1: We will incorporate ESG issues into investment analysis and decision-making processes.
- Principle 2: We will be active owners and incorporate ESG issues into our ownership policies and practices.
- Principle 3: We will seek appropriate disclosure on ESG issues by the entities in which we invest.
- Principle 4: We will promote acceptance and implementation of the Principles within the investment industry.
- Principle 5: We will work together to enhance our effectiveness in implementing the Principles.
- Principle 6: We will each report on our activities and progress towards implementing the Principles."

Support for responsible investment by institutional investors and others is driven by:

- recognition in the financial community that ESG factors play a material role in determining risk and return;
- understanding that incorporating ESG factors is part of investors' fiduciary duty to their clients and beneficiaries;
- concern about the impact of short-termism on company performance, investment returns, and market behavior;
- legal requirements protecting the long-term interests of beneficiaries and the wider financial system;
- pressure from competitors seeking to differentiate themselves by offering responsible investment services as a competitive advantage;
- beneficiaries becoming increasingly active and demanding transparency about where and how their money is being invested; and
- value-destroying reputational risk from issues such as climate change, pollution, working conditions, employee diversity, corruption and aggressive tax strategies in a world of globalization and social media.

Responsible investing then is differentiated from other investment strategies which stress a moral or ethical return. In contrast, responsible investment targets a wider group of investors whose primary purpose is financial return. It argues that ESG factors can have a material effect on the returns delivered to clients and beneficiaries and therefore they cannot be ignored in making investment decisions. Many of the social and ethical investment approaches incorporate specific often narrow themes, whereas responsible investment incorporates analysis of any information relevant to investment performance.

United Nations sustainable development goals

A key aspect of social and ethical investing is identifying the goals of those investments. Here, the United Nations has also been active in providing guidance. In 2015, 17 development goals were adopted. They are as follows:

- no poverty;
- zero hunger;
- good health and well-being;
- quality education;
- gender equality;
- clean water and sanitation;
- affordable and clean energy;
- decent work and economic growth;
- industry innovation and infrastructure;
- reduced inequalities;
- sustainable cities and communities;
- responsible consumption and production;
- climate action;
- life below water;
- life on land;
- peace, justice, and strong institutions; and
- partnerships for the goals.

These goals may seem overly vague and aspirational to some, but they provide a useful framework for categorizing investments. The Rise Fund, for example, looks to these goals as a starting point for identifying the potential social or environmental value of investment candidates.

Financial returns versus social and environmental returns

Fig. 2.4 presents a graphical summary of the various social investment styles. It compares these styles with reference to financial return on the vertical axis and social and environmental returns on the horizontal access. Conventional investment portfolios, with no consideration of ESG factors, will have a distribution of financial returns centered around a median market rate of return. Social and environmental returns to these conventional portfolios would be minimal. A portfolio designed to reflect ESG factors can be structured to have similar financial returns to conventional portfolios (empirical evidence of this will be reviewed in Chapter 9: Defining and measuring ESG performance) and will have a range of social and environmental returns superior to the conventional portfolio. The historical performance of divestment portfolios has been relatively poor, with few exceptions. Fig. 2.4 represents this investment style as having subpar financial performance, and some, albeit weak social and environmental influence as well. Mission investing and

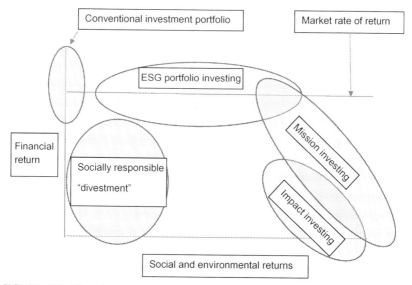

FIGURE 2.4 Financial return versus social and environmental return for various investment styles.

impact investing are shown as overlapping strategies. Both are more targeted than ESG investing. Some mission investing portfolios have been shown to yield market rates of return when designed to do so. In general, many mission investing strategies require a rate of return at least adequate to support the continuing operation of the organizational structure. Impact investing, however, includes at least some organizations which are comfortable with submarket and negligible financial returns. But it is assumed that their close focus will allow them to yield greater social and environmental benefits from their investments.

Global sustainable investment

This book focusses on ESG investment activity in the United States. Detailed coverage of ESG in other countries is beyond its scope. However, interested readers can find more information from the following organizations:

- African Investing for Impact Barometer (Africa)
- Belsif (Belgium)
- Dansif (Denmark)
- Eurosif (Europe)
- Forum pour l'Investissement Responsable (France)
- Forum Nachhaltige Geldanlagen (Germany/Austria/Switzerland)
- Forum per la Finanza Sostenibile (Italy)

- Japan Sustainable Investment Forum (Japan)
- KoSIF (Korea)
- LatinSIF (Latin America)
- Responsible Investment Association of Australasia (Australasia)
- Responsible Investment Association (Canada)
- Responsible Investment Research Association (India)
- SpainSIF (Spain)
- SWESIF (Sweden)
- UKSIF (United Kingdom)
- VBDO (the Netherlands)

Chapter 3

Theory of the firm

Chapter Outline

The social responsibility of business is
to increase its profits   29
Maximize shareholder welfare, not
market value   32

Maximizing welfare   34
Shareholder rights   36
Summary   39
Appendix   39

Environmental, social, and governance (ESG) investing at its core seeks to contribute assets to companies which are pursuing ESG goals, or to influence companies to do so. But some question to what degree companies should pursue nonfinancial goals. One of the most important writings on the purpose of a firm is Milton Friedman's "The social responsibility of business is to increase its profits" (Friedman, 1970). The majority of corporate executives, boards, and investment managers still agree with Friedman's view but after 50 years, many others think that this is not the whole answer. In this chapter, we will discuss Friedman's important paper and go on to look at competing views.

The social responsibility of business is to increase its profits

First, Friedman takes issue with discussions of the "social responsibilities of business." He points out that this is too vague, that inanimate constructs like corporations don't have responsibilities. It is people, proprietors, or corporate executives, who have responsibilities, and their fundamental responsibility is to conduct their business activities in accordance with the desires of their owners/employers. This means they will undertake "to make as much money as possible while conforming to the basic rules of society, both those embodied in law and those embodied in ethical custom" (Friedman, 1970). He notes that some corporations, for example, hospitals, might have an additional objective of providing certain levels of service. His point here is that the firm's managers are responsible to the owners of the corporation. These employees are free to support charitable or social activities on their own time, with their own income and wealth but have no basis to take it upon themselves to divert corporate resources to these purposes. Such an action would be taking money from others. It would reduce shareholder returns or

Environmental, Social, and Governance (ESG) Investing. DOI: https://doi.org/10.1016/B978-0-12-818692-3.00003-7

if these expenditures were funded by raising sales prices, it would siphon off customers' money. Shareholders and customers are, of course, always free to spend their own money on any cause as they see fit and, in this view, these are the appropriate sources of funding for charitable and social causes. A related question is to what extent corporate charitable acts might "crowd out" private contributions. One way to view employee spending on social activities is that they would be "taxing" shareholders and customers, and employees would be deciding on their own where "expenditures" of these tax dollars should go. But, Friedman points out, we have established elaborate governmental procedures to determine taxes and expenditures: democratic elections; elaborate checks and balances; executive, legislative, and judicial arms; federal, state, and local powers; important constitutional protections; and massive regulatory procedures. Imperfect as it may be, all this apparatus would be overturned or circumvented by a business manager, self-selected or appointed by a board of directors, who deems themselves simultaneously legislator, government executive, and jurist in pursuit of a specific social goal. Friedman goes further to consider that the corporate executive is hired to be an agent in promoting the interests of the owners of the corporation. To the extent that the executive departs from that goal in an attempt to further social purposes, then they become (unelected, unnominated, and unconfirmed) de facto public employees. Further questions arise as to how does the employee know how much to spend and how to spend it? How do they know what action to take to meet a specific social goal? What are the appropriate cost shares to assign to employees, shareholders, and customers? Many who support corporations' social activism do so only to the extent that their own preferences are aligned with those specific activities. However, they are less supportive or even critical of corporate activism which is at odds with their beliefs. So, it is not corporate social responsibility per se that they support, but instead it's the backing of specific causes that are important to them.

Friedman goes on to address the complaint that political and legislative processes are often too slow to address pressing social problems. He finds this argument objectionable in principle in that those who make this assertion have failed to persuade a majority of fellow citizens of their position and are nonetheless seeking to make an undemocratic claim of their validity. This argument also applies to activist stockholder proposals whereby a minority seek to impose their desire for favored causes on the company when those causes have consistently failed to attract support of a majority of the holders. And this is not a sterile debate from the 1970s. For example, large institutional investors are currently engaged with gun manufacturers on the issues of firearm manufacturing, sales and safety. As recently as March 2018, gunmaker American Outdoor Brands Corporation (formerly Smith and Wesson) posted a reply to these investors on its company website (Monheit and Debney, 2018):

"We do not believe that our stockholders associate the criminal use of a firearm with the company that manufactures it. We do believe, however, that there would be far greater reputational and financial risk to our company if we were to manufacture and market products containing features that consumers of our products do not desire, or if we were to take political positions with which consumers of our products do not agree." Though the company respects the current national gun-control debate, "the solution is not to take a politically motivated action that has an adverse impact on our company, our employees, our industry, our shareholders, the economies we support and, significantly, the rights of our law-abiding customers, but results in no increase in public safety." The company does, however, support greater enforcement of current laws and efforts to improve background checks.

After Friedman, a second influential paper is "Theory of the firm: managerial behavior, agency costs and ownership structure" (Jensen and Meckling, 1976). This paper provides a useful explanation for many corporate activities from the "agency-principal" perspective. In this model the principals (shareholders) cede decision making authority to agents (boards of directors and corporate managers). This delegation creates a generic problem which arises in many different arenas. The issue is that it is difficult for the principals to ensure that the agents act strictly in accordance with the best outcomes for the principals. Jensen and Meckling's analysis forms a basis for subsequent discussions of how to mitigate the agency problem using strategies such as establishing appropriate incentives for the agent and developing, at a cost, adequate monitoring solutions. Applying these concepts in the context of a firm's socially responsible actions, agent activities, and expenses not designed to enhance shareholder value would cause a loss of welfare to the principals.

Profit maximization has the virtue of being relatively simple, easy to understand, and easy to measure. Having other social purposes as goals leads to a risk of unintended, adverse outcomes. For example, here's one observer's interpretation of the demise of the failed blood testing company, Theranos:

> *I just finished reading John Carreyrou's "Bad Blood," the story of the fraud at Theranos Inc. and his work to uncover it. Theranos—in Carreyrou's view, and the view of federal prosecutors—issued tens of thousands of blood-test results to real patients using technology that it knew didn't work, endangering those patients' lives. There are a lot of passages in the book about Theranos founder Elizabeth Holmes inspiring and cajoling her employees to work harder, to get with the mission, to override their moral objections to faking the technology and push ahead.* **None of those passages mention shareholder value or profit maximization. They mention Holmes's vision of revolutionizing health care to save lives and treat cancer patients. If you want to inspire people to do terrible things, it is very useful to sell them on a grand vision, a higher purpose, a noble mission** *(emphasis added).*

Levine (2018).

Most of this chapter's discussion centers on the shortcomings of firms which focus only on maximizing profits or shareholder value. Levine's observations regarding Theranos point out the other side of the coin: a company may use a cloak of a grand vision while engaging in socially undesirable activities and being unprofitable at the same time.

Actions taken solely to effect social goals shouldn't be confused with similar actions which on the surface might seem to be altruistic, but in fact are designed to further corporate profitability. For example, an employer might provide amenities to a community such as paying for cleaning subways or ridding highways of litter. These "good will" activities can enhance the company's reputation and make it easier to attract employees or enhance a brand's image. But they are not germane to the question of a firm's more pervasive social responsibility. This kind of activity, promoting the company as environmentally or socially responsible but with little commitment, is sometimes called "greenwash."

Friedman's theory is based on an idealistic belief in the inherent value of freedom of individual choices and of democratic government principles. He rejects the imposition ("coercion") of artificial and ill-defined "social responsibility" as subversive of these institutions. This continues to be the position of many even in today's age of increased sensitivity to social issues. For example, Phil Gram and Mike Solon (Gramm and Solon, 2018) write the following in the Wall Street Journal on July 19, 2018: "...Arguments for imposing political and social objectives on business often are little more than rationalizations for forcing businesses to abide by values that have been rejected in Congress and the courts...America created the world's most successful economy by allowing private wealth to serve private economic objectives rather than political ones. The politicization of business decisions threatens to bring the massive inefficiencies of government into the private sector, cheating investors, workers and consumers in the process."

Maximize shareholder welfare, not market value

While Friedman's views are widely held, competing ideas have received increased attention. Some writers have taken the view that the modern corporation is as much a political adaptation as it is an economic or technological construct. Prior to the development in the 1970s of the view of the corporation as a nexus of contracts, particularly between shareholders and board members, there were interpretations of the firm as having corporate responsibilities to a wider group of constituents. Stakeholders are not just owners but also employees, customers, and the public at large. Another important stream of research looks at the firm from the point of view of property rights. Still others take issue with Friedman's theory on the basis that it too narrowly defines what it is that the owners of the business desire from their investment. Hart and Zingales (2017) argue that investors are not one-dimensional robots concerned only about monetary rewards. Yes, financial resources are important but individuals also have social and ethical concerns that do not end when evaluating corporate performance. Friedman makes the point that individuals should separate money-making activities from charitable acts which could be funded by those activities. But this separation argument assumes that individuals can gain the same scale and impact that a focused corporate action can have. Such is not always the case. Historically some corporate activities have resulted in significant negative social or environmental effects, but individuals acting on their own do not necessarily have the information, technology, or other resources to undo the damage. In these cases, having corporate involvement to address the negative effects might be the only credible solution. Government intervention either alone or with corporate participation is another alternative, although many agreeing with Friedman's profit maximizing argument would expect that corporate actions would be more efficient than government involvement.

Individuals are subject to the negative effects of "externalities" that may be generated by some corporate activities. Their welfare would be increased by direct corporate action to mitigate these externalities. In Friedman's idealized world, companies would simply make money and individuals and governments could use corporate income and taxes to address externalities. But Hart and Zingales argue that in many cases, money-making and ethical activities go hand in hand and are inseparable. They see Friedman's theory as requiring that consumers have scalable projects that are the mirror image of negative corporate activities. And further, that consumers receive enough funds to effect the offset, along with technology, information, communication, and other resources to bring this about. Clearly, this occurs rarely if ever. Government actions might be proposed as remedies but it's not obvious that focused government solutions can be provided efficiently in every instance. Nonseparable antisocial corporate activities are even more damning to Friedman's theory. The company's profit-making activities are intertwined with damaging results from those activities. And individuals do not have the technology, information, communication, and other resources to reverse the damaging results in a cost-effective manner. In this view, companies are better situated to address these issues.

Friedman's claim that government is the (sole) agent to effect social actions is also challenged. Laws and regulations don't necessarily cover every instance of desirable action. Even where there is the will to pass a law, the time it takes to gain enactment and enforcement can be excessive. And it may be more efficient for a business to act than for a government agency to be mobilized. The relative efficiency of corporate versus government action is surely supported by modern-day adherents to Friedman's theory.

These counter arguments are clouded somewhat by Hart and Zingale's use of examples of social issues which are controversial and have yet to receive overwhelming public support. And if there is no well-defined standard for the level of support required, there is a risk of self-interested behavior by managers and boards. Socially responsible actions by a business may well be justifiable, but there are still unanswered questions of who decides what actions and what level of resources.

Maximizing welfare

Stout (2013) makes the argument that boards and managers have latitude to maximize a wide array of possible objectives provided only that these actions themselves are legal and that they don't constitute a theft of corporate resources. She takes issue with the agent-principal analogy, noting that shareholder control is only indirect and in practice is difficult to exercise. Shareholders can replace boards, but this is rarely done. (A counter argument would be that this is rarely done because boards rarely act in an egregious manner. The threat of replacement and the recognition by the board of their responsibility to shareholders may act as a sufficient deterrent so as to make replacement unnecessary.) She notes that several strategies for shareholder profit maximization have been pursued in recent decades. Some of these strategies are as follows:

- Increasing the number of independent directors on the board.
- Tying executive compensation more closely to stockholder profits, especially share price appreciation.
- Remove staggering of director terms so as to make it easier to replace these directors and thereby encourage accountability.

Have these strategies been successful in increasing shareholder profits? Empirical studies are mixed, but Stout finds that at times, these strategies for increasing shareholder value have not been successful in increasing investor returns. Further complicating managing toward a goal of shareholder profit maximization is the realization that shareholders are a diverse bunch with many different objectives. Some may want short-term maximum profits, but others may be in the stock for the long run, with a distant retirement objective. This latter group of shareholders would presumably approve forgoing current profits in order to expand investment programs with a longer run payoff. Other investors may have a strong opinion on social goals. For example, a union pension fund would presumably be opposed to an aggressive workforce reduction to improve short-term quarterly results. Shareholder value then is an artificial concept that is in practice impossible to define. Using short-term share price as the only metric for success results in privileging those shareholders "...who are most shortsighted, opportunistic, undiversified, and indifferent to ethics or others' welfare." The desire to identify a single corporate purpose and optimize it may be appealing for its simplicity and for its usefulness when applying mathematics, but she thinks this is unrealistic and points out that many human activities pursue multiple objectives. For example, when eating a meal, we typically balance taste, healthfulness, and expense.

In a dramatic letter to corporate heads (Fink, 2018), the CEO of the world's largest asset manager expressed the opinion that in managing their companies, corporate leaders need to have a broader perspective:

> ...society increasingly is turning to the private sector and asking that companies respond to broader societal challenges. Indeed, the public expectations of your company have never been greater. Society is demanding that companies, both public and private, serve a social purpose. To prosper over time, every company must not only deliver financial performance, but also show how it makes a positive contribution to society. Companies must benefit all their stakeholders, including shareholders, employees, customers, and the communities in which they operate.

> ...Without a sense of purpose, no company, either public or private, can achieve its full potential. It will ultimately lose the license to operate from key stakeholders. It will succumb to short-term pressures to distribute earnings, and, in the process, sacrifice investments in employee development, innovation, and capital expenditures that are necessary for long-term growth. It will remain exposed to activist campaigns that articulate a clearer goal, even if that goal serves only the shortest and narrowest of objectives. And ultimately, that company will provide subpar returns to the investors who depend on it to finance their retirement, home purchases, or higher education.

While Fink's letter was well received by many investors and corporate CEOs, it failed perhaps unsurprisingly to convince others with more traditional views. These latter investors point out the difficulty in identifying agreed social purposes and in measuring results. They also revert back to Friedman-esque arguments that the purpose of the firm is to maximize shareholder value, pay taxes, and allow governments to address social issues. One investor pointed out that many of Blackrock's funds are "passive" and follow market indices (Lovelace, 2018). This investor believes it is inappropriate, even hypocritical for those funds to represent that they follow the market, but that fund management then says it will actively seek to influence decisions of those companies. Perhaps recognizing the difficulties in identifying appropriate social causes, this investor, himself an active philanthropist, said: "I didn't know Larry Fink had been made God."

In Stout's view, firms can pursue a course of addressing multiple objectives and doing a credible job with each. This is then a "satisficing" rather than "maximizing" strategy. By not seeking to "maximize" the outcome of any one group to the detriment of others, managers would have less pressure to resolve conflict among shareholders, customers and employees. A reasonable, even desirable, management strategy is to generate significant profits for investors, but also to take into account additional desired outcomes championed by other company stakeholders. Long-term as well as short-term shareholders' interests are balanced; customers are well served; working conditions are such that employment opportunities are eagerly sought; regulations are complied with; and the firm is run in a socially responsible manner. Corporate profits are important but not the sole focus of management. Satisficing multiple objectives would seem to be a good description of management behavior of some of the best performing companies in the United States.

Shareholder rights

The preceding discussion concerns the appropriate actions of the managers and boards of a firm. But what about the shareholders? Shareholders are sometimes said to "own" a company. While shareholders have several important rights, they technically do not "own" a company, it owns itself. What rights do shareholders have? In general, they have the following rights:

- The right to receive dividends, as declared by the board and subject to the priority of preferred stockholders.
- The right to inspect certain corporate documents such as books and records.
- A claim on assets in the event of bankruptcy.
- Rights to appraisal and access to certain information.
- The right to vote to elect, remove, or replace board members and to vote on certain corporate actions and other proposals.

Among these, the right to vote may be the most important. By exercising their right to vote, investor/owners can affect corporate oversight, management, and actions. Roughly 85% of US companies have issued stocks which provide for a one-share, one-vote structure. However, voting rights are watered down by companies which issue dual-class shares with differential voting rights attached to each class. In terms of voting rights, not all shares are created equal. Typically, the founders and other corporate insiders will retain stock with "super" voting rights which allow the founders to maintain voting control of the company. Stock issued to the public will have diluted voting rights. The most frequent voting ratio is for stock issued to founders, their families, and other insiders to have ten votes, while inferior shares have only one vote each. Some companies have dual-stock voting structures which are even worse than this. The dual-stock structure may have negative consequences in that it entrenches bad management unwilling to change its ways when the company fares poorly. But for a well-managed company it can also have the benefit of allowing forward thinking management to focus on long-term growth as opposed to merely maximizing this quarter's profits. Some examples of companies which have dual-class stock with skewed voting rights are Berkshire Hathaway, Ford, Facebook, and Alphabet. When Snap went public in 2017 it issued shares with no voting rights at all. The New York Stock Exchange for most of its existence would not list companies with dual-class voting rights. To compete with other exchanges with more liberal policies, it changed its rules and it now allows companies to initially list their shares in dual classes, but once they are listed the company cannot reduce the voting rights of existing shareholders or list new stock with super voting rights. More than 15% of the companies listed on US exchanges in 2015 had dual-class shares as opposed to only 1% in 2005.

Research on the question of whether companies with dual classes of stock underperform their peers show mixed results. While there is some evidence that closely held companies have historically taken on excessive debt and that increased insider voting rights is associated with reduced firm value, the recent public listing of growing technology companies and changes in public and private capital markets structure has, however, muddied the waters. Managers of these technology companies have had more freedom to successfully pursue long range projects than they might have had if they were more beholden to quarterly performance metrics. But disagreeing on the potential value of dual-class stock, some institutional investors include "one share, one vote" as a positive governance factor. Also, FTSE Russell, one of the largest providers of equity indexes, notified companies in 2017 that it would include in its indexes only those companies with at least 5% of voting rights in the hands of the public. This seems to be a low bar, but it would exclude companies such as Snap, Virtu, Hyatt and 45 others. If the bar were set at 25% of voting rights in the hands of the public, 230 companies would be excluded. The Appendix to this chapter contains the list of these companies. For its part, S&P Dow Jones barred the addition of dual-stock companies from the S&P 500 and other indexes, although existing companies were grandfathered.

One study (CFA, 2018) found the following from the history of dual-stock listings in the United States and from reviewing several case studies:

- The current boom in dual-stock listings in the United States and in Asia is similar to the experience in the United States during the 1920s and 1980s, including increased liquidity and outsized optimism.
- The booms in the 1920s and 1980s were each followed by a prolonged period of market turmoil.
- The rise and fall (and rise again) of dual-stock listings is neither inevitable nor unique, and there are many more options than a wholesale adoption of dual-stock structures.
- Stock exchanges are feeling competitive pressures to allow dual-stock listings.
- For family businesses with a dual-stock structure, it is much easier for major shareholders to abuse their position and take advantage of public shareholders, either through massive executive compensation packages or questionable consultancy arrangements.

- Major shareholders (usually the founders) are not incentivized to maximize the company's potential. They may have voting control, but they have low equity ownership and few benefits accrue to them.

The tension then is between founders' desire to maintain control and investors' desire for representation. A possible solution is to recognize that there may be some value in founders' keeping voting control in the early years of a company's life and growth, but to put a time limit on this structure. When the company is more mature, there are less grounds for arguing that super voting control should be in the hands of the founders' ancestors. The Securities and Exchange Commission (SEC) studied the relative valuation of companies with dual classes of stock. One group of companies gave insiders control of the company forever, and a second group had "sunset"

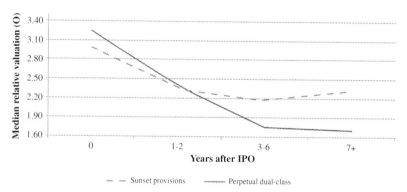

FIGURE 3.1 Valuation of dual-class firms. *Source: SEC https://www.sec.gov/news/speech/perpetual-dual-class-stock-case-against-corporate-royalty.*

Company	IPO year	Sunset trigger
EVO Payments	2018	3 years
Texas Roadhouse	2004	5 years (converted in 2009 to one share, one vote)
Groupon	2011	5 years (converted in 2016 to one share, one vote)
MuleSoft	2017	5 years (acquired in 2018 by Salesforce)
Bloom Energy	2018	5 years or superclass falls below 5% of outstanding common
MaxLinear	2010	7 years (converted in 2017 to one share, one vote)
Yelp	2012	7 years or superclass falls below 10% of outstanding common (converted in 2016 to one share, one vote)
Kayak Software	2012	7 years (acquired in 2013 by Priceline, now Booking Holdings)
Mindbody	2015	7 years
Apptio	2016	7 years or superclass falls below 25% of outstanding common
Twilio	2016	7 years
Smartsheet	2018	7 years or superclass falls below 15% of outstanding common
Veeva Systems	2013	10 years
Castlight Health	2014	10 years
Pure Storage	2015	10 years or superclass falls below 10% of outstanding common
Stitch Fix	2017	10 years or superclass falls below 10% of outstanding common
Alteryx	2017	10 years or superclass falls below 10% of outstanding common
Hamilton Lane	2017	10 years or founders and employees hold less than 25% of voting power
Okta	2017	10 years
Zuora	2018	10 years or superclass falls below 5% of outstanding common
Eventbrite	2018	10 years
Altair Engineering	2017	12 years or "executive holder" position falls below 10% of outstanding common
Fitbit	2015	12 years
Nutanix	2016	12 years
Workday	2012	20 years or superclass falls below 9% of outstanding common

FIGURE 3.2 Time-based approaches to dual-class stock. *Source: Council of Institutional Investors https://www.cii.org/dualclass_stock.*

provisions which provided for super voting control to expire either in a fixed number of years or on the death of the founder. Fig. 3.1 shows that seven or more years after their initial public offering (IPO), firms with perpetual dual-class stock trade at a significant discount to those with sunset provisions.

Sunset provisions can either be event based or time based. Events such as the death or departure of an insider could trigger provisions for higher vote shares to convert to lower vote shares. Time based sunset provisions range from 3 to 20 years after the company's IPO. Fig. 3.2 shows the time-based sunset provisions for several companies.

Summary

This chapter summarized some of the competing theories of the firm. The starting point is Friedman's seminal article making the case that maximizing shareholder value is and should be the goal of the firm. Subsequent authors point out that shareholders are a diverse bunch who have wants and needs that go beyond financial gains. Also supporting a broader range of frim objectives is the recognition that firms' actions may have adverse ESG consequences which are most efficiently addressed by the firms themselves. From a longer term view, the risk of negative ESG factors becomes even more important. Stout makes an attractive case for "satisficing" behavior that firms can and do take actions to meet the needs of different stakeholders. Finally, we looked in more detail at shareholder rights.

The theoretical discussion in the chapter also provides the background for addressing the question of whether ESG considerations are appropriate in managing a firm. In the next chapter, we will look at the duties and responsibilities of fiduciaries in managing investments and ask the similar question: "is it appropriate for investment managers to consider ESG criteria in asset allocation?" We will also discuss, in Chapter 8, Shareholder engagement, investor activism in terms of shareholder advocacy and engagement with corporate management to influence the firm's actions to be consistent with investor ESG goals.

Appendix

Analysis of securities affected by voting right hurdles set at 5% and 25%.

Ticker	Constituent name	Voting power in public ownership (%) (May 2018)
EV	Eaton Vance Corp	0.00
ERIE	Erie Indemnity Co	0.00
ARTNA	Artesian Resources Corp	0.00
SAM	Boston Beer Inc.	0.00
BRC	Brady Corp	0.00

(Continued)

Ticker	Constituent name	Voting power in public ownership (%) (May 2018)
CNBKA	Century Bancorp Inc.	0.00
EZPW	EZCorp Inc.	0.00
FII	Federated Investors Inc.	0.00
KELYA	Kelly Services Inc.	0.00
OPY	Oppenheimer Holdings Inc.	0.00
SNAP	Snap Inc.—A	0.00
GROW	US Global Investors, Inc.—A	0.00
CCO	Clear Channel Outdoor	0.58
NYLD	NRG Yield Inc. CL C	0.83
ARD	Ardagh Group SA	0.84
ATUS	Altice USA, Inc.—A	0.94
SDI	Standard Diversified Inc.	0.98
SCWX	Secureworks Corp	1.03
ANGI	Angi Homeservices Inc.—A	1.14
ZUO	Zuora Inc.—Class A	1.18
SMAR	Smartsheet Inc.—Class A	1.32
AC	Associated Capital Group	1.36
DBX	Dropbox Inc.—Class A	1.49
CIX	Compx International Inc.	1.60
MDB	MongoDB Inc.	1.98
GBL	Gamco Investors Inc.	2.11
SFIX	Stitch Fix Inc.—Class A	2.11
MDLY	Medley Management Inc.	2.15
VMW	VMware Inc.	2.21
VCTR	Victory Capital Holding—A	2.22
BAND	Bandwidth Inc.—Class A	2.29
MTCH	Match Group Inc.	2.38
CVNA	Carvana Co	2.50
BBGI	Beasley Broadcast Group	2.68
OCX	Oncocyte Corporation	2.70
ROAD	Construction Partners Inc.—A	2.76
ROSE	Rosehill Resources Inc.	3.04
UONEK	Urban One Inc.	3.24
DVMT	Dell Technologies	3.50
LAUR	Laureate Education Inc.	3.60
USM	United States Cellular	3.65
VIRT	Virtu Finl Inc.	3.85
RMR	RMR Group Inc.	3.98
APRN	Blue Apron Holdings Inc.—A	4.05
APPN	Appian Corp	4.26
PVTL	Pivotal Software Inc.—CL A	4.38
CSSE	Chicken Soup For The Soul EN	4.55
SNDR	Schneider National Inc.	5.12
HLNE	Hamilton Lane Inc.	5.28
TR	Tootsie Roll Industries	5.49
SWCH	Switch Inc.	5.57

(Continued)

(Continued)

Ticker	Constituent name	Voting power in public ownership (%) (May 2018)
H	Hyatt Hotels Corp	6.06
ALTR	Altair Engineering Inc.	6.30
PZN	Pzena Investment Mgmt	6.34
HUD	Hudson Ltd	6.91
NEXT	NextDecade	7.12
TEAM	Atlassian Corp PLC	7.12
APPF	Appfolio Inc.	7.15
IPIC	IPIC Entertainment Inc.	7.32
VHI	Valhi Inc.	7.38
HPR	High Point Resources	7.43
DVD	Dover Motorsports Inc.	7.71
HLI	Houlihan Lokey Inc.	7.72
INOV	Inovalon Holdings Inc.	7.78
AYX	Alteryx Inc.	7.96
PRPL	Purple Innovation Inc.	8.04
FLWS	1-800 Flowers Com	8.27
HMTV	Hemisphere Media Group	8.28
HOME	AT Home Group Inc.	8.35
ROKU	Roku Inc.	8.46
DISH	Dish Network Corp	8.47
CASA	Casa Systems Inc.	8.52
PAHC	Phibro Animal Health	8.79
GNPX	Genprex Inc.	9.05
COKE	Coca Cola Bottling	9.06
SATS	Echostar Corp	9.07
TLYS	Tillys Inc.	9.26
FDC	First Data Corporation	9.72
DDE	Dover Downs Gaming & Ent	9.73
BXG	Bluegreen Vacations Corp	9.88
YGYI	Youngevity International	10.25
CNA	CNA Financial Corp	10.38
SENEA	Seneca Foods Corp	10.48
SCCO	Southern Copper Corp	10.56
BOXL	Boxlight Corp	10.56
NYNY	Empire Resorts Inc.	10.68
WWE	World Wrestling Entmnt	10.76
NES	Nuverra Envtl Solutions	10.78
VALU	Value Line Inc.	11.05
ZS	Zscaler	11.58
RCUS	Arcus Biosciences	11.70
VICR	Vicor Corp	11.74
DGICA	Donegal Group Inc.	11.83
UMRX	Unum Therapeutics	11.86
PIXY	ShiftPixy	11.88
UBX	Unity Biotechnology	11.93
CBLK	Carbon Black	12.15

(Continued)

(Continued)

Ticker	Constituent name	Voting power in public ownership (%) (May 2018)
HEI/A	Heico Corp CL A	12.44
LBRT	Liberty Oilfield Service	12.45
EAF	Graftech International	12.48
QADA	QAD Inc.	12.50
DLB	Dolby Laboratories Inc.	12.57
JRSH	Jerash Holdings Inc.	12.63
NNI	Nelnet Inc.	12.81
ARL	American Rlty Invs Inc.	12.81
UBP	Urstadt Biddle Pptys Ins	12.95
DLTH	Duluth Holdings Inc.	13.01
BWL/A	Bowl America Inc.	13.49
ACMR	ACM Research	13.50
GWGH	GWG Hldgs Inc.	13.59
EL	Estee Lauder Companies	13.70
LINK	Interlink Electronics	14.00
ADT	ADT Inc.	14.02
METC	Ramaco Resources Inc.	14.78
RUSHA	Rush Enterprises Inc.	14.78
MJCO	Majesco	15.18
SALM	Salem Media Group Inc.	15.18
REV	Revlon Inc.	15.27
GTES	Gates Industrial Corp	15.28
VLGEA	Village Super Market Inc.	15.34
W	Wayfair Inc.	15.34
EEI	Ecology & Environment	15.35
EVFM	Evofem Biosciences Inc.	15.40
RDI	Reading International	15.68
APTI	Apptio Inc.	15.74
MOTS	Motus GI Holdings Inc.	15.78
EPE	EP Energy Corporation	15.96
S	Sprint Corp	16.04
DOCU	DocuSign	16.06
PANL	Pangaea Logs Solutions	16.16
GBLI	Global Indemnity Ltd	16.20
SAH	Sonic Automotive Inc.	16.27
RMNI	Rimini Street Inc.	16.28
WHLM	Wilhelmina Intl Inc.	16.33
OFED	Oconee Federal Financial	16.34
GRIF	Griffin Industrial Rlty	16.51
MANT	Mantech International	16.57
NMRK	Newmark Group Inc.	16.60
EVLO	Evelo Biosciences	16.67
GAIA	GAIA Inc.	16.77
CURO	Curo Group Holdings Corp	16.83
AMRC	Ameresco Inc.	16.87
NL	NL Industries Inc.	16.98

(Continued)

(Continued)

Ticker	Constituent name	Voting power in public ownership (%) (May 2018)
IBKR	Interactive Brokers Grp	17.02
MNI	McClatchy Co	17.17
CDAY	Ceridian HCM Holding	17.27
WDAY	Workday Inc.	17.33
RL	Ralph Lauren Corp	17.43
TFSL	TFS Finl Corp	17.59
NC	NACCO Industries Inc.	17.73
DNLI	Denali Therapeutics Inc.	17.73
LEVL	Level One Bancorp Inc.	17.84
BWB	Bridgewater Bancshares	17.92
CVI	CVR Energy Inc.	18.00
MCS	Marcus Corp	18.05
BOMN	Boston Omaha	18.07
AGR	Avangrid Inc.	18.10
HSY	Hershey Company	18.10
CLXT	Calyxt	18.22
QES	Quintana Energy Services	18.34
AMC	AMC Entertainment	18.41
ODC	Oil DRI Corp of America	18.48
QUAD	Quad/Graphics Inc.	18.52
NH	Nanthealth Inc.	18.65
AKCA	Akcea Therapeutics	18.75
TUSK	Mammoth Energy Services	18.79
MOV	Movado Group Inc.	18.84
IOR	Income Opp Realty Inv	18.88
BRID	Bridgford Foods Corp	18.91
TCI	Transcontinental Realty	19.05
IFMK	ifresh Inc.	19.30
KRO	Kronos Worldwide Inc.	19.38
ISCA	International Speedway	19.52
VTVT	VTV Therapeautics Inc.	19.60
FAT	FAT Brands Inc.	19.77
TSQ	Townsquare Media Inc.	19.83
HY	Hyster-Yale Materials	19.90
LASR	NLight	19.99
PSTG	Pure Storage Inc.	20.01
CBS	CBS Corporation	20.02
SEND	Sendgrid Inc.	20.10
MC	Moelis & Co	20.14
VIA	Viacom Inc. CL A	20.20
VIAB	Viacom Inc. CL B	20.20
AQB	Aquabounty Technologies	20.29
WK	Workiva Inc.	20.40
SQ	Square Inc.	20.42
FTSI	FTS International Inc.	20.52
PNRG	PrimeEnergy Corp	20.74

(Continued)

(Continued)

Ticker	Constituent name	Voting power in public ownership (%) (May 2018)
EROS	Eros Intl Plc	20.87
NTNX	Nutanix Inc.	21.02
STXB	Spirit of Texas Bncshres	21.08
AAME	Atlantic Amern Corp	21.09
PPC	Pilgrims Pride Corp	21.19
EOLS	Evolus Inc.	21.19
SBGI	Sinclair Broadcast Group	21.34
PNBK	Patriot Natl Bancorp Inc.	21.37
FNKO	Funko Class A	21.53
SCS	Steelcase Inc.	21.53
MPX	Marine Products Corp	21.55
NCSM	NCS Multistage Hold	21.71
APLS	Apellis Pharmaceuticals	21.75
SNFCA	Security Natl Finl Corp	21.99
FIBK	First Intst Bancsystem	22.14
MCHX	Marchex Inc.	22.16
CWH	Camping World Holdings	22.22
SEB	Seaboard Corp	22.29
QTRX	Quanterix Corporation	22.53
GMED	Globus Medical Inc.	22.75
TWLO	Twilio Inc.	22.94
JOUT	Johnson Outdoors Inc.	23.11
DCPH	Deciphera Pharmaceutical	23.12
ARMO	Armo Biosciences Inc.	23.15
RFL	Rafael Holdings	23.15
CLR	Continental Resources	23.17
TORC	Restorbio Inc.	23.24
RBCAA	Republic Bancorp Inc. KY	23.24
GNK	Genco Shipping & Trading	23.28
INTG	Intergroup Corp	23.28
SAIL	Sailpoint Technologies	23.38
DKS	Dicks Sporting Goods Inc.	23.70
GPRO	Gopro Inc.	23.72
ATRO	Astronics Corp	23.80
EQH	Axa Equitable Holdings	24.47
JBSS	Sanfilippo John B & Son	24.51
LBC	Luther Burbank Corp	24.90
FOR	Forestar Group Inc.	24.92
AMR	Alta Mesa Resources (A)	24.95
ODT	Odonate Therapeutics Inc.	25.00

Source: FTSE Russell Voting Rights Consultation-Next Steps. https://www.ftse.com/products/downloads/FTSE_Russell_Voting_Rights_Consultation_Next_Steps.pdf.

Chapter 4

Fiduciary duty in investment management

Chapter Outline

Addressing the Agency Problem	46	Freshfields Report	54
Fiduciary duty	48	Fiduciary II	56
Fiduciary obligations	48	United Nations Principles for	
"Prudent man" rule	49	Responsible Investing	57
Uniform Prudent Investor Act	51	Organization for Economic	
Uniform Prudent Management of		Cooperation and Development	58
Institutional Funds Act	53	Summary	58

Increasingly, corporations are including environmental, social, and governance (ESG) responsibility into their strategic planning, reporting, and day-to-day operations. This has been accompanied by growing support from institutional investors. And as we have seen, individual investors show a growing preference for ESG factors in their investment portfolios. But fiduciaries, who make financial decisions on behalf of others, have more complex considerations to make before adding ESG factors into their investment process. A fiduciary can be defined as an individual who has a duty to act in good faith and in a trustworthy manner toward another individual, especially in financial matters. There are many positions which often require the person to act in a fiduciary capacity: accountants, bankers, executors, trustees, financial advisers, board members, and corporate officers are some examples. Traditionally, financial return to beneficiaries has been their only objective, but today fiduciaries are increasingly being asked to consider additional dimensions beyond purely short-term monetary gains. Many investors are focused on the social value of making investments consistent with their ESG goals, and there is growing support for the idea that investments with negative ESG factors may increase the risk of negative financial performance, especially in the long run. For example, the Bank of England's Prudential Regulation Authority (PRA) has identified climate change as posing financial risks relevant to the Bank's objectives (PRA, 2018). It has recently undergone a transition in thinking from viewing climate change as a corporate social responsibility to viewing it as a core financial and strategic risk.

Environmental, Social, and Governance (ESG) Investing. DOI: https://doi.org/10.1016/B978-0-12-818692-3.00004-9

While the PRA's focus is on the impact to banks and insurance companies, the potential risks they identify are no less relevant to the financial performance of all investment portfolios.

So, what are the issues involved in fiduciaries' decision-making? Are fiduciaries violating their duties if they consider anything other than traditional financial objectives? Or conversely, if negative ESG actions can result in long-run financial underperformance, are fiduciaries negligent in ignoring these factors? We frame the discussion first from the perspective of the "Agency Problem."

Addressing the Agency Problem

The Agency Problem can be defined as a situation where an individual (the agent) takes actions on behalf of an asset owner (the principal). If the motivations of the agent and the principal are not perfectly aligned, opportunities exist for the agent to act in ways that are not beneficial, or even harmful to the principal. This problem can arise when corporate boards and executives don't act in the interests of shareholders, and in fact this potential conflict exists in a wide variety of interactions. It may be more pronounced in increasingly sophisticated financial markets where information asymmetries exist and potential rewards for bad acts can be substantial. For example, retail stock brokers have traditionally been paid commissions based on transactions rather than customer financial gains. If the customer's account is fully invested in the initial period, it may grow in value with gains in the invested assets. But if there are no additional trades, the commissions to the broker would be minimal. The more trades an account does, the greater the broker's income. This has occasionally led to illegal "churning" of accounts where brokers reaped the benefits of excessive buying and selling of stocks, with the owner of the account often suffering losses. (Many broker compensation plans have moved to charging a percentage of assets under management, thus limiting the impact of an over-trading incentive.) Another example: a real estate broker acting on behalf of a buyer is paid a commission as a percentage of the purchase price. The broker has an incentive to steer the client to a higher priced property. This may not be standard operating practice, but it would be naïve to think it never happens.

In the context of the firm, the agency problem can be illustrated as corporate managers taking actions that are detrimental to shareholders. Managers who are paid bonuses on short-term profits could take actions which boost quarterly earnings and bonuses but threaten the long-term viability of the company and its profitability for continuing shareholders.

The agency problem can be complicated when one adds the layer of complexity introduced by ESG factors. This would be the case where business managers who spend corporate time and assets on ESG issues could be seen by some shareholders to be squandering corporate assets if those shareholders don't have the same values as the managers. The flip side of this is the case where the investors want the business managers to undertake positive ESG actions, but the managers are in fact acting in ways detrimental to those shareholder values. Here's an example of senior corporate executives' negative actions dramatically affecting shareholders: media and resort companies have generally little adverse ESG impact (especially if we don't consider the extra carbon generated by the private jets favored by media stars and top executives!). But investigations in 2018 uncovered widespread hostile acts toward women by several prominent men in CEO positions. Shareholders who had invested in these companies in part because of their positive ESG scores were sorely disappointed to discover their managers were engaging in such negative actions. And the pain was not just in social and governance behavior, but it was financial as well. Shares in Wynn Resorts, for example, dropped roughly 40% and The Weinstein Company filed for Chapter 11 bankruptcy on March 19, 2018. Clearly, ESG factors can have substantial negative financial impact.

So, the agency problem can exist in corporate structures, but in investment management the potential for the agency problem is magnified by several factors. Investing requires significant knowledge about the instruments and their markets, some of which can be opaque and subject to extremely fast-moving events. It is therefore difficult for principals to identify with certainty when advisors or brokers are not acting in their best interests. Also, some investment managers have conflicting roles which can be difficult to fence off, even when they are disclosed. For example, an investment product sponsored by a broker's parent company may pay a higher commission to the broker but have higher fees or lower return to the owner than a similar but slightly different external product. It is almost impossible in practice for an investor to understand when this is happening. Fees and other incentives may thus not always be structured to optimally align the motives of agent and principals. And finally, there can be a lot of money at stake: large potential payoffs for taking steps not in the best interest of principals can lure some agents into crossing the line and taking actions which enrich themselves while causing harm to their investing clients.

So, as we mentioned, the person acting in an agency capacity in financial asset management is called a "fiduciary," which is derived from a Latin root meaning "trust," as in the beneficiary trusts that the agent will "do the right thing" in managing assets. There are both legal and ethical responsibilities required of fiduciaries and these have an important impact on ESG investing. Historically, investment managers have justified ignoring ESG factors by contending that to do anything other than manage investments to maximize financial returns would violate their fiduciary duty. But more recently, this view has been challenged. In the balance of this chapter, we will look at these arguments.

Fiduciary duty

This section is a review of fiduciary duty from an Economist's point of view, seen within the context of the agency problem and shaped by US regulations. However, it should not be considered in any way to be legal advice. Sources cited here may have opinions on these matters which might be challenged by others. It should come as no surprise to the reader that the lack of unanimity often seen among Economists is second only to the willingness of attorneys to differ on these questions.

Many if not most investment managers still hold to the traditional argument that they are not allowed to focus on anything other than financial returns. Increasingly, some authors disagree. Richardson (2007) for example, concludes that: "Contrary to common perceptions on the subject, SRI [Socially Responsible Investing] does not always or necessarily conflict with fiduciary duties of pension funds. Moreover, fulfilling fiduciary obligations can actually require careful attention to corporate social and environmental performance."

Where the only consideration is financial gain of the beneficial owners, responsibilities are straight forward. It's no wonder that many managers favor this simple approach, with convenient, noncontroversial metrics. But when broader investment objectives are included it gets more complicated. Proponents of including ESG factors point out that these are risk factors which may not be properly accounted for by traditional financial analysis. They argue that considerations of long-term preservation of capital should expressly take into account these factors. Thus they believe that consideration of these factors is not peripheral but is central and integral to a required, prudent focus on the economic interests of the beneficiaries. But what are the obligations of fiduciaries and do the regulations concerning managing investment funds allow for the consideration of ESG issues?

Fiduciary obligations

Private pension funds in the United States follow the requirements of the Employee Retirement Income Security Act of 1974 (ERISA). ERISA defines the responsibilities of a fiduciary as:

- Acting solely in the interest of pension plan participants and their beneficiaries and with the exclusive purpose of providing benefits to them;
- Carrying out their duties prudently;
- Following the plan documents; and
- Paying only reasonable plan expenses (ERISA, 2017).

State pension funds, mutual funds, and endowments tend to follow these rules as well as relevant state laws. The rules governing charities come from several different sources. In the United States, the majority of publicly traded companies follow the Delaware state laws for corporations. Delaware law provides for three primary fiduciary obligations: the duty of loyalty, the duty of impartiality, and the duty of care (for a good discussion of the issues, see Shier, 2017).

The first obligation requires the fiduciary to act in the best interests of the beneficiary, and only of the beneficiary. Self-dealing or conflicts of interest would violate this obligation. These concerns are pretty clear-cut when financial profit is the only consideration, but when ESG issues are factored in, it can become more complicated. There may be some specification of how to treat ESG factors in the original documentation establishing the fiduciary relationship, but historically this has not usually been the case. If there is no such statement, the desires of the beneficiary could be considered. In the case of multiple beneficiaries, the question becomes much more complicated again because there are potentially differences of opinion on including ESG factors. In that case the fallback position has been to simply consider maximizing financial return. The duty of loyalty would seem to make it difficult for the agent to make financial decisions based solely on her own beliefs with respect to including ESG issues without some guidance from the original document or from the beneficiaries.

A second obligation of a fiduciary is not to favor any one beneficiary over another. In the context of ESG investing, this is not an issue for funds whose beneficiaries have essentially identical goals. For example, a charitable foundation or pension fund would be expected to have investments which would not favor some individuals over others. However, where there is a pronounced diversity of interests in a pooled fund, the issue of impartiality can be important.

A third obligation for the fiduciary is one of care. Decisions must be carefully considered. Investment of funds must be prudent investments. This does not mean returns have to be maximized. The fiduciary can consider issues of risk and diversification. Although there are some differences in this obligation for different types of fiduciaries (public pension funds, charitable institutions, trusts managed by an individual or a corporation), they are very similar.

"Prudent Man" rule

The "Prudent Man" rule requires a trustee to manage trust assets as would a prudent investor, exercising reasonable care, skill, and caution. (In our more enlightened age, this rule would be named and referred to in a gender-neutral manner. However, in an effort to avoid confusion, I will use the original title of the rule.) The trustee has a duty to diversify the portfolio in keeping with the recognized benefits from doing so as understood from Modern Portfolio Theory. The trustee is further charged with exercising prudence in hiring necessary skilled advisors, accountants, lawyers, etc., while minimizing costs. Asset classes considered to be prudent investments have evolved over time to include equities, real estate, venture capital, and other investments previously thought to be excessively risky. Guidance has progressed to the point where no investment is per se prohibited, and rules have become general and flexible enough to accommodate prudent use of just about any suitable investment.

The Prudent Man rule was originally developed in the Commonwealth of Massachusetts in the early 1800s and later adopted by other states. Under "The Restatement (Second) of Trusts: Prudent Man Rule (1959)," when making investments the trustee is subject to the following:

- In the absence of provisions in the terms of the trust or of a statute otherwise providing, to make such investments and only such investments as a prudent man would make of his own property having in view the preservation of the estate and the amount and regularity of the income to be derived;
- In the absence of provisions in the terms of the trust, to conform to the statutes, if any, governing investments by trustees; and
- To conform to the terms of the trust (FDIC, 2007).

Unless the terms of the trust provide otherwise, the trustee is under a duty to the beneficiary to use reasonable care and skill to preserve the trust property and to make it productive. In making investments, the trustee has several requirements:

- Requirement of care. The trustee exercises due care in making an investment in considering both the expected return and risk. She may take into consideration advice and information from qualified attorneys, bankers, brokers, and others but must exercise her own judgment.
- Requirement of skill. The trustee is liable for a loss resulting from his failure to use the skill of a man of ordinary intelligence, and, if the trustee has a greater degree of skill than that of a man of ordinary intelligence, he is liable for a loss resulting from the failure to use such skill.
- Corporate trustees are held to a higher standard. If the trustee is a bank or trust company, it must use the facilities which it has or should have, and it may properly be required to show that it has made a more thorough and complete investigation than would an individual trustee.
- Requirement of caution. In making investments not only is the trustee under a duty to use due care and skill, but he must use the caution of a prudent man. The trustee must consider the safety of the principal as well as expected income.

The trustee, in considering the scope of investments that she should make, should take into consideration many circumstances, such as:

- the amount of the trust estate,
- the situation of the beneficiaries,

- the trend of prices and of the cost of living, and
- the prospect of inflation and of deflation.

It is noted that in some cases, income may be more important than pres-ervation of capital, and in other cases, the reverse may be true. Initially, the Rule specified a very limited list of acceptable low risk investments, but over time many other asset classes have been found to be consistent with prudent investing. The terms of the trust may provide for the category of investments that are allowable, but the trustee must still use "care and skill and caution" in selecting these investments. Trustee investment choices may be either "permitted" or "mandatory." The trustee may be "authorized or allowed" to make certain investments and thus has a privilege but not a duty to do so. On the other hand, the trustee may be "directed" to make those investments and must do so. If the terms of the trust provide that the trustee is authorized to make investments "in his discretion" the scope of allowable investments may be broadened, although he cannot lend trust money to him-self individually or purchase securities from himself individually. In all cases, investments must still be consistent with the actions of a "prudent man dealing with his own property and having primarily in view the preser-vation of the trust estate and the amount and regularity of the income to be derived." In the case of an informal trust where one gives money to another to invest for her, the suitability of investments may be governed by verbal instructions. The trustee has the same duty in making investments whether the trust is created verbally or by a formal document such as a will or deed.

In this 1959 formulation of fiduciary rules, delegation of duties is also not allowed. Where a trustee has the ability to make investment decisions, this function cannot be outsourced to others. We will see that this delegation prohibition is later lifted.

Uniform Prudent Investor Act

Recognizing the significant changes in investment theory and practice in the second half of the twentieth century, trust investment law was updated by the Uniform Prudent Investor Act (UPIA) of 1994. This Act drew on the Restatement (Third) of Trusts (1992) and leans heavily on theoretical and empirical work deriving from Modern Portfolio Theory. A fundamental result from this work is that diversification of assets results in superior port-folio performance as measured by either a lower risk for a given level of return, or higher expected return for a given level of risk (see more about this in Chapter 6: Financial markets: equities). Specific investments should not be considered on their own, but as part of an overall portfolio, recogniz-ing risk/reward tradeoffs, and the fact that uncorrelated or negatively corre-lated assets can lower overall portfolio risk. Assets such as commodities or real estate that on their own might be considered imprudently risky, are now seen as important, prudent sources of diversification. This Act provided for changes in five areas of the Prudent Man Rule:

- A trust account's entire investment portfolio is considered when applying the standard of prudence.
- The consideration and tradeoff of risk and return is identified as the fiduciary's central consideration.
- No category of investment is explicitly forbidden: the trustee can invest in anything that plays an appropriate role in achieving the risk/return objectives of the trust and that meets the other requirements of prudent investing.
- Diversification of investments is explicitly recognized in the definition of prudent investing.
- The earlier prohibition on delegation of investment and management functions is reversed, recognizing the increased complexity of capital markets and the value of specialists.

While not expressly considering ESG investment factors, this Act opens the door by removing arbitrary restrictions on investments, recognizing the portfolio value of alternatives, and incorporating risk factors in portfolio management. More fundamentally, it reflects a recognition of the need to incorporate updated and evolving concepts of prudent investing. Commentators have further raised the question of a trustee's ability to incorporate ESG issues in investment decision making. The concerns are analogous to those of a firm's board and managers, as discussed in Chapter 3: Theory of the firm. Are trustees bound to focus only on preservation of capital subject to risk tolerance and income needs, or can they properly take into consideration issues of morality, ethics, and public welfare? And if a trustee reasonably takes a longer-term view of risks, it's clear that negative ESG actions have severely harmed some companies which were otherwise favorably viewed by investors. With this historical perspective, aren't these ESG factors legitimately material even from a narrow focus on risk adjusted financial return? Over time, many commentators have come around to the conclusion that trustees may consider ESG factors in part due to a recognition that these issues can have a long-term impact on the risk of individual investments and the portfolio as a whole. A related question is: can a portfolio be constructed with positive ESG characteristics which has little or no diminution in return? We will look at empirical evidence of such portfolios in later chapters.

Over the years, the US Department of Labor (DOL) has issued several clarifications and guidance to the ERISA rules. With particular relevance to ESG consideration, DOL in its Field Assistance Bulletin issued in April 2018 (DOL, 2018), had this to say:

In 2015, the Department reiterated its longstanding view that, because every investment necessarily causes a plan to forego other investment opportunities, plan fiduciaries are not permitted to sacrifice investment return or take on additional investment risk as a means of using plan investments to promote collateral social policy goals...[but] when competing investments serve the plan's economic interests equally well, plan fiduciaries can use such collateral considerations as tie-breakers for an investment choice...if a fiduciary prudently determines that an investment is appropriate based solely on economic considerations, including those that may derive from environmental, social and governance [(ESG)] factors, the fiduciary may make the investment without regard to any collateral benefits the investment may also promote.

The bulletin goes on to state:

Fiduciaries must not too readily treat ESG factors as economically relevant to the particular investment choices at issue when making a decision. It does not ineluctably follow from the fact that an investment promotes ESG factors, or that it arguably promotes positive general market trends or industry growth, that the investment is a prudent choice for retirement or other investors. Rather, ERISA fiduciaries must always put first the economic interests of the plan in providing retirement benefits. A fiduciary's evaluation of the economics of an investment should be focused on financial factors that have a material effect on the return and risk of an investment based on appropriate investment horizons consistent with the plan's articulated funding and investment objectives.

This guidance has been interpreted by some to set a higher bar for consideration of ESG factors and consequently has made many defined contribution pension plan sponsors reluctant to offer ESG investment funds. Others, however, believe that this guidance does not conflict with offering ESG funds provided that sponsors are clear that the economic interests of the plan take precedence and that ESG considerations are well researched and are not random or used "to promote collateral social policy goals."

Uniform Prudent Management of Institutional Funds Act

Guidance for nonprofit and charitable organizations is provided by state laws and by the Uniform Prudent Management of Institutional Funds Act (UPMIFA) which updated a previous act which restricted the ability of a nonprofit to spend funds if its capital dropped below the original value of contributions. Fiduciaries acting for charitable organizations also have the duties of loyalty, impartiality, and prudent investment. The primary consideration is donor intent as expressed in documentation establishing gifts or donations. This documentation may explicitly provide for consideration of ESG factors. Fiduciaries must act in the best interest of the charity but may also consider the mission of the charity as a factor in making investment decisions. It would hardly make sense for the fiduciary to make investments which functioned at cross purposes to the charity itself. The key provision of UPMIFA specified that the institution could spend as much as it believed to be prudent, subject to donor instructions in the gift instrument. UPMIFA requirements specify that those managing funds for a charity must do the following:

- Give primary consideration to donor intent as expressed in a gift instrument, ... and shall consider the charitable purposes of the institution and the purposes of the institutional fund;
- Act in good faith, with the care an ordinarily prudent person would exercise;
- Incur only reasonable costs in investing and managing charitable funds;
- Make a reasonable effort to verify relevant facts;
- Make decisions about each asset in the context of the portfolio of investments, as part of an overall investment strategy;
- Diversify investments unless due to special circumstances the purposes of the fund are better served without diversification;
- Dispose of unsuitable assets; and
- In general, develop an investment strategy appropriate for the fund and the charity (UPMIFA, 2006).

In general, the duties of managers of charitable funds are in line with those discussed above in the section on UPIA. "Although the UPIA by its terms applies to trusts and not to charitable corporations, the standards of UPIA can be expected to inform the investment responsibilities of directors and officers of charitable corporations." Important sections of UPMIFA have to do with expenditures, which are out of scope for our discussion and have no impact on our interest in investment decisions related to ESG issues.

In 2016 the US Department of Labor proposed a "Fiduciary Rule" which would have expanded the definition of an "investment advice fiduciary." As initially crafted the new rule would strengthen measures designed to protect investors from conflicts that could lead advisors to choose investment products with unnecessarily high fees. Opponents of the rule countered that it was overly complex, would not prevent all abuses, would be costly, and could result in higher expenses. Shortly before the rule was to go into effect, in March 2018, the US Fifth Circuit Court of Appeals vacated the rule. While this proposed rule would have an impact on fiduciaries' potential conflicts of interest, it is not obvious that it would have an impact on our area of interest here, namely the ability of a trustee to consider ESG factors when making investment choices.

Freshfields Report

The discussion so far has been limited to US rules governing fiduciaries. International groups have looked at the issue in several different countries around the globe. The Asset Management Working Group of the United Nations Environment Programme Finance Institute (UNEP FI) commissioned a 2005 document known as the "Freshfields Report" (Freshfields Bruckhaus Deringer, 2005). The motivation for the report was stated as:

> ...the interesting questions concerning fiduciary responsibility come to the fore: are the best interests of savers only to be defined as their financial interest? If so, in respect to which horizon? Are not the social and environmental interests of savers also to be taken into account? Indeed, many people wonder what good an extra percent or three of patrimony are worth if the society in which they are to enjoy retirement and in which their descendants will live deteriorates. Quality of life and quality of the environment are worth something, even if not, or particularly because, they are not reducible to financial percentages. While not pretending to answer in the abstract what is right and what is good, we have sought to get expert opinion on the question whether the law restricts us, as asset managers, from seeking to attend to broadly accepted extra-financial interests of savers in conjunction with their financial interests.

The report was commissioned to address the following specific question:

> Is the integration of environmental, social and governance issues into investment policy (including asset allocation, portfolio construction and stock-picking or bond-picking) voluntarily permitted, legally required or hampered by law and regulation; primarily as regards public and private pension funds, secondarily as regards insurance company reserves and mutual funds?

The authors of the report looked at fiduciary duty in several jurisdictions and observe that:

> ...Despite the growing body of evidence that ESG issues can have a material impact on the financial performance of securities and an increased recognition of the importance of assessing ESG-related risks, those seeking a greater regard for ESG issues in investment decision-making often encounter resistance on the basis of a belief that institutional principals and their agents are legally prevented from taking account of such issues.

They analyze several different jurisdictions, but with respect to the United States specifically, they find:

> There is accordingly no reason why investment strategies should not include investments with positive ESG characteristics. The important limiting requirement is that imposed by the duty of loyalty: all investment decisions must be motivated by the interests of the fund's beneficiaries and/or the purposes of the fund. No investment should be made purely to give effect to the personal views of the decision-maker. Instead, all considerations must be weighed and assessed in the context of their expected impact on the investment portfolio. Moreover, as with all considerations, ESG considerations must be taken into

*account wherever they are relevant to any aspect of the investment strategy
(including general economic or political context, expected tax consequences,
the role that each investment plays within the overall portfolio, expected risk
and return, and the need for liquidity and/or capital appreciation). In addition,
where the beneficiaries have expressed investment preferences in the fund
instrument or otherwise, these preferences should also be taken into account.
In short, there appears to be no bar to integrating ESG considerations into the
day-to-day process of fund management, provided the focus is always on the
beneficiaries/purposes of the fund and not on unrelated objectives.*

They conclude:

*...the links between ESG factors and financial performance are increasingly
being recognized. On that basis, integrating ESG considerations into an investment analysis so as to more reliably predict financial performance is clearly
permissible and is arguably required in all jurisdictions.*

Fiduciary II

The Freshfields report was followed up in 2009 by a second study (UNEP
FI, 2009), known as "Fiduciary II." This report took the more aggressive
point of view that advisors and fund managers risk being sued if they do not
take ESG issues into consideration. It concludes:

- Fiduciaries have a duty to consider more actively the adoption of responsible investment strategies.
- Fiduciaries must recognize that integrating ESG issues into investment
  and ownership processes is part of responsible investment and is necessary to managing risk and evaluating opportunities for long-term
  investment.
- Fiduciaries will increasingly come to understand the materiality of ESG
  issues and the systemic risk they pose, and the profound long-term costs
  of unsustainable development and the consequent impacts on the long-
  term value of their investment portfolios.
- Fiduciaries will increasingly apply pressure to their asset managers to
  develop robust investment strategies that integrate ESG issues into financial analysis, and to engage with companies in order to encourage more
  responsible and sustainable business practices.
- Global capital market policymakers should also make it clear that advisors to institutional investors have a duty to proactively raise ESG issues
  within the advice that they provide, and that a responsible investment
  option should be the default position. Furthermore, policymakers should
  ensure prudential regulatory frameworks that enable greater transparency
  and disclosure from institutional investors and their agents on the

integration of ESG issues into their investment process, as well as from companies on their performance on ESG issues.
- Finally, civil society institutions should collectively bolster their understanding of capital markets such that they can play a full role in ensuring that capital markets are sustainable and delivering responsible ownership.

The tone of Fiduciary II was clearly much more aggressive than the earlier Freshfields report and probably did as much to antagonize skeptics as it did to convert them. Despite UNEP FIs strong position on including ESG in fiduciary considerations, the debate rages on and in 2016 UNEP FI launched a 3-year project charged with:

- Working with investors, governments, and intergovernmental organizations to develop and publish an international statement on fiduciary duty, which includes the requirement to integrate ESG issues into investment processes and practices.
- Publishing and implementing roadmaps on the policy changes required to achieve full integration of ESG issues in investment processes and practices across eight countries.
- Extending the research into fiduciary duties—and, more broadly, investor duties—to six Asian markets: China, Hong Kong, India, Korea, Malaysia, and Singapore.

United Nations Principles for Responsible Investing

The United Nations Principles for Responsible Investing (PRI) were developed by a group of the world's largest institutional investors, along with experts from intergovernmental organizations and civil society. The Principles, which are voluntary and aspirational guides to investment and were made public in 2006, are as follows:

- Principle 1: We will incorporate ESG issues into investment analysis and decision-making processes.
- Principle 2: We will be active owners and incorporate ESG issues into our ownership policies and practices.
- Principle 3: We will seek appropriate disclosure on ESG issues by the entities in which we invest.
- Principle 4: We will promote acceptance and implementation of the Principles within the investment industry.
- Principle 5: We will work together to enhance our effectiveness in implementing the Principles.
- Principle 6: We will each report on our activities and progress towards implementing the Principles.

The group behind the Principles considers ESG factors to be fundamentally important to fiduciary duty:

Fiduciary duty requires investors to act in the best interests of beneficiaries, and in doing so to take into account environmental, social and governance (ESG) factors, as these factors can be financially significant over the short and long term. The globally agreed SDGs [Social Development Goals] are an articulation of the world's most pressing environmental, social and economic issues and as such act as a definitive list of the material ESG factors that should be taken into account as part of an investor's fiduciary duty.

UNGC, 2017.

And, unequivocally:

Failing to consider all long-term investment value drivers, including ESG issues, is a failure of fiduciary duty.

Organization for Economic Cooperation and Development

In looking at ESG factors and investment governance in developed countries the Organization for Economic Cooperation and Development (OECD) concluded the following:

- Regulatory frameworks allow scope for institutional investors to integrate ESG factors into their investment governance. However, difficulties remain for investors in reconciling their obligations toward their beneficiaries with ESG integration. Lack of regulatory clarity, practical complexity and behavioral issues may discourage ESG integration.
- ESG factors influence investment returns through their impact on corporate financial performance and through the risks they pose to broader economic growth and financial market stability.
- There are technical and operational difficulties in measuring and understanding ESG-related portfolio risks; however, a growing number of tools are becoming available that enable institutional investors to integrate ESG factors to a greater or lesser extent (OECD, 2017).

Summary

In summary, the duties of fiduciaries are clearly to act in the best interests of beneficiaries. Over time, these responsibilities have been broadened to account for portfolio diversification and other risk issues primarily motivated by Modern Portfolio Theory. And an increasing number of writers believe that risks arising from ESG factors can and should be considered in the investment analysis, although at least in the United States, this is not currently the dominant opinion among investors.

Chapter 5

Overview of financial institutions

Chapter Outline

Information asymmetries, moral
hazard, and adverse selection   60
Commercial banks   63
Credit unions   64
Investment banks   66
   Trading and research   68
   Asset securitization   70
   Mergers and acquisitions   71
   Prime brokerage   71
Central banks   71
   Conventional monetary tools   73
   Unconventional monetary policy   74
   Other central banks   75
Shadow banking: other financial
intermediaries   76

Insurance companies   78
   Categories of insurance   78
   Prudential Financial Inc   83
   MetLife Inc   84
   Zurich Insurance Group   86
Pension funds   86
   Largest pension funds   89
   CalPERS   90
   Florida State Board of
   Administration   92
Asset managers   92
Hedge funds   94
Private equity   94

In later chapters, we will investigate several different environmental, social, and governance (ESG) investment styles and products. Literally trillions of dollars of capital are flowing into debt and equity assets. To understand these investments and potential future innovations we need a basic understanding of the US financial system. It's important to understand who the participants are: the investors, the issuers, and financial intermediaries; the fundamental reasons for their existence; the several types of institutions; and the range of services and products that they currently provide. In this chapter and in Chapter 6, Financial markets: equities, and Chapter 7 Financial markets: bonds, we will look at financial products, markets, and organizational entities. The starting point is understanding basic banking services which have evolved over a few thousand years from ancient forms of payment transfers and wealth management, such as it might have been. With the advent of the industrial revolution, society began to collect increasingly large surpluses which could be put to productive use. As these surpluses grew, so too did

Environmental, Social, and Governance (ESG) Investing. DOI: https://doi.org/10.1016/B978-0-12-818692-3.00005-0

banking institutions evolve to find the most efficient way to match up those with extra funds and the most productive uses for those funds. As the form of these banks have changed dramatically over time, so to have bank products evolved to cover a wide, ever-growing range. For banks to have survived over the ages there must be some basic economic role that they fulfill. At its core, the banking system provides an important economic function in paying a return to those with excess funds and delivering capital where it's needed. In a simple society, lenders could theoretically provide funds to borrowers directly, with no need for "intermediation" by a third party. But there are costs to borrowers to find those with funds to loan. And in parallel, people with money to loan or invest would need to spend time trying to find those with investable ideas. Then there is the issue of credit quality. How to tell a good risk from a poor one? Once a lender and a borrower found each other, contractual terms would have to be agreed and drawn up. How would payments be made and what would their frequency be? All these steps take time and require expertise. To address these and other issues, financial intermediation provided by banks and other institutions has thrived over the centuries. The latest Fintech peer to peer lending platforms also perform this economic function of intermediation, although with a much lighter touch than the largest banks.

Information asymmetries, moral hazard, and adverse selection

In addition to reducing transaction costs, financial institutions address several other problems which exist in lending, as well as other economic transactions. Borrowers and lenders often have different amounts of information about the details of financial transactions, especially when the lender is an individual or "retail" person. Typically, the borrower will know more about their business and their likelihood of repaying a loan than an individual lender would know. This information asymmetry puts an individual at a disadvantage. The classic example is the case of buying a used car. The average individual can't tell if it's in perfect running condition ("cherry"), or if it's on its last legs (a "lemon"). So, to protect themselves from crippling repair costs, the buyer must assume it's a lemon, budget for repairs and bid only what a lemon is worth. The seller doesn't want to sell a great cherry car for the low, lemon price, so they pull their cherry car out of the market. The seller of a lemon, however, sees this as a fair price, so the lemon stays in the market. If we generalize this example, we can say that where the buyer doesn't have sufficient information, the market will be dominated by bad or risky products and good products will not be offered. This situation is called "adverse selection." In banking, this means that if a lender can't tell a good deal from a bad deal, they would have less risk in assuming all deals are bad and budgeting accordingly. Consequently, they would offer terms suitable for bad deals and would be unlikely to see the good deals. Only bad deals would get funded.

The next issue that arises, also related to information asymmetry is "moral hazard." This refers to a situation where a borrower might take on excessive risk if the negative consequences of their actions would be borne by another party. An example in the insurance world would be if a failing restaurant owner has fire insurance, they might not be as careful about kitchen fires if they know that the insurance company will pay for the damage. Or take the case of mortgage lending. In the years leading up to the Global Financial Crisis, some mortgage "originators" would approve loans for borrowers who couldn't afford them. The originators would collect a fee for the mortgage, which would be passed on or sold to investors. When the borrowers eventually defaulted on the loans, it was the investors who took the loss and not the originators. (The Dodd-Frank Wall Street Reform and Consumer Protection Act created several mortgage-lending rules to address these poor lending practices, among others.)

Financial institutions play a key role in addressing these information asymmetries and consequent risk of adverse selection and moral hazard. Their research, monitoring, and other services are able to specialize in these areas and provide far better protection than any individual alone might be able to do. In addition, multiple layers of government regulation reinforce these efforts.

Here are some of the key factors accounting for the importance of financial institutions:

- Intermediation—Individuals and businesses with excess funds seek to earn a return on those funds, and borrowers need to raise funds for various purposes. Banks fulfill a role in matching those needs. There is also a temporal dimension to this intermediation. Depositors may wish to withdraw funds at any time for a variety of reasons, whereas loans typically have a fixed maturity. Banks provide the function of meeting the requirements of both groups of customers.
- Diversification—Without financial intermediaries, investors, especially those with smaller amounts of funds, would find it difficult to reduce their risk by diversifying into different assets. Modern banks offer a wide range of products in their "financial supermarkets."
- Information and Contracting Efficiencies—Banks can hire and train specialists to perform necessary due diligence to evaluate investments and to enter into effective contracts. Individuals are unlikely to develop these skills on their own.
- Payments—It is estimated that 95% of cash today exists as electronic entries at financial institutions. This attests to the usefulness of the banks' function as a center for payment transfers and record keeping.
- Security—Rather than stuffing cash in a mattress or burying gold in the backyard, most people take for granted the security of having financial assets maintained at a financial institution.

- Cost Savings: Economies of Scale and Scope—As banks have built up infrastructure for delivering financial products, the incremental cost for processing a given transaction has become dramatically reduced. There may be debates about potential diseconomies of scale due to increasing regulatory burdens that come with bank size, but, in general, for most financial operations, economies of scale would seem to be positive. It is also important to note that bank lending is the predominant source of funding for business, more important than equity and bonds in the United States and loans are even more important in other countries. "Economies of scope" refers to efficiencies in pursuing parallel lines of business. Economies are gained by virtue of expertise or shared overhead used in activities that are not identical. For example, experience in drafting contractual terms for one asset may yield a benefit in drafting contractual terms for a different asset. Relationships developed in one market may be useful in pursuing a second market.

Fig. 5.1 shows the largest commercial banks in the United States.

Bank name / Holding Co name	Nat'l rank	Bank ID	Bank location	Charter	Consol assets (Mil $)	Domestic assets (Mil $)	Pct domestic assets	Pct Cumulative Assets	Domestic branches	Foreign branches	IBF	Pct foreign owned
JPMORGAN CHASE BK NA/JPMORGAN CHASE & CO	1	852218	COLUMBUS, OH	NAT	2,194,835	1,639,236	75	14	5,070	33	Y	0.00
BANK OF AMER NA/BANK OF AMER CORP	2	480228	CHARLOTTE, NC	NAT	1,797,881	1,594,771	94	25	4,417	22	Y	0.00
WELLS FARGO BK NA/WELLS FARGO & CO	3	451965	SIOUX FALLS, SD	NAT	1,665,128	1,611,326	97	36	5,778	14	Y	0.00
CITIBANK NA/CITIGROUP	4	476810	SIOUX FALLS, SD	NAT	1,415,081	840,960	59	45	704	172	Y	0.00
US BK NA/U S BC	5	504713	CINCINNATI, OH	NAT	456,011	444,964	98	47	3,110	1	N	0.00
PNC BK NA/PNC FNCL SVC GROUP	6	817834	WILMINGTON, DE	NAT	368,602	364,556	99	50	2,459	2	N	0.00
TD BK NA/TD GRP US HOLDS LLC	7	497404	WILMINGTON, DE	NAT	294,331	294,331	100	52	1,248	0	N	100.00
CAPITAL ONE NA/CAPITAL ONE FC	8	112837	MC LEAN, VA	NAT	290,450	290,384	100	53	540	0	N	0.00
BANK OF NY MELLON/BANK OF NY MELLON CORP	9	541101	NEW YORK, NY	SMB	273,110	169,728	62	55	2	15	Y	0.00
STATE STREET B&TC/STATE STREET CORP	10	35301	BOSTON, MA	SMB	230,961	148,684	64	57	2	11	N	0.00
BRANCH BKG&TC/BB&T CORP	11	852320	WINSTON-SALEM, NC	SNM	216,129	215,913	100	58	1,958	1	N	0.00
SUNTRUST BK/SUNTRUST BK	12	675332	ATLANTA, GA	SMB	205,527	205,527	100	59	1,228	0	Y	0.00
GOLDMAN SACHS BK USA/GOLDMAN SACHS GROUP THE	13	2182786	NEW YORK, NY	SMB	179,244	179,244	100	60	1	1	N	0.00
HSBC BK USA NA/HSBC N AMER HOLDS	14	413208	TYSONS, VA	NAT	172,380	170,486	99	61	227	3	Y	100.00
ALLY BK/ALLY FNCL	15	3284070	SANDY, UT	SMB	151,077	151,077	100	62	0	0	N	0.00
MORGAN STANLEY BK NA/MORGAN STANLEY	16	1456501	SALT LAKE CITY, UT	NAT	141,013	141,013	100	63	0	0	N	0.00
FIFTH THIRD BK/FIFTH THIRD BC	17	723112	CINCINNATI, OH	SMB	139,986	139,389	100	64	1,170	1	N	0.00
KEYBANK NA/KEYCORP	18	280110	CLEVELAND, OH	NAT	136,905	136,382	100	65	1,189	0	N	0.00
NORTHERN TC/NORTHERN TR CORP	19	210434	CHICAGO, IL	SMB	131,900	85,035	64	66	57	5	Y	0.00
CHASE BK USA NA/JPMORGAN CHASE & CO	20	489913	WILMINGTON, DE	NAT	131,312	131,312	100	67	0	0	N	0.00

FIGURE 5.1 Largest insured US-chartered commercial banks ranked by consolidated assets. *From: Federal Reserve Board of Governors.* <https://www.federalreserve.gov/releases/lbr/current/>.

Commercial banks

Commercial banks, savings and loan associations, mutual savings banks, and credit unions share the basic banking functions of accepting deposits and making loans. Commercial banks raise funds through deposits, non-deposit borrowing, retained earnings, and stock issuance. Banks earn revenue through a combination of interest earned on lending and fees charged for a variety of products and services. Revenue-generating activities can be characterized as retail or individual banking, institutional banking, and global banking. Here are some of the services provided to individuals:

- checking and savings accounts,
- certificates of deposit,
- mortgages on residential and investment properties,
- home equity and other lines of credit,
- credit card lending,
- student loans,
- new and used car, motorcycle and boat loans,
- foreign exchange and remittance transfers,
- stock brokerage,
- wealth management,
- private banking, and
- insurance.

The following are typical institutional services offered by commercial banks:

- loans to financial and nonfinancial companies and governments,
- cash management and other corporate treasury services,
- leasing,
- commercial real estate,
- trade finance—letters of credit, bill collection, and factoring, and
- human resources services.

Global banking services involve many of the above services as well as capital markets activities. They may be carried out by affiliates of commercial banks or by stand-alone investment banks, which are discussed below. Smaller community banks tend to focus on more local business. Larger banks with a broader reach are called regional and superregional banks. The very largest banks are called money center banks and it is these banks which have global reach.

In their ongoing business, banks face many different risks:

- Credit risk—If a high proportion of borrowers' default on their loans, the bank will suffer losses.

- Interest rate risk—A bank's liabilities (deposits) are more often short-term while its assets (loans) are longer term. If interest rates rise, the bank will have to pay more for deposits, but might not be able to raise rates on all its loans.
- Trading risk—Banks have proprietary desks which take on risk in trading for the bank's own account. They also often acquire an inventory of financial products for sale to the bank's customers. Consequently, these trading positions are at risk to adverse moves in the various markets.
- Operational risk—Banks today have massive processing requirements. The September 11, 2001, terrorist attack made clear to many institutions that simply having a nearby redundant data center was not sufficient. For banks with Disaster Recovery (DR) sites in Manhattan, both centers were out of commission. Some later moved their DR centers across the river to New Jersey. But Super Storm Sandy on October 29, 2012, caused massive flooding in New Jersey as well as in New York. DR sites were able to come online, running on generators. However, many of these sites had only enough fuel for a day or two of operation and were soon shut down as well. It is sometimes said that "Generals plan to fight the last war." As thoughtful as operational risk planning may be, it often is the case that plans address previous crises and there are unforeseen issues that often arise.

Commercial banks play a crucial dual role in the economy: they hold citizens' wealth in the form of deposits and they play a vital role in the conduct of monetary policy. For these reasons, they are subject to regulatory overview by both state and, if nationally chartered, federal regulators. In return, deposits in insured banks are guaranteed by the Federal Depositors Insurance Corporation (FDIC), and the banks can borrow from federal facilities for liquidity and emergency purposes. In addition to state regulators, banks are subject to the rules and oversight of three federal agencies: the Federal Reserve, the Office of the Comptroller of the Currency and the FDIC. These agencies provide oversight with attention to the safety and soundness of the banks, minimizing systemic risk and providing deposit insurance.

Credit unions

Credit unions make consumer loans to a community of users. They are member-owned, not-for-profits and operate in order to deliver these financial services to their members. US credit union are subject to oversight by state regulators. If federally chartered, they may also be subject to oversight by the National Credit Union Administration (NCUA). When a credit union fails, NCUA conducts the liquidation and performs asset management and recovery. NCUA also manages an insurance fund which, like the FDIC, insures the deposits of account holders in all federal credit unions and a majority of state-chartered credit unions. While many credit unions have converted to commercial banks in past years, there are over 6500 credit unions in the United States, with more than $1 trillion in assets. The largest US credit union is Navy Federal Credit Union which serves US Department of Defense employees, contractors, and their families. In 2016 it had over 6 million members and $75 billion in deposits. Assets of the credit unions are predominately housing-related (first and second mortgages and home equity loans), new and used auto loans, and unsecured personal loans. There are also 12 wholesale credit unions, also known as corporate credit unions, central credit unions or "credit unions to credit unions," which provide services to individual credit unions. During the Great Financial Crisis, several of the wholesale credit unions failed when they sustained losses on mortgage-backed securities. Roughly 1% of then existing retail credit unions also failed and since 2008, between 10 and 20 credit unions fail each year.

Savings and loan associations (S&Ls) are also known as "thrifts." When the depositors and borrowers are members with voting rights, they are also known as mutual savings banks. They primarily fund mortgages although they are increasingly blurring the lines with commercial banks. As with other banks, an S&L may be state or federally chartered. During the Great Depression, many S&Ls failed with customers losing most or all their deposits. In response, Congress passed the Federal Home Loan Bank Act in 1932, thereby establishing the Federal Home Loan Bank Board (FHLBB) as overseer, and the Federal Savings and Loan Insurance Corporation was created to insure depositors' accounts. Up to the 1970s confidence had been restored in S&Ls and their business model was relatively simple: pay modest interest rates for deposits and charge a bit more for primarily housing-related loans. However, commercial banks began to offer depositors more innovative products at more attractive rates. To keep S&Ls as viable institutions, Congress began a deregulating process that allowed S&Ls to offer higher rates to depositors and to offer loans for purposes beyond housing finance. The Depository Institutions Deregulation and Monetary Control Act of 1980 allowed them to offer higher interest rates and additional money market and other products. On the asset side, the Garn-St. Germain Depository Institutions Act of 1982 expanded the range of S&L loans beyond traditional housing markets to include commercial loans, and state and municipal securities. These two Acts, along with weakening of accounting standards, resulted in a collapse of the industry. One notable failure was that of the Lincoln Savings and Loan in 1989. Its chairman was Charles Keating, who had been an active contributor to the political campaigns of several US politicians. Five Senators (Allan Cranston, Dennis DeConcini, John Glenn, John McCain, and Donald Reigle), later known as the Keating Five, were accused of improperly intervening on Lincoln's behalf on a matter behalf the FHLBB. By 1989, fully one-third of S&Ls, including Lincoln, had failed, and the Resolution Trust Corporation (RTC) was created, along with the

Office of Thrift Supervision, which replaced the FHLBB. RTC operated for 6 years and managed the disposal of failed thrifts assets. It was responsible for closing 747 thrifts and disposing of almost $500 billion in assets.

The Office of Thrift Supervision is considered to have been the weakest bank regulator in the period leading up to the Global Financial Crisis. Notable failed institutions that had been overseen by OTS were AIG, Washington Mutual, Countrywide, and IndyMac. OTS was closed in 2011 and its functions were rolled into other agencies, primarily the Office of the Comptroller of the Currency.

Competition in mortgage financing from many sources has resulted in reduced margins. Consequently, S&Ls have diversified and today increasingly resemble commercial banks by offering a wider range of loans and services.

Investment banks

Another category of financial institution is the investment bank. As previously discussed, commercial banks manage deposits and other savings accounts and make loans. Investment banks, on the other hand, perform two basic functions. For corporations and government entities which need funds, investment banks provide an array of services to assist in raising those funds. For investors, investment banks perform services as brokers and dealers in marketing financial services and products. While there are differences in their functions, some of the largest financial holding companies will have affiliates which are commercial banks and other affiliates which are investment banks.

Commercial banks were barred from many investment banking activities by the Banking Act of 1933, known as the Glass-Steagall Act. This act was overturned in 1999 with the passage of the Financial Services Modernization Act (FSMA). There are differences of opinion as to whether or not this liberalization of banking practices contributed to the Global Financial Crisis. It certainly contributed to the atmosphere of deregulation, but the major contributors to the crisis are believed to have had little direct relationship to FSMA.

Some investment banks are boutiques which focus on only one activity, such as mergers and acquisitions. Others, especially larger investment banks with distribution capability, provide a full array of services, such as:

- public offering of securities,
- trading,
- private placements,
- securitizations,
- mergers and acquisitions,
- merchant banking,

Global IB bank ranking

	FY 2018			FY 2017		
Bank	Revenue $m	% share	Rank	Revenue $m	% share
JPMorgan	6930.5	8.6	1	6767.1	8.1
Goldman Sachs	6240.2	7.7	2	6001.5	7.2
Morgan Stanley	5127.0	6.3	4	4936.6	5.9
BofA Merrill lynch	4487.2	5.6	3	5036.2	6.0
Citi	4006.1	5.0	5	4386.0	5.3
Credit Suisse	3452.6	4.3	6	3790.1	4.5
Barclays	3336.9	4.1	7	3498.7	4.2
Deutsche Bank	2455.6	3.0	8	2693.3	3.2
Jefferies LLC	1798.8	2.2	12	1638.5	2.0
UBS	1741.8	2.2	9	1881.6	2.3
Subtotal	39,576.7	49.0		40,629.6	48.7
Total	80,743.0	100.0		83,418.8	100.0

FIGURE 5.2   Global IB Bank revenue. *From: Wall Street Journal.* <*http://graphics.wsj.com/investment-banking-scorecard/*>.

- restructuring advice,
- securities finance,
- prime brokerage,
- clearing and custody services,
- origination and trading of derivatives, and
- asset management.

The largest investment banks are often classified as being in the "Bulge Bracket." This includes JP Morgan, Goldman Sachs, and Morgan Stanley, followed closely by Bank of America Merrill Lynch, Citi, Barclays, Deutsche Bank, Credit Suisse, and UBS. A second group, often challenging the Bulge Bracket firms, would include Wells Fargo, RBC, HSBC, BNP Paribas, Société Générale, BMO, Mizuho, and Nomura. And then there are the prestigious boutiques: Evercore, Moelis, Lazard, Allen, Greenhill, Qatalyst, and others.

Fig. 5.2 shows the top 10 investment banks and their revenues for 2017 and 2018.

Fig. 5.3 shows investment banking revenue by product or service area. Mergers and acquisitions was the top-performing area, and the leading bank was Goldman Sachs. For many years, fixed income, currencies and commodities had been the leading fee generator at Goldman and several recent CEOs

Top earners by product

Product	Revenue $m	% cge	Y-o-Y	Top bank	% share
Equity Capital Markets	15,543.5	14	⌄	JPMorgan	9.0
Follow-On	7686.1	21	⌄	JPMorgan	9.4
IPO	6226.6	8	⌄	Morgan Stanley	8.8
Mergers & Acquisitions	28,253.5	11	⌃	Goldman Sachs	10.7
Debt Capital Markets	19,890.0	16	⌄	JPMorgan	7.2
Corporate Bond-High...	3,874.6	40	⌄	JPMorgan	10.3
Corporate Bond-Inve...	10,560.5	8	⌄	BofA Merrill Lynch	6.7
Syndicated Lending	17,056.3	5	⌃	JPMorgan	9.4
Investment Grade	2,377.8	25	⌃	JPMorgan	12.0
Leveraged	14,678.5	3	⌃	JPMorgan	9.0

Dealogic revenue analytics are employed where fees are not disclosed

FIGURE 5.3 2018 Investment bank revenue breakdown. *From: Wall Street Journal. <http:// graphics.wsj.com/investment-banking-scorecard/>.*

had come from this area. However, in part due to the so-called Volker Rule limiting trading exposure, earnings from these products have declined as a percentage of investment banking revenue. Turning back to Fig. 5.3, we see that the second leading source of fees was debt capital markets, followed by syndicated lending and equity capital markets.

Trading and research

Investment banks play an important role in initial public offerings (IPOs). Often in IPOs and secondary offerings, the investment bank may need to take a principal position in the securities and may act to support markets This is just one of the circumstances which require trading operations and present opportunities for trading profits. Two additional trading activities that many investment banks engage in are risk arbitrage and proprietary trading.

Risk arbitrage is a strategy employed in speculating on the success of a merger of two companies. The trader typically buys the stock of the target company and sells that of the acquirer. When the merger or acquisition is consummated, there will have been a larger gain in the value of the target stock than the loss on the acquirer. Sometimes, however, a merger will fail to go through and the risk arb will suffer a loss. Arbitrage more generally involves going long one instrument and short another in the belief that their joint movement offers profit potential while presenting less risk than trading an outright position.

Proprietary trading, or speculation, is the use of the bank's capital as principal in a trading position. The bank will realize a profit or loss depending on the performance of the position. Banks' prop trading activity increased dramatically after the repeal of Glass-Steagall in 1999 and grew to be important profit centers for many. The range of markets traded included equity and debt markets, but also currencies, commodities, and other derivatives. The passage of the Dodd-Frank Act and the Volker Rule, however, has put some restrictions on bank speculative trading.

Banks also maintain significant research departments which provide analysis and investment opinions on the macroeconomic outlook, industries, and specific companies.

The independence of this research has been called into question at times. In August 2000, the Securities and Exchange Commission (SEC) issued Reg FD (full disclosure) which requires that all publicly traded companies must disclose material information to all investors at the same time. In 2003 10 Wall Street firms entered into an agreement with the SEC and other regulators which required them to pay $1.4 billion to settle charges that they had issued fraudulent research. This research was found to be routinely overly optimistic and was designed to assist the firms' investment banking units in gaining lucrative business from the covered companies. The 10 banks were Bear Sterns, CSFB, Goldman Sachs, JP Morgan, Merrill Lynch, Morgan Stanley, CitiGroup, Salomon Smith Barney, UBS, and Piper Jaffray. In addition, two individuals, Henry Blodgett and Jack Grubman were also subject to enforcement actions.

Among other requirements the SEC enforcement action required the banks to carry out the following structural reforms:

- The firms will separate research and investment banking, including physical separation, completely separate reporting lines, separate legal and compliance staffs, and separate budgeting processes.
- Analysts' compensation cannot be based directly or indirectly upon investment banking revenues or input from investment banking personnel.
- Investment bankers cannot evaluate analysts.
- An analyst's compensation will be based in significant part on the quality and accuracy of the analyst's research.
- Investment bankers will have no role in determining what companies are covered by the analysts.
- Research analysts will be prohibited from participating in efforts to solicit investment banking business, including pitches and roadshows.
- Firms will implement policies and procedures reasonably designed to assure that their personnel do not seek to influence the contents of research reports for purposes of obtaining or retaining investment banking business.

- Firms will create and enforce firewalls between research and investment banking reasonably designed to prohibit improper communications between the two. Communications should be limited to those enabling research analysts to fulfill a "gatekeeper" role.
- Each firm will retain, at its own expense, an Independent Monitor to conduct a review to provide reasonable assurance that the firm is complying with the structural reforms. This review will be conducted 18 months after the date of the entry of the Final Judgment, and the Independent Monitor will submit a written report of his or her findings to the SEC, NASD, and NYSE within 6 months after the review begins.

Despite these actions, a 2016 SEC investigation found that a Deutsche Bank analyst certified a Buy rating on a stock which was inconsistent with his personal view. The analyst did not downgrade a "Buy" rating on a company he covered because he wanted to maintain his relationship with the company's management (SEC, 2016).

For all these missteps, bank research at its best provides valuable insights into current and future prospects for companies and industries.

Asset securitization

Securitizations are the bundling together of many loans. The most popular form of securitizations has been mortgages, but other assets such as auto loans, student loans, and credit card receivables are also securitized. A common mortgage-backed security is the mortgage pass through. A trustee, which could be a bank or a government agency, services the underlying loans, collecting payments, and sending funds on to holders of the securities. Risks to investors in these products are that borrowers default, or if interest rates fall, they refinance and pay off their loans early. Collateralized bond obligations and collateralized debt obligations are additional types of securitizations which are backed by payments streams from different forms of existing debt obligations.

Mortgage-backed securities, especially those containing subprime mortgages, were a significant contributing factor to the financial crisis of 2007−08. In the overheated residential market of the early 2000s, many home buyers who did not have sufficient credit rating to qualify for a traditional mortgage were able to obtain a so-called subprime mortgage. Some of these loans had low, "teaser" interest rates, whereby the borrower had to make low payments for the first 2 years. At that time, the interest on the loans would increase to higher rates and the borrower's payments would escalate, often substantially. In the bubble years for real estate, the borrower could simply sell the underlying property for a higher price than they had paid for it. But when real estate prices started to drop in 2006 and 2007, these buyers were now under water or "upside down," owning property valued at less than their mortgage obligations.

Mergers and acquisitions

Mergers and acquisition activity by client companies represent a significant source of revenue for investment banks. Beginning in the 1960s, mergers were typically friendly transactions, wherein senior offices from each company would combine to form the management team of the new company. Later, the so-called corporate raiders popularized hostile takeovers of initially unwilling target companies. Many of these transactions were financed with funds raised by Michael Milken at Drexel. They were often characterized by increasing debt levels on target company balance sheets and gaining operating efficiencies by often large employee reductions. With the demise of Drexel, and the innovation of defenses such as poison pills and golden parachutes, hostile takeovers have become less frequent. Notably, some private equity firms have taken on the role of acquiring stakes in companies and pursuing aggressive agendas to change what they see as inefficient corporate practices.

Banks earn fees by giving advice to both acquirers and targets and may be involved in arranging financing. Some bankers may be involved in generating ideas for transactions and take those proposals to clients. In addition to the largest institutions, there are many niche advisors who play significant roles in transactions for particular companies and even industries.

Prime brokerage

Prime brokerage refers to the collection of services that banks will provide to hedge fund clients. This can include execution services, securities lending, risk management, and financing. Many banks will provide reporting services and technology support. They may even have departments which will assist in matching potential investors with hedge fund clients. Hedge funds represent a significant revenue source for banks, and they seek to provide whatever support funds may need to operate and grow their business.

Central banks

The central bank can be thought of as the bank for banks. In the United States, the central bank is the Federal Reserve System (Fed). Although proposed by Alexander Hamilton, the Fed as we now know it was created in 1913 in response to the Bank Panic of 1909. In comparison, the central banks of Sweden and England date to the 1600s. The focus in this section is on the US Fed, but it should be noted that there are other important central banks around the globe.

In general, the role of the central bank includes:

- Creation of money.
- Maintain interbank payments system.
- Execute government financial transactions.
- Supervise financial institutions.
- Conduct monetary policy to attain macroeconomic goals.
- Act as lender of last resort.

In the United States, the Federal Reserve System (FRS) is comprised of 12 regional banks, heavily weighted to the region east of the Mississippi River. This reflects the concentration of economic activity when the system was created in the early 1900s. Today, there are approximately 3000 banks which are members of the FRS. This includes all nationally chartered banks and state-chartered banks which meet certain requirements. There are an additional 17,000 depository institutions that are subject to Fed regulations. The Board of Governors of the Fed has 7 members who are appointed for 14-year terms. They are appointed by the President, subject to confirmation by the Senate. The President also appoints one of the governors as the chair, who presides over the Fed's independent conduct of monetary policy for a term of 4 years. The Fed has a large degree of independence. The lengthy terms of the governors mean that their tenure spans any President's time in office and would seem to make policy decisions less subject to political pressures. This independence is particularly important at times when the economy is growing too fast and the Fed needs to take measures to slow inflationary pressures and the growth of asset bubbles. Central banks in many other countries do not have this same degree of independence. Where the central bank is part of the executive branch of government, political pressures can be overwhelming and lead to a reluctance of the bank to slow growth. This can result in hyperinflationary conditions.

The US Fed has several roles:

- regulating and overseeing financial institutions;
- providing financial services to the banking system;
- executing monetary policy in support of macroeconomic goals;
- acting as lender of last resort;
- providing banking services to the US government; and
- issuing currency.

Fed regulations are extensive, and a full discussion is beyond our scope in this chapter. Here we will note that the Fed conducts examinations of banks to ensure their safety and soundness and sets reserve requirements. The Fed also assesses banks' compliance with consumer protection laws. The Consumer Finance Protection Board, established by the Dodd-Frank Act, is located within the Fed, but operates with a large degree of independence.

To assess the safety and soundness of a bank, the acronym "CAMELS" is used. The letters stand for: Capital adequacy, Asset quality, Management, Earnings, Liquidity, and Sensitivity to market risk. The Fed examiner will look at each of these issues in assessing the bank.

The Fed also provides many financial services. The Automatic Clearing House (ACH) provides electronic credit and debit services to banks. The FedWire Funds Transfer Service is an online wire transfer service for same day, typically very large fund transfers. The Fed also operates a nationwide check-clearing service, and is responsible for issuing currency. One other service of the Fed is acting as bank or fiscal agent for the US Government.

The macroeconomic goals of Fed policy are mandated by the Congress as maximum employment, stable prices, and moderate inflation. The Fed pursues these goals by influencing the quantity of money and banks' behavior in extending credit. It has more conventional tools for doing so, as well as more extreme measures developed after the Great Financial Crisis.

Conventional monetary tools

The Fed's three tools for implementing monetary policy are:

- open market operations,
- the discount rate, and
- reserve requirements.

Open market operations are the main means by which the Fed influences the amount of reserves in the system. Through the Domestic Trading Desk of the Federal Reserve Bank of New York, the Fed buys and sells financial instruments, usually Treasury bills and Treasury bonds. By buying these instruments from primary dealers, the Fed increases reserves available in those dealers' bank accounts. The banks then have more money to lend out to customers. This causes an expansion in the money supply. When the Fed instead sells those instruments, it drains reserves from the system, and banks have less money to lend. This results in a contraction in the money supply.

Reserve requirements are set by the Governors of the Fed. The reserve requirement specifies the percentage of deposits that banks must hold either in cash or in an account at the Fed. By lowering this ratio, the Fed allows banks to lend out a greater fraction of its deposits, thereby increasing money supply in the economy. If the Fed raises the reserve requirement, the banks will have less money to lend out and the effect will be contractionary. For example, if a bank has $400 million in deposits, and is subject to a 10% reserve requirement, then it has $360 million to lend. If the reserve requirement drops to 5%, then the bank would have $380 million to lend. This may not seem like a significant difference, but through the multiplier effect such a large reduction in the reserve requirement would be likely to result in inflationary pressures. On the other hand, an increase in the reserve requirement to 20% would result in only $320 million being available and would have a contractionary impact.

Funds held to meet the Fed's reserve requirement are called "required reserves." Banks may have "excess" reserves beyond the requirements and can lend them to each other. The rate at which they lend reserves is called the "Federal funds rate." One relatively new tool of Fed policy begun in 2008 is paying interest on reserves. This allows the Fed to exert more influence over the level of the Fed funds rate.

The Discount rate, or Primary Credit Rate, is determined by the Boards of Directors of the Fed regional banks and approved by the Board of Governors. It is the rate that the Fed charges for loans to banks. If a bank needs to borrow to meet its reserve requirement, it can borrow directly from the Fed' Discount Window at this rate. When the Fed was created in 1913, this was the principle instrument of the Fed's operations. It is now superseded by open market operations. These Discount Window loans are designed to relieve temporary pressure and systemic stress. The discount rate is set every 14 days. They are extended typically on an overnight basis but may stretch to a few weeks for generally sound institutions with short-term liquidity needs. There are several distinct categories: primary credit, secondary credit, seasonal credit, and emergency credit with different lending rates attached.

Unconventional monetary policy

The dramatic events surrounding the Global Financial Crisis caused policy-makers to move aggressively to use monetary policy to assist in rescuing the United States as well as the world financial system. The Fed resorted to several unconventional policy actions including Quantitative Easing (QE) and Operation Twist. Under QE, the Fed bought financial assets from banks, raising the price of those assets and increasing money supply. The first round of QE began in November 2008. A second program dubbed QE2 was begun in November 2010. A new policy called Operation Twist was started in September 2011. Its aim was to increase the average maturity of the bank's treasury portfolio. In September 2012, the Fed began QE3, buying close to $40 billion per month of mortgage-backed securities. Purchases under QE3 along with Operation Twist targeted $85 billion per month of long-term bonds. In December 2013, the Fed indicated a "taper" program, where the $85 billion spent per month would be reduced by $10 billion going forward. The initial response to the announcement of the taper program was a selloff in the stock and bond markets. This was termed the "taper tantrum." The markets did quickly recover however and in October 2014, the Fed indicated an end to the QE3 program.

QE programs have also been initiated in Europe and Japan. There are some differences among the various central banks' programs and some debate on the impact of these programs; they do seem to have had the following results: lower rates and higher prices for asset classes which were targeted for purchase; somewhat higher inflation; lower unemployment; higher GNP growth; and a reduction in systemic risk.

Other central banks

The Bank of England (BoE) was founded in 1694 and is nicknamed "The Old Lady of Threadneedle Street." Its mission is to promote the good of the people of the United Kingdom by maintaining monetary and financial stability. It issues currency, acts as lender of last resort in crises, manages failed institutions, and supervises 1700 banks and other financial infrastructure such as clearing houses, interbank payment systems, and securities settlement systems. BoE also acts as settlement and transfer agent for interbank payments and credit cards. Additionally, it provides banking services to the UK government and over 100 overseas central banks. A vital role of the BoE is conducting monetary policy to support its current inflation target of 2%. Its main policy tool is the Bank Rate which is the rate BoE charges on its loans to commercial banks. In earlier years, BoE rules were somewhat less formal than other central banks. If BoE had concerns, the commercial banker would be invited over for a cup of tea, which would usually be sufficient to bring about the central bank's desired change in behavior. Such informality seems to be a thing of the past.

The European Central Bank (ECB) was formed in 1998. Its mission is to serve the people of Europe by safeguarding the value of the euro and maintaining price stability, defined as an inflation rate of "below but close to 2% over the medium term." The basic tasks of the ECB are to set and execute monetary policy for the Eurozone, to manage foreign reserves and foreign exchange operations, and to promote smooth operation of the financial market infrastructure. The ECB also issues banknotes and contributes to financial stability and supervision.

The Bank of Japan (BOJ) was reorganized in 1942, after World War II. Having been modeled on the US FRS, it bears many similarities. Its mission includes the following:

- banknote issuance,
- conduct of monetary policy,
- implementation of monetary policy,
- interbank settlement services,
- ensuring systemic stability, and
- acting as bank for Treasury and other governmental needs.

The People's Bank of China historically has not been included in the list of the world's most influential central banks, but with the growth in importance of the Chinese economy, its influence should continue to increase. It was reorganized in 1995 to function more like the US Fed and focus on monetary policy, financial regulation, and foreign reserve matters. With the growth in importance of the Chinese economy, its influence should continue to increase. In 2003 its major functions were identified in the following detail:

- drafting and enforcing relevant laws, rules, and regulations that are related to fulfilling its functions;
- formulating and implementing monetary policy in accordance with law;
- issuing the Renminbi and administering its circulation;
- regulating financial markets, including the interbank lending market, the interbank bond market, foreign exchange market, and gold market;
- preventing and mitigating systemic financial risks to safeguard financial stability;
- maintaining the Renminbi exchange rate at adaptive and equilibrium level;
- holding and managing the state foreign exchange and gold reserves;
- managing the State treasury as fiscal agent;
- making payment and settlement rules in collaboration with relevant departments and ensuring normal operation of the payment and settlement systems;
- providing guidance to antimoney laundering work in the financial sector and monitoring money-laundering related suspicious fund movement;
- developing statistics system for the financial industry and responsible for the consolidation of financial statistics as well as the conduct of economic analysis and forecast;
- administering credit reporting industry in China and promoting the building up of credit information system;
- participating in international financial activities at the capacity of the central bank;
- engaging in financial business operations in line with relevant rules; and
- performing other functions prescribed by the State Council.

With the growth in importance of the Chinese economy, its influence should continue to increase.

Shadow banking: other financial intermediaries

Additional financial intermediation products are sold by affiliates of banks but also by stand-alone companies such as insurance companies, finance companies, hedge funds, private equity funds, and asset managers. Insurance products provide protection against risks. The providers collect funds in the form of premiums which are then invested in various markets. Over $6 trillion in assets are held by these companies. Finance companies provide loans to consumers and small businesses for purchase of products such as furniture, homes, cars, etc. Hedge funds and private equity funds pool investments from limited partners with typically large minimums required. The general partner of the fund may then invest in a wide range of assets, with these investments liquidated several years later and the proceeds distributed among the partners. Mutual funds pool investor funds in a shared diversified portfolio of stocks and/or bonds. Exchange-traded funds have some similarities to mutual funds in that returns track a diversified portfolio, but there are significant differences in structure, pricing and tax consequences. More about these products are given in Chapter 6, Financial markets: equities.

These and other types of financial services provide financing outside traditional bank structures and are currently subject to limited federal regulation. In fact, increasing regulation of more traditional financial products and markets has been a major contributor to the development of these alternatives. These products can be thought of as meeting credit needs outside of the typical banking channels. These activities are termed "shadow banking" and $34 trillion of credit is estimated to be provided via these channels (FSB, 2017). Many Fintech services fall into this general category.

These financing products are performed by some investment banks but also by the following range of participants:

- mortgage lenders,
- money market funds,
- insurance companies,
- hedge funds,
- private equity funds, and
- payday lenders.

The Financial Stability Board (FSB) notes that some people take the term "shadow banking" to be pejorative, but that these services provide economic value in extending credit where there are underserved needs and provide useful competition to traditional banks. There is a concern however for potential systemic risk.

The rise of shadow banking is just the latest manifestation of innovation in finance. Many Fintech products fall under this classification and the current wave of Fintech disruptors is debatably the most significant and wide-reaching force for innovation in financial markets, instruments, and institutions. And some commentators view the legacy banking structure as static and immovable. But this is definitely not the case. There have in fact been a series of substantial innovations in finance in recent history. Over time the financial environment has faced changes in technology, consumer preferences, regulation, increased competition from foreign banks, and other factors. These factors can be summarized as changes in demand for services and products, changes in their supply, and changes in regulation. With substantial profits at stake financial institutions are continually evolving to address these changes.

In the following sections, we will look at several different types of financial intermediaries all of which are increasing their sensitivity to ESG factors in investment choices.

Insurance companies

Insurance companies and pension funds are two of the largest sources of investment capital. US insurance companies had $6.5 trillion of cash and invested assets at the end of 2017. Understanding their business models, products, services, and obligations is important to understanding a significant segment of modern financial markets.

Insurance companies are in the business of risk sharing. The insured party faces an uncertain probability of a serious event with adverse economic effects. House fires and car accidents are common examples. The company and the individual enter into a contract that requires the company to make a payment to the insured if the specified adverse event occurs. In return for shifting this risk to the insurance company, the individual agrees to pay a fee or "premium."

Categories of insurance

There are as many categories of insurance as there are risks that an individual or a business may face. Here are some of the most common types.

- Life Insurance.
  - Term life insurance pays out an agreed amount if the insured dies within the time period set by the policy.
  - Whole life insurance builds up a cash value as well as providing a death benefit payout. The owner of the policy can withdraw the cash value or borrow against it. A major benefit is that the built-up cash value is not subject to taxation.
  - More complicated life insurance products consist of variants where the premia are either fixed or flexible and whether the cash value is fixed or variable.
- Health Insurance
  - There are many different health insurance plans in the United States and the rules, requirements, payments, and coverage are constantly changing and can vary from state to state. In general, people aged 25 and younger can be covered by their parents' policy. People 65 years or older can be covered by federal health insurance programs such as Medicare. Medicaid provides health care coverage for certain categories of individuals, with income restrictions.
  - There are plans established on the state level with various levels of coverage and costs. These plans can be used by individuals, families, and small businesses.

- Employer plans are the most common in the United States. The employer can select different options for the plans, and often the employee will have choices among these options, with higher premiums being charged for plans with greater coverage or lower deductibles. Employers and employees share the cost of these plans.
- Some common types of health insurance plans:
    - Health Maintenance Organization (HMO) requires the insured to choose a primary care doctor and requires a referral from this doctor in order to have a specialist visit be covered. The doctors included in the HMO are on an approved list and usually agree to a negotiated fee schedule.
    - Preferred Provider Organization (PPO) allows the insured to see a wider range of doctors, but there may be a higher charge for visits with doctors not in the PPO "network."
- The plans will have a deductible. The insured will pay the first, say $1000 of health care costs each year, and the plan coverage will kick in for the next dollar of expense. The level of deductible can usually be elected, with premiums decreasing for higher deductibles.

- Homeowners Insurance
    - Homeowner insurance provides coverage against property damage, casualty, and theft. Typical covered events can include wind, water and fire damage, visitors slipping and falling on the sidewalk, and theft of property. Homeowner insurance is considered to be prudent and a bank holding a mortgage on the property will require the homeowner to have home insurance.
- Auto Insurance
    - Most states require drivers to have insurance. Liability insurance covers damage to another person's car or property. Personal injury covers bodily damage, and collision insurance provides for repairing the car after the accident. Comprehensive insurance covers other events such as fire or water damage. Uninsured and underinsured motorist coverage provides for coverage if the accident involves another driver whose insurance would be expected to provide coverage, but this other driver has no or inadequate coverage.
- Annuities
    - Annuities provide a stream of income over the life of the insured. The purchaser provides an initial sum of money which the insurance company invests. The payment stream begins at a deferred date. For example, an individual may buy the annuity when he/she is 45, and elect to get an annual payment beginning at age 65, when they would expect to be retired.
- Casualty Insurance
    - This is a broad category of insurance which may cover a wide range of liabilities including loss of property, theft, autos, and a range of business liabilities as well.

- Catastrophe Insurance
  - Catastrophe insurance provides coverage for low probability high cost events that are usually excluded from more common policies. This would include events such as earthquakes, hurricanes, and terrorist attacks.
- Reinsurance
  - The common types of insurance provide for the insurance company to bear the risk of certain events. If an unusually large number of these events occur, the insurance company could become bankrupt. To mitigate this risk, the insurance company may want to lay off some of this exposure by purchasing insurance from another company. This is called reinsurance.
- Captive Insurance
  - This is a type of self-insurance where a parent group or a group of companies form their own insurance company to provide insurance for the group. This can result in lower costs and insurance products more tailored to the group's needs.
- Fraternal Life Insurance
  - This is life insurance covering individuals who are members of a nonprofit group that may have social, educational, religious, or similar bonds and purposes.

The success of an insurance company depends on several factors. It must be able to successfully gauge the risk of the adverse events it is insuring against. In some instances, it can accept or reject specific risks. In other instances, it will accept risks knowing that some percentage of the accounts will have a claim each year. Its profitability depends on its ability to accurately predict this percentage, and to charge an appropriate level of premium. A key component of insurance company profitability arises from the fact that premiums are paid in advance, and the company has the use of those funds until claims must be paid out. The company's profitability then is defined by the premiums received plus the investment income generated, minus operating expenses and claims paid out. Net profit for insurance companies ranges from 3% to 10% of revenues but varies sharply depending on the insurance products offered and investment returns.

Insurance companies consequently accumulate large amounts of cash from the premiums they receive as well as investment gains. The companies will invest these funds in a range of assets suitable for meeting their obligations. Favored assets are medium- and longer term fixed income, either tax exempt or taxable. The largest companies manage their funds internally but may also use external managers. External managers become more important for smaller companies and for investments in complex instruments where special expertise may be required.

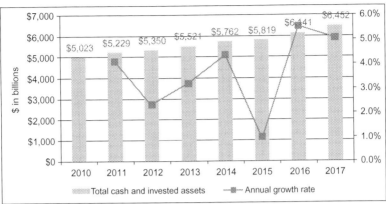

Note: Includes affiliated and unaffiliated investments

FIGURE 5.4   Total US insurance industry cash and Invested assets, 2010−17. *From: NAIC.*

Fig. 5.4 shows the growth in cash and invested assets for US insurance companies from 2010 to 2017.

Looking at the details of these investments, 65% of assets were in bonds and an analysis of the sources of funds shows that a similar fraction of total investments came from Life insurance companies (Fig. 5.5).

Fig. 5.6 lists the largest US Life insurance companies by assets, in 2017.

ESG investment practices and levels of commitment vary among insurance companies, and state insurance regulators have a substantial impact. Companies in California, for example, are required to have a greater awareness of environmental issues than are companies in many other states. In 2016 the California Department of Insurance began requiring insurers to disclose their fossil fuel investments and asked insurers to divest from thermal coal because of the risk that thermal coal could become a stranded asset on the books of insurance companies as consumers, businesses, markets, and governments transition away from coal as a source of energy. But there is disagreement on this issue, especially in states where producing energy is a big part of the economy—Oklahoma, North Dakota, Montana, and Texas. Insurance commissioners and attorneys general in these states believe the California initiatives are an "affront to sound insurance regulation." Twelve state attorneys general and one state governor signed a letter to the California insurance commissioner threatening legal action. These officials believe the California requirements are immaterial to a well-functioning insurance market and that the disclosures would harm consumers rather than help them by providing tangential information that might cloud disclosure about insurance products being offered. They also believe the California requirements insert political disagreements over environmental policy into the domain

Asset class	Life	P/C	Health	Fraternal	Title	Total	% of total
Bonds	2,982,586	1,003,354	116,948	106,703	4858	4,214,449	65.3%
Common Stock	166,027	598,478	37,510	4486	2460	808,962	12.5%
Mortgages	477,051	18,119	134	11,583	81	506,968	7.9%
Schedule BA (Other Long-Term Assets)	177,694	159,418	11,312	4783	210	353,416	5.5%
Cash & Short-Term Investments	105,008	117,258	46,189	2925	1196	272,575	4.2%
Contract Loans	129,027	3	-	2884	-	131,915	2.0%
Derivatives	58,661	233	1	48	-	58,942	0.9%
Real Estate	23,550	12,849	5544	286	227	42,457	0.7%
Securities Lending (Reinvested Collateral)	16,870	4476	724	571	-	22,640	0.4%
Other Receivables	11,652	9785	652	67	5	22,161	0.3%
Preferred Stock	10,514	5522	454	612	402	17,504	0.3%
Total	4,158,640	1,929,496	219,468	134,946	9,440	6,451,989	100%
% of Total	64.5%	29.9%	3.4%	2.1%	0.1%	100.0%	

FIGURE 5.5   Total US insurance industry cash and invested assets by asset class and insurer type, 2017. *From: NAIC.*

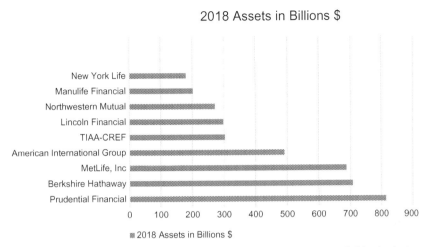

FIGURE 5.6   Largest US life insurance companies in 2017, by assets. *Compiled by the Author from company reports.*

of insurance carrier investments. Despite the debate, many insurers are including at least some ESG factors in their investment decisions. Here are a few examples of what some of these companies are doing.

Prudential Financial Inc

The largest of these insurance companies, Prudential Financial states that it recognizes that "investments could—and should—generate a financial return and create positive, measurable social impact." "To that end the company has a program of impact investing targeting a 2020 total of $1 billion in social enterprises, financial intermediaries and real assets." The company references its founding in 1875 with the original name of "The Widows and Orphans Friendly Society," a "social-purpose enterprise dedicated to bringing an affordable form of burial insurance to the working poor." Prudential's investment portfolio intentionally maintains a great deal of asset flexibility, as it includes both direct and indirect investments, debt and equity, real assets and operating businesses, mortgages, securitizations, private placements, and various other types of alternatives. This allows the company to take advantage of attractive opportunities in affordable housing equity (but less so when debt seems unattractive). It also participates in lending to education and workforce development projects. Investment outcomes that are targets include financial inclusion, affordable housing preservations, educational excellence, workforce development, sustainable agriculture, and others.

Three portfolios are managed:

- Impact Managed Portfolio. This accounts for 80% of the ESG portfolio. The investments are larger than those in the other two portfolios and have generated above market returns. One notable example is charter school lending. The superior investment results of this portfolio offset the concessions in the next two.
- Catalytic Portfolio. These are smaller investments in for-profit entities, projects, or financial structures. They are often startups or otherwise have little or no track record and as such entail more risk that the Impact Managed Portfolio investments. They are usually equity investments that have significant R&D value and if successful, can lead to bigger investments. One example focuses on stormwater runoff mitigation. This portfolio has trailed the financial performance of the Impact Managed Portfolio, but the projects show great promise for significant social impact.
- Philanthropic Portfolio. This portfolio is managed on behalf of The Prudential Foundation and provides concessionary capital to nonprofits. Low-interest loans are provided to support organizations where cheaper capital can be provided directly to an end user or beneficiary, for example, community development finance institutions or the Disability Opportunity Fund.

MetLife Inc

The impact investment portfolio of MetLife Inc. grew to $50 billion in 2017, an increase of 12% year-over-year from 2016. Its MetLife Foundation reached more than 6 million low-income individuals through the fourth year of its 5-year, $200 million-dollar commitment to financial inclusion. In 2018 it enhanced its ESG platform by forming a new Responsible Investments Strategies group. The company puts its ESG philosophy into practice by beginning with a bottom up research process that includes a focus on ESG considerations. This is followed by a long-term "Buy and Manage" investment approach which evaluates ESG factors at the time of initial purchase as well as in periodic reviews of continuing investments. In addition, the company engages with management in an ongoing dialogue to ensure the investee company's goals and actions are aligned with ESG principles.

Fig. 5.7 shows the distribution of MetLife's investments in four categories: Community and Affordable Housing Investments; Infrastructure; Green Investments; and Municipal Bonds.

Roughly 5% of the Responsible Investments portfolio is invested in the first category, Community and Affordable Housing Investments, the remaining 95% is split relatively evenly, 30%−34% each, among the remaining three categories.

Pursuing Responsible Investments

As an investor interest in ESG issues accelerates worldwide, evidence is mounting that incorporating these factors into investment decision-making can positively support portfolio performance and returns. MIM has a long history of responsible and impact investing, with a focus on four core areas:

Green Investments

We have a long track record of support for green buildings and renewable energy projects, including wind and solar. At December 31, 2018, we held equity stakes in 60 LEED-certified real estate properties and made further investments in renewable offshore wind projects in the U.K.

Investments held at Dec. 31, 2018: **$16.6B**

Impact and Affordable Housing Investments

We invest in impact and affordable, high-quality housing projects that build financial health and bring tangible benefits to communities. In 2018, we increased the supply of loans to micro-, small- and medium-sized businesses in unbanked and underserved markets globally.

Investments held at Dec. 31, 2018: **$2.6B**

Infrastructure Investments

We create local jobs and economic benefits via infrastructure projects that build or upgrade airports, ports, roads, pipelines, transmission lines and power generation — including wind and solar projects. In 2018, we also invested in U.S. not-for-profit hospitals and healthcare facilities in underserved communities.

Investments held at Dec. 31, 2018: **$17.1B**

Municipal Bonds Investments

We support infrastructure, education and community services, spanning around 600 municipalities in 47 states and Washington D.C. In 2018, we invested in Pennsylvania's Planning and Construction Workbook program, which facilitates loans to school districts for eligible school construction projects.

Investments held at Dec. 31, 2018: **$16.3B**

We also strive to support financial services firms that embrace diversity.

In 2018, we conducted over $2 billion in business with capital markets firms owned by, or focused on employing, women executives, minority executives, women and disabled veterans.

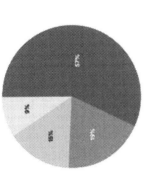

MIM Responsible Investments Committed in 2018

57%
9%
13%
19%

Infrastructure: $4.3 Billion
Municipal Bonds: $1.4 Billion
Green Investments: $3.1 Billion
Impact and Affordable Housing Investments: $0.7 Billion

FIGURE 5.7 MetLife impact investments. *From: MetLife.*

Zurich Insurance Group

Zurich Insurance Group is one of the world's largest insurers. It manages assets of approximately $200 billion and believes that sustainable investment is integral to its goal of earning superior risk-adjusted returns while "doing good" at the same time. It accomplishes this by integrating ESG factors into its investment approach and by making significant impact investments. It embarked on a "5-5-5" program of investing $5 billion in impact investments, targeted to avoid 5 million tons of atmospheric CO_2, affecting 5 million people. Toward this end, it had achieved a goal in 2017 of investing $2 billion in green bonds.

Pension funds

US retirement assets in 2018 totaled over $29 trillion. About 19%, $5.6 trillion were in 401(k) plans. These plans usually offer several different investment fund options for an individual to select from. Public pension funds are some of the largest institutional investment pools in the US. Retirement plans in the United States take several different forms: Individual Retirement Accounts (IRA), Defined Benefit Plans, and Defined Contribution Plans. Years ago, the Defined Benefit Plan was the typical retirement plan for corporations and government. Under this type of plan, the employer, or sponsor, commits to paying retired employees a specified sum, or benefit, during the retirement years. This structure imposes significant risks on both the employer and employee. The risk to the employer is that retirement obligations may increase unsustainably, due to increasing life expectancy and other factors. The risk to the employee is that the corporation goes bankrupt and is unable to pay out the retirement benefit. Qualified benefit plans are guaranteed by the Public Benefit Guarantee Corporation (PBGC); however, this is not a guarantee by the US Government, and PBGC may not have sufficient resources to cover all defaulted plans. The percentage of commercial corporations offering Defined Benefit Plans has shrunk to roughly 10%, while 75% of government plans are Defined Benefit.

In a Defined Contribution Plan, the employer, or plan sponsor is responsible only for making specified contributions on behalf of participants. The sponsor is not responsible for payments at the time of retirement. Thus the risk to the employer is greatly diminished. The amount received by the participants will depend on the size of the contributions and the growth in the value of those assets. The risk to the employee is then that the assets might not grow sufficiently to support a particular level of spending in retirement. Some popular plans are 401 (k) and employee stock ownership plans.

Another type of retirement fund is the individual retirement plan (IRA). This plan has certain tax advantages in that investment gains are allowed to accumulate tax free. They are not taxed until investment income is

Trillions of dollars, end-of-period, selected periods

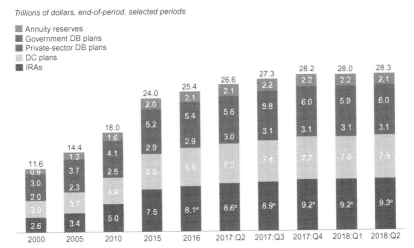

FIGURE 5.8   US retirement assets by account type. *From: Investment Company Institute.*

withdrawn. So, the beneficiary earns a return on what would otherwise have been tax payments. In a traditional IRA, the account is funded with pretax dollars. Tax is paid when these dollars are paid out to the individual. In a Roth IRA, the account is funded with after-tax dollars. In IRAs as well as many Defined Contribution plans, the choice of investments is up to the individual.

Fig. 5.8 shows the distribution of retirement market assets by type of plan.

Assets in Annuities and private sector Defined Benefit Plans have increased slightly since 2000, but there have been dramatic increases in the other categories: Government Defined Benefit Plans, Defined Contribution Plans, and IRAs.

Contributions from employers and employees are a significant source of pension fund revenue, but the largest share of pension fund revenue comes from accumulated investment earnings. The funds' investments are typically allocated to several different asset classes. On average, a pension fund will have the following distribution of investments across asset classes:

- public equities: 47.6%;
- fixed income: 23.2%;
- real estate: 6.6%;
- alternative investments: 18.3%; and
- cash and other: 4.3%.

Fig. 5.9 lists some of the largest US public pension funds. Eleven of them are close to, or substantially in excess of $100 billion.

Plan	Total assets
CalPERS	$336,684
CalSTRS	$216,193
New York State Common	$201,263
New York City Retirement	$189,794
Florida SBA	$167,900
Texas Teachers	$146,326
New York State Teachers	$115,637
State of Wisconsin Investmen Board	$109,960
North Carolina Retirement	$106,946
Washington State Investmen Board	$104,260
Ohio Public Employees	$97,713
New Jersey Division of Investment	$80,486
Virginia Retirement Sysem	$79,238
Oregon Public Employees	$77,495
Ohio Teachers	$76,458
Michigan Retirement	$75,550
Georgia Teachers	$73,089
Minnesota State Board of Investment	$72,672
Massachusetts PRIM	$69,496
Tennessee Consolidated	$55,112
Los Angeles Country	$53,832
Pennsylvania Public Schools	$52,891
Colorado PERA	$51,476
Maryland State Retirement	$50,297
Illinois Teachers	$49,863
Missouri Public School	$42,307
Illinois Municipal	$39,811
Nevada Public Employees	$39,721
Alabama Retirement	$38,800
South Carolina Public Employees	$37,263

FIGURE 5.9 Largest US public pension funds. *From: Pensions & Investments.*

Largest pension funds

The goal of pension funds is to provide retirement income for beneficiaries. The risk to adding ESG factors is that the fund will underperform. This can result in a shortfall in income to retirees and resulting hardship. It can also lead to the firing of investment managers and board members. If those managers and board members are very public about their support for ESG investing, they can become easy targets, even if the ESG investments have little to do with the poor performance of the fund. As discussed in an earlier chapter, ERISA rules govern private pension funds and these rules are also often followed by public funds. Over time the Department of Labor has issued several guidance Bulletins on ESG investing. The most recent 2015 and 2018 Bulletins clarified that ESG factors may directly affect the economic returns of an investment and may be incorporated when assessing an investment.

Early forms of socially responsible investing consisted of simply divesting holdings of companies engaged in negative activities. Activities that resulted in the divestiture of shares included investments or operations in apartheid-era South Africa, and the so-called sin stocks in the alcohol, tobacco, and casino industries. In most cases, this strategy of divesting was seen to have little or no impact on the target companies, but negative impact on the investment performance of the funds. More recently, ESG investing has taken a positive approach of "screening" candidate companies for ESG impacts. Companies with positive impacts can be included in the portfolio and in more sophisticated approaches, the companies can be selected so the overall portfolio return can be expected to mirror a benchmark index that otherwise includes both included and screened out companies.

The two key questions for ESG investing by pension plans are:

- Can ESG-screened portfolios meet the same return/risk objectives as nonscreened portfolios?
- Are public plans the right vehicle for advancing ESG goals?

As we will see in later chapters, empirical evidence of ESG investment performance is mixed, with older studies showing that funds which used only a divestment approach were generally underperforming. But using more nuanced ESG investment criteria can result in a portfolio with the expectation of comparable performance.

On the second question, social investing is a prerogative of private investors, but for it to be appropriate for public pension funds, there must be assurances that it won't yield lower returns and that all fiduciary responsibilities are met. It should come as no surprise that there are supporters on both sides of these two questions, with the majority of investment managers still focusing exclusively on financial returns. (See Munnell and Chen, 2016 for a discussion of these questions.) For public pension funds as a whole, financial returns and the level of funding are increasingly falling short of future requirements. A 2018 study (Pew, 2018) found that for 2016, the most recent data available, the state pension funding gap was increasingly widening. This gap, the difference between fund assets and liabilities, showed that states cumulatively had a deficit of $1.4 trillion, an increase of $295 billion from the previous year. And subpar investment returns were a major cause of the increase in the gap. The median public pension plan's investments returned about 1% in 2016, far below the median assumption of a 7.5% increase. With such poor returns it is exceedingly difficult for fund managers to build a consensus on an investment strategy with a focus other than maximizing financial return.

Next, the ESG investment activities of some of the large pension funds will be discussed.

CalPERS

CalPERS, the California Public Employees' Retirement System, is the largest public pension fund in the United States. It has over $350 billion in total assets and 1.9 million members. It was one of the earliest institutional investors to become active in ESG investing. It is a founding signatory of the UN Principles for Responsible Investing, an investor alliance formed to advance sound ESG practices. In 2005 it joined CERES, a nonprofit organization of investors, environmental organizations, and public interest groups working with companies to address sustainability challenges. Its work with CERES dates back to 2003.

The foundation of CalPERS ESG investing rests on an economic framework of integrating financial performance with ESG factors.

CalPERS considers that long-term value creation requires the effective management of three forms of capital—Financial, Physical, and Human. This provides an economic approach to ground the sustainable investment agenda into their fiduciary duty to generate risk-adjusted returns for CalPERS' beneficiaries. They have identified five core issues which they believe have a long-term impact on risk and return:

- Investor Rights
- Board Quality: Diversity, Independence and Competence
- Executive, Director and Employee Compensation
- Corporate Reporting
- Regulatory Effectiveness

These five core issues are illustrated in Fig. 5.10.

The fund identified climate change, water scarcity and quality, income inequality, and disruptive technologies as important areas of focus. An executive of CalPERS acted as chair of Climate Action 100 Plus, a coalition of investors active in environmental issues. The biggest impact of CalPERS strategy seems to be through the application of its corporate governance

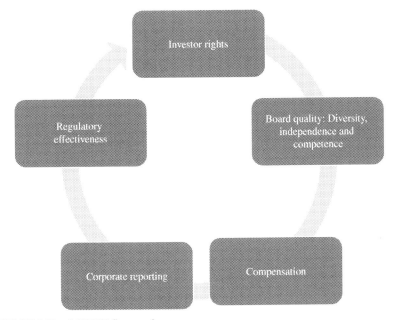

FIGURE 5.10   CalPERS' five core issues.

program focusing on the five core issues. Its direct investments in ESG focused strategies are modest compared to its massive portfolio. In March 2018, a CalPERS board member proposed that the retirement system should divest holdings of assault rifle retailers and wholesalers, but the board voted 9-3 against this proposal.

Significantly, through the end of 2017 CalPERS investment performance lagged slightly behind other state pension funds and the S&P 500. CalPERS was 69% funded in 2016, which was higher than the national average of 66%, but trailed other states, such as New York's 91% funded level. An improvement in 2017 investment returns boosted the funding level to 71%; however, the lingering gap and projected modest future investment earnings mean that contributions to the fund will have to increase sharply or retirement benefits will be cut, or both. Given CalPERS prominence in supporting ESG issues and organizations, some critics have attributed the System's financial difficulties to CalPERS' ESG investment choices. CalPERS however rejected this argument, pointing out that they had very small allocations in the worst performing ESG funds and that individual investments should not be evaluated outside of the overall portfolio diversification and investment approach. They further reaffirmed that working with companies to address ESG issues has a positive impact on long-term, risk-adjusted financial performance. But reflecting concerns about the fund's performance, the board president, who was a strong supporter of ESG investing and a board member of UN PRI, lost an October 2018 election to a challenger who questioned the fund's social investment focus.

Florida State Board of Administration

Florida's State Board of Administration (SBA) is required to invest assets and discharge its duties in compliance with fiduciary standards and in accordance with Florida law which requires the SBA and its staff to:

- Make sound investment management decisions that are solely in the interest of investment clients.
- Make investment decisions from the perspective of subject-matter experts acting under the highest standards of professionalism and care, not merely as well-intentioned persons acting in good faith.

The SBA acts as a long-term investor and supports the internationally recognized governance structure for public companies, which includes shareowner rights, strong independent boards, performance-based executive compensation, accurate accounting, and audit practices and transparent board procedures and policies.

Some of the areas in which SBA votes, engages, and advocates for improved handling of risks and disclosure are:

- environment and sustainability,
- greenhouse gas emissions,
- energy efficiency,
- water supply and conservation,
- political contributions and expenditures,
- operations in protected or sensitive areas,
- community impact assessments,
- supply chain risks,
- corporate diversity, and
- human rights risks.

SBA specifically rejects divestiture in favor of active engagement with investee management. It believes that divestiture seldom results in sustained lower share prices or limited capital market access for affected companies. Over the long term, divestiture will increase costs (execution, custom indices reflecting excluded securities, etc.) while potentially reducing diversification and returns. In contrast, the fund has a long history of actively engaging with boards and management to focus corporate attention on issues of concern.

Asset managers

Asset management companies handle investments on behalf of clients, both individuals and institutions such as insurance companies, pension funds,

Largest U.S. asset managers	
BlackRock	$6.44 trillion
Vanguard Group	$5.1 trillion
State Street Global	$2.8 trillion
J.P. Morgan Chase	$2.733 trillion
Fidelity Investments	$2.46 trillion
Bank of New York Mellon	$1.9 trillion
Capital Group	$1.87 trillion
Goldman Sachs Group	$1.54 trillion
Prudential Financial	$1.39 trillion
Northern Trust Asset Management	$1.2 trillion

FIGURE 5.11 Largest US asset managers. *Data compiled by the author from various public reports.*

government entities, and others. Some asset managers are business units of larger bank holding companies and some are very large stand-alone entities. They are sometimes called investment managers, money managers, or portfolio managers. Fig. 5.11 lists the largest US asset managers.

Asset managers provide their clients with investment services which may include research, advice, and execution related to asset selection, execution, and subsequent performance monitoring and analysis. They are often thought-leaders and advisors in these fields. These companies employ a full range of professionals to carry out these functions. They are compensated based on a percentage of assets under management (AUM), with additional fees attached to some products and services. This fee structure is attractive to the firm in that it is recurring, as long as the customer is happy with the manager's performance. The return on each fund offered by the asset manager is measured, or benchmarked, against a specific index. If the fund outperforms or is "reasonably" close to the benchmark index, the asset manager can expect most clients to be happy and continue to use their services. But if the fund underperforms the benchmark, clients may move their funds to a different manager (the asset manage experiences an "outflow" of assets) and the income of the asset management company will fall. Consequently, there is a substantial emphasis placed on investment performance and successful portfolio managers are handsomely compensated. As we will discuss in Chapter 6, Financial markets: equities, there is an increasing movement to invest in passive index funds, which seek to simply mirror the performance of a specific index fund which is taken as the benchmark. There is no active management into or out of particular assets in the index. This type of investment carries a much lower fee from the asset manager, often less than 20 basis points.

The biggest asset managers have aggressively moved into offering their clients a range of ESG investment choices. The biggest, BlackRock, offers a full range of screens to exclude the "sin" stocks; to invest in companies which rank high in ESG factors; and to identify and invest in companies for "impact" on social and environmental issues. Larry Fink, BlackRock's Chairman and CEO has publicly challenged corporate CEOs to manage their companies with more emphasis on ESG issues.

Hedge funds

Hedge funds collectively manage in excess of $3 trillion in client funds. They make investments in a wide assortment of assets. Capital is pooled from investors, called "limited partners" and is invested by professional managers employed by the fund company which is called the "general partner." The original investment strategy of hedge funds was to both go long and go short equity markets at the same time. If the market went higher, the gain on the longs would outweigh the loss on the shorts. But if the market went lower, gains on the shorts would outweigh losses on the longs. Hence, the investor was "hedged" (at least partially) against a falling stock market. Hedge fund strategies have evolved to where these funds now invest in the full range of assets available, including equity, debt, real estate, foreign exchange, and commodities. As with other investment managers, some hedge funds are now beginning to offer investment funds with an ESG sensitivity. A recent survey of 80 hedge funds found that 40% of the respondents said they were doing at least some investing using "responsible" investing principles. Roughly 10% of AUM were being invested responsibly (AIMA, 2018).

Private equity

Private equity funds are similar in structure to hedge funds: limited partners contribute capital and the general partner allocates the investments. The principle difference is in the type of investment: private equity funds buy nonpublic or private equity, often physical assets. Venture capital can be considered to be a subset of private equity investment, with the distinction that venture capital usually is invested in startup or early stage companies, many of which fail. Private equity more typically invests in mature companies. Private equity firms have also been associated with the strategy of buying companies using leverage or high levels of borrowings. They would then engage in restructuring the company and selling the resulting entity at great profit to the partners. More recently, some of these firms such as TPG's RISE fund and Bain Capital's Double Impact Fund, have begun investing in companies and projects with significant ESG impact. Also, Blackstone Group, KKR & Co., and others have senior officers and teams working with portfolio companies to improve ESG practices within those companies. One advantage both hedge funds and private equity funds enjoy is that they are able to operate with a longer time horizon. Investor capital is often tied up for 7−10 years or longer, giving time for projects and companies to weather early years where economic performance may be uneven.

Chapter 6

Financial markets: equities

Chapter Outline

Risk, return, and diversification	98	Collective investment vehicles: mutual	
Capital asset pricing model	100	funds and exchange-traded funds	107
Efficient market hypothesis	101	Equity indexes	108
Random walk	101	ESG indexes	109
Types of orders	101	MSCI	110
Equity trading venues	103	FTSE Russell	111
Regulation	105	Morningstar	113
Investing in equities	106	Robo-advisors	115

Much of environmental, social, and governance (ESG) investing involves considered ownership of corporate equities, either individually or in the form of baskets of companies. But what do these securities represent? What is the theoretical basis for combining multiple holdings into a diverse portfolio? Where and how do equities trade? Why are exchange-traded funds (ETFs) suddenly favored and how do they differ from mutual funds? What are the features of ESG Indexes and multiinvestor funds? In this chapter we will seek to answer these questions and more.

Equity, or common stock, represents ownership interest in a company. The equity holders have a claim on the profits of the company, but this claim is junior to other creditors such as the company's suppliers, bondholders, and other lenders. In the event of a bankruptcy all these claimants would be in line ahead of the owners of the common stock. Stockholders however are not liable for the obligations of the company. Shareholders can only lose the value of their stock holdings. In general, stockholders have the right to vote on certain proposals and on the election of members of the board of directors. Executives of the company manage the business. There are exceptions to this model which restrict the voting rights of stockholders while maintaining their rights to profits of the company. The lack of voting rights may seem unfair to stockholders, but if the nonvoting character of the stock is revealed in advance and if an investor still chooses to buy it, then there may be little basis for any complaint. The argument in favor of nonvoting stock is that it leaves control of the company in the hands of the founders, who believe that their vision is important for the prospects of the company. The

Environmental, Social, and Governance (ESG) Investing. DOI: https://doi.org/10.1016/B978-0-12-818692-3.00006-2

argument goes further to contend that too many public companies become focused on very short-term results, to the detriment of the longer-term prospects of the company. One company which issued common stock with no voting rights is Snap. It had an IPO in 2017, issuing public shares with no voting rights and although there were some complaints, the offering was "snapped up" by institutional investors. Those complaints however, led to an announcement by index provider FTSE Russell that it would exclude from its indexes any company which had less than 5% of voting rights outstanding to public shareholders. It remained to be seen if being excluded from indexes would be enough of a concern to Snap for it to change its voting rights.

In addition to common stock there is an interesting class of stock that shares the features of both debt and equities. This is called "preferred stock." These instruments pay the holder a dividend which may be fixed or floating. Preferred dividends are paid out before any dividends are paid to holders of common stock. If the company is unable to pay the dividend at some point, the missed dividends can be accrued and be fully paid at a later date. This class of preferred stock is called "cumulative preferred stock" and contrasts with "noncumulative preferred stock," where a missed dividend is simply foregone, and not made up at a future time. Holders of cumulative preferred stock have seniority over common stock with respect to dividend payments and the distribution of assets in the event of bankruptcy. "Convertible preferred stock" is preferred stock which includes an option for the investor to convert the shares into common stock at a preset price. If the common trades higher over time, then the convertible holders will be able to participate in that appreciation by converting their preferred shares at the lower preset price.

Risk, return, and diversification

For an investor, purchasing the shares of one company may yield a positive gain, but comes with the risk that the investor could lose money or otherwise fall behind gains that might have been achieved by buying shares of a different company or a basket of companies. By buying only one company she takes on the associated risk that those shares may not keep pace with market averages or some other benchmark. Numerous studies have shown that investment risk can be reduced by buying shares in a group of companies. This diversification may be beyond the financial means of most individuals, but these investors can buy participation in one or several alternative pooled investment funds. Mutual funds and ETFs are pooled investment vehicles which offer diversification with often small minimum levels of investment. To understand the purpose of these funds, a brief discussion of the theory underlying portfolio diversification is warranted. So-called "Modern Portfolio Theory" (MPT) dates back to the 1950s(!) and earned its pioneer, Harry Markowitz, a deserved Nobel Prize in Economics in 1990. The theory makes several assumptions which some economists believe limit its value, but other economists have modified those assumptions to develop extensions with more relevance to real-world behavior and limitations. Despite its limiting assumptions, as a theoretical construct, MPT has stood the test of time as a valuable starting point for thinking about portfolios and especially about the interaction and tradeoffs of risk and reward in their construction. The starting point is the assumption that investors are risk averse. They would like to minimize the risk for a given return, or alternatively, they would like to maximize return for a given level of risk. Portfolios which meet these requirements are called efficient portfolios, and in homage to his pioneering work, are sometimes called "Markowitz efficient portfolios." To achieve diversification, a portfolio can be spread across multiple asset classes: bonds, equities, commodities, and other alternative assets. Within an asset class, a portfolio can also be diversified. For example, an equity portfolio can be spread across companies in various industries, countries, and size.

To achieve an efficient portfolio, how should these investments be allocated? And within a set of efficient portfolios, how can one find the best or optimal portfolio? MPT provides a solution in terms of maximizing expected return for a given level of risk as measured by standard deviation or variance of the portfolio. A full presentation of MPT is beyond our scope, but key points are summarized here. The expected value of the portfolio return can be calculated as the weighted average of the individual asset returns. Measuring the portfolio variance is more complicated. It requires measuring the variance of the individual assets as well as the covariance between every pair of assets. The covariance or correlation between two assets measures how closely they move together. If the covariance is high, the portfolio will tend to have more risk. If Assets A and B are highly correlated, then when A loses value, B is likely to also lose value and the total portfolio percentage loss will be greater than either asset separately. Conversely, if Assets A and B have low or negative correlation, when A loses value, B is likely to be much less affected and the total portfolio percentage loss will be less than the percentage loss in A alone. Therefore to minimize portfolio risk, the correlation between assets should be minimal or even negative. In practice, constructing a portfolio with the highest level of expected return for a given level of risk would require massive computation. Critics of MPT point out some other limiting assumptions in the theory:

- Expected return and variance in the portfolio are not the whole story— Other concerns include "fat tails" or unexpectedly frequent occurrences of outlying results, or "Black Swans."
- Assumption of risk aversion—Appetite for risk varies considerably.
- Homogeneous expectations—The theory assumes investors have the same expectations of risk and return for assets, when clearly markets demonstrate that there are differences.

- One-period time horizon—It is not clear what the appropriate period is, but having some investors with short-term investing horizons, and other investors with long-term horizons clearly makes the one-period horizon a limiting assumption.

While MPT is a valuable starting point and economists have extended that model to incorporate more elaborate assumptions, investors have developed useful shortcuts over time that are not necessarily inconsistent with the MPT principles. For example, some financial advisors suggest that 10%–20% of annual gross income should be allocated to savings, and those savings should be invested into a diversified portfolio of, say 35% bonds, 60% equities, and 5% alternatives, such as real estate or commodities. Within each of these allocations further diversification is advised, and the percentages might be adjusted to reflect the career stage of the individual. People at an earlier stage of their working lives might have a lower percentage of bonds, whereas those approaching retirement might have a higher percentage of income generating investments. Finally, the adviser might suggest that the portfolio be periodically rebalanced in a tax efficient manner.

Capital asset pricing model

Following up on the tradeoffs of risk and expected return, a model developed to use these concepts to price securities is the capital asset pricing model (CAPM). This and other asset pricing models seek to determine the theoretical values of assets given their expected returns. The model assumes there is a risk-free rate of return, typically the yield on US Treasuries, and there is also a broad market return. For Stock A, the variability of A is compared to the broader market. This relative volatility is called "beta." Stocks with a beta of 1.0 would move precisely with movements in the broad market index. A beta of less than 1.0 reflects less volatility, and greater than 1.0 would indicate more volatility. The basic CAPM formula then is:

$$R_A = R_F + \beta_A(R_M - R_F)$$

where R_A is the return required of stock A; R_F is the rate of return on the risk-free asset; R_M is the market rate of return; and β_A is beta, or the volatility of Stock A compared to the volatility of the market.

What the model says is that the expected return from an asset should be equal to a risk-free rate plus a premium which reflects the relative volatility in that asset's return, as compared to the market return. These principles have relevance in understanding asset pricing even if the model itself has some difficulty in being applied to real-world circumstances. There are other asset pricing models which have extended the CAPM concepts and incorporate a variety of risk factors. These factor models may rely on purely statistical inputs, on macroeconomic indicators, or on company fundamentals.

Efficient market hypothesis

The efficient market hypothesis (EMH) is a theory of investments in which investors have perfect information and act rationally in acting on that information. And it doesn't require that all investors are omniscient. If only some are, they will buy undervalued assets and sell those that are overvalued, thereby driving prices to the efficient value. Consequently, it is impossible to "beat the market." There is no edge to be gained as an active investor. Stock analysis and market timing both have no incremental value. An investor can only earn the market rate of return, unless they take on more risk. EMH underlies the belief by many that the best investment strategy is to buy a low-cost, diversified portfolio with passive management. Other market observers, however, point to the success of some investors in performing classic fundamental stock analysis and of yet other investors who use various quantitative methods to trade.

Random walk

"Random Walk" refers to the movement of any variable (in this case stock prices) where the next period value is a random step, not dependent on the current value. If markets are efficient, then movement in the market is unpredictable and price action is random. The next period movement in price is equally likely to be positive or negative. This hypothesis was popularized by Malkiel (1973) in the book *A Random Walk Down Wall Street*. Proponents of the EMH hold to its basic tenets that traders will act to buy assets which are underpriced relative to risk and return, and they will sell assets which are overpriced. Other economists believe there is more at work in the markets, as evidenced by periodic crashes and bubbles that cannot be explained simply because of new information.

Types of orders

In equities trading, as well as other asset markets, there are several different order types:

- Market order—One of the two most common types of orders. The order is filled at the best price in the market. The risk to the buyer (or seller) is that the order will be filled at a time when there is a "liquidity gap," that the best price in the market is temporarily adverse.
- Limit order—This is the second of the two most common order types. The investor specifies a price at which the order is to be executed. The order can be filled only at that price or better. The risk to the investor is that the market is slightly worse than the limit price and the order goes unfilled. In the case of a buy order, the investor presumably believes that there is upside potential in the stock. By specifying too low a limit price,

the investor misses out on getting their order filled and the stock may run away to the upside without them.

- Stop order—These are conditional orders. In the case of a sell stop, this order specifies that the stock is to be sold if it trades down below a specified price. (A buy stop would specify that the stock is to be bought if it trades above a specified price.) For example, Apple stock may be trading at 150. A trader might enter a sell stop at 135. If Apple trades at or below 135, the order to sell is activated. The sell stop is often used in a protective manner: an investor is long a stock. If it trades below a certain level, the thesis underlying the investment may be invalid, or the risk of greater loss requires exiting the position. Therefore the investor commits to exiting the position if the stock trades below a certain level. In our example, that would be if Apple trades 135 Note that the sell stop may be used to take profits if the market has risen since the stock was bought, and the investor wants to take profits if the stock shows signs of weakness. In this case, the investor may have bought Apple at 50 or less. The stop order is activated if the market trades at the specified price and the investor books the profit. The stop order is also combined with either a market or limit order. A stop market order would be: sell Apple at the market on a 135 Stop. In this case, if Apple traded 135, there would be a sale order activated at the best bid in the market. The risk to the investor is that the next best bid could be substantially lower, only to bounce back. Of course, the market could continue straight down as well. A stop limit order might look like: sell Apple 135 Stop, 135 limit. In this case, if Apple trades 135, the order is activated and becomes a sell order with a 135 limit. It can be filled at 135 or better, but not worse. The risk is that the investor never gets filled and the market runs away to the downside.
- Open only orders—These orders can be filled only in the day's opening range.
- Close only orders—Orders to be filled during the closing range of the day.
- Fill-or-kill orders—These orders are exposed to the market, and must be filled immediately or they are canceled.
- Good-till-canceled—Unless otherwise stated, all orders are good only for the current trading session. GTC orders are good orders for continuing trading sessions until the investor cancels them.

Institutional investors often place large size orders, called "blocks" and many engage in "program trading" where many different stocks, or "baskets" will be executed essentially simultaneously. These trades may at times accentuate volatility in markets. Another group of traders with distinctive styles are the high frequency traders (HFT). HFT traders use computerized algorithms and low latency connectivity to exchanges to rapidly post bids and offers and to trade against orders in the market. There are many different styles of HFT trading but it general, their trade size tends to be relatively small, and are often closed out in a relatively short time period. Many of the HFT are not highly capitalized and do not carry large positions over night. While the size of their individual trades may be small, they trade very often. HFT traders often act as market makers and provide crucial depth to many markets. In fact, it is estimated that HFT trading may account for more than 50% of total US equity trading. Some observers believe HFT trading contributes negatively to increased volatility in markets, while others point out that HFT traders provide irreplaceable liquidity to the markets. Some market observers who think HFT is a negative, have proposed the creation of "speed bumps" to slow these traders down. These proposals have not won widespread support, in part due to concerns that they might dramatically reduce liquidity in many markets.

Equity trading venues

In the United States, equities are traded on either an exchange or on an alternative trading system (ATS). There are several smaller and regional exchanges, but the three largest US exchanges are:

- NYSE, the New York Stock Exchange, is also nicknamed "The Big Board" and is a subsidiary of the InterContinental Exchange (ICE). It is the largest venue by market capitalization of its listed companies. It operates side by side electronic and floor based trading, with the former dominating traded volumes.
- NASDAQ is second to NYSE in market capitalization of its traded companies. Its parent company owns and operates several smaller US exchanges as well as Nordic and Baltic Exchanges. NASDAQ was the first of the exchanges to trade exclusively electronically.
- BATS, owned by CBOE, is the largest US equities market operator by volume, with four active exchanges: BATS BZX Exchange, BYX Exchange, EDGA Exchange, and EDGX Exchange.

In addition to exchanges, equities are traded on what is known as alternative trading systems (ATS), which can be either "lit" pools (they provide pre-trade transparency about orders and posttrade transparency about executed trades) or "dark" pools (there is no pretrade information, but after trading, transactions are reported). Electronic communications networks (ECNs) are lit services which display bids and offers in the market and are available to investors with direct market access. They do not require connection through brokers. Some examples of ECNs are Bloomberg Tradebook, LavaFlow, and Track ECN.

Dark pools are facilities which permit institutional investors to execute or "cross" trades with each other without disclosing bids or offers in advance of the trade. These facilities developed out of concerns about information leakage. If an institutional investor showed a bid for very large size to the market, traders might "front run" the order by jumping ahead of the investor. Any offers remaining in the market would quickly back up and the investor would end up paying a hefty premium or would not even be able to fill their order. There are several different alternative forms of dark pools with variations on minimum order size, ownership of the pool, pricing, and other factors. There are pools owned by broker-dealers: Barclays, Credit Suisse, Citi, Goldman Sachs, JP Morgan, and Morgan Stanley all operate dark pools which are popular with investors. Other dark pools are operated on an agency basis by brokers or exchanges. These include pools operated by Instinet, Liquidnet, BATS, and NYSE Euronext. There are also dark pools maintained by proprietary electronic trading firms who often act as principal to transactions. One such firm, Virtu, describes its "Virtu Matchit" ATS as an anonymous crossing venue with nondisplayed liquidity from numerous sources including: liquidity providers, institutional brokers, Virtu's own client market-making business, Virtu proprietary flow, direct market access from third-party broker-dealers and algorithmic order flow from third-party broker-dealers, and Virtu Electronic Trading.

Numerous alternative trading platforms have been built to compete with the existing ATS and exchanges. Some have interesting technology, but none have yet seen overwhelming levels of adoption by traders. One key is liquidity, a feature of the "network effect." The network effect refers to the characteristic of a good or service whereby it becomes more valuable when more people use it. If Facebook, Instagram, or other social services had few users, they would have little value, but everyone uses them, so they are the go-to places for social interaction. This effect is also important in markets: if many or most traders use a particular market or platform, then that is where the tightest bid-asked spreads and the largest volumes would be. In markets, success in attracting liquidity begets further liquidity. If a market has excellent liquidity, the technology only has to be good enough. Volume of trading activity thus builds a competitive moat around the biggest exchanges and makes it extremely difficult for a disruptor to gain traction.

NASDAQ itself was the first electronic platform for trading equities. As early as 1971, it linked a distributed network of traders, and it continues to upgrade and invest in technology. NYSE has historically been identified with exchange members trading stocks on its iconic physical exchange floor but entered the electronic age with the 2006 merger with Archipelago Holdings and the subsequent renaming of the electronic business as NYSE Arca. In 2012 NYSE was acquired by the InterContinental Exchange, known as ICE. This accelerated the move to electronification of the equity markets as ICE brought a culture of tech innovation from its commodity exchange operations. While an old timer by current Fintech standards, ICE followed a development path being emulated by many startups today. ICE's Chairman and CEO, Jeff Sprecher, originally bought an energy trading platform in

Atlanta in 1996, for $1 and the assumption of debt. This platform became an online marketplace for trading energy in 2000. Sprecher later accelerated the "digitization" of equity trading to where it is the dominant force today.

Regulation

There are several layers of regulation of equities markets in the United States. The Securities and Exchange Commission (SEC) is the primary federal entity charged with carrying out securities laws passed by Congress. The SEC was created by the Securities Exchange Act of 1934 which was intended to correct some of the causes of the Great Depression. The SEC's mission is to protect investors; maintain fair, orderly, and efficient markets; and facilitate capital formation. It has the following five divisions:

- Division of Corporation Finance—This division ensures that investors have material information when companies initially offer securities and on an ongoing basis.
- Division of Enforcement—Enforcement staff conduct investigations and prosecutes civil suits in federal courts and administrative proceedings.
- Division of Economic and Risk Analysis—This group integrates financial economics and data analytics in order to support policy-making, rule-making, enforcement, and examination.
- Division of Investment Management—This division regulates variable insurance products, federally registered investment advisers and investment companies, including mutual funds, closed-end funds, unit investment trusts, and exchange-traded funds.
- Division of Trading and Markets—This division establishes and maintains standards for fair, orderly, and efficient markets. It regulates the major securities market participants such as broker-dealers, stock exchanges, FINRA, and others.

The Financial Industry Regulatory Authority (FINRA) was created by Congress but is not a government agency. It is a not-for-profit organization whose mission is investor protection and market integrity through regulation of broker-dealers. It carries out this mission by the following activities:

- Writing and enforcing rules governing broker activities
- Examining firms for compliance with these rules
- Fostering market transparency
- Investor education

While the SEC and FINRA are national level regulators, each state also has securities laws and their own regulators. These state laws are called "blue sky laws" and are focused on investor protection. There are some differences among the states and securities offerings will often contain wording to the effect that the issues are not available to residents of certain states.

In addition to the above regulators, the exchanges themselves have rule-books and participants agree to be bound by those rules. The exchanges also have some disciplinary powers including fines and denying market access to rule violators.

Investing in equities

Investing in equities can take several forms. The simplest is the individual or retail investor buying a specific stock for their own account. Trading volume, however, is dominated by institutional investors: pension funds, insurance companies, hedge funds, and other managers of large pools of capital. The latter investment styles can be characterized as active where the manager seeks to outperform the market averages or passive where the goal is to match a benchmark, usually one of the indexes described later in this chapter. Investment strategies may further target a specific industry, certain company size (measured by market capitalization of the component companies) or geography. Active investment managers have a significant percentage of their compensation determined by their success as measured against specific relevant benchmarks. A typical compensation agreement for a hedge fund provides for hedge fund managers (employees or partners of the General Partner of the fund) to be paid a management fee of 2% of assets under management (AUM) and 20% of profits. These percentage vary depending on market conditions and demand for a particular manager's services, and size and bargaining power of limited partners. There is another level of investment management called "fund of funds." These managers charge a fee for selecting and monitoring investment allocations to fund managers. These fees are in addition to the fees charged by those fund managers. These high fees have created an opportunity for Fintech companies to offer lower cost investment management services termed "robo-advisors." Many people have pointed out the difficulty for investors to outperform market averages when all the fees are accounted for. One such critic is Warren Buffet, arguably the greatest investor of his generation. In his 2016 letter to investors in Berkshire Hathaway (Buffet, 2016), he gave results of a challenge he had issued in 2008. His thesis was that over a 10-year period a passive investor in a low fee index fund would outperform a portfolio of funds of hedge funds with all fees and other costs included. This challenge was accepted, and results are shown in Fig. 6.1.

The results are that for the period shown the low-cost passive index outperformed the active managers when all fees and other costs are included. A qualifying argument in favor of the active management side is that these funds seek to generate positive returns at times when the overall market may be negative and would therefore outperform the passive index at times of stress in the market. This was the case in 2008 when the passive index fund lost 37% of value while the fund of funds were down lesser amounts.

Year	Fund of funds A	Fund of funds B	Fund of funds C	Fund of funds D	Fund of funds E	S&P index fund
2008	−16.5%	−22.3%	−21.3%	−29.3%	−30.1%	−37.0%
2009	11.3%	14.5%	21.4%	16.5%	16.8%	−26.6%
2010	5.9%	6.8%	13.3%	4.9%	11.9%	15.1%
2011	−6.3%	−1.3%	5.9%	−6.3%	−2.8%	2.1%
2012	3.4%	9.6%	5.7%	−6.2%	9.1%	16.0%
2013	10.5%	15.2%	8.8%	14.2%	14.4%	32.3%
2014	4.7%	4.0%	18.9%	0.7%	−2.1%	13.6%
2015	1.6%	2.5%	5.4%	1.4%	−5.0%	1.4%
2016	−2.9%	1.7%	−1.4%	2.5%	4.4%	11.9%
Gain to date	8.7%	28.3%	62.8%	2.9%	7.5%	85.4%

FIGURE 6.1   Performance of six managed funds versus an S&P index fund. *Source: Berkshire Hathaway.*

The end results could also be different if the ending year of the Buffet Challenge was a down year for the market. It should be noted that Buffet's argument focusses on the detrimental effect of excessive fees. It does not necessarily imply that all active investors will underperform the market average. In fact, Berkshire Hathaway itself stands as an example of successful active management (for more on Buffet, see Mathews, 2014).

Collective investment vehicles: mutual funds and exchange-traded funds

Given the importance of diversification in an investor's portfolio, financial institutions have developed investment vehicles which allow investors with limited funds to have the benefit of a wide distribution of assets in one investment purchase. One such vehicle is the mutual fund. Units or shares of a mutual fund are sold to individual investors. The manager of the fund then invests the proceeds in a diversified portfolio. Investors buy or sell shares of the fund at the fund's net asset value as calculated at the close of the day's trading. Each investor shares proportionally in the gains or losses of the fund's overall performance. Mutual funds can be either open-ended or close-ended. Open-ended funds continuously buy and sell units and are priced at the underlying net asset value of the funds' holdings. Closed-ended funds have a fixed, specific number of units. These units are then bought and sold in the open market, with the price determined by supply and demand for the units.

Mutual funds are attractive to investors in that they provide diversification, have lower costs of contracting and information gathering, and professional investment management. They come in many different flavors: there are bond funds and stock funds, and within stock funds, there are growth, income, and blended funds. They can also be passive or actively managed.

A newer collective investment vehicle which has become extremely popular, is the ETF. ETFs are securities which track a specific index of equities, bonds, or other assets. Unlike a mutual fund, buyers of an ETF do not have a fractional ownership interest in the underlying stocks or bonds, but instead own shares of the ETF itself which are bought and sold on exchanges, on an intraday basis. The exchange-traded market is actually a secondary market for ETFs. The primary market involves specialist firms, usually high frequency traders, who are involved in the creation and redemption of the shares. These institutional professionals are classified as authorized participants for a specific ETF. They perform a crucial arbitrage function by acquiring the necessary basket of securities which the ETF tracks. Like mutual funds, ETFs allow investors wide diversification and can be bought or sold on exchanges. There are also ETFs with a wide variety of investment styles and asset classes. There are some differences which account for the relative attractiveness of ETFs versus mutual funds. Investors don't have to wait until the end of the day to discover the price of the fund. ETFs trade throughout the day based on their constantly updated net asset value. If mutual funds have trading profits, then there may be tax liabilities for each of the fund shareholders. For an ETF, shares in the ETF itself are bought and sold so the sale by one investor may have tax consequences for that investor, but not for those investors who have not changed their position.

Mutual funds and ETFs can consist of securities of a narrowly focused group of companies or can reflect industry groups or even the market as a whole. In the last few years, funds focusing on ESG factors have become increasingly popular. More about these are given below and in Chapter 10, ESG in managing institutional investor funds.

Equity indexes

While the major exchanges have extensive lists of individual company equities, investing in a diversified group of companies and tracking the performance of that group is made easier by looking at stock market indexes. These indexes are used to assess the overall performance of industries or the condition of the market and to benchmark the performance of investment portfolios. The most important and widely watched indexes are:

- Dow Jones Industrial Average—This is a price weighted average of 30 large and widely held US industrial companies.
- New York Stock Exchange Composite Index—This, and the below indexes are all weighted by market capitalization (size) of the included companies' stocks. This benchmark is a sum of all the companies traded on the NYSE.
- NASDAQ Composite Index—Summarizes the value of all stocks traded on the NASDAQ system.
- Standard and Poor's 500 stock index—A committee of the S&P Corporation selects companies traded on NYSE, NASDAQ, and OTC markets to reflect the best representation of overall market sentiment.

- Wilshire 5000—This index seeks very broad market representation by including over 6500 different companies.
- Russell 1000—A broad index of 1000 larger companies.

There are also indexes that are important benchmarks for non-US markets. Some of the more closely watched indexes are:

- Tokyo Stock Price Index—TOPIX. This is an index of all the shares in the Tokyo market's First Section which lists the largest and most actively traded company stocks.
- Nikkei 225—This is an index of the 225 largest companies listed in the First Section.
- Hang Seng Index—This is a capitalization weighted index of the 50 largest companies traded on the Hong Kong exchange.
- Financial Times Stock Exchange 100 Index—This index includes the 100 largest companies traded on the London Stock Exchange and represents roughly 81% of its total market capitalization.
- DAX—This is an index of the 30 largest companies trading on the Frankfurt Stock Exchange.
- CAC 40 Index—The Cotation Assistee en Continu 40 is a capitalization weighted index of the 40 largest companies trading on Euronext Paris.
- Swiss Performance Index—The SPI includes roughly 230 companies trading on the Swiss Exchange and includes only those domiciled in Switzerland.
- S&P/TSX Composite—Formerly the TSE 300, this index includes prices of roughly 250 companies trading on the Toronto Stock Exchange. This represents about 70% of total market capitalization.
- Morgan Stanley Capital International (MSCI) World Index—This is a global index comprised of 1654 companies across 23 markets.

Most of these indexes have further subindexes reflecting industry, size, or geographic concentration.

ESG indexes

Several companies have constructed equity indexes that reflect ESG criteria. Many of these indexes are designed to "do well while doing good." The goal is to develop indexes which include companies with superior ESG characteristics but at the same time, have overall portfolio financial performance roughly equal to that of more conventional portfolios. These index products are designed to provide the institutional investment community with investment vehicles which have certain risk and return characteristics and are in compliance with ESG mandates and policy benchmarks. The indexes are used as benchmarks to assess investment performance and are used to create other financial products such as institutional and retail funds, ETFs, structured products, and derivatives. In Chapter 9, Defining and measuring ESG performance and Chapter 10, ESG in managing institutional investor funds, we will look in more detail at how these indexes are constructed and at how some institutional investors are using them. Here, we will briefly describe some of the available indexes.

MSCI

MSCI began developing global equity indexes in 1969. Today their products are used by a wide variety of institutional investors. Asset owners use their research, data, indexes, and multiasset class risk management tools to determine whether the managers they hire are delivering appropriate risk-adjusted returns. Chief investment officers use their data to develop and test investment strategies, and they also use MSCI models and performance attribution tools to understand the drivers of return in their portfolios. Active managers use their factor models, data and portfolio construction, and optimization tools to build portfolios and keep them aligned with their investment objectives, while passive managers use index data, equity factor models, and optimization tools to construct their index funds and ETFs. Finally, chief risk officers use MSCI risk management systems to understand, monitor, and control risk in their portfolios.

Over $180 billion have been allocated to ESG indexes constructed by MSCI. These indexes can be grouped into the following main categories:

- MSCI Global Sustainability Indexes—These benchmarks target the highest ESG-rated companies making up 50% of the adjusted market capitalization in each sector of the underlying index. The indexes are designed for investors seeking exposure to companies with strong sustainability profiles with relatively low tracking error to the underlying equity market. In using these indexes, investors hope to mirror the return of the underlying index but do so by investing only in the companies with the best ESG scores.
- MSCI Global SRI Indexes—These benchmarks consist of companies with the highest ESG ratings making up 25% of the adjusted market capitalization in each sector of a parent MSCI index, after excluding companies involved in alcohol, tobacco, gambling, civilian firearms, military weapons, nuclear power, adult entertainment, and genetically modified organisms (GMOs).
- MSCI Global ex Controversial Weapons Indexes—These benchmarks are designed for investors who wish to avoid investments in cluster bombs, land mines, chemical and biological weapons, and depleted uranium weapons.
- MSCI Global Environmental Indexes—This Index family provides low carbon, fossil fuels exclusion, and other indexes designed to support various low carbon investment strategies.

- Barclays MSCI ESG Fixed Income Indices—This group comprises more than 500 standard and custom ESG fixed income indices. More about fixed income markets and indices can be found in Chapter 7, Financial markets: bonds.
- Custom MSCI ESG Indices—Bespoke indices are constructed to meet specific investor interests and mandates.
- MSCI ACWI (All Country World Index) Sustainable Impact Index—This index is comprised exclusively of companies whose core business addresses at least one of the world's social and environmental challenges, as defined by the United Nations Sustainable Development Goals. To be eligible for inclusion in the index, companies must generate at least 50% of their sales from one or more of the sustainable impact categories and maintain minimum environmental, social, and governance (ESG) standards.

FTSE Russell

FTSE Russell, a wholly owned subsidiary of the London Stock Exchange Group's Information Services Division, provides numerous indexes to institutional investors to use as benchmarks and for the creation of investment funds, ETFs, structured products, and index-based derivatives. In total, approximately $16 trillion in assets are benchmarked to their indexes. ESG Indexes offered by FTSE Russell can be classified into the following groups:

- FTSE Global Climate Index Series—This Series is designed to reflect the performance of a global, diversified basket of securities where their weights are varied based on three types of climate-related analysis (carbon emissions, fossil fuel reserves, and green revenues data).
- FTSE ESG Index Series—In this series, company weights within each index are "tilted" using FTSE Russell's ESG Ratings. Subsequently, industry neutral reweighting is applied so that the industry weights in each index match the underlying index universe. As a result, the FTSE ESG Indexes have risk/return characteristics similar to the underlying universe with the added benefit of improved ESG metrics.
- FTSE 4Good Index Series—Using clearly defined ESG criteria, this family of indexes is designed to measure the performance of companies demonstrating strong ESG practices.
- FTSE Green Revenues Index Series—This series is designed to obtain increased exposure to companies engaged in the transition to a green economy, based on FTSE's Green Revenues data model. The indexes are designed to capture changes in the revenue mix of companies as their business models shift to the delivery of goods, products, and services that allow the world to adapt to, mitigate or remediate the impacts of climate change, resource depletion, and environmental erosion.

- FTSE Divest-Invest Index Series—This Series is designed to combine fossil fuel divestment with thematic investment in low carbon and green solutions.
- FTSE Environmental Markets Index Series
    - FTSE Environmental Technology Index Series measure the performance of companies globally whose core business is in the development and deployment of environmental technologies, including renewable and alternative energy, energy efficiency, water technology, and waste and pollution control. Companies are required to have at least 50% of their business derived from environmental markets and technologies in order to be eligible.
    - FTSE Environmental Opportunities Index Series measure the performance of global companies that have significant involvement in environmental business activities, including renewable and alternative energy, energy efficiency, water technology, and waste and pollution control. Companies are required to have at least 20% of their business derived from environmental markets and technologies in order to be eligible.
- FTSE EPRA Nareit Green Indexes—These indexes provide investors with a tool for integrating climate risk into their listed real estate portfolio. These indexes provide a sustainability-focused extension to the FTSE EPRA Nareit Global Real Estate Index Series, the world's leading series of listed real estate benchmarks. The FTSE EPRA Nareit Green indexes weight constituents based on two sustainable investment measures: green building certification and energy usage.
- FTSE ex Fossil Fuels Index Series—Some market participants are looking to manage carbon exposure in their investments and reduce write-off or downward revaluation risks associated with stranded assets. Stranded assets are fossil fuels deposits, including oil, gas, and coal, that must remain unburned or in the ground in order for the world to avoid the worst impacts of climate change. The FTSE ex Fossil Fuels Index Series is designed to represent the performance of companies in FTSE Russell and FTSE RAFI indexes after the exclusion of companies that have certain exposure to fossil fuels.
- The FTSE All-World ex Coal Index Series is designed to represent the performance of companies in specific market segments of the FTSE All-World Index after the exclusion of companies that have certain exposure to coal mining or general mining.
- FTSE Women on Boards Leadership Index Series—This series is designed to represent the performance of companies that have a higher proportion of women on their boards and have strong social policies.

In late 2018, FTSE announces the creation of several new green indexes in the listed real estate sector as well as a partnership with Sustainalytics to create new ESG versions of the Russell 1000, 2000, and 3000 Indexes.

Morningstar

Morningstar is an investment research and investment management firm which, among other services, provides an influential rating of investment funds. In 2016 it developed a tool for evaluating funds based on sustainability criteria. The Morningstar Sustainability Rating uses company ESG ratings developed by Sustainalytics. The Morningstar rating is a measure of how well companies held in a portfolio are managing their ESG risks and opportunities relative to other portfolio companies in the same category. Portfolios which do not intentionally incorporate sustainability criteria can still be evaluated for how well they may be doing on these measures.

Morningstar produces an annual "Landscape" report which reviews financial and sustainability performance of funds. Some key takeaways from the 2018 report (Morningstar, 2018):

● More funds than ever incorporate ESG or sustainability themes in the United States.
● Sustainable funds can now be found in 56 Morningstar Categories.
● Assets under management and net flows have reached all-time highs.
● Sustainable funds are competitive on price and performance.
● Performance skews positive over both the short term and long term.
● Sustainable funds consistently receive high Morningstar Sustainability Ratings

The review defined the US sustainable funds universe as those open-ended funds and exchange-traded portfolios that, by prospectus, state that they incorporate ESG criteria into their investment processes or indicate that they pursue a sustainability-related theme or seek measurable sustainable impact alongside financial return. It excludes funds that only use values-based exclusionary screening. Fig. 6.2 shows the increase in new sustainable funds added in each year from 2013 to 2017.

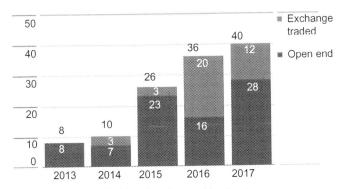

FIGURE 6.2   New sustainable fund launches. *Source: Morningstar.*

FIGURE 6.3 Sustainable funds span a range of Morningstar categories. *Source: Morningstar.*

	2017		2016		2015	
	#	%	#	%	#	%
Top quartile	45	24	41	28	33	28
Second	55	30	39	27	35	29
Third	47	26	44	30	29	24
Bottom quartile	37	20	21	15	22	19
N=	184		145		119	

FIGURE 6.4 Sustainable funds performance relative to Morningstar category, 2015–2017. *Source: Morningstar.*

In addition to these new funds, several funds began adding sustainability criteria to their existing funds. The combination of new funds and the adaptations of some existing funds has resulted in broad coverage of sustainable funds across many categories, as shown in Fig. 6.3.

So, how have these sustainable funds performed? The Morningstar review concludes that their performance is consistent with the observation that "... the weight of the research evidence suggests no systematic performance penalty associated with sustainable investing and possible avenues for outperformance based on reduced risk or added alpha." For 2017, 54% of these funds ranked in the top half of their Morningstar Category for the year. The performance over the 3-year period ending in 2017 was similar, even as the number of funds increased from 119 to 184 (Fig. 6.4).

Robo-advisors

Investment management is an area of growth for new, disruptive Fintech startups. Sometimes referred to as "Wealth Tech," these companies provide a variety of services to improve the delivery of products designed to assist investment and wealth management. These products range from incremental, technology-enabled services augmenting existing products to more disruptive wholistic solutions. Perhaps the most successful of these latter services are "Robo-advisors" which are online, primarily automated investment management services. The typical business model is to have online customer access with no physical presence and little if any human interaction. The customer specifies individual investment preferences in terms of risk, desired return, and investment amounts. The company's investing algorithms then identify investment choices and weightings for each. The investments are typically in different ETFs although some services may offer a choice of assets among stocks, bonds commodities, and others. There may also be a choice offered between passive and active investment vehicles. In terms of investment choices, the robo services are like those offered by the wealth management divisions of the big financial institutions. What is different is the focus on online delivery and lack of physical infrastructure and human interaction. This allows robos to present an enhanced digital customer experience and keeps costs to very low levels.

The two leading robo-advisors are Wealthfront and Betterment. Attesting to its popularity, Wealthfront had $10 billion in assets under management (AUM) as of early 2019. It has a very low minimum requirement for opening an account of only $500 and charges no management fee for accounts of less than $10,000. For amounts in excess of $10,000, Wealthfront charges a flat fee of 0.25%. This is in line with fees charged by Betterment and other robos. Wealthfront offers a service called Path that will assist setting up a retirement plan. The user responds to a questionnaire and links Path to their checking account. Based on goals, habits, and financial condition, tailored strategies are recommended. The service centers on building a diversified strategy, optimized to minimize taxes and with low fees. Daily tax loss harvesting is a central feature. Investments which are losing money are sold, generating a tax loss, and highly correlated alternative investments are added, leaving the overall portfolio profile unchanged. Another feature is Advanced Indexing. This portfolio tool allocates capital to a combination of large and mid-cap US stocks and one or two additional ETFs. The weights are shifted based on a multifactor methodology which identifies securities which are likely to have higher expected returns and are therefore overweighted. In terms of ESG investing, Wealthfront offers investors an option, within their Stock-Level Tax-Loss Harvesting feature, to exclude specific stocks from their portfolios. This allows investors to choose any "sin" stocks which they wish to omit. Wealthfront has seen client exclusion requests in four categories: tobacco, deforestation, fossil fuels, and weapons. Wealthfront clients with over $500,000 to invest can make use of the company's "Smart Beta" service to provide further granularity in company exclusions. As we have noted in previous chapters, simply excluding specific stocks, with no consideration of portfolio impact can (and historically has) resulted in sup-par financial performance. Individual investors, of course, may choose to accept the potentially lower financial returns associated with such a divestment strategy.

Betterment was founded in 2008 and has many similarities to Wealthfront and some differences. Both services offer a range of IRA and other accounts, with extensive online access. Customers establish their risk tolerance and optimal portfolios are designed. The portfolio is rebalanced if it falls out of alignment with objectives. Both offer Socially Responsible Investing choices. Customer account balances are insured by the Securities Investor Protection Corporation, up to a maximum of $500,000. While focused on technology solutions, Betterment also puts emphasis on availability of professionals and licensed experts. It has a minimum requirement of just $1. Betterment will cap fees at a maximum of $5,000 and will also automatically make bank deposits if the balance exceeds a specified amount. It will harvest cash in a customer's account and invest it even if it results in fractional shares.

Betterment has taken a sophisticated approach to developing a Socially Responsible Investment (SRI) option based on MSCI ESG ratings of companies. In their SRI portfolio they have replaced conventional portfolio holdings with SRI focused companies in each of the following categories: US total stock market; US large value; mid-cap and small growth; and emerging markets. Based on historical performance, the resulting SRI portfolios are expected to closely track conventional, core portfolios.

Chapter 7

Financial markets: bonds

Chapter Outline

Future value and present value 118
Internal rate of return 120
Credit instruments 121
Fisher's law 122
Term structure and yield curve 122
Types of debt instruments: money market instruments 124
Types of debt instruments: US Treasury securities 127
Types of debt instruments: agency securities 129
Types of debt instruments: corporate bonds 129
Types of debt instruments: municipal securities 132
Types of debt instruments: sovereign debt 133
Fixed income trading 133
Fixed income indexes and funds 136
   ESG bond funds 136
   ESG bond fund managers 139
   Green bonds 141

Credit markets provide a huge amount of capital to businesses and governments alike. ("Fixed income," "bonds," and "credit" markets are often used interchangeably to refer to interest-bearing securities.) In terms of dollar value, credit markets are much larger than equity markets, and they are increasingly being used for environmental, social, and governance (ESG) investment. Institutions and individuals can invest in ESG bond funds, which buy fixed income instruments from issuers with positive ESG characteristics. Or they can buy "green bonds" which are issued for specific projects which are consistent with the investors' ESG goals. Or they can buy ESG ETFs or other derivatives based on ESG indexes. Before we investigate these products, we need an understanding of the theory behind bonds and the range of instruments that are available in fixed income markets.

Money has been loaned for thousands of years. European Kings and Queens have issued (and defaulted on) loans for funding wars and other purposes. Modern governments continue to borrow money (and default) in today's modern credit markets. Corporations also depend on these markets for funding operations and capital projects. An important feature of credit products is that the issuer pays interest to the provider of capital. The starting point for thinking about interest rates is understanding the individual preferences for consumption today versus consumption tomorrow. A consumer could choose to buy a bundle of goods for current consumption or keep

Environmental, Social, and Governance (ESG) Investing. DOI: https://doi.org/10.1016/B978-0-12-818692-3.00007-4

some resources (save) for future use. This can be called the rate of time preference. Some consumers might prefer to consume all their resources now, but could be convinced to defer some consumption to future periods, if there is some compensation, or payment, to do so. Another way to think of it is that lending has opportunity costs: lenders have the alternative to consume now. Borrowers must offer an incentive for lenders to forego current consumption, and that incentive is called "interest." Would you prefer to have $1000 today or $1000 next year? Almost everyone would prefer the $1000 today and would insist on some additional payment to wait until next year and to account for the risk that they won't get paid back.

Future value and present value

Interest payments can take different forms and have different frequencies. The typical arrangement is for borrowers to make a monthly or quarterly payment to lenders. Interest payments on bonds are often semiannual. Some bonds only make one lump sum payment of interest when the bond is redeemed at maturity. To compare bonds with different payment streams we have two related concepts that provide consistent measurement. Future Value (FV) quantifies what an investment will be worth a specified time in the future, and Present Value (PV) quantifies the current worth of future investment results. In the example of deferring $1000 for 1 year, assume there is a simple rate of interest of 5% annually. The interest earned would be 1000×0.05 or $50. The FV of the investment at the end of 1 year would equal the PV plus all interest payments or: $1000 + (\$1000 \times 0.05) = \$1000 \times (1 + 0.05) = \$1050$.

This can be expressed as:

$$FV = PV + \text{Interest}$$

Noting that interest is a fraction of PV, this can be expressed as:

$$FV = PV \times (1 + r)$$

where r is the interest rate.

Dividing both sides of the equation by $(1 + r)$ gives the relation for deriving PV when knowing FV and the interest rate:

$$PV = \frac{FV}{(1 + r)}$$

If the investment continues for a second year, on the same terms, the interest earned is again 5%, but on the new principal of $1050. In second and subsequent periods, interest is earned on the original principal and on the earlier interest. This paying interest on interest is called the "compounding of interest" and is a powerful multiplier in long-term investment results. In this example, in the second year, the FV can be calculated as the sum of the new principal at the end of the first year (1050) plus interest earned of $1050 \times 0.05 = \$52.50$, or a total of $1102.50.

Noting that the principal at the end of the first year is made up of the original principal plus first year's interest, this can be expressed as:

The original $1000 + Interest on $1000 in Year One + Interest on $1000 in Year Two + Interest in Year Two on the Interest earned in Year One,

or

$1000 + \$1000 \times 0.05 + \$1000 \times 0.05 + ((\$1000 \times 0.05) \times 0.05)$, or

$$FV = PV + (PV \times r) + (PV \times r) + ((PV \times r) \times r)$$

With some modest manipulation, we get:

$$FV = PV \times \left(1 + r + r + r^2\right)$$
$$= PV \times \left(1 + 2r + r^2\right)$$

And noting that $(1 + 2r + r^2) = (1 + r)^2$,

$$FV = PV \times (1 + r)^2$$

$$\$1000 \times (1.05)^2$$

More generally,

$$FV = PV \times (1 + r)^n$$

where r is the interest rate and n is the number of periods.
In our example above,

$$FV = \$1000 \times (1.05)^2$$
$$= \$1102.50$$

So, after 2 years of earning 5% per year, the $1000 would be equal to $1102.50.

This formula can be used to calculate the total amount of money that an investor would receive from any investment with a fixed, compound rate of return. Note that it is more than just multiplying the annual rate of interest by the number of years: there is additional interest earned on the interest from earlier years. The Future Value formula can be used to calculate the amount of money that would be gained from any investment with a fixed payment. Take for example, an investment of $1000 at 5% interest for 5 years. Plugging these parameters into a readily available financial calculator would show a total amount of $1276.28. After 10 years the total would be $1628.89. While a calculator is needed to determine the precise amounts, there is a handy rule of thumb that can be used to estimate how many years it takes for an investment to double. Called the "rule of 72," simply take the interest rate, as a whole number and divide it into 72. For example, if the interest rate is 7%, divide 72 by 7 and the result is a bit more than 10. It takes approximately 10 years for an investment to double if it increases by 7% each year. If the interest rate is 6%, it would take 12 years to double ($72/6 = 12$). From the formula, $FV = PV \times (1 + r)^n$ notice that FV is greater with increases in PV; with increases in r, the rate of interest; and with increases in n, the number of periods.

So, the Future Value formula can be used to show what to expect in the future from an investment made now. Financial calculators make it simple to just plug in the parameters and quickly see the results. The next question is: if the amount earned in the future is known, what is it worth today? Using the previous example, $1050 next year, at a 5% interest rate, would have a Present Value of $1000. So, if the equation for FV is:

$$FV = PV \times (1 + r)^n$$

then dividing both sides of the equation by $(1 + r)^n$ gives:

$$PV = \frac{FV}{(1 + r)^n}$$

Note that, with FV held constant, PV falls as interest rates rise; and falls with a larger number of periods. PV will be greater with increases in FV, if r and n are held constant. In our example, $1050 next year at 5% interest has a PV of $1000, but at 7% interest it has a PV of only $981.31. Alternative investments might have different payment streams. By comparing PV of each of the streams, an investor can easily determine which is preferred. An important feature of PV is that it is additive. If investment returns are paid out in a series of payments, rather than a lump sum, the PVs of the individual payments can be summed to get a total PV for the entire stream of payments.

Internal rate of return

One application of using PV is in evaluating investments which return a stream of payments. If the stream of payments is known, then the interest rate which would make that stream just offset the original cost is called the internal rate of return (IRR). IRR can be used to calculate expected returns from a wide range of projects, such as purchasing new plant and equipment. It can thus be used to compare, and rank, diverse projects. The calculated IRR can them be compared with the company's hurdle rate or minimum acceptable return. For example, a micro brewer might purchase equipment totaling $1 million and expect to earn $200,000 per year in beer sales. Using the PV formula, the PV of the first year's sales is equal to

$$\frac{200,000}{(1 + r)}$$

where r is the IRR.

The PV for year two would be:

$$\frac{200,000}{(1+r)^2}$$

Assuming there is a 10-year life to the equipment, then we can solve the following equation for the IRR of purchasing the new equipment:

$$\$1,000,000 = \frac{200,000}{(1+r)} + \frac{200,000}{(1+r)^2} \ldots + \frac{200,000}{(1+r)^{10}}$$

Using a financial calculator, this equation can be solved for r, the IRR which equates this stream of payments with the original cost. In this example, the IRR equals 15.098%. If the micro brewer's hurdle rate is substantially less than 15%, this would be a profitable investment for them.

Credit instruments

Credit market instruments have many different forms. We can start by grouping them into four categories:

- Simple loan. This is a traditional transaction where the lender provides funds and the borrower repays the principal at maturity, plus an additional amount of interest.
- Fixed payment loan. This is most familiar as a mortgage or auto loan, where the borrower makes the same payment at regular intervals. Each payment includes interest plus a partial return of the original principal.
- Coupon bond. Coupon bonds pay the owner a fixed amount each period. At maturity, a specified amount, the face value, is paid to the owner.
- Zero-coupon bond. These are also known as Discount Bonds, and are sold at a price less than its face value. No interest is paid. Instead, at maturity, the owner receives full face value which includes a positive premium above the purchase price.

In order to compare the returns of these instruments with different cash flows and different maturities, another concept is necessary, and it is called the Yield to Maturity or YTM. YTM can be defined as the interest rate that makes the Present Value of the cash flow from the instrument equal to the price of the instrument. Recall the formula for PV:

$$PV = \frac{FV}{(1+r)}$$

For a Coupon bond, FV would be the series of coupon payments (CP) plus the face value of the bond. So, PV for a 1-year bond would equal the coupon (actually two semiannual coupons) plus the face value, properly discounted, or

$$PV = \frac{CP}{(1+r)} + \frac{Face\ Value}{(1+r)}$$

The value of r which solves this equation is called the Yield To Maturity. If we multiply both sides of this equation by $(1 + r)$, we get

$$(1 + r)PV = CP + \text{Face Value}$$

If PV = Face Value, namely the purchase price equals Face Value, then YTM is simply the coupon rate. If price is above Face Value, then YTM is below the coupon rate, and if price is below Face Value, then YTM is above the coupon rate.

Fisher's law

The foregoing discussion is in terms of nominal interest rates. That is, there is no discussion of inflation. Fisher's law, named after the economist Irving Fisher considers that the rate of change of prices in the real economy has an impact on required rates of return on financial instruments. This can be stated as:

$$i = r + p$$

where i is the nominal rate of interest; r is the real rate; and p is the expected rate of inflation.

Intuitively, Fisher's law says that the nominal rate equals the real rate plus inflation.

Note also that

$$r = i - p$$

or that the real rate equals the nominal rate minus inflation. As an example, if the nominal rate on a bond is 4% and inflation is 2%, then an investor receives a real rate of return of 2%. The practical application is that if investors expect higher rates of inflation, they will demand higher rates of interest from bond issuers.

Term structure and yield curve

Credit instruments have different maturities. US federal debt maturing in less than 1 year is called "Treasury Bills." "Treasury Notes" have a maturity of between 1 and 10 years, and "Treasury Bonds" mature in more than 10 years. Corporate debt can have a similar wide range of maturities. The relationship between interest rates and bond yields of different maturities is called the term structure of interest rates or the yield curve. In general, the longer the time to maturity the greater the required yield. Fig. 7.1 shows a typical shape for the yield curve.

A typical positive yield curve demonstrates increasing yields with longer maturities. A flat yield curve would have a constant yield across all maturities and an inverted yield curve would show higher yields for shorter maturities. In September 2011 the Federal Reserve engaged in "Operation Twist,"

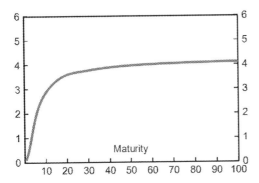

FIGURE 7.1 Yield curve.

which was so named because its objective was to "twist" the yield curve. The Fed wanted to bring down longer term interest rates, so it bought long-term Treasury bonds while at the same time selling short-term Treasuries. (There was an earlier Fed "Operation Twist" in 1961. This was also the time of a dance craze, called the Twist, made popular by Fats Domino and Chubby Checker.)

The difference between any two maturities is called a yield curve spread or a maturity spread. This is most commonly used in looking at Treasuries. A complication in comparing corporate maturities is that credit quality differences between issuers is also important. The US Treasury yield curve acts as the benchmark for setting yields and pricing bonds globally.

Two important concepts in bond pricing are duration and convexity. Duration is a measure of the sensitivity of the price of the instrument to a change in interest rates. It is defined as the rate of change in price with respect to a change in yield. Convexity is a measurement that indicates how rapidly duration changes. It is the second derivative of price with respect to yield.

What factors impact bond prices? We can start with the factors that influence demand for bonds. These include:

- Wealth. The more resources an individual has, the greater the amount of bonds they are likely to purchase.
- Expected return. The greater the payoff from bonds, the more likely they will be favored versus other uses of funds.
- Risk. The greater the certainty of the expected return, relative to other assets, the more likely the bonds will be purchased.
- Liquidity. A high expected return is great, but if there are liquidity concerns, the investor may have less certainty of being able to realize those returns.

Bonds with the same maturity would be expected to have the same interest rate, but there are other factors to consider, namely:

- Default risk. US Treasuries are considered globally to be the risk-free reference instrument. Other corporate bonds and the debt of other countries include a risk premium that reflects an assessment of their credit worthiness. Rating agencies (the largest are Moody's, Standard and Poor's, and Fitch) provide credit ratings. Corporate bonds are rated as Investment Grade (low credit risk) or High Yield (high credit risk). High Yield bonds were once called Junk bonds, but High Yield may be a term with more appeal to investors. Within the Investment Grade, those rated triple A (AAA or Aaa) are said to be prime, double A (AA or Aa) are of high quality, single-A issues are called upper-medium grade, and triple-B issues are medium grade. Fig. 7.2 shows how the yield on the highest quality Aaa corporate bonds have changed over time.

- Liquidity. It is important that bids exist when an investor wants to sell a bond. If liquidity is unavailable when the investor wants to exit the position, the investor risks suffering losses or missing out on other reinvestment opportunities. The US Treasury market is the world's most liquid market. The next most liquid market is the market for money market funds. On the other hand, many corporate bonds have very limited liquidity.

- Tax treatment. The relevant return for an investor to consider is the after-tax return. This gives a funding advantage to the various municipalities which issue bonds to fund their outlays. Municipal bond interest is exempt from federal taxes, and in most states, interest on bonds issued within that state are exempt from state taxes as well. Tax paying investors need to consider the after-tax payout when comparing taxable corporate bonds with tax-free municipals. For example, depending on specific tax rates of an individual investor, a municipal paying 4.7% interest tax free would be competitive with a taxable corporate issue paying 5%. Also, these relative rates are sensitive to changes in tax policy. If income tax rates rise, then tax-free municipals are more attractive and could offer lower rates. Conversely, if income tax rates are reduced, then municipals are less attractive and would need to increase the interest rate they pay, relative to the taxable corporate rate. Fig. 7.3 shows bond yields for a variety of issues and maturities.

Types of debt instruments: money market instruments

Money market instruments are financial instruments which are issued with a maturity of one year or less. They provide a market for investors to earn a return on liquid assets; borrowers who need short-term liquidity have access to these funds; and they provide the Fed with a means to effect monetary policy. The money markets include the following different types of instruments, each with different purposes. Banks lend to each other in what is called the "interbank funding (or lending) market." Unsecured lending takes place through the federal funds market while secured lending occurs in the repo market. The rate at which banks borrow from each other is the "fed

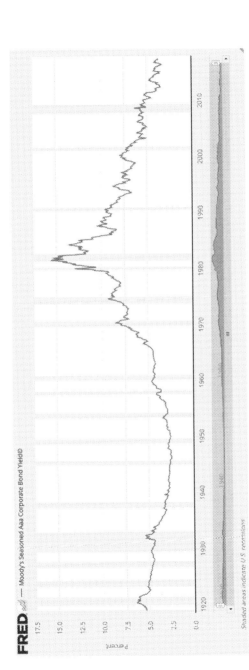

FIGURE 7.2 Moody's Seasoned Aaa Corporate Bond Yield. *Source: From Moody's, Moody's Seasoned Aaa Corporate Bond Yield [AAA], retrieved from FRED, Federal Reserve Bank of St. Louis; https://fred.stlouisfed.org/series/AAA, November 2, 2019.*

	3months	6months	9months	1year	2years	3years	5years	10years	20years	30years+
CDs (New Issues)	1.20%	1.30%	1.35%	1.50%	1.70%	1.95%	2.30%	2.80%	3.10%	–
BONDS										
US Treasury	1.03%	1.19%	1.28%	1.36%	1.49%	1.66%	1.95%	2.34%	2.61%	2.87%
US Treasury Zeros	–	–	–	1.33%	1.47%	1.67%	1.97%	2.44%	2.83%	2.94%
Agency/GSE	1.29%	1.40%	1.38%	1.53%	1.83%	1.86%	2.17%	3.00%	3.42%	–
Corporate (Aaa/AAA)	–	–	1.39%	1.49%	1.67%	1.84%	2.34%	2.73%	3.48%	4.02%
Corporate (Aa/AA)	1.32%	1.48%	1.57%	1.60%	1.88%	2.01%	2.49%	3.12%	3.76%	4.51%
Corporate (A/A)	1.49%	1.53%	1.66%	1.88%	1.98%	2.33%	2.75%	4.19%	4.91%	4.94%
Corporate (Baa/BBB)	1.71%	1.72%	1.91%	1.90%	2.95%	2.66%	3.77%	5.80%	6.08%	6.26%
Municipal (Aaa/AAA)	0.95%	0.99%	1.07%	1.04%	1.17%	1.44%	1.60%	2.50%	3.21%	1.90%
Municipal (Aa/AA)	1.09%	1.05%	1.08%	1.23%	1.44%	1.59%	2.00%	3.15%	3.55%	3.92%
Municipal (A/A)	1.22%	1.20%	1.21%	1.23%	1.59%	2.05%	2.13%	3.45%	3.86%	4.00%
Taxable municipal*	0.82%	1.43%	1.54%	1.55%	2.04%	2.32%	2.91%	3.92%	3.60%	3.64%

FIGURE 7.3   Bond yields for a variety of issues and maturities.
*Taxable Municipal ratings cover a rating range from Aaa to A3 from Moody's or AAA to A-from S&P. *Source: Fidelity Investments.*

funds rate." In London, the rate at which banks borrow from each other is the London InterBank Offered Rate or LIBOR. LIBOR has become the underlying reference rate for a huge amount of floating rate debt. Roughly $400 trillion dollars of financial instruments are based on LIBOR.

A repurchase agreement (repo) is a short-term sale of a security with a promise to buy it back, usually the next day. The agreement from the buyer's perspective is called a reverse repo: the purchase of a security with an agreement to sell it back. The security that's exchanged stands as collateral for the loan advanced to the seller. The seller, usually a dealer, thereby has access to lower cost funds, while the buyer can earn a return on a liquid, secured transaction. Collateral are most often Treasuries and agency securities but can include mortgage-backed securities, other asset-backed securities (ABS), and pools of loans.

Commercial paper (CP) is an alternative to bank borrowing by corporations with high credit ratings. Most CP matures within 90 days but can extend further. When the CP expires, it is usually replaced with a new issue, in a process called "rolling over." Some CP is issued by nonfinancial companies, but financial companies with large funding needs have come to dominate this market. The volume of CP outstanding prior to the Global Financial Crisis totaled over $2 trillion. Since the GFC, volumes have been barely half that level.

Certificates of Deposit are issued by banks and have a term and denomination. The large denomination CDs are $10 million and over. CDs may be nonnegotiable, requiring the owner to wait until the maturity date to redeem, or negotiable, in which case the owner can sell the CD on the open market at any time.

Banker's Acceptances are financing agreements, guaranteed by the issuing bank, which are created for use in transactions involving imports and exports as well as storing and shipping goods within the United States. An importing business, for example, can provide a banker's acceptance to an exporting business thereby limiting the risk to the shipper of nonpayment. The banker's acceptance substitutes the financial institution's credit standing for that of the importing business.

A Funding Agreement is a life insurance contract providing a guaranteed return of principal and interest to the buyer. There are a number of different variations which provide for a fixed or floating rate of interest, maturities of 3–13 months and there may be a put provision, which allows the investor to demand early repayment.

Money Market Funds have approximately $3 trillion in assets. They are invested in short-term financial instruments with an objective of obtaining the highest return subject to certain restrictions and a mandate to maintain a net asset value of $1 or more. Money market funds were created in the 1970s in part to provide a return on funds that were in checking accounts and were prohibited from earning interest. A net asset value of less than $1 is called "breaking the buck" and was of great concern during the Global Financial Crisis. In September 2008 Lehman Bros. filed for bankruptcy. At the time the Reserve Primary Fund took losses on Lehman debt and its net asset value dropped to 97 cents. Investors were concerned that other money market funds might have similar issues and a large net capital outflow ensued. Actions by the U.S. Department of the Treasury to temporarily insure these funds prevented what might have become a run on money market funds and freezing the ability of firms to fund short-term needs. Fig. 7.4 shows the level of total financial assets in money market mutual funds over time.

Types of debt instruments: US Treasury securities

The US Treasury is the largest issuer of debt in the world, and the market for this debt is the most liquid.

- Treasury Bills have a maturity of 1 year or less. They do not pay interest, but pay a fixed amount at maturity and sell at a discount to that face value.
- Treasury Notes have maturities from 2 to 10 years and pay interest semi-annually. They repay the principal at maturity.
- Treasury Bonds have maturities greater than 10 years and also pay interest semiannually, with the principal repaid at maturity.

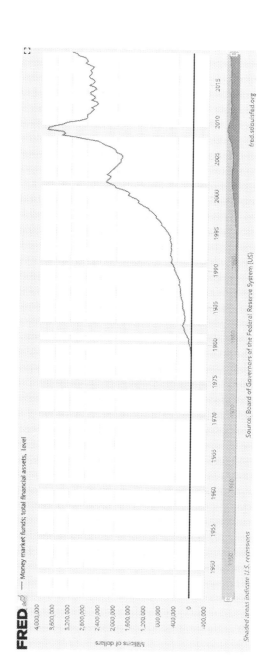

FIGURE 7.4 Money market mutual funds: total financial assets. *Source: From Board of Governors of the Federal Reserve System (US), Money market funds; total financial assets, Level [MMMFFAQ027S], retrieved from FRED, Federal Reserve Bank of St. Louis; https://fred.stlouisfed.org/series/MMMFFAQ027S, November 2, 2019.*

- Treasury Floating Rate Notes make quarterly payments based on the 3-month Treasury bill rate.
- Treasury Inflation Protected Securities (TIPS) pay at rates based on the Consumer Price Index.
- Treasury Strips. There is also trading in derivatives which represent the coupon payments separately from the principal of Treasury securities.

The Department of the Treasury holds quarterly refunding auctions in February, May, August, and November. Only recognized "primary dealers" participate in these auctions. These 22 dealers then provide further distribution by maintaining continuous, liquid Over The Counter markets. The most recently auctioned issue is referred to as the "on the run" issue, and others are called the "off the run" issues. Total federal debt is shown in Fig. 7.5. Total federal debt as a percent of GDP is shown in Fig. 7.6.

Types of debt instruments: agency securities

Several Federal Agencies provide funding support for specific sectors of the US economy and issue a variety of debt instruments in support of those functions. These entities include the following:

- Fannie Mae: The Federal National Mortgage Association supports liquidity in the secondary market for mortgages.
- Freddie Mac: The Federal Home Loan Mortgage Corporation provides support for conventional mortgages. Both Fannie Mae and Freddie Mac suffered huge losses in the Global Financial Crisis and both were placed under the conservatorship of the Congress on September 7, 2008.
- Farmer Mac: The Federal Agricultural Mortgage Corporation provides for improved access to mortgages for farmers and other rural businesses.
- TVA: The Tennessee Valley Authority provides flood control, electric power, etc. Obligations are not guaranteed by the US government but are rated AAA.

Types of debt instruments: corporate bonds

Most corporate bonds are issued with a term of 20−30 years, and specify the periodic payment of a percentage of par or face value. Bonds may be issued with a call provision, which allows the issuer to redeem the bond earlier than at maturity. There are also bonds with put features, which allow the buyer to sell the issue back to the issuer at par, with certain conditions. A bond with a sinking fund provision requires the issuer to redeem a predetermined amount prior to maturity. Convertible bonds have a provision that grants the buyer an option to convert the bond into shares in the issuing company. This feature is similar to warrants which also are options to purchase stock. Corporate bonds receive credit ratings by rating agencies and are also

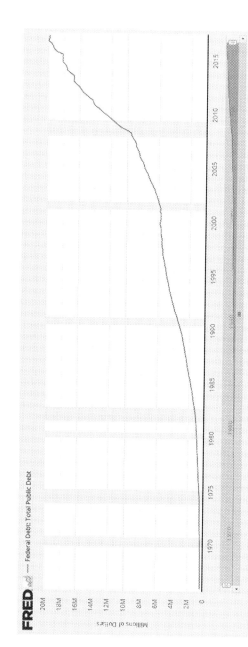

FIGURE 7.5 Federal debt: total federal debt. *Source: From U.S. Department of the Treasury. Fiscal Service, Federal Debt: Total Public Debt [GFDEBTN], retrieved from FRED, Federal Reserve Bank of St. Louis; https://fred.stlouisfed.org/series/GFDEBTN, November 2, 2019.*

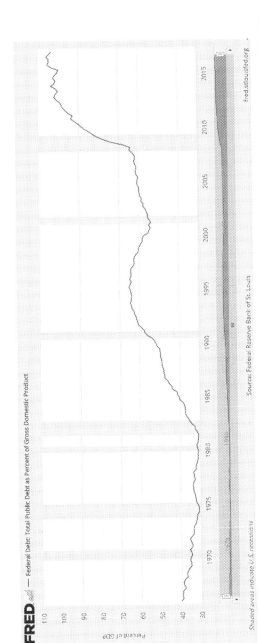

FIGURE 7.6 Federal debt: total public debt as percent of gross domestic product. *Source: From Federal Reserve Bank of St. Louis and U.S. Office of Management and Budget, Federal Debt: Total Public Debt as Percent of Gross Domestic Product [GFDEGDQ188S], retrieved from FRED, Federal Reserve Bank of St. Louis; https://fred.stlouisfed.org/series/GFDEGDQ188S, November 2, 2019.*

classified more broadly as Investment Grade (IG) or High Yield (HY). Trading in the secondary market for corporate bonds occurs in the over the counter market and has less liquidity than in many other markets. It is still dominated by broker-dealers using telephone and chat messaging services, although bond-trading platforms have made some inroads. These platforms have several different models: single dealer platforms allowing a specific dealer to offer online access to its clients; interdealer systems allowing only the large dealers to trade with each other; dealer–client systems which are open to buy side institutional clients as well as dealers; and auction systems. Whether executed on a platform or through traditional means, reporting of corporate bond transactions is required on the Trade Reporting and Compliance Engine (TRACE) operated by the Financial Industry Regulatory Authority (FINRA).

An intermediate debt instrument between Commercial Paper and longer maturity bonds is the Medium Term Note (MTN). These notes have lower costs associated with them and afford the issuer more flexibility in term and size of the offering.

Types of debt instruments: municipal securities

Roughly 44,000 different US entities have issued municipal debt, most of which has tax-advantaged status. These issuers include states, counties, cities, school districts, sewer, water, and other authorities. The traditional attraction of these securities is that they are exempt from federal taxation, and may be exempt from state and local taxes in the jurisdiction in which they are issued. Institutional investors also are active in trading these markets, but are more interested in seeking capital gains rather than tax advantages. Because of the tax advantages, municipals can offer lower rates of interest and still be competitive with corporate bonds with the same maturity. Municipal debt can have different sources of backing, for example:

- General Obligation debt can be unlimited and would be secured by the full faith and credit of the issuer. It can also be limited by restrictions on tax rates of the issuer.
- Moral Obligation bonds have nonbinding pledges of tax revenue.
- Revenue Backed bonds are issued to support funding for a specific purpose and are backed by a claim on revenues generated by that purpose. For example, airport revenue bonds or sports facility bonds.

Municipalities also issuer shorter term obligations for a period of 12 months, although maturities can be longer or shorter than this. These securities include tax and revenue anticipation notes, tax-exempt commercial paper, and others.

A risk to municipal bond holders is that the issuing jurisdiction defaults. Some muni issuers have access to Chapter 9 reorganizations, but municipal bankruptcies can be complicated. Many states do not allow municipals to file for bankruptcy and many others impose certain conditions before granting approval. The fear is that a municipal filing for bankruptcy could have a chilling effect on the ability of other government entities to raise funds in the future. Some examples of recent Chapter 9 bankruptcy filings are Orange County, California in 1994 and Detroit, Michigan in 2013. One notable entity that was not allowed to file for bankruptcy is Puerto Rico. In June 2016 President Obama signed the Puerto Rico Oversight, Management and Economic Stability Act (PROMESA), a law creating a federal oversight board with authority to negotiate a bankruptcy-like restructuring of the $70 billion in debt owed by the island, which had defaulted on portions of its debt several times in 2016.

Types of debt instruments: sovereign debt

Sovereign debt is the obligation of a country's central government. It can be internal debt, owed to the country's residents, or external debt, funded by foreign lenders. Internal debt carries lower risk because it can theoretically be repaid by raising taxes, reducing spending, and printing money. Basically, the country's residents are repaying themselves in various forms. Repaying debt to external lenders can be more problematic, especially if the country's currency suffers an adverse movement in foreign exchange markets. The rating agencies provide separate ratings for internal debt and external debt of each country.

Having the financial commitment of a country's central government might seem to provide a risk-free guarantee to sovereign debt, but Fig. 7.7 shows the significant incidence of default since 1800. And the fact that many of these countries have defaulted 7 and even 8 times shows that defaults are not a barrier to future access to the world's capital markets.

Fixed income trading

Trading of equities is dominated by organized exchanges. Bond trading is more complicated. A corporation typically has one stock but may have many bonds outstanding. Each bond may trade only infrequently, and the size of a typical bond trade is much large than a stock purchase. Taken together, these factors make it difficult for traders to maintain broad inventories and post bid/offer markets. Consequently, bond trading has evolved little over the years and still consists mainly of one-off transactions where investors call or electronically chat with brokers or dealers to find bonds and determine prices.

But with the advent of technology, bond trading no longer relies completely on traditional modalities of telephone and chat messaging. Instead there are Request For Quote (RFQ) systems and electronic platforms

Selected countries (*number of defaults*)
July 31, 2014

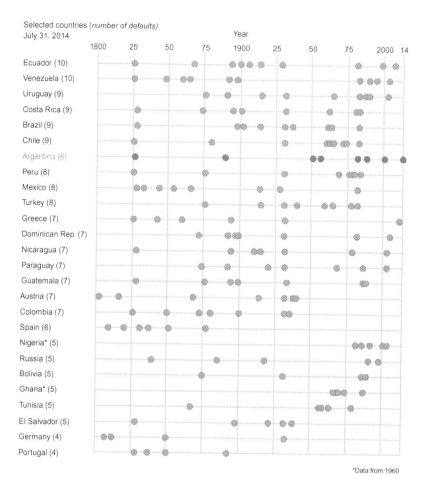

*Data from 1960

FIGURE 7.7 External sovereign defaults since 1800. *Source: Carmen Reinhart and Kenneth Rogoff.*

which have growing liquidity and trading volume. The RFQ systems have a few variants but represent a type of hybrid trading system where one party will ask for a market in an issue with no commitment to trade. The responding party may offer a tradable market, or just an indication. The two parties then may progress to a trade which is either broker assisted or involves posting on a platform. A major event was the opening up of some of these platforms to "all to all" trading. Previously, dealers preferred to only deal with each other on interdealer platforms, and transact with buy side clients through traditional means. Electronic trading of corporate bonds increased to 26% of the total in the second quarter of 2018. Of the electronic platforms offering bond trading, MarketAxess accounted for 85% of corporate bond trading by institutions.

One platform with an interesting history is BondPoint. BondPoint operates an electronic marketplace with over 500 financial firms as participants.
It started life as ValuBond and was acquired by KCG, a financial firm that
specialized in high-frequency market making. In 2012 KCG suffered a
famous $465 million loss in less than an hour when its trading software mal-
functioned, apparently due to faulty updates to existing algorithmic trading
software. The devastating losses resulted in KCG being sold to GETCO, and
later to Virtu, both also financial firms specializing in high-frequency market
making. In January 2018 BondPoint was acquired by exchange operator ICE.

The largest volumes of Treasuries are traded on interdealer (between
dealer banks) platforms operated by Brokertec, eSpeed, and TradeWeb.
Brokertec dominates fixed income trading with approximately 80% market
share. BGC, which sold eSpeed to Nasdaq in 2013 began a new Treasury
trading platform in the summer of 2017.

The rise of electronic platforms has shown that there are many advantages to this form of trading, but there are some disadvantages also. Some of
the advantages and disadvantages are as follows.

Advantages of electronic trading:

- Trading efficiencies.
- Access.
- Better price discovery.
- Index trading requirements for liquidity. The growth of index trading has
  resulted in a need for financial firms to have access to larger volumes of
  an array of bonds. This is facilitated more easily in electronic systems.
- Network effects. As more and more participants use a platform, that plat-
  form has significantly more value.
- Back Office. Automated straight through processing with minimal human
  intervention increases processing speed and minimizes error risk.
- Reporting, compliance, and risk.
- Fewer errors.
- Faster.

Challenges to the growth of electronic trading:

- Heterogeneity and market fragmentation. There is a massive array of
  bonds with multiple dimensions of issuer, maturity, etc. This makes it
  difficult to offer a comprehensive solution.
- Liquidity. Most trading occurs in roughly 1000 of the 15,000 or so bond
  issues. The other 14,000 have limited liquidity which makes them
  unlikely candidates to be posted on platforms.
- Smaller size. Platforms often have small minimum order size. This
  attracts more potential participants who might have smaller capitalization,
  but can be a nuisance or even a liability for a participant who needs to
  move large volumes.

- Inertia, cost of new systems. All current traders have a system that works for them at the present time. Large institutions have massive investments in legacy systems. To put in something new requires clear justification.
- Business risk for dealers and buy side institutions. Dealers do not want to lose customers to anonymous platforms, and buy side institutions fear losing access to services that can be provided only by the largest dealers who have increased their market share since the Global Financial Crisis.
- Information leakage. If a seller with a large position posts an offer on the screen, there is a risk that this information will cause others to front run the sell order or to back up any potential bids. Similarly, if a partial quantity trade occurs and is posted on the screen, this public information could hurt the seller's ability to complete the required size of the total issue.

Fixed income indexes and funds

Following on Modern Portfolio Theory concepts developed for equity markets, there are broad-based bond indexes and funds which provide investors with convenient investment vehicles and benchmarks for diversification in fixed income portfolios. Fixed income indexes have been constructed by sector, maturity, risk, geographic coverage and other factors. For example, geographic fixed income indexes exist for the United States, Canadian, European, Emerging Markets, Global, and other categories.

Fixed income ETFs have become an increasingly popular vehicle for broad-based investing in fixed income securities. In the United States, close to 400 fixed income ETFs have about $640 billion in combined AUM. These ETFs have some interesting features, beyond the investment diversification they offer. The underlying value of an ETF will track an index of the bonds it is designed to replicate, but it trades conveniently as a single security on an exchange. The price of the ETF is subject to the bids and offers traders place for the ETF and may differ somewhat from its underlying value. Some single bonds trade infrequently and can be difficult to source and price, especially in active markets. But in general, there is likely to be a tighter, more liquid market for the ETF than there would be for each of the underlying bonds. Bond ETFs also pay out monthly interest and do not "mature." Individual bonds do, of course, mature, and may pay semiannual interest, but the ETF will constantly buy issues as older holdings mature and will have a stream of different interest payments which can be paid out on a regular monthly schedule.

ESG bond funds

Managers of fixed income portfolios have made increasing efforts to make investments in the bonds of companies which have positive ESG factors.

Through careful analysis of issuers and the bonds' yield, duration, credit quality, and other criteria, they have been able to design portfolios which are likely to mirror existing bond funds but add the dimension of positive ESG. While these funds are seeing increased interest, their size is still relatively modest. Institutional investors have increasingly added ESG factors to their criteria for equity investments, but fewer fixed income analysts and portfolio managers take ESG factors into consideration than do their equity counterparts. One possible explanation is that owning bonds is different than owning equity. Bond fund managers may engage with companies on ESG issues, but they have a different kind of access to corporate management. Equity owners, unlike fixed income holders, can vote on shareholder proposals and have a voice in board member selection. Bond owners do not have such a vote. However, CEOs and CFOs will certainly give an audience to those who are significant buyers of their debt issues.

Fig. 7.8 shows the results of a CFA-PRI survey which found that institutional investors surveyed were much more likely to consider ESG factors in equities than they were in credit markets.

Despite the more limited attention from fixed income participants, there are now ESG bond funds available across a wide range of issuer categories (Fig. 7.9).

So how does the financial performance of bond funds with favorable ESG scores compare to bond funds with low ESG scores? One recent study (Barclays, 2018) constructed high- and low-ESG portfolios using security-level data from Bloomberg Barclays bond indices. The analysis was performed twice, using ESG ratings from two different providers: MSCI ESG Research and Sustainalytics. To isolate the impact of ESG, the analysis controlled for credit rating, spread, duration, and distribution across industry sectors for a 9-year period. This is important to the analysis as tilting the exposure to high-ESG bonds can cause the portfolio to have different characteristics. The data imply that companies with strong credit quality tend to have higher ESG scores. So, a high-ESG portfolio would show the lower yield associated with stronger credit quality. It is therefore important to control for these other factors in the analysis.

	Equity analysis	Credit analysis
Governance issues	56%	42%
Environmental issues	37%	27%
Social issues	35%	27%

FIGURE 7.8 Respondents who often/always integrate material ESG issues into their investment analysis. *Source: CFA Institute.*

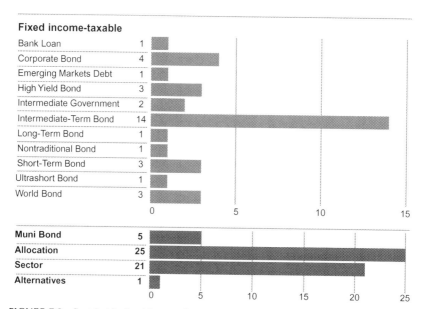

FIGURE 7.9 Sustainable fixed income funds span a range of Morningstar categories. *Source: Morningstar.*

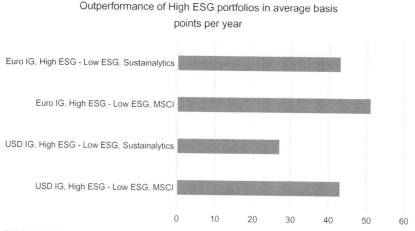

FIGURE 7.10 Portfolios of high ESG Investment Grade issuers outperformed portfolios of low ESG Investment Grade issuers in both the USD and Euro markets for the period 2009–2018.

As shown in Fig. 7.10, the high-ESG portfolio for Investment Grade US issues outperformed the low-ESG portfolio by 43 and 27 basis points for the portfolios constructed using data from the two different providers. In the European market, the outperformance was stronger: 51 and 43 basis points.

Some other conclusions for US issuers:

- European companies ESG scores are higher than their US counterparts.
- Companies with higher ESG ratings had lower borrowing costs in Europe, but not in the United States.
- For High Yield portfolios, high-ESG bonds also outperformed low-ESG bonds.
- Different categories of ESG factors had different levels of impact across alternative industries:
  - Environmental factors were most important for noncyclical consumer goods and transport and energy industries. Governance was second. Social factors had a negative impact in transport and energy.
  - Governance factors were most important for banking and brokerage, with social also being important and environmental having little impact.
- Increased interest in ESG investing has not driven up the price of high-ESG bonds. It is possible that high-ESG bond prices could get bid up, making returns lower, but this is not supported by the data.

The authors believe their study of relative portfolio performance for the period 2009–18 confirms their analysis done for an earlier period, released in 2016. They conclude that incorporating ESG factors into investment decision making has been broadly associated with positive portfolio performance, with environmental and governance factors being most significant. The authors go on to caution against over-interpreting the industry-specific results and point out that ESG factors are rarely the only consideration in portfolio construction.

For example, an ESG filter can help screen out securities with weak ESG attributes, at the risk of reducing the investment universe and, hence, the potential for generating returns. On the other hand, portfolios can be constructed with the aim of achieving a high average ESG score without excluding any securities ... and at the same time choosing securities that have desirable characteristics such as relative value or momentum. In that case, it could be acceptable to an investor to find a low-ESG issuer in a portfolio, considering the trade-off between ESG and purely financial characteristics.

ESG bond fund managers

Recognizing the growing investor interest, the large fixed income asset managers all offer ESG bond funds to their clients. Here we summarize key features of the funds offered by two of the largest providers.

PIMCO

PIMCO is one of the world's largest fixed income asset managers. As of the third quarter of 2018, it had over $1.72 trillion in AUM. PIMCO launched its first socially responsible bond fund way back in 1991, a similar fund in Europe in 2010 and in 2017 it launched a series of core ESG bond strategies. In 2011 it was a signatory of the United Nations Principles of Responsible Investment. There are four key beliefs in PIMCO's investment approach:

- ESG analysis is consistent with PIMCO's long-established investment process, which stresses long-term thinking.
- ESG investing does not need to sacrifice financial performance in order to achieve positive social impact.
- Engagement is a crucial component of social investing.
- ESG issuance is inclusive of a wider range of factors than green bonds only.

PIMCO has formalized its approach by creating an ESG profile for each issuer and developed a proprietary scoring system for every government and sovereign issuer. The process for building specialist ESG portfolios starts with top down views of long-term global economic themes as well as more cyclical factors. Guidelines are developed for key risk factors such as duration, curve, credit, currency, and volatility. These are common factors for all of the company's portfolios. Three further steps are undertaken in constructing the ESG portfolios: exclusion of companies whose practices are fundamentally inconsistent with ESG principles; assess individual issuers and evaluate portfolios; and engage with individual issuers and industry groups to further ESG practices and goals. These three steps are illustrated in Fig. 7.11.

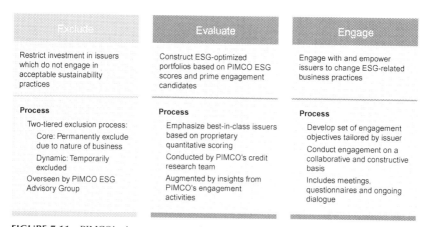

FIGURE 7.11 PIMCO's three-step approach to building ESG fixed income portfolios. *Source: PIMCO.*

Fidelity

Fidelity Investment Inc. is one of the world's largest investment management companies, with almost $7 trillion in customer assets as of mid-2018. It offers three sustainability index funds covering all fixed income asset classes:

- Fidelity Sustainability Bond Index Fund
- Fidelity U.S. Sustainability Index Fund
- Fidelity International Sustainability Index Fund

Investors can find additional ESG investment offerings at Fidelity, including an actively managed mutual fund—Fidelity Select Environment & Alternative Energy Portfolio—and Fidelity's FundsNetwork program, which include more than 100 ESG funds. Resources available to investors include company-level ESG research and mutual fund and ETF screening tools.

Green bonds

So ESG bond funds buy the debt of companies that score well on ESG metrics. The companies issuing the debt are free to use the proceeds for many different purposes. This debt is not typically identified with a specific "green" project. But another way to invest in fixed income instruments with positive ESG attributes is to buy individual "green bonds" themselves. Green bonds are securities issued for specific projects which are designed to achieve environmental goals. They are basically conventional bonds, but the proceeds are targeted for environmentally friendly uses. Similar bonds are called blue bonds, social bonds or sustainable bonds. Projects may be aimed at energy efficiency; pollution prevention; sustainable agriculture, fishery, and forestry; clean transportation; water management; and others. These bonds usually also have tax incentives, are certified by third parties, and provide for follow-up impact reporting. The green bonds usually have the same credit rating as the issuer's outstanding bonds, and the green bond buyers, therefore are not taking on additional risk.

Issuers can be financial companies, nonfinancial companies, development banks, local governments, government-backed entities, and sovereign governments. While there are now a diverse set of issuers and investors, green bonds account for only 1% of total bonds. But investor interest and total issuance have grown sharply from the first green bond issued in 2007 by the European Investment Bank. Total global green bond issuance in 2017 reached $155.5 billion, up 78% from 2016's total of $87.2 billion. 2018 issuance, estimated at $162 billion, was slightly up on 2017.

The World Bank issued its first green bond in 2008 and 10 years later had raised a total of $12.6 billion through 150 green bonds. Here are two examples of the terms of recent World Bank issues. A 7-year

USD-denominated bond carried a semiannual coupon of 3.125% per annum and matures on November 20, 2025. It offers investors a yield of 3.214% (semiannual), which is equivalent to a spread of 14.9 basis points over the 3.00% US Treasury note due October 31, 2025. The 9-year EUR-denominated bond carried an annual coupon of 0.625% per annum and matures on November 22, 2027. It offers investors a yield of 0.685% (annual), which is equivalent to a spread of 40.4 basis points over the 0.50% German Bund note due August 15, 2027. The joint lead managers for the bonds were Bank of America Merrill Lynch, Credit Agricole CIB, Deutsche Bank, and SEB. These issues were oversubscribed by a diverse group of international institutional investors.

The largest issuer in the United States was Fannie Mae which raised $24.9 billion from its Green Mortgage Backed Securities (MBS) facility. The Fannie Mae Green MBS is a fixed income security designed to have a positive impact in three dimensions:

- Financial: Lower credit risk, higher cash flows, and higher property value
- Social: Greater affordability and higher quality, healthier, more durable housing
- Environmental: Lower use of energy and water resources, and greater resiliency

Green bond indexes and ETFs

The green bond market includes a broad array of issuers and green bond funds can have risk and return expectations consistent with a conventional high quality global fixed income portfolio. Some institutional investors are comfortable that a green bond allocation can replace part of their global fixed income portfolio while maintaining similar yield, duration, and other metrics. Some of the green bond indexes are as follows:

- Bloomberg MSCI Barclays Green Bond Index—Consists of investment grade, corporate, government issues with green criteria assessed against six MSCI defined eligible categories. USD only and EUR only subindexes are available.
- BAML Green Bond index—Investment grade debt of corporate and quasi-government entities, excluding securitized and collateralized securities. Qualifying bonds must have a clearly designated use of proceeds that is solely applied toward projects or activities that promote climate change mitigation or adaptation or other environmental sustainability purposes. General debt obligations of corporations that are involved in green industries are not included.
- S&P Green Bond Index—May include HY as well as IG securities. Corporates, government, and multilateral issuers. Climate bond initiative (CBI) green designation required.

The S&P Green Bond Select Index, for example, comprises all issuer types available in the global green bond market excluding tax-exempt US municipal bonds. It has the characteristics of a high quality, core global bond investment and can be considered for a sustainable allocation in such a portfolio.

Investors can buy one or more of the green bonds, but for diversification purposes, they can also buy ETFs indexed to the broad-based green bond indexes. The first green bond ETF was the VanEck Vectors Green Bond Fund (GRNB), listed in March 2017. It tracks the performance and yield characteristics of the S&P Green Bond Select Index. In November 2018 Blackrock launched the iShares Global Green Bond ETF (BGRN). This ETF tracks the value of the Bloomberg Barclays MSCI Green Bond Select (USD Hedged) Index, which holds approximately 180 different green bonds. The BGRN fund has an effective duration of 6.96 years and an average yield to maturity of 3.65% like GRNB before it; BGRN is designed to offer institutional investors an easily tradable vehicle which can be the core of a global bond allocation, or as an environmentally responsible satellite in a diversified portfolio.

The International Capital Market Association (ICMA) provides guidance for the governance of the Principles for Green, Social and Sustainability Bonds. It defines these bonds as any type of fixed instrument security where the proceeds will be applied exclusively to eligible environmental or social projects. It also maintains a database of these bonds.

There are many firms that act as external reviewers, working with issuers to confirm that the proceeds of bond offerings will meet green, sustainable, or social objectives. These reviewers include:

Bureau Veritas
Carbon Trust
China Chengxin Credit Management Co., Ltd.
Cicero
DNV GL
ERM Certification and Verification Services
EthiFinance
Kestrel Verifiers
S&P Global Ratings
Sustainalytics
TUV NORD CERT
Vigeo Eiris

Chapter 8

Shareholder engagement

Chapter Outline

Using engagement to create value
for both investors and companies **146**
   Shareholder activism 147
   Shareholder voting by proxy 149
Key corporate governance and
shareholder voting trends **150**
Recent shareholder proposals **152**
Examples of shareholder
engagement policies **155**
   Blackrock 156

   CalPERS 156
   T. Rowe Price 158
   The New York City
   Comptroller's Office 159
   Vanguard 159
Institutional investors acting together **161**
   The Investor Stewardship Group 163
   The 30% Club 164
   Sustainability Accounting
   Standards Board 165

A common goal of environmental, social, and governance (ESG) investing is to influence companies to conduct themselves in a manner that is consistent with the investors' ESG beliefs. One method of attempting to nudge corporate behavior is to engage with company boards and executive management. This engagement can take the form of either an ongoing dialogue or by the exercise of shareholder rights to vote on proposals in support of specific actions. Shareholders may make these formal proposals which are then presented to all the company's shareholders and subjected to a vote. Proponents of shareholder activism believe this sort of engagement is the most productive way to bring about changes in corporate behavior, from the inside.

An alternative argument sometimes made is that shareholders of large public companies can always sell their shares if they don't like the way the company is being run. If there is a large liquid market, the shareholders will not necessarily suffer a significant loss in doing so. In fact, this is just like the divestment strategy that's often pursued on moral or ethical grounds. But this argument seems to turn the control relationship on its head. The popular understanding is that shareholders have the owners' ability to control a company's actions, even if it's only indirectly through their ability to elect board members. For corporate executives, (employees) to take actions which result in shareholders feeling forced to sell their ownership interests seems a bit like the tail wagging the dog. Here's a sports analogy: the owners aren't pleased with the team's losing record, players' lackluster performance and the coach's poor strategy. The coach says: "if you don't like it, sell the team." It's unlikely that that coach will be running the team for long!

This continues to be an ongoing debate among activists: is the better strategy engagement or divestiture? Selling shares does nothing to advance the cause of activists who want a change in some aspect of the company's behavior. For example, many who are concerned with reducing carbon recognize that the move from fossil fuel consumption will be difficult and progress will most likely stretch over decades. Consequently, they advocate a range of policies including engagement, correctly pricing the risk premium associated with fossil fuels, transparency and the closure of high cost, and high carbon projects. These investors believe they need to own these companies so that their voices can be heard. On the other hand, those favoring divestment believe engagement is too slow if it is working at all.

But for many concerned investors, they don't see that the impact of selling shares in suspect companies will accomplish their ESG goals. First, the size of the holdings to be sold may not be material to the price of the target shares. And if all the concerned shareholders sell their holdings, then the remaining shareholders would presumably be less likely to encourage the company to engage in more ESG friendly actions. Most institutional funds were created prior to the advent of ESG investing. Divesting stocks for social purposes can call into question these managers' responsibilities to beneficiaries and tax payers, especially if the fund underperforms, or becomes significantly underfunded. Several empirical studies have found that funds which merely excluded "sin" stocks historically suffered from underperformance. Another concern for institutional investors is that there are costs associated with divestment, both transaction costs and diversion of staff resources. For all these reasons, engagement has proven to be a popular alternative to divestment.

Using engagement to create value for both investors and companies

A recent study (Gond et al., 2018) investigated the gains from engagement for both investors and their investee companies. The study was based on 36 interviews with large listed companies, combined with prior research on engagement practices of 66 institutional investors. Building on earlier studies showing that ESG engagement does contribute to enhanced returns, this study focused on how ESG engagement creates value for investors and companies alike. The study adopted a broad definition of value to include enhanced exchange of information ("communication value"); the production and diffusion of new ESG-related knowledge ("learning value"); and the political benefits that can be derived from engagement, for instance, through enhanced executive support for ESG issues ("political value"). Fig. 8.1 provides an overview of each of these three streams of value creation.

Value creation dynamics	Corporations	Investors
Communicative Exchanging information	Clarifying expectations and enhancing accountability	Signaling and defining ESG expectations
	Managing impressions and rebalancing misrepresentations	Seeking detailed and accurate corporate information
	Specifying the business context	Enhancing investor ESG communication and accountability
Learning Producing and diffusing knowledge	Anticipating and detecting new trends related to ESG	Building new ESG knowledge
	Gathering feedback, benchmarking, and gap spotting	Contextualizing investment decisions
	Developing knowledge of ESG issues	Identifying and diffusing industry best practice
Political Deriving political benefits	Enrolling internal experts	Advancing internal collaboration and ESG integration
	Elevating sustainability and securing resources	Meeting client expectations
	Enhancing the loyalty of long-term investors	Building long-term relationships

FIGURE 8.1 Mechanisms of engagement value creation. *Source: From How Esg Engagement Creates Value For Investors And Companies, Principles for Responsible Investment. Used with permission from UNPRI.*

The study provides key recommendations for both companies and investors. For companies, they can improve communication with investors by more closely coordinating internal ESG information systems, ESG engagement information, and ESG reporting practices. Companies are also encouraged to act more proactively, rather than only responding to investors, on ESG policies and management systems. And finally, companies can benefit from improved internal coordination among investor relations, sustainability personnel, and C-level and board members with respect to investor meetings.

For investors, the study recommends that they improve transparency and communication of their engagement objectives and how engagement processes are initiated, executed, and evaluated. Learning values can be enhanced by strengthening the feedback loop between new ESG information and insights gained by engagement and by active participation rather than reliance on outsourcing engagement activities. And finally, benefits can be obtained by financial analysts working more closely with ESG staff on engagement and by having clients and beneficiaries involved in developing or refining engagement policies and objectives.

Shareholder activism

For large institutional investors, ESG engagement strategies have evolved over time. Often it began as issuing generalized guidance principles. It then advanced to proxy voting in public markets and issuing broader statements on views of best practices. And finally, many firms have adopted a more holistic engagement strategy consisting of active dialogue combined with voting.

In earlier times, shareholder activism was associated with colorful, controversial personalities such as Wilma Soss, Lewis D. Gilbert, and Evelyn Y. Davis. Davis was said to have bought $2000 worth of stock, the minimum required to propose a resolution, in 120 different companies. For decades she attended annual meetings and proposed resolutions dealing with various governance issues such as executive compensation and term limits for board members. The actions of Davis and some of these other individuals were greeted with a range of forbearance, hostility, ridicule, and occasional good humor, but infrequently with serious consideration.

Another group of shareholder activists is typified by Carl Icahn. This type of investor buys a stake in a company they believe is undervalued and uses this ownership position to gain seats on the board of directors and redirect company policies so as to unlock corporate value. Various strategies, some controversial, may be employed. In the 1980s, some investors bought shares and threatened the target company's leadership with a hostile takeover. The investors used these threats to force the company to buy back their shares (and only their shares) at a premium. This practice was termed "greenmail" and is generally condemned as enriching some shareholders at the expense of others. Several laws were passed to make these practices more difficult. But these investors may also have more legitimate interests in corporate restructuring, including for example a sale of assets, mergers, or splitting operating divisions apart to the benefit of all shareholders. A common focus of these activists is also on governance issues such as excessive executive pay and misuse of corporate assets. In general, this category of activists has been less interested in social and environmental issues not directly related to increasing short term equity value.

A curious and controversial case of shareholder voting occurred in February 2018 at the Annual General Meeting (AGM) of Sinovac Biotech Ltd., a China-based biopharmaceutical company with 3300 shareholders, a listing on the NASDAQ exchange and a market capitalization of $447 million. In the formal notice of the meeting, the company identified three items of business: (1) the reelection of the existing board of directors; (2) approval of the financial statements; and (3) the appointment of independent auditors. However, at the meeting, and apparently without prior notice, dissenting shareholders proposed a new ballot, and delivered a majority of votes electing a new board of directors. These shareholders were not corporate "gadflies" but included Citibank and JPMorgan. The ballots filed by JPMorgan alone were for proxies of over 26 million shares, representing over 45% of the shares outstanding. With a majority of the votes, the dissenting shareholders seemed to have elected a new board. However, the counter argument was that all shareholders were deprived of full, fair, and plain disclosure and a reasonable opportunity to express their will on company matters. The dissenting shareholders had not provided advance notice of their competing ballot or slate of directors to other shareholders. In this and previous shareholder meetings, few holders attended in person and would have no opportunity to receive notice or to review the dissent proposals. Further, the dissenting shareholders were said to have acted in secret and colluded in a breach of an agreement with the company and in violation of US Securities law. Both sides insisted that their board was the "true" board and the matter went to the courts. Sinovac is incorporated in Antigua and Barbuda, and the court there decided in favor of the incumbent board and management, effectively confirming that procedures need to be followed. A further curiosity in this case, is that the company decided that the attempt to install a new board triggered a "poison pill" takeover defense which resulted in new shares being issued and the holdings of the dissenters were dramatically diluted.

Shareholder voting by proxy

The majority of shareholder votes on corporate resolutions are made by investment managers who vote the proxies given to them by the beneficial owners of the stock. Investor participation in corporate governance has grown dramatically: 72% of S&P 500 companies reported engaging with shareholders in 2017, compared to just 6% in 2010. In the 2017 proxy season, retail shareholders voted approximately 28% of their shares, while institutional investors voted approximately 91% of their shares. The largest investment managers do their own research on these proposals, but smaller managers receive recommendations on how to vote by proxy advisory firms. These firms provide a useful service in aggregating information about companies and proposals, but critics point out that these advisory firms have no obligation to shareholder interests, have potential conflicts of interest and have little competition. Two firms, Institutional Shareholder Services (ISS) and Glass, Lewis & Company together control 97% of the proxy advisory industry. Concern about the influence of these two companies led the Securities and Exchange Commission (SEC) in 2018 to open up discussion of the roles, activities, and impact of the proxy firms.

Studies on the importance of the advisory firms' ratings show mixed results. There is evidence that in at least some cases corporate policies are influenced by the advisory firms' rating criteria. The ratings also have some influence on voting behavior, but this is muted by the fact that the largest investment managers do their own research.

Reliance on the independent agency recommendations is thought to in some way remove or "cleanse" any conflict of interest on the investment managers' part. The managers can represent that they are voting with the recommendation of an independent authority. However, this imposes a burden of understanding the potential conflicts on the part of the proxy advisory firms themselves and the potential influence on these firms from commercial relationships with reporting companies.

Let's look at how the proxy advisory firms come up with their recommendations. These voting recommendations are developed and updated through an iterative process, involving analysis of regulatory requirements, industry practices, and discussions with market participants. Corporate issuers and institutional investors are engaged in the development and updating of voting policies, such as criteria for assessing the independence of board directors and executive compensation packages. The advisory firms will communicate with corporate issuers and allow them to review the data used to make voting recommendations before they are finalized.

Critics point to the potential conflicts of interest that arise. For example, ISS provides consulting services to companies wishing to improve their corporate governance. Firms may feel it necessary to retain these services in order to get a favorable rating. (ISS believes it has taken steps to disclose and mitigate this potential conflict.) In addition to concerns about conflicts of interest, the advisory firms have been criticized for insufficient transparency on their recommendation process and occasional inaccuracies.

Glass Lewis believes that it does not exert undue influence on investors. During the 2017 proxy season, Glass Lewis recommended voting FOR 92% of the proposals it analyzed from the US company meetings it covers (the board and management of these companies recommended voting FOR 98% of the same proposals). Yet directors received majority FOR votes 99.9% of the time and say-on-pay proposals received majority FOR votes 99.1% of the time. Also, directors received support of 96% and say-on-pay proposals received support of 93% compared to Glass Lewis' FOR recommendations of 89% and 84%, respectively. These results give some support to the notion that shareholders are voting independently of both Glass Lewis and company management.

For its part, ISS notes that its recommendations are also not blindly followed. Approximately 85% of ISS's top 100 clients used a custom proxy voting policy and during calendar year 2017, approximately 69% of the ballots processed by ISS on behalf of clients globally were linked to clients' custom policies. This represented approximately 87% of the total shares processed by ISS during this period.

Key corporate governance and shareholder voting trends

Here are some key facts about corporate governance and shareholder voting trends in 2018, based on over 4000 annual meetings (Broadridge, 2018):

- Institutional ownership of public company shares declined slightly to 70% (from 71% in 2017). Retail ownership increased to 30% from 29%.
- Institutional shareholder voting participation remained high at 91%. Retail shareholder participation declined slightly to 28% this season.
- Shareholder support for say-on-pay proposals at companies where the CEO pay ratio was disclosed was the same, on average, as it was at companies that were not required to disclose the pay ratio. "Say on Pay" refers to resolutions that would give shareholders a vote on executive compensation.
- Institutional shareholder support for social and environmental proposals increased over the past 5 years from 19% in 2014 to 29% in 2018.

- Institutional and retail support of corporate political spending proposals has increased over a 5-year period from 20% overall in 2014 to 28% this season.
- The number of proxy access shareholder proposals declined over the last 4 years from 81 in 2015 to 34 in 2018. This is partially due to the fact that many companies have voluntarily adopted proxy access—including 65% of S&P 500 companies. Proxy access proposals refer to the ability of shareholders or groups of shareholders to propose candidates for election to board seats, subject to certain restrictions such as a minimum percentage of shares held by the group. Notably this past season, institutions opposed shareholder proposals that sought to lower existing thresholds or remove limits on the number of shareholders required to reach the ownership threshold.

The increasing support for social and environmental proposals is demonstrated in Fig. 8.2, which shows the percentage of votes cast in favor of ESG shareholder proposals.

Some notable institutional investor engagement developments:

- BlackRock engaged with companies on topics including CEO overcompensation, board diversity, gun violence, director performance evaluations, and director succession.
- NYC Comptroller Scott Stringer and the NYC pension funds continued to advance their Boardroom Accountability Project 2.0, pushing for

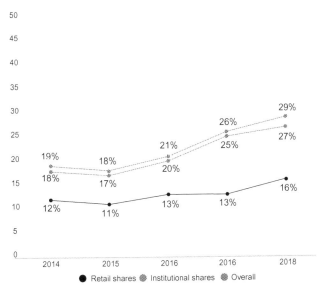

FIGURE 8.2 Social/environmental proposals: percentages of shares voted "for". *Source: Broadridge + PWC.)*

diverse, independent and "climate-competent" boards. Forty-nine of the 151 boards have appointed 59 new directors who are either female or people of color.

- The California Public Employees' Retirement System (CalPERS) reported that they engaged with over 500 companies in the Russell 3000 on their lack of board diversity and that they withheld votes from 271 directors at 85 companies as a result.
- T. Rowe Price (TRP) reiterated its position as a long-term investor and detailed its philosophy on shareholder activism. Additionally, TRP stated it will engage with companies directly, and privately, to resolve differences constructively. For contested solicitations, it will apply a long-term lens to determine which side is more likely to foster long-term performance by the company.

Recent shareholder proposals

For many years, independent shareholders have offered proposals for policy changes or disclosures. These proposals have historically received few votes and were offered more to make a statement than with any real hope of passage. In the last few years, some of these proposals have actually gotten majority votes, but their impact has been greater than that. Corporate boards and management have taken note of the substantive issues raised and the growing support these proposals have gotten from mainstream investors. Consequently, these proposals have had much greater impact on corporate policies and disclosures than one would suspect solely by looking at the number which were approved in formal voting.

So what issues are presented in shareholder proposals? While 2018 saw somewhat lower absolute numbers of ESG proposals than in 2017, the mix of issues and success rate is interesting. Nine environmental and social proposals received majority votes in 2018, a record number (Westcott, 2018). Eighteen other proposals received significant support of roughly 40%. The successful proposals receiving majority votes were:

- Requirement for Kinder Morgan to report on preparations for a "2DS" scenario of a 2-degree Celsius increase in global temperatures, considered to be the upper limit of global warming to avert serious economic consequences.
- Similar 2DS requirement for Anadarko Petroleum. (The success of these 2DS proposals and three similar ones in 2017 has had an impact on company willingness to do such reporting voluntarily and resulted in the withdrawal of many such proposals from voting.)
- Requirement for a report on coal ash risk at Ameren.
- Reporting on methane emissions management at Range Resources.
- Sustainability at Kinder Morgan and at Middleby.

- Setting goals for greenhouse gas emissions at Genessee & Wyoming.
- Reporting on risks resulting from the opioid epidemic—Depomed.
- Report on gun safety and the mitigation of harm—Sturm Ruger

Fig. 8.3 shows the distribution of environmental proposals filed in the 2018 proxy seasons.

Many resolutions involved proxy access. Traditionally, corporates boards select candidates to stand for election to those boards. Proxy access resolutions seek to open the director nomination process up to allow investors to present nominations. Other proposals concerned executive compensation (say on pay) and retention of auditors in cases where questionable corporate activities were only recently revealed. Board gender diversity and sexual misconduct mitigation and risk management issues also were the subject of proposals.

The figures that follow show details of voting results for 2017 and 2018 for many different categories. Fig. 8.4 shows the results for environmental proposals.

Note: (1) Includes floor proposals; excludes proposals on ballots that were not presented or were withdrawn before the annual meeting. 2017 figures are for the full year and 2018 figures are through June 8, 2018. (2) Based on votes FOR as a percentage of votes FOR and AGAINST.

Seven environmental proposals received majority votes in 2018, and eight of the ten categories saw significant support of about 25% or more. The largest categories of proposals were in the areas of GHG emissions reduction, sustainability reporting, and 2DS reporting.

Fig. 8.5 shows the results for social proposals.

Only two social proposals received majority votes, the aforementioned opioid and firearms proposals. The average support for all categories of social proposals, however, was significantly over 25%. The largest categories of proposals were in the areas of lobbying, board diversity, election spending, and workplace diversity.

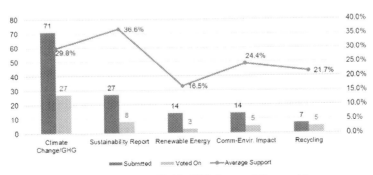

FIGURE 8.3 Environmental proposals filed in 2018. *Source: Alliance advisors.*

Environmental Proposals	2018 Submitted	2018 Voted on[1]	2018 Majority votes[2]	2018 Average support[2]	2017 Submitted	2017 Voted on[1]	2017 Majority votes[2]	2017 Average support[2]
Coal	2	1	1	53.2%	2	2	0	36.8%
Fugitive methane	10	4	1	35.5%	13	4	0	30.0%
2-Degree scenario report	20	5	2	36.8%	19	16	3	45.4%
GHG emissions reduction	31	9	1	32.1%	24	9	0	22.9%
Energy efficiency and renewable energy	12	3	0	16.8%	14	8	0	21.5%
Palm oil and deforestation	4	2	0	24.9%	8	3	0	19.7%
Recycling	8	4	0	20.4%	15	6	0	23.5%
Board environmental risk committee	4	1	0	48.6%	1	0	0	N/A
Director with environmental expertise	1	1	0	26.5%	4	3	0	13.3%
Sustainability report	30	8	2	37.0%	23	10	1	32.1%

FIGURE 8.4 Votes on environmental proposals 2018 and 2017. *Source: Alliance advisors.*

Social proposals	2018 Submitted	2018 Voted on[1]	2018 Majority Votes[2]	2018 Average support[2]	2017 Submitted	2017 Voted on[1]	2017 Majority Votes[2]	2017 Average support[2]
Board diversity - liberal	30	3	0	24.5%	38	9	2	27.7%
Workplace diversity	23	7	0	38.8%	19	10	1	32.4%
Student loans	1	1	0	42.8%	1	0	0	N/A
Opioid crisis	11	2	1	51.8%	0	0	0	N/A
Antibiotics and factory farms	4	2	0	29.3%	8	3	0	25.1%
Lobbying - conservative	2	2	0	27.9%	11	1	0	1.9%
Lobbying - liberal	50	26	0	26.2%	51	39	0	26.0%
Election spending	27	16	0	34.4%	33	19	0	28.0%
Hybrid - lobbying/election spending	5	3	0	33.2%	4	3	0	26.6%
Firearms	5	1	1	68.8%	0	0	0	N/A
Cybersecurity	2	1	0	29.5%	0	0	0	N/A

FIGURE 8.5 Votes on social proposals 2018 and 2017. *Source: Alliance Advisors.*

Fig. 8.6 shows the results for governance proposals.

Thirty-two governance proposals received majority votes in 2018. This is a substantial drop from the 2017 level. This can be explained primarily by the drop in proxy access proposals which received heavy support in 2017. Many companies recognized the need to revise their proxy access rules and have done so or are doing so voluntarily, thereby reducing the need for independent proxy access proposals. All categories of governance proposals have received average support in access of 25%, and the categories with the largest number of proposals are: special meetings, independent chair, written consent, proxy access, and supermajority voting. "Written consent" refers to the ability of shareholders to act by writing as opposed to appearing at a meeting. Many companies had put in their original articles of incorporation that shareholders could act only in voting at meetings, or by unanimous written consent.

Fig. 8.7 shows the results for compensation proposals.

No compensation proposals received a majority of votes in either 2017 or 2018. The largest number of proposals was filed in the categories of gender/racial pay equity and link pay to social issues and clawbacks. Categories

Governance proposals	2018 Submitted	2018 Voted on[1]	2018 Majority Votes[2]	2018 Average support[3]	2017 Submitted	2017 Voted on[1]	2017 Majority Votes[2]	2017 Average support[3]
Declassify board	14	5	5	84.5%	16	9	6	64.8%
Majority voting	10	3	2	63.8%	18	14	9	65.5%
Proxy access — adopt	27	11	3	38.8%	108	31	19	57.5%
Proxy access — amend	27	21	0	28.4%	67	26	0	28.1%
Supermajority voting	25	12	9	62.3%	24	13	12	72.1%
Dual-class stock	10	8	0	29.2%	13	12	0	28.0%
Special meetings	79	57	7	41.6%	28	24	4	42.1%
Written consent	44	36	6	42.3%	17	15	3	45.5%
Independent chairman	55	41	0	30.8%	53	44	0	30.5%

FIGURE 8.6   Votes on governance proposals 2018 and 2017. *Source: Alliance advisors.*

Compensation Proposals	2018 Submitted	2018 Voted on[1]	2018 Majority Votes[2]	2018 Average support[3]	2017 Submitted	2017 Voted on[1]	2017 Majority Votes[2]	2017 Average support[3]
Accelerated vesting of equity awards	6	3	0	31.4%	7	6	0	30.7%
Revolving door payments	3	3	0	28.2%	5	4	0	28.3%
Clawbacks	13	8	0	38.3%	7	6	0	13.9%
Retention of equity awards	1	1	0	28.1%	5	4	0	23.3%
Gender/racial pay equity	27	5	0	14.8%	30	14	0	14.7%
Link pay to social issues	21	10	0	15.4%	11	8	0	11.5%

FIGURE 8.7   Votes on compensation proposals 2018 and 2017. *Source: Alliance advisors.*

receiving greater than 25% of votes were clawbacks, accelerated vesting of equity awards, revolving door payments, and retention of equity awards. Clawbacks refer to the company taking back compensation previously awarded based on performance. If financial results in later periods are negatively impacted by past actions, the company can "clawback" some or all that compensation. For example, the trader implicated in JP Morgan's "London Whale" scandal was reportedly paid between $6 and $7 million annually. After the bank booked an estimated $6.2 billion by the end of 2012, it was reported to have "clawed back" 80% of the trader's compensation. Accelerated vesting of equity awards refers to the practice of paying executive compensation based on stock grants at an earlier date than the original grant specified. The concern is that the original grant specified certain performance requirements that were presumably designed to be appropriate incentives and advancing the vesting of these awards circumvents those incentives and lessens retention leverage. Revolving door payments are compensation to executives who move between government and private employment. Retention of equity awards proposals seeks to require executives to hold on to their grants of equity to continue their economic exposure to the company's fortunes.

Examples of shareholder engagement policies

Some of the largest public and private investment managers have become more aggressive in engaging investee companies, both by proactive discussions with managements and boards and also by active participation in corporate resolution voting. Next, we will summarize the policies of several of these large, active investment managers.

Blackrock

Blackrock is the world's largest asset manager with over $6 trillion in assets under management (AUM). It engages with investee companies in a constructive manner asking questions rather than instructing company actions. But if it finds a company's business or governance practices have shortcomings it will enter into a dialogue and expect a response consistent with its perspective as a long-term investor. Where warranted it will vote against management in order to protect the long-term economic interests of its clients. Blackrock established several key engagement priorities for the 2-year period 2017−18. They are focused on five areas:

- Governance
  - Board composition, effectiveness, diversity, and accountability.
- Corporate strategy
  - Board review of corporate strategy is key.
- Compensation
  - Executive pay policies should link closely to long-term strategy and goals.
- Climate risk disclosure
  - Enhance understanding, through consistent disclosures, of the processes each company has in place to manage climate risks.
- Human capital
  - In a talent constrained environment, a high standard of human capital management is a competitive advantage.

Many companies have developed policies for engagement of ESG issues, but the people driving these policies may not necessarily be at the C-level in those companies. This is not the case at Blackrock, where Chairman and CEO Larry Fink's 2018 letter to corporate CEOs challenged then to make positive contributions to society in the areas of climate change, human capital management, diversity, and executive pay (Fink, 2018).

CalPERS

CalPERS, the California Public Employees' Retirement System, is the largest public pension fund in the United States. It has over $300 billion invested in more than 10,000 public companies. It sees itself as an investor with a long-term investment horizon and as such, believes it must consider ESG factors across all of its day-to-day investment business. It believes long-term value results from effective management of financial, physical, and human capital. This economic approach grounds their sustainable investment agenda in their fiduciary duty to generate risk-adjusted returns for their beneficiaries. The four drivers of its corporate engagement program are:

- environmental practices, including but not limited to climate change and natural resource availability;
- governance practices, including but not limited to alignment of interests;
- human capital practices, including but not limited to fair labor practices, health and safety, responsible contracting, and diversity; and
- risk management practices.

CalPERS has a Focus List Program which involves engaging with companies to improve their governance practices. This engagement has focused on:

- board quality and diversity—leadership structure, independence, skill-sets, and diversity;
- corporate reporting—transparency of environmental-social-governance (ESG) practices, business strategy, and capital deployment;
- investor rights—voting rights and director terms;
- risk management of environmental and social issues; and
- shareholder alignment on executive compensation practices.

An analysis of the results of this engagement looked at the stock performance of 188 companies targeted from 1999 through 2013. The performance of the companies subject to this engagement was found to be 15.27% above the Russell 1000 Index and 11.90% above their respective Russell 1000 sector indices.

CalPERS also sees proxy voting as the primary way to influence a company's operations and governance. Its proxy voting practice is stated thusly:

We implement our proxy voting responsibility in a manner that is consistent with these Principles unless such action may result in long-term harm to the company that outweighs all reasonably likely long-term benefit; or unless such a vote is contrary to the interests of the beneficiaries of the System. It is therefore important for shareowners such as CalPERS to exercise their rights to participate and make their voting decisions based on a full understanding of the information and legal documentation presented to them. Our proxy voting responsibilities cover a wide range of corporate governance issues centered around various management and shareowner proposals. Specific voting topics may include board quality, investor rights, executive compensation, corporate reporting, capital structure, environmental and social related issues. When exercising our voting rights, we will cast votes "for" or "against", individual management and shareowner proposals consistent with the interest of our beneficiaries and consistent with the Principles. We will vote "against", an individual or slate of director nominees at companies that do not effectively oversee these interests. We will also withhold our vote in limited circumstances where a company has consistently demonstrated long-term economic underperformance. As part of our commitment to transparency, we publish our proxy voting activities at over 11,000 companies' annual general meetings.

CalPERS (2018)

A cursory review of publicly available records of CalPERS proxy votes shows that they often vote against the recommendation of company management and will regularly support independent shareholder proposals on governance matters. In 2017, for example, CalPERS was active in helping pass resolutions at ExxonMobil and Occidental Petroleum that required climate risk reporting.

T. Rowe Price

TRP is a US firm with $1 trillion in AUM. It states that "As a global investment management firm, we recognize the influence we have on social and environmental issues through our investment portfolios... The central mission of our company is to help our clients reach their long-term goals... Consistent with that mission, we have an obligation to understand the long-term sustainability of a company's business model and the factors that could cause it to change. We do this by incorporating environmental, social, and governance (ESG) considerations into our investment process."

TRP is a signatory of the Principles for Responsible Investment (PRI) and supports the PRI framework as an effective means to encourage better dialogue and improve company disclosure. Analysts and portfolio managers are supported by two groups of internal specialists: the Responsible Investment and Corporate Governance teams. The investment approach follows these principles:

- Collaboration—among companies, investors, and governments, all have a role to play.
- Accountability—investment analysts are responsible for assessing the full range of factors likely to have a meaningful impact.
- Fundamental research—ESG analysis and engagement are most effective when led by experienced investors who know the company well.
- Stewardship—responsibilities as diligent investors do not cease with the decision to purchase a security. It is important to maintain regular dialogue with the management of portfolio companies.
- Materiality—the focus is on the ESG factors considered to be most likely to have a material impact on client portfolios.

Material ESG factors vary by country, industry, and company. They may include: capital stewardship, accountability, transparency, leadership quality, strategy and execution, the competitive dynamics in the industry, management of human capital, and efficient use of resources.

The New York City Comptroller's Office

The New York City Comptroller's Office (NYCCO) manages investments on behalf of the New York City Pension Funds. A Corporate Governance and Responsible Investment team develops and implements the corporate governance programs for the five New York City Pension Funds, including voting proxies, engaging portfolio companies on their environmental, social and governance policies and practices, and advocating for regulatory reforms to protect investors and strengthen shareowner rights.

For the 1-year period of July 1, 2017, to June 30, 2018, NYCCO had the following proxy voting statistics:

- Of 69,360 proxy proposals, 69,131 votes were cast.
- Votes were cast with management 76% of the time and against 24% of the time.
- 7054 meetings were attended.

As shown in Fig. 8.8, the largest category of proposals was related to Directors, with a fairly wide distribution of other issues.

Fig. 8.8 shows the distribution of proposal issues, divided between management sponsored and shareholder sponsored.

Vanguard

The Vanguard group, with over $5 trillion in AUM is the largest provider of mutual funds and the second-largest provider of Exchange Traded Funds (ETFs). It has historically been the leader in implementing very low charges for its funds. It also is a leader in engagement with investee companies. In its 2017 fiscal year, its Investment Stewardship team voted on 171,000 proxies at nearly 19,000 shareholder meetings and held more than 950 engagements with company leaders and directors. Vanguard believes that long-term investor success is improved when companies have:

- high-performing boards that are fit for purpose,
- governance structures that empower shareholders,
- compensation plans that appropriately incentivize sustained outperformance, and
- a framework for overseeing and managing significant risks.

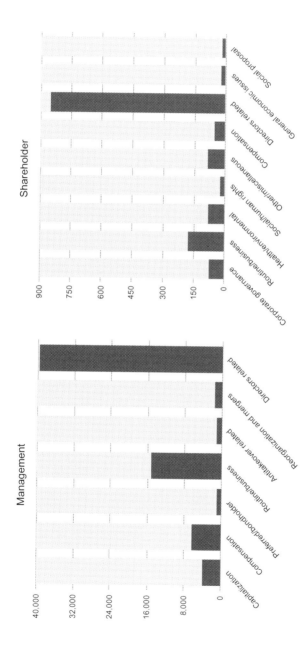

FIGURE 8.8 Shareholder proposals for NYCCO companies. *Source: From NYCCO, 2018. Pension/Investment Management. City of New York. Used with permission from ISS Analytics.*

Some issues that Vanguard perceives as threats to shareholders' economic interests include traditional governance issues such as misaligned executive compensation packages, unequal shareholder voting rights, ineffective boards, climate risk disclosure, and gender diversity on boards. Beginning in 2017, Vanguard has supported shareholder resolutions regarding climate change, which the firm now believes poses a long-term risk to companies in certain industries.

The firm "... takes positions on these matters not because they are inherently good or noble, but because they are tied to the long-term economic value of your funds' investments. We express our views in our meetings with individual companies, in our public advocacy, and ultimately in the way we vote proxies on behalf of Vanguard funds."

Institutional investors acting together

We've seen how several large institutional investors have engaged with investee companies. The next level of engagement may be to form an alliance of like-minded investors to bring additional weight to proposals. For example, in November 2018, 13 investors, together with the Harvard Advanced Leadership Initiative, united to pressure gun manufacturers and sellers to make firearms safer, more secure, and easier to trace. The investment group consisted of:

- CalPERS
- California State Teachers' Retirement System (CalSTRS)
- Connecticut Retirement Plans and Trust Funds
- Florida State Board of Administration
- Maine Public Employees Retirement System
- Maryland State Retirement and Pension System
- Nuveen, the asset manager of TIAA
- OIP Investment Trust
- Oregon Public Employees Retirement Fund
- Rockefeller Asset Management
- San Francisco Employees' Retirement System
- State Street Global Advisors
- Wespath Investment Management

These investors have cumulative AUM of almost $5 trillion. They united to create and promote Principles for a Responsible Firearms Industry. They state that they believe in the rule of law and respect the 2nd Amendment of the US Constitution, but they also believe they have a duty to their beneficiaries to assume responsibility for reducing risks if and when they hold a financial interest in firearms-related enterprises. Further, they believe that enterprises involved in the manufacturing, distribution, sale, and enforcement of regulations of the firearms industry are well positioned to support pragmatic transparency and safety measures that contribute to the responsible use of firearms. Through this framework, they assert their role as investors in encouraging such practices and identify expectations for the firearms industry that will reduce risks and improve the safety of civil society at large. They also commit to monitoring progress by companies over time and engaging with them regularly.

The Principles are meant to be sensible and not intended to be prescriptive in nature. There are many ways to apply a principle; companies are free to apply the Principles in a manner they deem appropriate. The group also recognizes that the civilian firearms industry is highly regulated by both federal and state entities with respect to the manufacture, sale, use, and transfer of firearms, but believes that more can be voluntarily done by companies to advance safety and the responsible use of civilian firearms. The investor group calls on civilian firearms companies to publicly demonstrate and publish their compliance with each of these principles, failing which, they state, somewhat ominously, "we will consider using all tools available to us as investors to mitigate these risks."

The five Principles are:

- Principle 1: Manufacturers should support, advance, and integrate the development of technology designed to make civilian firearms safer, more secure, and easier to trace.
- Principle 2: Manufacturers should adopt and follow responsible business practices that establish and enforce responsible dealer standards and promote training and education programs for owners designed around firearms safety.
- Principle 3: Civilian firearms distributors, dealers, and retailers should establish, promote, and follow best practices to ensure that no firearm is sold without a completed background check in order to prevent sales to persons prohibited from buying firearms or those too dangerous to possess firearms.
- Principle 4: Civilian firearms distributors, dealers, and retailers should educate and train their employees to better recognize and effectively monitor irregularities at the point of sale, to record all firearm sales, to audit firearms inventory on a regular basis, and to proactively assist law enforcement.
- Principle 5: Participants in the civilian firearms industry should work collaboratively, communicate, and engage with the signatories of these Principles to design, adopt, and disclose measures and metrics demonstrating both best practices and their commitment to promoting these Principles.

Time will tell how successful the group will be. Despite their cumulative size, they are not among the largest shareholders of the two largest public gun makers: Sturm, Rogers & Co. and American Outdoor Brands Corp. (formerly Smith and Wesson). In its defense, the latter firm stated that it does not believe that its stockholders associate the criminal use of firearms with the company that manufactures them. BlackRock, the largest shareholder, issued a message to clients in March 2018 stating that it had a two-pronged approach to firearms companies. First, for clients seeking to exclude firearms from their portfolios, it created new ETFs with screens to exclude civilian firearms. Second, it engages with firearms manufacturers and retailers regarding business practices connected with the production and sale of firearms. Perhaps to explain why it doesn't go further in challenging gun companies, the firm states that "BlackRock manages money for a diverse set of investors, including pension plans, insurers and individual investors, who have a wide range of views on firearms. It is ultimately our clients' choice about the types of funds they invest in. It is our privilege to serve them, and we will continue to engage with all of our clients to understand their needs and preferences so that we can effectively meet their investment objectives."

The formation of this alliance of institutional investors may signal a new trend in investor engagement going beyond the recent emergence of activism by individual institutions. Despite the size and significance of these individual institutions, they are realizing that acting alone they still account for only a minority of votes, but by banding together they present a much more formidable force for the changes they wish to effect.

Several investment industry organizations have been formed to advance the state of corporate governance. Most of the large investors mentioned in this chapter are supporting or founding members of these groups. Some of the most important are the following:

- Investor Stewardship Group (ISG)
- 30% Club
- Sustainability Accounting Standards Board (SASB)

The Investor Stewardship Group

The ISG is an investor-led initiative of some of the largest US-based institutional investors and global asset managers. There are more than 60 US and international institutional investors with combined assets in excess of US$31 trillion in the US equity markets. The group's goal is to establish a framework of basic investment stewardship and corporate governance standards for US institutional investor and boardroom conduct. To that end they have developed stewardship and governance principles:

ISG stewardship framework for institutional investors

Principle A: Institutional investors are accountable to those whose money they invest.

Principle B: Institutional investors should demonstrate how they evaluate corporate governance factors with respect to the companies in which they invest.

Principle C: Institutional investors should disclose, in general terms, how they manage potential conflicts of interest that may arise in their proxy voting and engagement activities.

Principle D: Institutional investors are responsible for proxy voting decisions and should monitor the relevant activities and policies of third parties that advise them on those decisions.

Principle E: Institutional investors should address and attempt to resolve differences with companies in a constructive and pragmatic manner.

Principle F: Institutional investors should work together, where appropriate, to encourage the adoption and implementation of the Corporate Governance and Stewardship principles.

ISG corporate governance framework for US listed companies

Principle 1: Boards are accountable to shareholders.

Principle 2: Shareholders should be entitled to voting rights in proportion to their economic interest.

Principle 3: Boards should be responsive to shareholders and be proactive in order to understand their perspectives.

Principle 4: Boards should have a strong, independent leadership structure.

Principle 5: Boards should adopt structures and practices that enhance their effectiveness.

Principle 6: Boards should develop management incentive structures that are aligned with the long-term strategy of the company.

The 30% Club

The 30% Club was founded in London and in October 2016 issued a Statement of Intent that club members will use their ownership rights and undertake stewardship to encourage progress on gender diversity. The Statement of Intent includes supporting the following targets by 2020:

- Thirty percent women on FTSE350 boards and
- Thirty percent women at senior management level of FTSE100 companies.

  Commitments of the group include:

- Engagement with investee companies

Active engagement with board chairs and nomination committees on the issue of board diversity.

Raise questions where there is evidence that there has been a failure in the nomination process with respect to board diversity.

May choose to vote against the reelection of the chair of the board or nomination committee, particularly where there continues to be no evidence of board diversity, and engagement with the board has not led to any satisfactory outcome.

- Exercise of ownership rights

As a general approach, this could involve voting actions in listed companies in two areas:

Directors (re)elections—Board Chair and/or Nominations Committee Chair. The nominations committee should ensure that the board has the appropriate range and balance of skills, experience, independence, and knowledge. The chair of this committee shares a responsibility with the board chairman for ensuring that directors are appointed on merit, against objective criteria and with due regard for the benefits of diversity. Investors could consider not supporting the nominations committee chair and/or board chair of those companies that still fall short of expectations.

Report & Accounts

Companies should include disclosure on their diversity policy and implementation. Investors could consider not supporting the Report & Accounts resolutions if the diversity statement is not considered satisfactory or there is no clear evidence that diversity is being sufficiently considered by the board.

Sustainability Accounting Standards Board

Financial Accounting Standards Board (FASB) has established rules for financial accounting and now, since its founding in 2011, the SASB seeks to provide similar rules for social and environmental issues, with particular relevance to SEC Form 10K filing requirements for US companies. It has an Investor Advisory Group comprised of most of the large investment managers, representing roughly $25 trillion in AUM. SASB's activities will be discussed in more detail in Chapter 9, Defining and measuring ESG performance.

Chapter 9

Defining and measuring ESG performance

Chapter Outline

ESG factors in portfolio construction   167
Standards for companies to report
their ESG impacts   168
    Global Reporting Initiative   169
    Sustainability Accounting
    Standards Board   173
    United Nations Global Compact   174
    The United Nations Guiding
    Principles   175
Quality issues in ESG reporting   175
Corporate ESG reporting: findings   176
Services providing an assessment
of corporate ESG   177
    Sustainalytics   177

    MSCI   177
    RepRisk ESG Business Intelligence   178
    Ceres   178
    JUST Capital   179
How do mutual funds and ETFs
rate ESG performance of
portfolio companies?   180
    Does ESG investing require lower
    returns?   180
    Conceptual critiques of ESG
    investing   180
    Empirical studies   181

Previous chapters discussed various financial instruments available to environmental, social, and governance (ESG) investors. But are those investments doing what investors believe them to be doing? How are ESG factors defined, measured, and reported? And how have ESG portfolios performed over time? It is important to have a thorough understanding of all of these aspects of ESG investment performance.

ESG factors in portfolio construction

In earlier chapters, we saw how investors are increasingly concerned about ESG issues and are showing an increased interest in investing in companies with positive characteristics. But how is an investor to assess a company's performance? Wanting to build an ESG portfolio might be a relatively easy decision but working through the details of constructing such a portfolio can require much more effort. First, the investor must decide on the key qualities that are important to her. Many ESG scores are provided as a single metric,

Environmental, Social, and Governance (ESG) Investing. DOI: https://doi.org/10.1016/B978-0-12-818692-3.00009-8

but there are many separate factors which go into building this score. A particular issue may be of overwhelming importance to one investor, but a second investor may think the same issue is unimportant, or worse, have a diametrically opposed view. Modern databases can contain hundreds of different ESG variables, with scores for each. Proliferation of artificial intelligence (AI) amplifies the problem because this procedure still requires an analyst to provide a structure to the AI application, but the AI process is typically opaque to the investor. With many possible indicators, the investor must determine the relative merits of each. Some choose instead to follow other investors with similar professed ESG goals. This route has the virtue of simplicity, and it may allow the investor to defer criticism to a third party. But it also entails the risk that the other investors' portfolio may not accurately reflect stated goals. Index providers, institutional investment managers, and mutual fund and ETF sponsors all can provide a solution to this information problem by having the necessary resources to take on investigating the ESG performance of companies.

With hundreds of socially responsible mutual funds and ETFs trading in US markets, there is a broad range of investment choices now available to investors. Some providers offer bespoke services where the investor can pick and choose portfolio components, but a more popular option is for the investor to simply participate in one of the many off the shelf pooled ESG investment products. While this offers investors simple execution, and a great selection it also poses the challenge of understanding each approach and the differences among these funds. Some of the funds have simply added an ESG supplement to an existing investment process while others take a more outcome-oriented approach designed to deliver a sustainability or impact return alongside a financial return. This somewhat simplistic approach may meet the needs of some investors but there's a risk that the fund is not delivering on the ESG objectives. Consequently, other investors desire a more results-based approach. Analyzing ESG funds then can require understanding not only their risk-return profiles but also their approach to sustainability. To provide an ESG rating, the analyst or rating service must identify the ESG factors that are important, develop some means of measuring those factors, and then have a way to assess each company's performance.

Standards for companies to report their ESG impacts

The easiest way to rate a company is to simply rely on historical reputation for the company or its industry. But this method can underappreciate efforts companies are making to improve their performance, and conversely, can fall victim to inaccurate or misleading corporate advertising. For example, the Dow Chemical Company would score low on ESG based on some historical products and the general perception of the chemical industry. However, more recently Dow has become one of the leaders in its industry in embracing the need for sustainable operations and products. To exclude it from an ESG portfolio based on historical data would be short sighted, given a desire to encourage activities which support a better future. Or take the case of Volkswagen. The auto manufacturer heavily marketed its "clean diesel" technology and clean air compliance for decades. It was then found to have falsified emissions test data and pled guilty to violating the Clean Air Act. It subsequently paid $4.3 billion in fines in the United States and billions more in Germany. It spent additional billions to buy back cars sold under false pretenses. If one had put VW in an ESG portfolio, its presence would have done little to advance an environmental objective not to mention the financial cost of its transgressions.

There is also a complication in that ESG considerations are multidimensional. A company's performance can be measured in many areas such as air, water, and energy impacts; employee and customer sustainability effects; gender and minority hiring, training, and promotion practices. How best to measure and weight all of these? The difficulty in gathering and analyzing information on a wide range of ESG factors has led companies and investors to rely on outsourced services to do the research and to provide guidance on ESG issue identification, compliance, and reporting.

There are several services providing frameworks for reporting sustainability or ESG performance: Global Reporting Initiative (GRI) Sustainability Reporting Guidelines, SASB, the United Nations Global Compact (UNGC), the UN Guiding Principles on Business and Human Rights, OECD Guidelines, International Organization for Standardization (ISO) 26000, and the International Labour Organization (ILO) Tripartite Declaration. In the following section, we will look at several of these different frameworks for ESG measurement and reporting.

Global Reporting Initiative

Eighty-nine percent of reporting firms use a formal framework or guidance for their reporting, and the most popular framework was established by the GRI. GRI is an independent organization, formed in 1997 by CERES, the TELLUS Institute, and the United Nations Environment Programme. The GRI Standards were most recently updated in 2016. In 2017 63% of the largest 100 companies in reporting countries, and 75% of the Global Fortune 250 used the GRI reporting framework. The Standards are grouped into three topic-specific categories: economic, environmental, and social. In addition, there are three universal Standards to guide reporting organizations in preparing a sustainability report. They guide reporters in using the Standards, reporting an organization's relevant contextual information, and reporting how its topics are managed.

Under Economic topics, the broad categories of Standards are:

- Economic Performance
- Market Presence
- Indirect Economic Impact
- Procurement Practices
- Anti-corruption
- Anti-competitive Behavior

The broad categories for Environmental Standards are:

- Materials
- Energy
- Water and Effluents
- Biodiversity
- Effluents and Waste
- Environmental Compliance
- Supplier Environmental Assessments

The Social Standards categories are:

- Employment
- Labor/Management Relations
- Occupational/Health and Safety
- Training and Education
- Diversity and Equal Opportunity
- Non-discrimination
- Freedom or Association and Collective Bargaining
- Child Labor
- Forced or Compulsory Labor
- Security Practices
- Rights of Indigenous Peoples
- Human Rights Assessment
- Local Communities
- Supplier Social Assessment
- Public Policy
- Customer Health and Safety
- Marketing and Labeling
- Customer Privacy
- Socioeconomic Compliance

Under each of these categories there are detailed topic-specific Disclosure Standards. For example, the first category under Economics is Economic Performance. This topic has four Disclosures:

Disclosure 201-1: Direct economic value generated and distributed. The requirements are:

The reporting organization shall report the following information:

a. Direct economic value generated and distributed (EVG&D) on an accruals basis, including the basic components for the organization's global operations as listed below. If data are presented on a cash basis, report the justification for this decision in addition to reporting the following basic components:

   i. Direct economic value generated: revenues;
   ii. Economic value distributed: operating costs, employee wages and benefits, payments to providers of capital, payments to government by country, and community investments;
   iii. Economic value retained: 'direct economic value generated' less 'economic value distributed'.

b. Where significant, report EVG&D separately at country, regional, or market levels, and the criteria used for defining significance.

Disclosure 201-2: Financial implications and other risks and opportunities due to climate change. The requirements are:

The reporting organization shall report the following information:

a. Risks and opportunities posed by climate change that have the potential to generate substantive changes in operations, revenue, or expenditure, including:

   i. a description of the risk or opportunity and its classification as either physical, regulatory, or other;
   ii. a description of the impact associated with the risk or opportunity;
   iii. the financial implications of the risk or opportunity before action is taken;
   iv. the methods used to manage the risk or opportunity;
   v. the costs of actions taken to manage the risk or opportunity.

Disclosure 201-3: Defined benefit plan obligations and other retirement plans. The requirements are:

The reporting organization shall report the following information:

a. If the plan's liabilities are met by the organization's general resources, the estimated value of those liabilities.

b. If a separate fund exists to pay the plan's pension liabilities:

   i. the extent to which the scheme's liabilities are estimated to be covered by the assets that have been set aside to meet them;
   ii. the basis on which that estimate has been arrived at;
   iii. when that estimate was made.

c. If a fund set up to pay the plan's pension liabilities is not fully covered, explain the strategy, if any, adopted by the employer to work towards full coverage, and the timescale, if any, by which the employer hopes to achieve full coverage.

d. Percentage of salary contributed by employee or employer.

e. Level of participation in retirement plans, such as participation in mandatory or voluntary schemes, regional, or country-based schemes, or those with financial impact.

Disclosure 201-4: Financial assistance received from government. The requirements are:

The reporting organization shall report the following information:

a. Total monetary value of financial assistance received by the organization from any government during the reporting period, including:
  i. tax relief and tax credits;
  ii. subsidies;
  iii. investment grants, research and development grants, and other relevant types of grant;
  iv. awards;
  v. royalty holidays;
  xvi. financial assistance from Export Credit Agencies (ECAs);
  xvii. financial incentives;
  xviii. other financial benefits received or receivable from any government for any operation.

b. The information in 201-4-a by country.

c. Whether, and the extent to which, any government is present in the shareholding structure.

These four Economic Standards illustrate the level of detail provided by GRI. (The complete list of Standards can be found on the GRI website: https://www.globalreporting.org/standards/gri-standards-download-center/ ?g = 1aba153b-bfea-492c-bb5c-134bee736572.)

One criticism of the GRI Standards is that they do not give guidance on the impact of "contextual" factors. These are the limits and demands placed on economic, environmental, or social resources, at the global, regional, local, or sector level. There is such wide diversity across nations that application of the Standards necessarily varies. The implication relevant to the discussion in this chapter is that two reporting organizations can be reporting based on dramatically different interpretations of the Standards because of sectoral, local, or regional factors. It is also important to repeat that these Standards are guidelines for corporate reporting. GRI does not review company or government reports for accuracy. And this is a crucially important short-coming: no matter how detailed the Standards are, organizations self-report their performance. One must question the resulting accuracy of the data.

While GRI is the most popular source of sustainability reporting guidance, there are several other organizations with different, competing reporting methodologies.

Sustainability Accounting Standards Board

The Sustainability Accounting Standards Board (SASB) has developed a series of industry-specific sustainability accounting standards that help companies disclose financially material, decision useful ESG information to investors. The group's work, as signaled by the acronym is parallel to that of the Financial Accounting Standards Board or FASB. FASB is an independent organization that establishes financial accounting and reporting standards that are consistent with Generally Accepted Accounting Principles. This group's work is an attempt to provide better, consistent metrics like those available in purely financial accounting. To that end they have developed a series of industry-specific issues, 78% of which are quantitative. SASB's Sustainable Industry Classification System identifies 11 sectors and 77 industries. The industry groupings are shown in Fig. 9.1.

FIGURE 9.1 SASB'S sustainable industry classification system. *Source: From SASB'S SUSTAINABLE INDUSTRY CLASSIFICATION SYSTEM*^R ©*SICS. Reprinted with permission from The SASB Foundation. All rights reserved.*

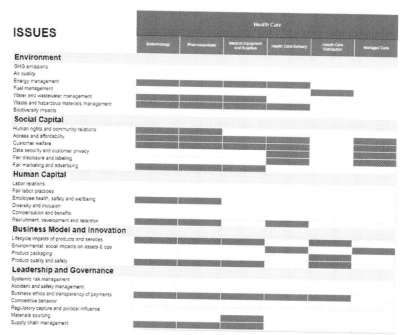

FIGURE 9.2 SASB materiality map for health care industries. *Source: From SASB'S SUSTAINABLE INDUSTRY CLASSIFICATION SYSTEM*® ©*SICS. Reprinted with permission from The SASB Foundation. All rights reserved.*

Within an industry certain ESG issues are more important or "material" than others. SASB digs into each industry to identify which issues are relevant. The detailed issues can be displayed as a "Materiality Map" for each industry. Fig. 9.2 shows such a map for Health Care Industries.

The SASB criteria are particularly useful for US companies in reporting ESG risks in SEC Form 10-K filings, and in this regard are more focused than the somewhat more general GRI criteria.

United Nations Global Compact

United Nations Global Compact (UNGC) is the world's largest corporate sustainability initiative. It provides 10 principles for businesses to incorporate into their strategies, policies, and procedures (UNGC, 2018). These principles are:

Human Rights
- Principle 1: Businesses should support and respect the protection of internationally proclaimed human rights; and
- Principle 2: make sure that they are not complicit in human rights abuses.

Labour
* Principle 3: Businesses should uphold the freedom of association and the effective recognition of the right to collective bargaining;
* Principle 4: the elimination of all forms of forced and compulsory labour;
* Principle 5: the effective abolition of child labour; and
* Principle 6: the elimination of discrimination in respect of employment and occupation.

Environment
* Principle 7: Businesses should support a precautionary approach to environmental challenges;
* Principle 8: undertake initiatives to promote greater environmental responsibility; and
* Principle 9: encourage the development and diffusion of environmentally friendly technologies.

Anti-Corruption
* Principle 10: Businesses should work against corruption in all its forms, including extortion and bribery.

The United Nations Guiding Principles

The United Nations Guiding Principles on Business and Human Rights (UNGP) also provide guidance for global governments and businesses in preventing and addressing business-related human rights abuses. Company disclosures with respect to UNGP are collected and can be viewed on a public website: https://www.ungpreporting.org/database-analysis/explore-disclosures/. Reports can be filtered by sector, location, salient issue, company, or year of review. They can also be filtered by type of information: governance or respect for human rights; defining the focus of reporting; and management of salient human rights issues.

Quality issues in ESG reporting

While there are several frameworks for reporting, there are questions about the quality of these reports. Some of the concerns expressed about the data are (Esty and Cort, 2017):

* Materiality—are the factors being measured or reported important or fundamental to the company's efforts.
* Uniform reporting versus industry specifics—an emphasis on uniform reporting across all industries may miss the fact that some factors are far more important or alternatively irrelevant for different industries.
* Required versus self-reported data—Government agency regulations require reporting of useful data which can provide the basis of reasonable

comparisons. In contrast, much other data consists of voluntary self-reporting which may contain gaps and can be difficult to compare across companies.

- Coached results and conflicts of interest—many rating companies also sell benchmark and consulting services which raise the potential for conflicts of interest.
- Monitored versus estimated data—There is some data available from pollution monitoring equipment, but much more frequently "data" are estimated using often opaque methods of questionable value.
- Verification—much of the data are self-reported by the companies themselves. Roughly half of these companies have some sort of third-party verification, but the methods used are often opaque.
- Coverage—less than 5% of the world's publicly listed companies report their emissions. The percentage reporting on other issues is even lower.
- Gap filling—data quality is further impacted by missing observations and little transparency on methods used when there are estimates.
- Reporting consistency and methodological rigor—an overall concern is that there are no systematic reporting standards covering all factors and companies.
- Normalization—little or no effort is made to recognize scale or scope across companies.
- Outcomes versus inputs—where measures of outcomes are not available, such as actual amount of emissions, resort is often made to measuring inputs such as budget or staffing which can be identified as addressing emissions. But the efficacy of inputs can be highly variable: a company devoting significant inputs to pollution issues may yet have higher emissions than a company with half that level of inputs.
- Analysis—given all the uncertainties in the data, it is important to have transparency on analytic methods used to evaluate the data.
- Aggregation and weighting—a score for a company may be based on say 10 factors. Any weighting of these factors will contain some level of subjectivity.

Corporate ESG reporting: findings

The preceding identifies several different sources of guidance on corporate ESG reporting and some of the shortcomings of these services. But how many companies report ESG performance and on what basis? A survey conducted in 2017 provides a detailed look at the corporate responsibility and sustainability reporting of 4900 companies across the globe (KPMG, 2017). Some of its significant findings are:

- For the 100 largest companies in each of 49 countries, the majority of companies (60% or more) in all industries report on corporate responsibility and sustainability.

- Most of the biggest companies integrate financial and nonfinancial data in their annual reports.
- Although a majority of reporting companies disclose targets for reducing carbon emissions, only a minority of companies acknowledge climate risk, and very few attempt to quantify or model their risk.

It is important to note that these are "self-reported" results. The companies provide their own assessments, which raises issues of the usefulness and consistency of the data. In order to assess the quality of the assessment process and the accuracy of the resultant reports, some companies have made use of external verification or "assessment" services. These external services were used in two-thirds of the companies surveyed overall, but in only 45% of the largest companies.

Services providing an assessment of corporate ESG

The discussion so far has been about services which provide guidance to companies and governments on their self-reporting of ESG performance. But there are several services which provide research on corporate ESG performance.

Sustainalytics

Sustainalytics provides data on over 70 indicators. Each indicator is weighted by an assessment of its relative importance in each of 42 industry groups. The indicators are organized in three "pillars" of E, S, and G issues. Each company rated is scored on each factor according to its preparedness, disclosure, and performance relevant to that factor. The resulting scores are scaled between 1 and 100 and each company is then assigned a percentile ranking within its industry group. This process is updated annually. While there is a huge amount of detail and effort in these rankings, there is obviously a substantial amount of judgement required for the underlying qualitative assessments. Yet, one would expect that these judgements would be more objective than those coming from self-reporting by organizations. In addition to these ESG ratings, Sustainalytics also monitors daily news feeds for any events that may have negative impacts. This service allowed Sustainalytics to provide early warning of Volkswagen's scandal relating to falsified diesel emissions testing.

MSCI

MSCI also provides ESG ratings. It generates such ESG ratings for 7500 companies (13,500 total issuers, including subsidiaries) and more than 650,000 equity and fixed income securities. Fig. 9.3 illustrates its approach to developing these ratings.

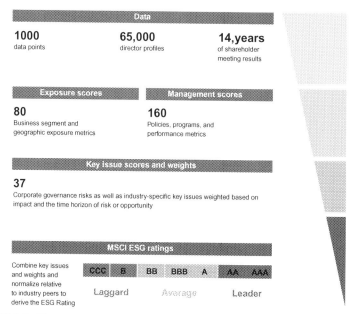

FIGURE 9.3   The making of an MSCI ESG rating.

One point to note is that the correlations between the Governance scores from MSCI and those from Sustainalytics have been persistently lower than for the other pillars. This is most likely explained by the fact that MSCI's G score measures the quality of corporate governance, focusing on issues such as the composition of the board and executive compensation while Sustainalytics' comparable metric includes some of these issues, but also gives a large weight to the company's governance of environmental and social issues.

RepRisk ESG Business Intelligence

RepRisk ESG Business Intelligence is another global research firm and provider of ESG risk data. RepRisk monitors the companies in the Norwegian Pension Fund's portfolio for defined ethical issues such as severe human rights violations, particularly regarding child labor, forced labor, and violations of individual rights as well as environmental and corruption.

Ceres

Ceres is a Boston based nonprofit which has developed a set of core principles forming the basis of a code of corporate environmental behavior. The 10 Ceres Principles are:

- Protection of the biosphere
- Sustainable use of natural resources
- Reduction and disposal of wastes
- Energy conservation
- Risk reduction
- Safe products and services
- Environmental restoration
- Informing the public
- Management commitment
- Audits and reports

Ceres founded and directs the Investor Network on Climate Risk which includes more than 100 institutional investors. It also was one of the founders of the Global Reporting Initiative, mentioned above. Among other resources, its investor guide on agriculture supply chain risk, called "Engage the Chain" (Ceres, 2017), provides investors and companies with an overview of the environmental and social issues involved with the production of several common agricultural products. It identifies reputational, market, operational, litigation, and regulatory risks. Ceres' SEC Sustainability Disclosure Search Tool is used to search annual filings of reporting companies.

An important point to note is that ratings based on historical data especially that which is self-reported by companies, are backward looking. They reflect actions taken in the past and may or may not be relevant to future events. Also, sustainability ratings encapsulate a wide range of issues and it can be challenging to understand how best to apply them in the investment process.

JUST Capital

JUST Capital was founded in 2013 with a mission "to build a more just marketplace that better reflects the true priorities of the American people" (JUST, 2018). The JUST methodology consists of three steps:

- a poll to determine the factors/issues which matter most;
- evaluate companies based on these issues; and
- rank the largest publicly traded US companies based on these evaluations.

The company defines seven major sets of issues, with an underlying set of 39 component factors. Each of these receives a weight according to quantitative polling of individuals. Each company in the database is then rated on each of these weighted components. These rankings have been used to create an investible index called "JUST US Large Cap Diversified Index."

How do mutual funds and ETFs rate ESG performance of portfolio companies?

Morningstar

Morningstar is probably the premier fund rating service. It analyzes fund performance and its recommendations have a significant effect on investor flows into and out of these funds. In rating ESG funds, it relies heavily on Sustainalytics ratings, along with an assessment of ESG-related controversies. Morningstar provides investors with Sustainability Ratings for approximately 20,000 mutual funds and ETFs. The rating scale is one through five corresponding to a relative ranking within the investment's industry group. A rating of one (actually one globe) indicates the investment is at the bottom of the range, three indicates an average rating and a five indicates an investment at the high end of the ESG performance range for that industry group. Some investors find these weightings useful in deciding among targeted sector funds. They may prefer a traditional fund to investments identified as SRI (or ESG) because those investments may have industry weightings or other characteristics which are not consistent with the investor's mandate or the investor believes it could result in underperformance. But by using the Morningstar Sustainability Ratings, the investor can gain ESG value while maintaining a specific investment style. For example, if the investor wants to be in a large-cap growth fund, she can select a large-cap growth fund with a five ESG rating over a fund with only a one rating.

Does ESG investing require lower returns?

Let's jump ahead to this author's conclusion: *ESG investing does not necessarily require accepting lower returns.* But the issue has many nuances and there is little consensus. A recent article in Barron's (Serafeim and Seessel, 2018) is typical of treatment in the financial press: two equal sides make the respective cases affirming and denying positive returns to ESG investing. But based on reviewing many individual empirical studies and several meta studies, we believe that one can construct an investment portfolio using ESG criteria that has reasonable prospects of equaling the financial performance of a suitable benchmark portfolio. If longer run risks are taken into account, the balance tips more in favor of the positive ESG portfolio. Two caveats: the ESG criteria must be carefully selected and metrics to identify investee company performance must be clearly understood.

Conceptual critiques of ESG investing

First, it is important to realize that an investment process that is simply a negative screen is unlikely to provide financial performance equal to a neutral approach. Some of the differences in opinion on the success of ESG investing lies in the confusion of investing styles: ESG investing is much more than just a negative screen. Negative screening is often used to build ethical portfolios with some believing that if enough investors avoid the sin stocks, their prices would drop, and management would be forced to change their ways. However, others point out that lower prices could lead to a situation where the firm's price to earnings ratio would be lowered, making the stock look like a buying opportunity. "Value" investors, looking for cheap, or underpriced stock would then rush in. Furthermore, to the extent that ethical investors do not own the stock, they would not have voting rights and be locked out of any discussion on managing the company. And negative screens excluding tobacco companies have resulted in underperformance as those companies have done well over certain periods of time.

A further conceptual issue is the exclusion effect: if one looks at a universe of 1000 stocks, and excludes say 10% without regard to financial performance, then there is a chance that at least some of those stocks would outperform the average. By limiting the universe of possible stocks, the investor is at risk to selecting a portfolio which would underperform the average. But instead of using a naïve negative screen, some ESG investors use a more sophisticated factor approach which incorporates consideration of specific favorable ESG actions a company is taking along with financial analysis. Often this is done in comparison with peer companies, with the more responsible company being favored for investment. And this type of factor analysis can be done not just for the more controversial environmental and "sin" categories, but also for more mainstream financial (or governance) issues such as excluding companies known to use unusually optimistic accounting and growth projections.

Empirical studies

What does the data tell us? While there are many individual studies showing conflicting results, a number of meta-studies support the conclusion that companies with strong ESG performance also score highly on traditional financial metrics. Here we summarize some of these reviews. One study (Clark et al., 2014) surveyed over 200 sources and concludes that:

- Ninety percent of the studies show that sound sustainability standards lower the cost of capital.
- Eighty-eight percent of reviewed sources find that companies with robust sustainability practices demonstrate better operational performance, which ultimately translates into cashflows.
- Eighty percent of the reviewed studies support the conclusion that companies with strong ESG performance also score highly on traditional financial metrics.

Another paper (Fulton et al., 2012) reviewed more than 100 academic studies, 56 research papers, 2 literature reviews, and 4 meta studies. Their key finding: "The evidence is compelling: Sustainable Investing can be a clear win for investors, and for companies. However, many SRI fund managers, who have tended to use exclusionary screens, have historically struggled to capture this. We believe that ESG analysis should be built into the investment processes of every serious investor, and into the corporate strategy of every company that cares about shareholder value. ESG best-in-class focused funds should be able to capture superior risk-adjusted returns if well executed."

Some results of this review:

- All of the academic studies agree that companies with high ESG ratings have a lower cost of capital in terms of debt and equity.
- Eighty-nine percent of the studies show that companies with high ESG ratings exhibit market based outperformance, while 85% of the studies show these companies exhibit accounting based outperformance.
- The most important factor is Governance.
- Eighty-eight percent of studies of actual fund returns show neutral or mixed results, with the complication that most of these funds are using negative screens. Fund managers have struggled to capture outperformance in the broad SRI category of strategies, but "they have, at least, not lost money in the attempt."

Yet another review (Mudaliar and Bass, 2017) of dozens of studies of the financial performance of impact investing concluded that returns for market rate seeking impact investments were comparable to those of conventional investment portfolios.

A 2015 paper (Friede et al., 2015) examined approximately 2200 academic studies that had looked at the relationship between ESG and financial performance. This study appears to be the most complete and exhaustive overview of academic research on the topic to that date. The results of the study support the business case for ESG investing. Ninety percent of the studies reviewed find a nonnegative relation between ESG and financial performance and the large majority of studies find a positive relationship. Of the three categories of factors, Governance displays the strongest correlation with positive financial performance. It is also noted that in addition to positively impacting fund performance, ESG can uncover nonfinancial risks that may become costly for companies in the future.

Finally, BlackRock compared traditional and ESG-focused equity benchmarks for the period 2012–18. As shown in Fig. 9.4, one could conclude that ESG portfolios offer some protection against ESG-related risks as well as having historical performance comparable to that of conventional portfolios.

	United States	
	Traditional	ESG Focus
Annualized Return	15.8%	15.8%
Volatility	9.5%	9.6%
Sharpe ratio	1.62	1.60
Price to earnings	19.4	19.5
Dividend Yield	2.1%	2.1%

FIGURE 9.4 Comparison of traditional and ESG-focused equity benchmarks by region, 2012–2018. *Source: Author Construction from published source.*

It is important to note that all of these studies are based on historical data, and there are no guarantees that future investment performance will follow these historical patterns. But in summary, the case for ESG investing having comparable financial performance appears to be empirically well founded.

Chapter 10

ESG in managing institutional investor funds

Chapter Outline

BlackRock	188	Goldman Sachs	198
Sustainable investment choices	188	J.P. Morgan	200
Fidelity	193	Betterment	201
PIMCO	194	JUST Capital	203

The dramatic increase in interest in environmental, social, and governance (ESG) investments has led to the creation and popularity of ESG offerings at every major investment management firm. ESG investing solutions are gaining traction with all categories of investors: individual investors, consultants, wealth managers, and large institutional investors, both domestic and around the globe. This chapter looks at what some of the large financial institutions are doing to facilitate these investments. In 2012, US ESG assets totaled $3.7 trillion. The next 4 years saw an average annual growth rate of 135%. A study by the Forum for Sustainable and Responsible Investment (USSIF, 2018) calculates that total US assets under management (AUM) using socially responsible investing (SRI) strategies grew from $8.7 trillion at the start of 2016 to $12.0 trillion at the start of 2018 (Fig. 10.1).

The ESG issues which received the most consideration from institutional investors and money managers in 2018 were: climate change, conflict risk, tobacco, gun control, human rights, board issues, and executive pay. To address these concerns, investment choices have moved significantly beyond simple divestment strategies. There are now equity indexes constructed to mirror the risk/reward profiles of traditional indexes, but also designed to favor companies with positive ESG characteristics. For investors interested in green energy there are also now several benchmark indexes such as S&P Global Clean Energy Index, NASDAQ Clean Edge Green Energy Index, and World Alternative Energy Index. Another interesting index is the MSCI ACWI Sustainable Impact Index. To qualify for inclusion in this index, a company must maintain minimum ESG standards and generate at least 50%

Environmental, Social, and Governance (ESG) Investing. DOI: https://doi.org/10.1016/B978-0-12-818692-3.00010-4
185

SOURCE: US SIF Foundation.

FIGURE 10.1 Sustainable and responsible investing in the United States 1995-2018. *Source: From US SIF Foundation, Report on US Sustainable, Responsible and Impact Investing Trends 2018 (2018), available at https://www.ussif.org/trends.*

of its sales from one or more of the Sustainable Impact categories of nutritious products, treatment of major diseases, sanitary products, education, affordable housing, loans to small and medium size enterprises, alternative energy, energy efficiency, green building, sustainable water, and pollution prevention. Fig. 10.2 shows how closely the financial performance of this Sustainable Impact index tracks a traditional broad-based equity index.

In 2016 the traditional index outperformed the Sustainable Impact Index (7.86% vs 4.64%) but the latter index did better in both 2017 (27.45% vs 23.97%) and in 2018 (−7.41 vs −9.41). Fig. 10.3 gives some more detail on the risk and return characteristics for the two indexes through April 2019.

As these metrics point out, there are now ESG favorable indexes which have historical risk and return characteristics which are quite similar to traditional indexes. Investors have a reasonable expectation that they can achieve benchmark performance and at the same time support ESG issues.

With owners of large pools of capital showing increased interest in ESG investing, it should come as no surprise that the large financial institutions now offer suitable investment products, reflecting not only their own newly discovered ESG sensitivities but also a keen commercial sense for what their institutional customers are requiring. Investment offerings run the gamut from impact investments with less focus on market rates of return to sophisticated, often "quant"-based strategies which take a portfolio approach to ESG-sensitive investing, while maintaining risk and return profiles similar to traditional benchmarks. These latter strategies include ESG oriented mutual funds and exchange-traded funds (ETFs) as well as investor-driven "bespoke" solutions. Here are some examples of the funds offered:

CUMULATIVE INDEX PERFORMANCE ~ NET RETURNS (USD) (NOV 2015 – APR 2019)

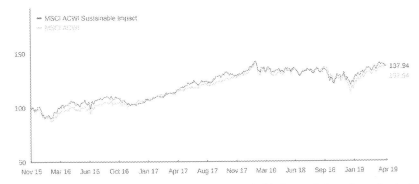

FIGURE 10.2   Performance of the MSCI ACWI Sustainable Impact Index mirrors the traditional broad-based index.

INDEX PERFORMANCE ––– NET RETURNS (%) (APR 30, 2019)

FUNDAMENTALS (APR 30, 2019)

	1 Mo	3 Mo	1 Yr	YTD	3 Yr	5 Yr	10 Yr	Since Nov 30, 2015	Div Yld (%)	P/E	P/E Fwd	P/BV
MSCI ACWI Sustainable Impact	3.62	4.59	3.29	11.39	9.53	na	na	9.87	2.55	18.93	16.41	2.29
MSCI ACWI	3.38	7.48	5.06	15.96	11.36	na	na	9.87	2.47	17.63	15.24	2.33

INDEX RISK AND RETURN CHARACTERISTICS (NOV 30, 2015 – APR 30, 2019)

	Beta	Tracking Error (%)	Turnover (%)	3 Yr	5 Yr	10 Yr	3 Yr	5 Yr	10 Yr	Since Nov 30, 2015	(%)	Period YYYY-MM-DD
MSCI ACWI Sustainable Impact	0.92	5.28	37.48	10.07	na	na	0.82	na	na	0.77	15.88	2018-01-26—2018-12-25
MSCI ACWI	1.00	0.00	2.56	10.11	na	na	0.98	na	na	0.80	17.30	2018-01-26—2018-12-25

¹ Last 12 months   ² Based on monthly net returns data   ³ Based on ICE LIBOR 1M

FIGURE 10.3   Detailed performance characteristics: Sustainable Impact MSCI ACWI mirrors traditional MSCI ACWI.

- iShares Global Clean Energy ETF
- iShares MSCI USA ESG Select ETF
- iShares MSCI KLD 400 Social Index Fund ETF
- iShares MSCI ACWI Low Carbon Target ETF
- Invesco Solar ETF
- Invesco Wilderhill Clean Energy ETF
- First Trust Nasdaq Clean Edge Green Energy Index Fund
- Pax Global Environmental Markets Fund
- Green Century Balanced Fund
- New Alternatives Fund
- SPDR SSGA Gender Diversity Index ETF
- Parnassus Core Equity Fund
- Parnassus Endeavor Fund
- Vanguard FTSE Social Index Fund
- TIAA-CREF Social Choice Fund
- Ariel Fund Equity Fund

Some of the financial institutions sponsoring these funds were early signatories of the United Nations' principles for responsible investment (PRI),
but others have more recently jumped on the band wagon. There are now
over 340 US investment managers who are PRI signatories, with 72 having
been added in 2018. Globally, there are about 1700 investment manager signatories. In the following sections, we look at ESG investment offerings
ranging from those of the largest US financial institutions to those of a
Fintech "robo-advisor" and an alternative index and fund based on the work
of the nonprofit Just Capital Foundation.

BlackRock

BlackRock is the world's largest investment manager with roughly $6 trillion
in AUM. The firm and its CEO, Larry Fink, have aggressively embraced sustainability. Fink famously wrote a letter to corporate CEOs in January 2018
in which he told them that they are responsible not only for corporate profits
but also to make a positive contribution to society. Fink called for action on
specific issues such as employee development, innovation, and longer term
focus but also urged these executives to take a leadership role in making the
world a better place. Had the letter come from an activist outside of the
financial community, CEOs might have at best given a polite response along
the lines of "whatever the importance of social issues, investors want profits." But coming from the CEO of the largest investment manager, the letter
was a bold stroke, one that amped up the conversation in board rooms.
While the letter has been generally well received, passionate supporters on
both sides took strong issue with Fink. Some traditionalists questioned his
authority to instruct investee companies, while social activists attacked
BlackRock for not going much farther.

So, with the CEO leading the charge, BlackRock has fully committed to
sustainability. It believes incorporating business relevant sustainability issues
can contribute to an investee company's long-term financial performance
and are important considerations to incorporate into Blackrock's investment
research, portfolio construction, and stewardship processes. The company
also considers the importance of ESG factors in its own operations.

Sustainable investment choices

As the largest asset manager, BlackRock offers clients a smorgasbord of
ESG choices: green bonds; renewable infrastructure investments; thematic
strategies aligned with UN Sustainable Development Goals; sustainable
ETFs, including the industry's largest low carbon ETF; and one of the largest
renewable power funds. It integrates sustainable investing and ESG considerations in its real assets and global real estate and infrastructure investments. The company also designs and builds customized alpha-seeking and

index strategies, across public equity and debt, private renewable power, commodities, and real assets. BlackRock believes that it is not necessary to sacrifice financial return for social outcomes, that scalable investment solutions can be designed to enhance long-term returns, improve financial outcomes, and contribute to the adoption of global sustainable business practices. As noted in the last chapter, BlackRock provides metrics showing many sustainable investments have historically had similar financial performance to that of comparable traditional investments. For example, for investors focused on limiting potential risks associated with the transition to a low carbon economy, there is the MSCI ACWI Low Carbon Target Index. It is based on the traditional MSCI ACWI Index and includes large and mid-cap stocks selected from 23 Developed Markets and 24 Emerging Market countries. This index overweights companies with relatively low carbon emissions, resulting in a difference in carbon intensity between the two indices of 58%. Fig. 10.4 shows the close tracking of the low carbon and traditional indexes.

For the period 2011 through 2015, the low carbon index outperformed the traditional index. For the more recent period the traditional index did slightly better: 7.86 versus 7.27 in 2016, 23.97 versus 23.59 in 2017, and −9.41 versus −9.78 in 2018. Despite these differences, the two indexes have quite similar risk and return characteristics, both with a Beta of 1.00 and the low carbon index slightly outperforming the traditional index for the period November 30, 2010 to April 30, 2019 (8.87 vs 8.75). Fig. 10.5 has more comparative detail on risk and return of these two indexes.

BlackRock's investment products include mutual funds, ETFs (branded as "iShares"), closed-end funds, other equity and fixed income investments, and multiasset strategies combining different types of assets including stocks,

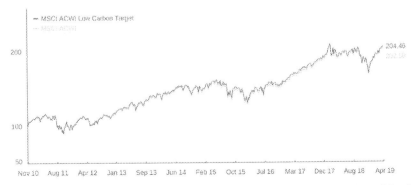

CUMULATIVE INDEX PERFORMANCE - NET RETURNS (USD) (NOV 2010 – APR 2019)

FIGURE 10.4 Performance of the MSCI ACWI low carbon target index mirrors the traditional broad-based index.

INDEX PERFORMANCE — NET RETURNS (%) (APR 30, 2019)   FUNDAMENTALS (APR 30, 2019)

	1 Mo	3 Mo	1 Yr	YTD	3 Yr	5 Yr	10 Yr	Since Nov 30, 2010	Div Yld (%)	P/E	P/E Fwd	P/BV
					ANNUALIZED							
MSCI ACWI Low Carbon Target	3.48	7.61	4.96	16.23	11.13	6.94	na	8.87	2.44	17.83	15.34	2.37
MSCI ACWI	3.38	7.48	5.06	15.96	11.36	6.96	na	8.75	2.47	17.63	15.24	2.33

INDEX RISK AND RETURN CHARACTERISTICS (NOV 30, 2010 – APR 30, 2019)

	Beta	Tracking Error (%)	Turnover (%)	3 Yr	5 Yr	10 Yr	3 Yr	5 Yr	10 Yr	Since Nov 30, 2010	(%)	Period YYYY-MM-DD
				ANNUALIZED STD DEV (%)			SHARPE RATIO				MAXIMUM DRAWDOWN	
MSCI ACWI Low Carbon Target	1.00	0.42	14.68	10.16	11.18	na	0.95	0.57	na	0.70	19.57	2018-03-26—2018-12-25
MSCI ACWI	1.00	0.00	2.56	10.11	11.13	na	0.98	0.58	na	0.69	19.30	2018-01-26—2018-12-25

¹ Last 12 months ² Based on monthly net returns data ³ Based on ICE LIBOR 1 M

FIGURE 10.5   Detailed performance characteristics: MSCI ACWI low carbon target index mirrors traditional MSCI ACWI.

bonds, real estate, and others. BlackRock presents the investment process in a three-step framework as follows:

- First, know what you own. Starting with traditional portfolio analytics, understand current ESG characteristics of your current investments.
- Next, translate into effective action. Based on current investments, set targets to improve the ESG features of your portfolio.
- Then, measure your performance. Track sustainable and traditional portfolios for performance.

BlackRock goes on to offer three investment ideas to drive the investor's goals:

- Thematic
  - Seek to reduce the carbon footprint of your portfolio.
- ESG
  - Incorporate ESG into the core of your portfolio.
- Impact
  - Target measurable impact and consistent returns.
  To address these goals, the firm offers several different investment choices:
- Thematic
  - iShares MSCI ACWI Low Carbon Target ETF—this Exchange Traded Fund tracks the MSCI ACWI Low Carbon Target index and:
    - seeks to maintain global equity exposure while reducing carbon footprint of the portfolio;
    - supports companies less dependent on fossil fuels by overweighing them relative to peers which emit more carbon; and
    - delivers a low-cost, socially responsible investment solution.
  - iShares Global Clean Energy Index ETF—this ETF tracks the index composed of global equities in the clean energy sector and:
    - provides exposure to companies that produce energy from solar, wind and other renewable sources;

- provides targeted access to clean energy stocks around the world; and
- is used to express a global sector view.

- ESG
  - iShares ESG USD Corporate Bond ETF—seeks to track the investment results of an index composed of US dollar–denominated, investment-grade corporate bonds issued by companies that have positive ESG characteristics while exhibiting risk and return characteristics similar to those of a comparable traditional index. Its purpose is to:
    - obtain exposure to companies that have higher ESG ratings through a broad range of US dollar–denominated investment-grade corporate bonds;
    - seek stability and income in a sustainable portfolio with similar risk and return to the Bloomberg Barclays US Corporate Index; and
    - provide a low-cost, sustainable building block for the core of a portfolio.
  - iShares ESG 1–5 Year USD Corporate Bond ETF—this ETF is similar to the iShares ESG USD Corporate Bond ETF but focuses on US dollar–denominated investment-grade corporate bonds having remaining maturities between 1 and 5 years. Issuing companies have positive ESG characteristics while exhibiting risk and return characteristics like those of the parent index of such index.
  - iShares ESG MSCI USA ETF—this ETF seeks to track an index of US companies that have positive ESG characteristics as determined by MSCI analysis of over 6000 securities based on 37 industry-specific issues weighted based on the industry's impact and the time horizon of the risk/opportunity. This ETF allows the investor to:
    - obtain exposure to higher rated ESG companies while accessing US large and mid-cap equities;
    - seek similar risk and return to the comparable traditional index; and
    - use a low-cost, sustainable building block for the portfolio core.
  - iShares ESG MSCI EAFE ETF—this ETF seeks to track an index of large and mid-cap developed market equites, excluding US and Canada, that have positive ESG characteristics. It provides exposure to high-rated ESG equities while accessing large- and mid-cap stocks in Europe, Australia, Asia, and the Far East.
  - iShares ESG MSCI EM ETF—this ETF seeks to track an index of large and mid-cap emerging market equites that have positive ESG characteristics. It provides exposure to emerging market stocks with superior ESG ratings while seeking similar risk and return as a traditional, comparable index.

* iShares ESG MSCI USA Small-Cap ETF—this ETF seeks to track a capitalization weighted index of small-capitalization US equites that have positive ESG characteristics. It provides exposure to companies with superior ESG ratings while seeking similar risk and return as a traditional, comparable index, namely the MSCI USA Small-Cap Index.
* iShares ESG US Aggregate Bond ETF—this ETF tracks the investment results of an index composed of US dollar–denominated, investment-grade bonds from issuers with favorable ESG ratings while exhibiting risk and return characteristics similar to those of the broad US dollar–denominated investment-grade bond market as represented by the Bloomberg Barclays US Aggregate Bond Index.
* iShares MSCI USA ESG Select ETF—this ETF tracks the investment results of an index composed of US companies and:
  - provides exposure to companies which have positive ESG ratings (and excludes tobacco companies);
  - accesses 100 + large and mid-cap stocks with positive ESG ratings; and
  - reflects investors' values.
* iShares MSCI KLD 400 Social Index ETF—this ETF tracks an index which is a capitalization weighted index of 400 US securities that provides exposure to companies with outstanding ESG ratings. It excludes companies involved in nuclear power, tobacco, alcohol, gambling, military weapons, civilian firearms, genetically modified organisms (GMOs), and adult entertainment. The index is designed to maintain similar sector weights as the MSCI USA Index, and the selection universe is large, mid, and small-cap companies in the MSCI USA IMI Index. This index is designed to track performance of the large-, mid-, and small-cap segments of the US market. It has over 2400 constituents and covers 99% of the US market. The index is float-adjusted market capitalization weighted. Companies that are not existing constituents of the MSCI KLD 400 Social Index must have an MSCI ESG Rating above "BB" and the MSCI ESG Controversies score greater than 2 to be eligible. At each quarterly index review, constituents are deleted if they are deleted from the MSCI USA IMI Index, fail the exclusion screens, or if their ESG ratings or scores fall below minimum standards. Additions are made to restore the number of constituents to 400. All eligible securities of each issuer are included in the index, so the index may have more than 400 securities.
* Impact
  * BlackRock Impact US Equity Fund is a portfolio of equities in companies with positive aggregate societal impact outcomes as determined by BlackRock. It seeks to deliver performance against the

Russell 3000 on an aggregate impact outcome basis. The Fund is actively managed, making use of BlackRock's proprietary "Systematic Active Equity Impact Methodology." The principal societal impact outcomes that are currently considered are: corporate citizenship (employee satisfaction), green innovation, carbon intensity, ethics controversy, high impact disease research, and litigation.

* iShares MSCI Global Impact ETF seeks to track the investment results of MSCI ACWI Sustainable Impact Index, an index composed of companies that derive a majority of their revenue from products and services that address at least one of the world's major social and environmental challenges as identified by the United Nations Sustainable Development Goals. Investors in this fund aim to receive global equity exposure while advancing goals such as education or climate change. Target companies employ socially conscious practices and build their businesses with an eye to driving positive change.

* BlackRock Impact Bond Fund. By investing across multiple fixed income sectors and instruments, this Fund aims to provide a combination of income and capital growth. It is actively managed, making use of BlackRock's proprietary "Systematic Active Equity Impact Methodology." The principal societal impact outcomes that are currently considered are: corporate citizenship (employee satisfaction), high impact disease research, greenhouse gas emissions, ethics controversies, and litigation.

Fidelity

Fidelity Investments Inc. is a Boston-based firm with over 30 million individual customers, $6.7 trillion in total customer assets, and $2.5 trillion in AUM. Clients interested in sustainable investments can use Fidelity stock, ETF, and mutual fund screeners to identify desired investments based on ESG characteristics. Other investors may prefer to invest in a fund designed to achieve ESG goals, with risk and return characteristics in line with traditional investments. Fidelity offers these clients several ESG fund choices:

* Fidelity US Sustainability Index Fund—this is a domestic equity fund tracking a benchmark that targets the highest ESG-rated companies. It's designed for investors seeking exposure to domestic US companies with strong sustainability profiles. Its objective is to provide investment results that correspond to the total return of the MSCI USA ESG Index. The investment strategy entails normally investing at least 80% of assets in securities included in the MSCI USA ESG Index, which represents the performance of stocks of large- to mid-capitalization US companies with high ESG performance relative to their sector peers, as rated by MSCI ESG Research. Statistical sampling techniques are also used to attempt to

replicate the benchmark index performance. Factors analyzed include capitalization, industry exposures, dividend yields, price/earnings and price/book ratios, earnings growth, country weightings, and the effect of taxes.

- Fidelity International Sustainability Index Fund—this fund is normally 80% invested in companies in the MSCI ACWI ex USA ESG Leaders Index. This index provides exposure to a capitalization weighted index of international equities of companies rated high on ESG issues by MSCI ESG Research. Statistical sampling techniques are also used to attempt to replicate the benchmark index performance. Factors analyzed include capitalization, industry exposures, dividend yields, price/earnings and price/book ratios, earnings growth, country weightings, and the effect of taxes.
- Fidelity Select Environment & Alternative Energy Portfolio (FSLEX)

    A sector fund investing in companies with a business focus on alternative and renewable energy and other environmental support services.
- Fidelity Sustainability Bond Index Fund (FNDSX)

    A bond index fund tracking a benchmark comprised of investment-grade government, corporate, and asset-backed securities designed for investors seeking income and exposure to issuers with strong sustainability profiles.
- Fidelity Women's Leadership Fund

    This fund invests in equities of companies with a woman on the senior management team, a board composed of at least one-third women, and/or policies that attract, retain, and promote women. Its objective is long-term capital growth.

PIMCO

Pacific Investment Management Company LLC (PIMCO) manages $1.7 trillion with a focus on fixed income products. It is an autonomous subsidiary of Allianz SE. Until 2014 it was headed by cofounder and former Chief Investment Officer Bill Gross who was nicknamed "The Bond King." PIMCO is a provider of mutual funds and other portfolio management and asset allocation services for millions of investors worldwide. Its investment product offerings include core bonds and credit, structured credit, alternatives, real assets, private credit, and currencies. PIMCO's clients include retirement savers, public and private pension plans, educational institutions, central banks, government agencies, sovereign wealth funds, foundations, endowments, and financial intermediaries.

PIMCO believes it is possible to achieve both attractive financial returns and positive change. It manages ESG-focused mutual funds and separate accounts. In 2017 it launched a range of fixed income ESG strategies combining portfolio construction, active engagement, and transparent reporting. Their process consists of three prongs:

- Exclude—restrict investment in issuers deemed inconsistent with sustainability practices. Examples include companies involved in weapons, tobacco, pornography, and coal.
- Evaluate—emphasize investment in issuers with best-in-class ESG practices such as good environmental practices, strong corporate governance, and social policies.
- Engage—interact collaboratively with issuers to improve ESG-relevant practices. Sample engagement issues: climate risk reporting, parental leave policy, and culture and conduct committees. In 2018, PIMCO contacted 147 corporate issuers, 56% in North America, 36% in Europe, and 8% in the Asia Pacific region.

To support its ESG investing, PIMCO has built a dedicated team of seven ESG developers to work with portfolio managers in analyzing ESG data and corporate credit capital structures. Its ESG Technology Process is illustrated in Fig. 10.6:

Fig. 10.6 provides an overview of four proprietary tools:

- ESG ANALYTICS (Data Warehouse)—centralizes internal and external ESG data and allows portfolio managers and analysts to perform analysis on individual bonds and portfolios. It also facilitates customizable reporting, data dissemination, and integration of ESG as a core part of the investment process.

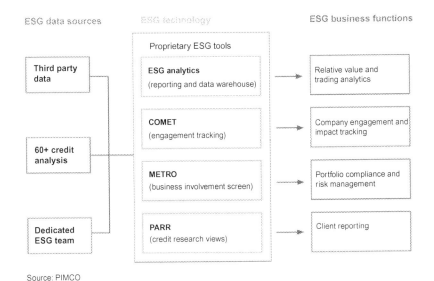

Source: PIMCO

FIGURE 10.6 PIMCO's ESG technology process.

- ESG COMET (Company Engagement Tool)—captures issuer information on ESG activity and impact factors. It also provides reports on ESG engagement priorities and supports tracking progress of ESG engagement efforts, progress milestones, and follow-ups.
- ESG METRO (Business Involvement Screen)—tracks the involvement of issuers in activities such as coal, firearms, etc. It provides a more granular view than that provided by third-party data vendors.
- PARR (PIMCO Analyst Research and Recommendations)—tracks the credit views of PIMCO's credit team, including proprietary credit scores.

Fixed income products fall into four categories: corporates, sovereigns, mortgages, and US municipals. In the corporate bond sector, PIMCO applies its ESG process to green, social, and sustainability bonds that focus on the UN Sustainable Development Goals. It analyzes the alignment of the issuer's ESG strategies with the bond's objectives and the use of the proceeds. It assesses the bond's impact by evaluating evidence of significant positive outcomes, compared with "business as usual" outcomes. Finally, it screens for "red flags" and controversies which could threaten expected positive impacts.

In evaluating sovereign debt markets, PIMCO conducts in-depth, bottom-up risk analysis, assessing financial, macroeconomic, and ESG variables. The analysis includes explicitly scoring the sovereign on several individual ESG factors including the following:

- Environmental
    - Greenhouse gas emissions per capita
    - Fossil fuel usage
    - Renewable energy
    - Notre Dame Country Index
- Social
    - Life expectancy
    - Mortality rate
    - Gender equality
    - Gini coefficient
    - Health score
    - Years of education
    - Years of higher education and training
    - Labor market indicators
    - Perception of corruption
- Governance
    - Political stability
    - Voice and accountability
    - Rule of law
    - Control of corruption
    - Government effectiveness
    - Regulatory quality

Some additional factors allowing for a more granular assessment of environmental risk are:

- Climate transition risk measures, including share of fossil fuels, renewables, and CO_2 emissions. Countries with a large dependence on fossil fuels may experience budget and other pressures.
- Climate physical measures, including assessing the impact on the cost of capital for governments in vulnerable countries.
- Environment and health indicators, including measures of air pollution.
- Natural resources assessment indicators, which consider longer term environmental risks, including deforestation risk, biodiversity decline, overfishing, and ocean health deterioration.

Turning to the mortgage market, PIMCO has developed a proprietary responsible investing scoring model. Its philosophy in mortgages has four objectives:

- Support homeownership.
- Increase access for underserved communities.
- Promote responsible lending.
- Discourage predatory lending.

The fourth category of fixed income investment is the US municipal bond market. The majority of tax-exempt munis have some social or public purpose, but some have greater relevance for sustainable objectives than do others. PIMCO's proprietary analysis ranks each issuer on a range of ESG pillars:

- Environmental
  - Waste disposal
  - Drinking water treatment and recycling
  - Energy efficiency and carbon emissions
  - Regulatory efforts and response
- Social
  - Wealth distribution/poverty
  - Graduation rates
  - Employment profile
  - Affordable housing
- Governance
  - Accreditation issues
  - Management diversity
  - Accounting/reporting philosophy and pension funding discipline
  - Political coordination and budget accord

Each issuer is scored relative to peers within each of the three ESG factors. These separate scores receive weights based on industry relevance, creating a total ESG score for each individual credit (different credits from the same issuer can receive different ratings.) This is an important distinction. PIMCO can assess the ESG focus of individual issues by making use of these issue specific metrics, along with insights from an independent third-party ESG specialist and with consideration of the issuer itself and intended use of the issue's proceeds. PIMCO also is able to develop a qualitative assessment of issuers by virtue of its position as a major participant in the muni bond market.

Goldman Sachs

Goldman Sachs Asset Management (GSAM) provides products and services to support clients who wish to integrate ESG considerations into their investment decisions. GSAM believes that in certain instances, ESG factors can be material drivers of long-term, risk-adjusted returns, and that some clients have more targeted values, priorities, or investment objectives concerning ESG issues. GSAM itself became a signatory of the UN PRI in 2011, is a Carbon Disclosure Project (CDP) signatory, and a signatory to the UK and Japan Stewardship Codes and Green Bond Principles. It also joined the Investor Stewardship Group, the US-based asset manager group focused on promoting US stewardship and governance. GSAM also supports the Singapore Stewardship Principles, and staff have served as advisors or board members to many ESG and impact investing industry groups. In related ESG investment activities, Goldman Sachs has established a clean energy target of $150 billion in financings and investments by 2025. From 2001 to 2018, Goldman's Urban Investment Group has also deployed over $7.6 billion into underserved US communities and has innovated many public—private partnership financing models.

GSAM defines Assets Under Supervision (AUS) as AUM and other client assets for which Goldman Sachs does not have full discretion. As of the end of 2018, GSAM supervised over $17 billion in ESG and impact-oriented client assets, and another $64 billion invested with ESG considerations. GSAM views ESG and impact investments sitting on a continuum of increasing social effectiveness, but potentially diminished financial returns. On the low or no financial return end of the spectrum, clients may wish to undertake concessionary impact investing, which seeks to have positive impact but can result in below market rates of return, or philanthropy which entails donations. While these are not a focus of GSAM, the group can provide advice to interested clients. The other end of the ESG and impact investing spectrum consists of Alignment, ESG Integration and Impact Investing Strategies. These strategies are:

- Alignment
  - Avoiding objectionable exposures while optimizing desired exposures.
  - Seeks to improve ESG quality with minimal financial impact.

- ESG Integration
  - Integrate ESG factors into active investment analysis.
  - Seeks better performance by incorporating financially material ESG factors.
- Impact Investing
  - Invest to generate measurable social or environmental impact.
  - Seeks to have tangible impact and produce alpha in private markets.

To support client ESG and impact investing, GSAM has investment teams and dedicated ESG and Impact offerings in six different product areas:

- Fundamental Equity
  - US Equity ESG
  - Global Equity Partners ESG
  - International Equity ESG
  - Emerging Markets ESG
- Fixed Income
  - ESG Enhanced Separately Managed Accounts
    - Corporate Credit Debt (Investment Grade and High Yield)
    - Emerging Market Debt (Corporate and Sovereign)
    - Securitized Credit
    - Municipal Credit (Traditional and Taxable)
    - Short Duration Liquidity
- Quantitative Investment Strategies
  - S&P Environmental and Socially Responsible Strategies
  - Risk Aware, Low Emissions Strategy
  - Tax aware and factor-based equity strategies with ESG
  - Custom ESG Equity Insights
  - ESG-focused product that provides GSAM clients with broad exposure to US large cap companies with favorable ESH ratings
- GSAM Private Real Estate
  - ESG Integrated, commingled and customized portfolios of real estate assets
- GSAM Credit Alternatives
  - Renewable energy strategy
- Alternative Investments and Manager Selection
  - Customized public and private market ESG and Impact portfolios across asset classes and impact themes
  - Commingled private market impact investing vehicles

In each of these strategies GSAM has integrated ESG and impact capabilities in two approaches: holistic integration and engagement of ESG issues across traditional investment approaches, and for more proactive clients, a dedicated platform to tailor ESG and impact focused portfolios.

J.P. Morgan

J.P. Morgan Asset Management (JPMAM) has been a signatory of the UN PRI since 2007 and is committed to incorporating ESG factors into investment practices, where material and relevant. To that end JPMAM established a Sustainable Investment Leadership Team (SILT) to implement a strategy for sustainable investing globally. SILT's mandate includes:

- promoting internal best practices, including identification and assessment of ESG issues;
- driving thought leadership and innovation;
- deepening and broadening current investment capabilities, including portfolio analytics, measurement and reporting; and
- sharing views and helping clients better understand JPMAM capabilities.

To meet client investment goals in sustainable investing, JPMAM defines its ESG capabilities across four ESG categories of ESG Integration, Best in Class, Values/Norms-Based Screen, and Theme-Based/Impact Investing. Some examples of investment solutions in these categories are:

- ESG Integration—systematic and explicit consideration of ESG factors in the investment decision-making process, such as:
  - equities: US, Global, EM;
  - global real estate; and
  - infrastructure.
- Best in Class—investment in companies based on positive ESG performance relative to industry peers, such as:
  - equities: US, European.
- Values/Norms-Based Screen—avoiding certain companies or industries that do not align with investor values or meet other norms or standards, such as:
  - faith-based investing and
  - tobacco/firearms screens.
- Theme-Based/Impact Investing—investments based on specific environmental or social themes or assets related to sustainability, such as:
  - municipals;
  - aging population; and
  - carbon reduction.

Portfolio managers draw on research analysts, corporate governance specialists, and third-party data to address ESG issues. Investment Directors work with Chief Investment Officers, Portfolio Managers, and Risk Managers to monitor portfolios.

J.P. Morgan has also developed a quantitative tool, called ESGQ, designed to help investors pick stocks that are both consistent with ESG considerations, and that also show promise of outperforming a broader index.

The methodology behind this index recognizes that MSCI and other ESG ratings and scores are slow reacting, typically published only annually. ESGQ makes use of long-term corporate responsibility data combined with faster moving data points from two providers: Arabesque and RepRisk. The analysis then adds momentum indicators to capture changes in sentiment and price behavior.

For ESG conscious clients, JPMAM offers investments in the following asset categories with ESG considerations refined to reflect relevance and specific impact in each asset class:

- equities;
- global fixed income, currency, and commodities;
- private equity;
- global hedge fund solutions;
- global real estate;
- infrastructure; and
- beta strategies.

Betterment

Betterment is an online, automated investing service, one of the more successful of the so-called robo-advisors. Its client demographic skews younger than the established financial institutions discussed earlier, and it can be expected to have a robust ESG offering for these customers. For clients who prefer to invest according to their values, Betterment offers an SRI option. As SRI is a developing field, Betterment recognizes the challenges involved in building an SRI portfolio and considers its approach to SRI to be aspirational and evolving. It has created a portfolio strategy designed to be iterated over time, while maintaining core principles of balanced cost and proper diversification. In developing its SRI Portfolio for customers, Betterment addressed five questions:

- How is SRI defined?
  - Betterment uses ESG factors to define and score the degree to which the portfolio is socially responsible. Its approach has two fundamental dimensions:
    - Reduce exposure to companies involved in nonsocially responsible activities and environmental, social, or governmental controversies.
    - Increase investments in companies that work to address solutions for core environmental and social challenges in measurable ways.
- What are the challenges for implementing SRI today?
  Using quantitative measures to assess ESG performance is an appropriate action in principle, but there are some practical considerations that require consideration.

- Poor quality of ESG scoring data. Some companies disclose ESG data, some don't. And disclosed data may be inconsistent. Betterment uses MSCI data as the best source that's currently available.
- Many existing SRI products on the market have serious shortcomings. There are products that sacrifice desirable diversification and there are others that invest based on competing, often inconsistent ESG issues/themes.
- Few SRI-oriented ETFs have sufficient liquidity. The most active traditional ETFs have median daily dollar volumes in excess of $400 million. The largest SRI funds trade a median of barely $2−4 million dollars per day. ETFs are low-cost pooled investments but entering and exiting ETF positions where there is thin liquidity can result in unreasonably high execution expense or "slippage." This can threaten the viability of the investment strategy. Accordingly, Betterment has selected the SRI favorable ETFs with the greatest AUM for its SRI Portfolio.

- How is Betterment's SRI portfolio constructed?

    To meet requirements for lower cost and higher liquidity, the Betterment SRI portfolio focusses on large US companies with high ESG ratings. But this alone would be overly concentrated so in an effort to properly diversify the portfolio, Betterment's SRI portfolio allocates to additional funds with value and smaller cap companies which do not have SRI mandates.

    Compared to Betterment's core, traditional portfolio, there are two main changes. US large cap stock exposure is replaced with an allocation to a broad US ESG ETF, DSI. Another broad-based US ESG stock market ETF, SUSA, is the alternative for DSI which is utilized by Tax Loss Harvesting + . Second, traditional portfolio allocation to emerging market equities is replaced by a broad-based emerging market ESG fund, ESGE.

    DSI filters out companies involved in tobacco, military weapons, civilian firearms, GMOs, nuclear power, alcohol, and adult entertainment. SUSA screens out tobacco and companies that have run into controversies. ESGE excludes tobacco, certain weapons companies and companies with severe business controversies.

    The main differences between Betterment's SRI portfolios and core, traditional portfolios are:

- Removal of exposures to the US total stock market and US large cap value funds
- Incorporation of DSI in order to replace the US large cap stock exposures. DSI also completely absorbs the allocation to large cap value of Betterment core portfolios.

- Addition of mid-cap and small-cap growth funds in order to account for mid-cap and small-cap growth allocations within total US equity funds.
- Maintenance of allocations to mid-cap and small-cap value funds to account for the mid-cap and small-cap value allocations within total US equity funds and the value tilt of Betterment core portfolios.
- Replacement of a market cap-based emerging market stock fund with SRI-focused emerging market stock fund, ESGE.

  Betterment recognizes the limitations of its approach. For example, there may be conflicts among ESG categories. Some companies which rate poorly on environmental grounds, may still be included because they are rated highly on social and governance grounds. Also, due to diversification requirements, the SRI portfolio still holds exposure to companies that do not necessarily score well on ESG criteria. Recognizing these and other shortcomings, Betterment considers its SRI commitment to be an ongoing process.

- How socially responsible is the SRI portfolio?

  The stocks of many US large cap companies with negative social impact are removed from the SRI portfolio. Using MSCI ESG Quality scores for each company in the portfolio an overall fund level ESG Quality score can be calculated. This score reflects the ability of the underlying holdings to manage key medium- to long-term risks and opportunities arising from ESG factors. Based on this data, US large cap stock and emerging market stock holdings of Betterment's SRI portfolios have an MSCI ESG Quality score that is approximately 40% higher on average relative to those of Betterment core portfolios.

- Are there expected differences in an SRI portfolio's performance?

  Based on historical data the performance of SRI portfolios ended up being about the same as that of core portfolios for the 10-year period ending on June 30, 2017. There are, of course, no guarantees that future performance will follow the historical path.

JUST Capital

The foregoing institutions offer various ESG investment products based on ESG ratings of companies. These rating are obtained through some combination of data provided by external vendors such as MSCI, by internal research staff or from exclusionary criteria such as participation in tobacco, weapons, etc. But one company goes in a different direction: it asks people what they most want to see from the nation's biggest businesses and ranks companies according to which ones are the best at doing the right thing. JUST Capital was founded in 2013 with a mission "to build a more just marketplace that better reflects the true priorities of the American people." The JUST methodology consists of three steps

- A Poll to determine the factors/issues which matter most. The top answers were pay workers fairly, treat customers well and protect their privacy, produce quality products, minimize negative environmental impact, give back to communities, commit to ethical and diverse leadership, and create jobs.
- Evaluate companies based on these issues.
- Rank the largest publicly traded US companies based on these evaluations.

The company defines seven major sets of issues, with an underlying set of 39 component factors. Each of these receives a weight according to quantitative polling of individuals. Each company in the database is then rated on each of these weighted components. These rankings have been used to create an investible index called "JUST US Large Cap Diversified Index" (JULCD). For 2018, 9 of the top 10 companies were technology related, with Proctor & Gamble the only outlier.

The JULCD tracks the JUST-ranked top rated 50% of the Russell 1000. It began trading in November 2016 and consistently outperformed the traditional benchmark index. From inception through the first quarter of 2019, JULCD returned an annualized 14.9%, 120 basis points better than the Russell 1000 return. In June 2018, GSAM launched the Goldman Sachs JUST US Large Cap Equity ETF which was designed to track the performance of JULCD. Through the first quarter of 2019, there were approximately $122 million invested in this ETF.

Chapter 11

ESG in managing college and university endowments

Chapter Outline

Hampshire College   209
  Yale University   212
  University of California   214
  Brown University   215
  Harvard   217
  Columbia University   220
  ESG investing in other schools 221
Organizations providing analysis,
support, consulting, and investing
services for endowment management 222

Commonfund   222
The Intentional Endowments
Network   222
National Association of College
and University Business Officers 223
The Forum for Sustainable and
Responsible Investment   224

University campuses have been at the forefront of action for social change on many issues. So, it would be logical for us to assume that college and university endowments are at the vanguard of the growing movement to include environmental, social, and governance (ESG) issues in investment decisions. And we would be wrong. If the overall percentage of investments going to ESG from all sources is now about 25%, colleges and universities are lagging. A recent study showed that only 18% of 802 reporting academic institutions considered ESG criteria in their portfolio investment decisions. Fig. 11.1 shows the results of the 2018 survey of US College and University Endowments.

There are several explanations for why endowment managers are lagging in the trend toward ESG investing. Some of the difficulties in implementing ESG investment programs are the following:

- Lack of unanimity. Lack of unanimity of board members on whether or not to include ESG factors in investment decisions. Some board members may be open to ESG investing but others share the fiscal conservatism of the general population of investment managers. This traditionalist approach, prevalent in the investment community at large, has resulted in

Environmental, Social, and Governance (ESG) Investing. DOI: https://doi.org/10.1016/B978-0-12-818692-3.00011-6

	Total institutions	Over $1 billion	$501 million $1 billion	$501–$500 million	$101–$250 million	$51–$100 million	$25–$50 million	Under $25 million
Total institutions	802	104	85	88	195	154	103	73
Seek to include investments ranking high on ESG criteria								
Yes	18%	19%	20%	24%	17%	12%	23%	8%
No	66%	51%	62%	60%	73%	75%	60%	71%
No answer	16%	30%	18%	16%	10%	13%	17%	21%
Exclude or screen out invsetments inconsistent with institution's mission								
Yes	21%	21%	20%	24%	20%	21%	26%	14%
No	62%	47%	64%	62%	68%	67%	52%	68%
No answer	17%	32%	16%	14%	12%	12%	22%	18%
Include impact invsetments furthering institution's mission								
Yes	10%	15%	14%	10%	12%	18%	6%	8%
No	67%	50%	59%	71%	71%	72%	68%	74%
No answer	23%	35%	37%	19%	17%	20%	26%	21%

*Multiple responses allowed.

FIGURE 11.1 Percentage of college and university endowments that used SRI strategies in FY18. *Source: NACUBO.*

historical financial performance which is generally at least acceptable to the university community as a whole.

- Differences of opinion on which ESG factors are important. As in American society as a whole, there are differences of opinion on climate change, gun rights, abortion, and on and on. It would be rare to find unanimity of opinion on all these issues in any diverse group.
- Differences of opinion on how best to impact specific ESG factors. And if somehow the endowment investment board agrees that climate change, for example, is an important factor to consider, they can still disagree on the effectiveness of fossil fuel divestment in having an impact on climate change and whether the potential financial cost is worth the potential gain.
- Investability. Can specific ESG issues be accommodated in investment vehicles that are available to the investment managers? Sometimes yes and sometimes no. A separate but related issue is that the typical endowment will have external managers and may be invested in "commingled" funds with other investors. The endowment board can express its ESG goals but may have limited ability to perfectly execute on those goals. Those colleges and universities which manage some of their endowment internally may have more control but may still be challenged to find the right investment.

- Boards have to balance the interests of different stakeholders in the university community. Faculty and/or students may come together to support specific ESG issues, but staff, alumni, political/government figures, and future generations may have conflicting thoughts. And ESG goals themselves can turn out to have conflicting investment implications. For example, technology companies may score well on environmental issues but have abysmal records on women and minority hiring and promotion.
- Concerns about "fiduciary" duty. Some endowment contributions are bequeathed with restrictions. This "donor intent" can limit ESG investment. More generally, as discussed in Chapter 4, Fiduciary duty in investment management, fiduciary duty has several obligations. The latest Department of Labor guidance may provide leeway to consider ESG factors especially in the context of long-run risks, but many board members and managers continue to be reluctant to take an aggressive interpretation of their ability to deviate from traditional investment portfolio approaches.
- Confusion/skepticism about the returns of traditional investments versus ESG informed investments. For fiduciaries, financial return is obviously important, and as we have pointed out, simple divestment strategies have often turned out to yield poor financial performance. And most of the pressure on endowment trustees and managers has been on simple strategies to divest companies involved in fossil fuels, guns, or other "sinful" industries. In fact, it can be argued that aggressive demands for divestment may be causing endowment managers to reject any ESG proposals, even those that would have the potential to achieve ESG goals and also yield market rates of return.
- Inertia. In any organization there is always an inertial force. "We have always done it this way, and it has been successful." The burden is on those who want change to demonstrate that any new approach would yield a better outcome. Some boards are more reluctant to embrace change and require greater assurances that ESG will achieve the promised goals.
- Employment risk. Even successful university endowment managers have faced bitter criticism from parts of the university community. Embarking on a new investment philosophy with a risk of financial underperformance, and with fragmented stakeholder support entails employment and even career risk. If there is a significant part of the portfolio allocated to ESG investments and the portfolio underperforms, the managers will be subject to second-guessing, and possibly getting fired. On the other hand, if the portfolio mirrors traditional benchmarks, results are likely to be in line with those of other endowments and managers can more easily defend their results.

The "Endowment Model" refers to a style of investing with a long time horizon and a relatively aggressive position in taking on risk. This investing

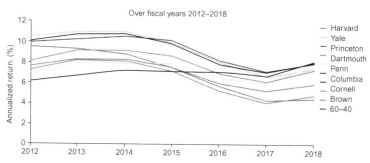

FIGURE 11.2 Ivy league endowment rolling ten year performance. *Source: Analytics and research provided by Markov Processes International, Inc. (MPI).*

style is most associated with David Swenson and his team at Yale but has been widely copied. It entails significant allocation of capital to private often illiquid investments. This style has generally served university endowments well. In 2018 the median return on endowment investments for a broad range of colleges and universities was 8.3%. For the Ivy schools, returns ranged from a low of 9% (Columbia) to 15.7 % (Brown). Looking at investment performance in eight Ivy League schools for 20 years up until Fiscal Year 2018, Ivy investment performance had outperformed a 60/40 equity/fixed income allocation. Given that these portfolios have higher risk profiles, they suffered significant losses during the Global Financial Crisis, only to outperform during the subsequent rebound. Fig. 11.2 shows the performance of the endowments of eight Ivy League schools over the period 2012−18.

Some notable points are:

- While 2017 and 2018 gains were strong, 2018 is the first year that an analysis of 10 year rolling averages showed Ivy investment performance lagging a 60/40 portfolio. For 20 years up until Fiscal Year 2018, Ivy investment performance had outperformed a 60/40 equity/fixed income allocation. And if 15- or 20-year averages are used instead of the 10 year, the Ivies still appear to have an edge.
- Columbia was the only school with gains less than 10%.
- Harvard continues to rank among the low performers.
- Estimated risk in the Ivy portfolios, with their significant exposure to long-term private equity, venture capital, and real estate, remains significantly higher than a 60/40 portfolio.
- The Ivies' Sharpe ratio indicates that their portfolios have a higher degree of risk for the return earned, showing that they are less efficient than the 60/40 portfolio. (The Sharpe Ratio is the average return earned minus the risk-free rate of return divided by the standard deviation of return.)
- Gifts to endowments are tax-deductible to the donors and endowment income has traditionally been tax-free to educational institutions. But the

tax reform package passed in 2018 places an annual 1.4% excise tax on net investment income at institutions with at least 500 students and net assets of $500,000 per student. It remains to be seen if there will be changes in endowment giving or investment to avoid this tax, or if institutions will simply seek to maximize pretax revenue.

These statistics are interesting, but our concern here is not the size of endowment returns, or whether the endowment model is better or more successful than a more conservative style or even passive investing in market indices. We are interested in the consideration given to ESG issues, regardless of risk appetite or public versus private investments. Remember that barely 18% of college and university endowment assets are invested with consideration given to ESG factors, or 81% are invested with more traditional concerns. A typical university investment office policy then might be something like this:

The mission of the investment office is to provide prudent stewardship of endowment assets for current and future generations. To that end the investment objective is to achieve the highest return consistent with a modest level of risk. Risk is mitigated by a distribution across many different asset classes, public and private. Part of the portfolio is managed internally, with several, carefully vetted external managers handling the balance. Income from the endowment supports student financial needs and social services, faculty and research salary and benefits and maintenance of the physical plant. Distributions from the endowment are set by a university committee and will average in the area of 5% of assets. This level provides funding for current needs but maintains the value of the endowment for future generations as well.

This generic mission statement does not explicitly address ESG issues and as such may be representative of policy at many colleges and universities. However, there are several endowment investment offices where ESG and sustainable investing are explicit drivers. Next, we will discuss ESG investing at several of those schools.

Hampshire College

Hampshire College was one of the first to address ESG issues in its endowment investing strategy. It was the first to divest from South Africa in 1976. It divested from weapons contractors in 1982, from fossil fuels in 2011, and private prisons in 2015. In 1977 Hampshire established its initial investment policy, adopted a more comprehensive socially responsible policy in 1982 and updated it in 1994. Students along with college leaders spurred these developments and subsequent revisions. Since 2011, the school's ESG policy has moved to positive screens rather than simple divestments. It looks for companies aligned with the following favored criteria:

- Providing beneficial goods and services such as food, clothing, housing, health, education, transportation, and energy.
- Pursuing research and development programs that hold promise for new products of social benefit and for increased employment prospects.
- Maintaining fair labor practices including exemplary management policies in such areas as nondiscriminatory hiring and promotion, worker participation and education, and in policies affecting their quality of work life.
- Maintaining a safe and healthy work environment including full disclosure to workers of potential work hazards.
- Demonstrating innovation in relation to environmental protection, especially with respect to policies, organizational structures, and/or product development; giving evidence of superior performance with respect to waste utilization, pollution control, and efforts to mitigate climate change risk.
- Using their power to enhance the quality of life for the underserved segments of our society and encourage local community reinvestment.
- Having a record of sustained support for higher education.

So, the above criteria are business practices which the Hampshire Board believes are consistent with the school's broader mission. On the other hand, there are practices which they would not support and are identified as:

- Having significant operations in countries with human rights violations.
- Engaging in unfair labor practices.
- Practicing oppression or discrimination based on race, gender, identity, ethnic origin, sexual orientation, or disability, or promote or profit therefrom.
- Demonstrating substantially harmful environmental practices.
- Marketing abroad products that are banned in the United States because of their impact on health or the environment.
- Having markedly inferior occupational health and safety records.
- Manufacturing or marketing products that in normal use are unsafe.
- Refusing to make their performance records concerning above guidelines available upon reasonable request.

Based on these factors, the College maintains a list of disfavored industries. The list is intended to give further guidance to its policy and is meant to evolve with time, as issues arise while avoiding a "recency" reaction to "the latest concerns expressed on campus." The list of disfavored industries:

- Fossil fuel/carbon producers and related businesses
- The weapons and firearms industry
- The private-prison industry and related businesses

The College's trustees have made several comments over the years explaining its approach: "Hampshire acknowledges that nonprofits have a duty to serve the public —a quid pro quo for tax-favored status...This trade-off strongly suggested to the Board that all of the college's actions should be aligned with its mission. This includes how it sources its food, qualifies and admits its students, and how it invests its endowment."

And: "The policy requires the college to favor investments that do right by the environment, employees and supply chains, and are governed with transparency and fairness."

And this: "Too often the first response of administrators and trustees in rejecting divestment is, investment decisions must be made solely on financial considerations and never subject to moral and political questions. That argument — making money is too important to allow talk of morality, social well-being, or the future of the students for whom the institution exists — is discordant for a mission-driven institution. Organizations can align their investment strategy with their educational and social mission without forfeiting financial returns."

The College has become fully open and transparent about its endowment investments. It reports its individual securities investments to the campus community on a quarterly basis. This complete transparency, tight scrutiny, and stated emphasis on the school's mission over financial gain would lead one to believe that the endowment's investment performance might trail the market. Its modest endowment of $52 million is not big enough to have access to some of the private markets where behemoths like Harvard have made outsized gains. However, "In the 5-year period ending June 30, 2017, the portfolio's annualized return broadly exceeded its Policy Indices, as well as a 70/30 Global stock/bond benchmark." Over this 5-year period, the Total Managed Fund returned an annualized 8.0%, versus a Policy Index return of 6.8% and the 70% MCSI ACWI 30% Barclays Global Aggregate Bond Index return of 7.6%.

Hampshire identifies its challenges and concerns as:

- Limited universe of institutional quality investment vehicles with strong ESG experience across asset classes.
- Size of endowment limiting ability to access certain private investments and actively managed separate accounts.
- Additional time to educate the college community (e.g., students and Board) on ever-evolving ESG issues.
- Transparency of endowment holdings at the level of individual securities
- Concerns about resistance from alumni.

But while there are some challenges ahead, Hampshire sees the following positives in its ESG policy and practices:

- Strong investment performance since realigning the portfolio.
- Allowance for continued and measured approach in monitoring investments and their results in both financial and ESG performance.

- Encouraged greater transparency and thereby stronger governance practices in managing the endowment.
- Facilitated greater dialogue among key stakeholders, including students, staff consultant and the Board.

Yale University

Yale was also one of the earliest pioneers in ESG investing under the direction of its legendary Chief Investment Officer, David Swenson. The size of its endowment, $29.4 billion, is second only to that of Harvard. It recently announced that it would apply to its private market investments the same ESG investment standards that it applies to its public market investments.

The $29.4 billion endowment is comprised of thousands of funds with various purposes and restrictions. Roughly three quarters are restricted gifts providing long-term funding for specific purposes. For the year ending June 30, 2018, Yale's endowment earned a 12.3% return. Over the last 20 years, Yale has earned a market-leading return of 11.8%. Over the last 30 years, it has returned 13% per annum. It credits its success to "sensible long-term investment policies, grounded by a commitment to equities and a belief in diversification." These results once again add ammunition to those who say that consideration of ESG issues need not have adverse financial implications.

Socially responsible investing at Yale traces its roots back to a 1969 Seminar "Yale's Investments" which explored the ethical, economic, and legal implications of institutional investments. This Seminar formed the basis for the 1972 book "The Ethical Investor" which established criteria and procedures for ESG investing. It formed the guidelines for Yale's investing as well as serving as a blueprint for other universities. Yale went on to form the Advisory Committee on Investor Responsibility (ACIR) which would address social responsibility issues of US investing in apartheid era South Africa, defense contracting, political lobbying, and environmental safety. ACIR now provides advice and performs policy implementation for the Corporation Committee on Investor Responsibility (CCIR) which recommends policy to the full Yale Corporation, and is charged with implementing the approved policy. ACIR also advises the CCIR on voting corporate proxies dealing with ethical issues and engages directly with members of the Yale community on ethical investment activities.

Yale has taken substantive actions on several major issues:

- South Africa. From 1978 to 1994, Yale initiated dialogue with companies active in South Africa and eventually divested shares of 17 companies, representing a total market value of about $23 million. In February 1994 positive changes had occurred in South Africa and investment restrictions were lifted.

- Tobacco. In 1994 the Yale Corporation established guidelines for voting in favor of proxies of tobacco companies that:
  - call upon tobacco companies to place health warnings about the dangers of addiction, disease, and death caused by smoking on all advertising and
  - place warnings on promotional items for tobacco products distributed throughout the world;
  - request companies to cease advertising tobacco products to minors, including all uses of the company's brand names and associated symbols for sponsorships;
  - request tobacco companies to support enforcement mechanisms at all governmental levels to prevent illegal sales of tobacco products to minors;
  - request tobacco companies to take actions designed to reduce the health risks to minors; and
  - call upon tobacco companies to report publicly accurate information relating to the ingredients of their products that have probable adverse health effects.
- Sudan. Because of genocidal atrocities in the region of Darfur, Sudan, the Corporation put certain oil and gas companies on the restricted list, due to their operations in the region. As a result, Yale divested from one company.
- Climate change. In 2014 Yale adopted the following proxy-voting guidelines:

  Yale will generally support reasonable and well-constructed shareholder resolutions seeking company disclosure of greenhouse gas emissions, analyses of the impact of climate change on a company's business activities, strategies designed to reduce the company's long-term impact on the global climate, and company support of sound and effective governmental policies on climate change.

  The Chief Investment Officer also sent a letter to all its active Endowment managers encouraging them to account for the costs of greenhouse gas emissions and to avoid companies that refuse to acknowledge the costs of climate change.
- Private prisons. In 2018 the Corporation adopted guidelines for voting proxies to support resolutions related to improvements in the corporate social responsibility of private prisons.
- Assault weapon retailers. In 2018 the Corporation adopted a policy of not investing in any retail outlets that market and sell assault weapons to the general public.

Not all activist concerns have resulted in investment policy changes. For example, it is interesting to contrast Yale's treatment of the above issues with pressure to divest or forgive holdings of Puerto Rican debt. A coalition of activists called on investors, including Yale, to disclose all investments in Puerto Rican bonds, cancel all those held by Yale, and fire investment managers who refuse to sell or forgive the debt. The ACIR concluded in January 2018 that divestment or forgiveness of Puerto Rican debt was not warranted when an investor is abiding by the applicable legal framework in a process in which the debtor's interests are appropriately represented.

University of California

The University of California (UC) endowment totals $12.3 billion. It grew 8.9% for the fiscal year ending June 30, 2018 and has averaged 6.7% for the preceding 20 years. The endowment, along with other UC assets (pension fund, working capital, retirement savings program funds, and captive insurance assets) are managed by the UC Office of the Chief Investment Officer (OCIO). UC's investment decision-making considers sustainability to be a fundamental input, using a definition of sustainable development as "economic activity that meets the needs of the present without compromising future generations' ability to meet their own needs." They phrase the concerns for maintaining financial returns while investing sustainably in the following way: "We must meet the needs of our current operations and the current requirements of our retirees without compromising our ability to serve future students, staff members and faculty. While many of our stakeholders are focused on sustainability from a values perspective, we consider sustainability in risk assessment and due diligence." In eschewing divestment, they say "[We] believe that investing in solutions will have more impact than our decisions about how and when we exit certain markets or assets."

OCIO has identified the following, fluid list of core ESG risk issues:

- Climate change
- Food and water scarcity
- Inequality
- Aging population
- Diversity
- Human rights
- Circular economy
- Ethics and Governance

In order to incorporate sustainability issues into its investment decision-making, OCIO rejects "simply... creating exclusionary lists or applying software applications that determine "metrics" whose scientific bases are not clear or precise. Rather, we need to integrate sustainability as an integral part of our high-performance culture...By considering sustainability in every decision, we can best meet our obligations. ..."

Some explicit actions OCIO has taken are:

- Joining with others to strengthen its voice

  OCIO is a signatory of the UN Principles for Responsible Investing and participates in Ceres' Investor Network on Climate Risk and CDP.
- Putting its capital to work advancing solutions to the world's most pressing environmental and societal challenges.

  OCIO has committed to allocating $1 billion over 5 years to climate solutions.
- Leveraging the University of California ecosystem to access and scale sustainable investment opportunities.

  OCIO is dedicated to collaborating with the UC community to deepen its knowledge of ESG issues.

OCIO further believes it has a responsibility as shareholders to promote transparency and disclosure, corporate social responsibility, and corporate sustainability to help ensure a healthy economy and preserve the ability to achieve sustainable long-term returns. It intends to develop guidelines to align its sustainability beliefs in engaging with portfolio companies in dialogue, shareholder resolution, and proxy voting. It also aims to partner with external fund managers, asset owners, and industry initiatives. OCIO also plans to implement asset class specific manager selection and monitoring guidelines that will: "integrate ESG criteria into manager due diligence, incorporate ESG criteria into manager agreements, and review manager performance against a set of key ESG performance indicators." Other steps include engagement and partnering with stakeholders in the UC community; collaborating with like-minded peer investors; expanding resources and capabilities around sustainable investing; and improve and expand transparency and accountability in reporting sustainable investing activity and thought leadership.

Brown University

Brown University has an endowment of $3.8 billion. Investment management is provided by the Brown Investment Office (BIO) which is subject to oversight from the Investment Committee of the Corporation of Brown University. The purpose of the endowment is to provide financial stability and support to the current and future generations who participate in Brown's educational mission. BIO manages the endowment with a focus on "preserving and prudently growing the endowment's value over the long term." Over a 20-year period, the endowment has had an annualized return of 8.3%. For the 1-year period ending June 30, 2018, the endowment had a stellar 13.2% return.

The Advisory Committee on Corporate Responsibility in Investment Policies (ACCRIP) is a group of students, faculty, staff, and alumni who consider issues of ethical and moral responsibilities in Brown's investment policies. Some major actions and divestments recommended by ACCRIP:

- On December 6, 2010, ACCRIP recommended that Brown not reinvest in HEI Hotels and Resorts based on concerns about labor/management relations and work conditions at HEI-operated properties.
- Sudan/Darfur. On February 25, 2006 on a recommendation from ACCRIP, Brown voted to exclude from the university's direct investments, those companies found to be supporting the Sudanese government in its continuing genocidal actions. In 2012 this policy was modified to approve the use of the Conflict Risk Network's targeted divestment approach. Any company defined by CRN as "scrutinized" is included on Brown's divestment list.
- Tobacco. On May 7, 2003, ACCRIP passed a resolution recommending that tobacco companies by excluded from Brown's direct investments and from those of Brown's separate account investment managers.
- More recent "Actions in Progress" concern fossil fuels, coal and "Justice in Palestine." It is interesting to note that discussions on these issues reflect a range of opinions on the issues and effective actions. For example, ACCRIP voted down a proposal for divestiture of coal companies. Brown's President Paxson stated that: "Among the arguments in favor of divestment are that coal is a serious environmental hazard and that the mining and burning of coal make significant contributions to the problems of climate change and environmental degradation — consequences so grave it would be inconsistent with the goals and principles of the University to accept funds from that source. Arguments against divestment include concerns about the practical difficulties of monitoring which companies should be excluded from the portfolio, as well as the view that encouraging clean coal technologies might be a better approach until there exist viable alternatives to fossil fuels."

In 2017 BIO partnered in establishing the Brown University Sustainable Investment Fund (BUSIF). This fund provides a new giving option for donors, and "embraces Environmental, Social and Governance (ESG) considerations, promoting active solutions to the challenges of climate change, among other environmental and societal concerns, while seeking superior financial performance." Some features of the fund are that it will invest in companies with strong ESG characteristics; it will accept donations of any size, with no minimums; the fund's payout will be at the Administration's discretion with a bias toward sustainability projects; and the fund will not invest in companies engaged in the extraction, exploration, production, manufacturing, or refining of fossil fuels.

Brown formed a Task Force on Climate Change and Business and Investment Practices which was expected to:

- Advise the President on how to align Brown's commitment to environmental sustainability and addressing climate change with the University's business and investment practices and external relations;
- Assess whether Brown's policies and practices in the choice of external vendors and contractors reflect best practices in environmental sustainability;
- Make recommendations on guidelines for proxy resolutions concerning issues of environmental responsibility to assist ACCRIP with the fulfillment of its charge;
- Identify best practices on issues of environmentally sustainable investing for consideration by the Brown University Investment Office;
- Coordinate efforts with Brown's Sustainability Strategic and Planning Advisory Committee; and
- Consider whether a standing committee should be established to sustain and enhance the work of the task force on an ongoing basis.

Harvard

Harvard's endowment at the end of 2018 totaled over $38 billion, the largest of any school. It consists of over 13,000 separate funds and supports a wide range of University activities, most notably financial support for faculty and undergraduates, graduate fellowships, and student "life" and activities. A majority of the funds in the endowment have restrictions directing their use to specific programs such as dedicated scholarships and endowed chairs or named professorships. Roughly 80% of the funds are dedicated by the donor specifically to one of Harvard's twelve Schools. Any appreciation in the endowment's value beyond the amount distributed for these and other purposes is retained by the endowment. The endowment distributed $1.8 billion in the fiscal year ending June 30, 2018, roughly one-third of Harvard's total operating revenue for the year. Over the years, various critics have questioned the proportion of the funds going to undergraduate education versus faculty support versus research. Expenditure decisions have necessarily sought to balance these competing interests, each of which contributes to the reputation and quality of the University. Another often-heard criticism is that there should be a higher payout from the endowment. Distributions have typically been between 5% and 5.5% over the last 10 years, with a range of 4.2%−6.1%. It was determined that this range will provide a steady, dependable stream of income to support current needs while preserving the value of the endowment and the future stream of income for generations to come. To accelerate the rate of payout would benefit the present at the expense of the future. Many endowment gifts have restrictions on their distribution, but most are intended to benefit not just current students and faculty but future generations as well. Undoubtedly, any way the pie is sliced would lead to some parties convinced that it should be done a different way.

Another controversy involving the Harvard endowment concerned the fees paid for its management. In 1974 Harvard set up the nonprofit Harvard Management Company to manage the endowment largely internally. As a $5 billion pool of capital by 1990, it required highly skilled managers who would need to be compensated accordingly. In 1990 Harvard hired Jack Meyer to run the endowment. Through 2005, Meyer and his team outperformed most other endowments and grew total assets to $23 billion. However, he became something of a victim of his success, as his compensation of $7.2 million was completely out of scale with faculty salaries. Amidst increasing criticism, Meyer left Harvard, along with many of his colleagues, to found private investment firms. Harvard now uses external mangers much more extensively. It is not clear if the University actually pays less in compensation to its fund managers now than it formerly did, but the issue is now out of the public spotlight. While there are mutual funds and ETFs which have fees that are 10 basis points or less, hedge funds, private equity, and venture capital funds typically have fees that are based on 2% of assets under management and 20% of profits. It has been estimated that Universities with the largest endowments, Harvard, Yale, Princeton, Stanford, and the University of Texas, all pay their external managers more in fees than the amount they provide for tuition assistance. This may be appropriate where the managers are delivering outsized returns, and the assets are so huge, but the optics are still troubling to many inside the university community.

Harvard is an active member of many climate-sensitive investor groups. It was the first US endowment to become a Signatory of the UN-sponsored Principles of Responsible Investing. Harvard Management Company (HMC) is an active member of the PRI Working Group on Corporate Climate Change Lobbying. Harvard is also a signatory to the Investor Expectations on Corporate Climate Lobbying and is a signatory of PRI's Global Statement on Investor Obligations and Duties. Members of HMC's Compliance team have joined the PRI's Hedge Fund Advisory Committee and Harvard is also a signatory to the climate change program of CDP, formerly known as the Carbon Disclosure Project. Harvard is also affiliated with CERES and SASB.

HMC updated its Sustainable Investment Policy in November 2016. It states that HMC makes a commitment to consider material ESG factors in underwriting, analysis, and monitoring investments. It defines material ESG factors as those that can have direct impact in eroding the economic value of the company's assets, across all asset classes, sectors, and markets. Some of these ESG factors are energy consumption, greenhouse gas emissions, climate change, resource scarcity, water use, waste management, health and safety, employee productivity, diversity and nondiscrimination, supply chain risk management, human rights (including respect for worker rights), and effective board oversight. The specific factors vary by industry in terms of their relevance and materiality. The commitment to considering ESG factors, however, is framed by concern for the endowment's financial strength. The funds have been given to Harvard to "advance academic aims, not to serve other purposes, however worthy." The endowment is conceived fundamentally as an economic resource, "not as a lever to advance political positions or to exert economic pressure for social purposes, which could entail serious risks to the independence of the academic enterprise and the ideal of free inquiry."

There are some, rare occasions when HMC will consider divestment. These are cases where companies' activities are deeply repugnant or unethical, such as perpetuation of apartheid in South Africa, the manufacturing of tobacco products, and enabling genocide in Darfur. These restrictions are applied to direct holdings by internal portfolio managers as well as segregated external holdings. In cases where HMC funds are commingled at external managers with those of other investors, these restrictions are not extended to those entities.

HMC also works closely with the University's Corporation Committee on Shareholder Responsibility (CCSR) and Advisory Committee on Shareholder Responsibility (ACSR) on issues pertaining to proxy voting. Since 1972, these two committees have been active in considering the University's shareholder responsibilities. ACSR is comprised of students, faculty, and alumni and considers shareholder resolutions of HMC investee companies. It presents its recommendations to the CCSR which determines how Harvard votes on these social responsibility proxies.

HMC has a three-pronged approach to sustainable investing:

- ESG integration

  ESG factor considerations are tailored to fit each specific asset class, recognizing that different factors may be material in some industries but not others. Integration of ESG issues continue throughout the investment cycle. HMC uses an operational due diligence framework to ensure that ESG issues are addressed in the analysis of prospective investments in public equity, private equity, absolute return, real estate, and natural resources. After an investment is made, HMC continues to monitor any identified ESG risks and engages with external managers to ensure effective oversight. For direct investments in natural resources HMC conducts, as appropriate, on-site ESG due diligence to identify project related ESG risks and impacts. HMC also is committed to working with third-party organizations, such as the Forest Stewardship Council ("FSC"), which are devoted to encouraging responsible management of the world's forests.

- Active ownership

  Active ownership is an important means to support good corporate governance and has two prongs: engagement with investee companies and exercising the right to vote on shareholder resolutions. HMC works with the ACSR and CCSR to determine positions on voting proxies on social and environmental issues. Shareholder resolutions on governance matters are typically addressed by HMC.

- Collaboration

    As mentioned above, Harvard is an early signatory of the PRI and other groups promoting sustainable investing initiatives. Such interaction with peers is an important part of the process.

Columbia University

The Columbia Investment Management Company (IMC) is a wholly owned subsidiary of Columbia University and is charged with managing the bulk of the University's endowment which consists of approximately 5500 separate funds. Columbia's endowment totaled $10.9 billion at the end of the 2018 fiscal year. It earned a 9% return during the year, the worst performance among all Ivies and short of the University's benchmark. In March 2000 Columbia University established the Advisory Committee on Socially Responsible Investing (ACSRI). Its purpose is to advise the University Trustees on ethical and social issues pertinent to endowment investments. The legal and fiduciary responsibility for the management of the University's investments lies with the University Trustees. As a result, ACSRI recommendations are advisory in nature. The Subcommittee on Shareholder Responsibility deliberates and takes final action upon the recommendations of the ACSRI. In some circumstances, the Subcommittee may bring ACSRI recommendations to the full Board of Trustees for action. ACSRI consists of 12 voting members, representing students, faculty and alumni, along with two nonvoting University officers. The Committee votes on issues such as proxy-voting rights, shareholder initiatives, and investment screening, and makes recommendations to the University Trustees. Formal recommendations and the subsequent action or response by the Trustees are reported. In one action, ACSRI recommended that the University should establish a separate "fossil free" investment vehicle to receive the contributions of alumni who would prefer such investment management for their contributions. The Committee also monitors divest/noinvest lists of companies with operations relevant to private prisons, Sudan, and tobacco. These lists are provided to Columbia Investment Management Company, which verified that as of the end of Fiscal Year 2018, none of the companies on these lists were in the directly held public equity portfolio.

The ACSRI has been consistently active on one issue in particular: divestment from thermal coal. In March 2017, the University's Trustees voted to support a recommendation from the ACSRI to divest from companies deriving more than 35% of their revenue from thermal coal production and to participate in the Carbon Disclosure Project's Climate Change

Program. In February 2018, however, ACSRI declined to support a further measure to divest from indirect holdings in investments with significant earnings derived from thermal coal. These indirect holdings generally arise from investments in funds managed by external managers.

Divestment, as we have pointed out several times in this book, is generally understood to be marginally effective at best. This was well understood by ACSRI at the time they voted to divest from thermal coal, but they felt that the symbolism (symbolic-speech-through-divestment) is important:

> *The Committee is aware that divestment from coal producers would be a form of symbolic speech. Other buyers will step in, stock prices will not directly be affected, and coal producers will not stop producing coal. Nevertheless, divestment from fossil fuel producers has become the subject of an international campaign aimed at university endowments and others as a way to signal the seriousness of the climate change threat: a form of self-restraint that is meant to mobilize a broader public constituency.*

ACSRI (2017)

ESG investing in other schools

We noted in the beginning of this chapter that only 18% of colleges and universities report that they seek to include companies ranking high in ESG criteria in their investment portfolios. But many schools exclude, screen out or divest from companies or industries which are deemed to be inconsistent with the school's mission, ethos, or investment philosophy. Some of that divestment activity is described in the preceding discussion of the investment activities of several colleges and universities. Here we will briefly summarize the actions of a few other schools:

- The University of Massachusetts divested its coal industry holdings in 2015 and in 2016 became the first public university to divest holdings of fossil fuels.
- Also, in 2015, Syracuse University announced that it would "not directly invest in publicly traded companies whose primary business is extraction of fossil fuels and will direct its external investment managers to take every step possible to prohibit investments in these public companies as well."
- In 2019 Middlebury College announced that it will divest its holdings in fossil fuel companies, in a phased program stretching over 15 years.

These are just a few of the colleges and universities who have divested coal and or fossil fuel companies. It is estimated that roughly 150 educational institutions globally have done so.

Organizations providing analysis, support, consulting, and investing services for endowment management

Several organizations provide services and support for university endowment management, including ESG investing. Among them are: Cambridge Associates, Commonfund, The Forum for Sustainable and Responsible Investment (US SIF), The Intentional Endowments Network, National Association of College and University Business Officers, NMS, Responsible Endowments Coalition, Second Nature, Sustainable Endowments Institute, and Wilshire Associates. Here are summaries of the activities of a few of these organizations.

Commonfund

Commonfund is a leading asset management firm, with $25 billion in AUM. It was founded in 1972 with a focus on not-for-profit institutions. It now has 1300 institutional clients, including educational endowments, foundations, philanthropic organizations, hospitals, healthcare organizations, and pension plans. Its Commonfund Institute provides investors with research, commentary, and advice on a range of topics. Some posts relevant to ESG investing which were released in recent years are:

- What are the differences between SRI and ESG?
- ESG Investing becomes mainstream
- Integration of ESG factors in practical steps
- ESG—what is it?
- ESG: sharpening the point?
- From SRI to ESG: the changing world of responsible investing
- ESG and your institution
- Getting started in responsible investing

The Intentional Endowments Network

In March 2016, 77 founding institutions launched The Intentional Endowments Network (IEN), a peer network designed to support endowment investment practices that address ESG and sustainability factors in order to enhance financial returns and align with institutional mission and values. The founding members included: Arizona State University, ASU Foundation, Becker College, California State University, Calvert Investments, Carleton College, Hampshire College, Hanley Foundation, Litterman Family Foundation, Middlebury College, Portland State University, San Francisco State University Foundation, Wallace Global Fund, UBS Asset Management, University of Maine, and University of Massachusetts Foundation. The founding of IEN followed up on earlier forums of higher education, foundation, and nonprofits to address questions such as:

- Why should we consider aligning investments with ESG goals? How does this fit with our mission as educational and philanthropic institutions? Our responsibilities as fiduciaries?
- What are financial costs and benefits of such alignment? Can we get good ROI with such alignment?
- What is happening across higher education and foundations and how can we learn from others who have moved forward in this area?
- How might we discover and assess the range of strategies and products available for aligning investments with ESG goals?
- How might we effectively facilitate a constructive conversation and decision-making process across all our stakeholders?
- How might we keep informed about and support each other in addressing these issues in the future?

Today, IEN is a leading network of more than 150 higher education leaders, their stakeholders, financial industry practitioners, and academics. Members share knowledge and resources in the interest of helping endowments develop best practices and facilitate connections with experts and peers to support administrators and trustees in enhancing approaches to sustainable investing and addressing stakeholders' concerns. Some of IEN's strategic activities are:

- Convening key stakeholders: bringing together senior-level decision-makers and key stakeholders for learning from peers and experts.
- Knowledge exchange: creating venues for education, knowledge exchange and constructive dialogue.
- Creating resources and thought leadership: developing white papers, articles, case studies, and other resources.
- Capacity building: providing opportunities for building capacity around the broad range of SRI/ESG investing and organizational change leadership through various media (webinars, publications, conference presentations, etc.).
- Peer networks and partnerships: working with and through the many organizations and initiatives that are active in related areas to foster collaboration and leverage synergies.

National Association of College and University Business Officers

The National Association of College and University Business Officers (NACUBO) is a membership organization representing chief business and financial officers from more than 1900 colleges and universities. It supports its members through advocacy efforts, community service, and professional development activities. NACUBO's mission is to advance the economic viability, business practices, and support for higher education institutions in fulfillment of their missions. It provides a broad range of resources:

- Conferences, Workshops, Continuing Professional Education, Leadership Programs, and E-Learning
- Research
- Publications
- Advocacy
- Leadership Initiatives
- Content Focused on Specific Topics Research
  - Accounting
  - Finance
  - Student Financial Services
  - Analytics
  - Leadership
  - Tax
  - Endowment Management
  - Risk Management and Campus Security
  - Grants Management
  - Facilities and Environmental Compliance
  - Planning and Budgeting
  - Privacy and Data Security

The Forum for Sustainable and Responsible Investment

The Forum for Sustainable and Responsible Investment (US SIF) has a mission to: "rapidly shift investment practices toward sustainability, focusing on long-term investment and the generation of positive social and environmental impacts." US SIF has over 300 members with over $3 trillion in AUM. Its membership includes investment management and advisory firms, mutual fund companies, asset owners, research firms, financial planners and advisors, broker-dealers, community investing institutions, and nonprofit organizations. Since inception, its goal has been to influence investors to pursue practices which create social and environmental benefits alongside competitive returns. Services to the membership and activities advancing its mission include:

- Cutting edge research on sustainable investment
- Educational resources, such as live and online courses, fact sheets, and guidebooks
- Outreach to federal legislators and regulators to advance policy initiatives
- Media and public engagement
- Networking opportunities through national conferences and other events

In undertaking these activities, US SIF is guided by six core values:

- Commitment
- Knowledge

- Collaboration
- Inclusion
- Accountability
- Optimism

This chapter has summarized the ESG and sustainable investment activities of several College and University endowment investment offices, and some organizations which offer supporting services. As a group, endowments are less concerned with ESG investing than other asset pools but given US and global trends and ESG awareness in university communities, it is likely that there will be substantial increases in ESG considerations in endowment management.

Chapter 12

ESG in managing sovereign wealth and government sponsored funds

Chapter Outline

Transparency issues and concerns 229
Linaburg–Maduell Transparency
Index 232
ESG investing by SWFs 232
ESG investing policy in selected
sovereign wealth funds 235
   Norway's Government Pension
   Fund-Global 235
   The French Pension Reserve Fund 238
   Temasek Holdings Private Limited 239
   China Investment Corporation 240

New Zealand Superannuation Fund 241
Future Fund, Australia's Sovereign
Wealth Fund 242
Middle East Sovereign Wealth
Funds 243
Mubadala Investment Company
(Abu Dhabi) 243
Public Investment Fund of Saudi
Arabia 244
Other sovereign wealth fund
activities 245

As an individual, with skill, hard work and possibly some luck, you will have your income exceed your level of spending. You will save the surplus, and if it becomes a large enough sum, you will seek to invest it for your future needs. And so it is also with governments. At times, governments will find themselves with accumulating surpluses, and will seek to invest for future needs or future generations. Often these surpluses occur somewhat unexpectedly due to, for example, a sudden increase in commodity pricing. "Sovereign Wealth Fund" (SWF) is the term used for these funds which are often of major economic importance to the country of origin. They can also be of major significance to the firms they invest in as well as the country of origin of those firms. These funds are distinct from funds which may be held at central banks for currency stabilization or liquidity management purposes. Some distinguishing features of SWFs are that they usually have a long-term focus, invest in wide ranging global assets and act for the benefit of the state. They are also managed directly or indirectly by the government. Environmental, social, and governance (ESG) investing by these funds is complicated by pressures to show financial returns, by investing

Environmental, Social, and Governance (ESG) Investing. DOI: https://doi.org/10.1016/B978-0-12-818692-3.00012-8

conservatism common as well in other institutional investors and in some cases by local customs and traditions which need to be respected when considering more progressive social and governance issues. That being said, SWFs are making significant investments with an ESG focus, especially in renewable energy.

Sovereign wealth funds have been around for quite some time but became increasingly significant in the late 20th and early 21st century. This is explained in part by the rise in hydrocarbon prices, and in fact oil wealth accounts for roughly half of all assets in SWFs. Other sources of wealth include copper, diamonds, phosphate, increased foreign exchange reserves, government budget surpluses, and pension fund contributions. Fig. 12.1 lists the largest SWFs.

The largest SWF fund is the $1 trillion Government Pension Fund-Global of Norway, which was established in 1990 as revenues from North Sea Oil accumulated to meaningful sums. The top 10 SWFs have a combined total assets under management (AUM) of over $5.254 trillion and account for roughly three quarters of the assets of all SWFs. The total AUM of all SWFs exceeds that of the global private equity and hedge fund industries... combined! And is projected to grow to over $15 trillion in 2020.

SWFs can be categorized as follows (IMF, 2008):

- Stabilization funds. The primary objective is to insulate the budget and the economy from destabilizing swings in the price of a volatile commodity, like oil.

Rankings by Total Assets

Rank	Profile	Total Assets	Type	Region
1	Norway Government Pension Fund Global	$989,934,000,000	Sovereign Wealth Fund	Europe
2	China Investment Corporation	$941,417,000,000	Sovereign Wealth Fund	Asia
3	Abu Dhabi Investment Authority	$696,660,000,000	Sovereign Wealth Fund	Middle East
4	Kuwait Investment Authority	$592,000,000,000	Sovereign Wealth Fund	Middle East
5	Hong Kong Monetary Authority Investment Portfolio	$509,353,000,000	Sovereign Wealth Fund	Asia
6	SAFE Investment Company	$439,836,526,800	Sovereign Wealth Fund	Asia
7	GIC Private Limited	$390,000,000,000	Sovereign Wealth Fund	Asia
8	Temasek Holdings	$374,896,000,000	Sovereign Wealth Fund	Asia
9	National Council for Social Security Fund	$341,354,000,000	Sovereign Wealth Fund	Asia
10	Qatar Investment Authority	$320,000,000,000	Sovereign Wealth Fund	Middle East

FIGURE 12.1 Largest Sovereign Wealth Funds.

- Savings funds. Today's budget surplus might be based on a nonrenewable resource. When the revenue from that resource runs out, future generations will have the benefit of income from this type of fund.
- Reserve investment funds. The assets of these funds are classified as reserve assets, and the fund is established to earn a return on those assets.
- Development funds. These funds support industrial policy or socio-economic projects designed to raise a country's potential future output.
- Contingent pension reserve funds. These funds provide for the government's future pension liabilities.

Transparency issues and concerns

In the early years of the 21st century foreign assets and reserves rapidly accumulated in commodity-based countries and others with growing export economies. Concerns built over the rise in importance of the somewhat opaque SWFs. These funds became increasingly important investors and there were questions raised about their being used to acquire sensitive strategic or economic assets to advance political aims of a state In the United States, national security issues were raised around SWF intentions in several important US transactions such as China National Offshore Oil Corporation's (CNOOC) bid for oil company Unocal, and Dubai Ports World's purchase of US (and European) ocean port assets. As the size of these funds continued to grow, and with limited transparency on their policies and intentions, there was a perception and concern that protectionism could grow, limiting the free flows that make global financial markets work to the benefit of all countries. Additional concerns were raised about the potential for destabilizing financial forces and a weakening of the ability of governments and central banks to provide oversight. Against this background, The International Working Group of Sovereign Wealth Funds (IWG) was established in 2008 (later renamed the International Forum of Sovereign Wealth Funds or IFSWF) to develop a code of conduct for SWFs.

The guiding objectives of this group were:

- To help maintain a stable global financial system and free flow of capital and investment;
- To comply with all applicable regulatory and disclosure requirements in the countries in which they invest;
- To invest on the basis of economic and financial risk and return-related considerations; and
- To have in place a transparent and sound governance structure that provides for adequate operational controls, risk management, and accountability.

The IWG members either implemented or intend to implement the principles and practices, on a voluntary basis, subject to home country laws, regulations, requirements, and obligations. These are the principles (called the "Santiago Principles") and practices enacted (IWGSWF, 2017):

- GAPP 1. Principle. The legal framework for the SWF should be sound and support its effective operation and the achievement of its stated objective(s).
  - GAPP 1.1. Subprinciple. The legal framework for the SWF should ensure legal soundness of the SWF and its transactions.
  - GAPP 1.2. Subprinciple. The key features of the SWF's legal basis and structure, as well as the legal relationship between the SWF and other state bodies, should be publicly disclosed.
- GAPP 2. Principle. The policy purpose of the SWF should be clearly defined and publicly disclosed.
- GAPP 3. Principle. Where the SWF's activities have significant direct domestic macroeconomic implications, those activities should be closely coordinated with the domestic fiscal and monetary authorities, to ensure consistency with the overall macroeconomic policies.
- GAPP 4. Principle. There should be clear and publicly disclosed policies, rules, procedures, or arrangements in relation to the SWF's general approach to funding, withdrawal, and spending operations.
  - GAPP 4.1. Subprinciple. The source of SWF funding should be publicly disclosed.
  - GAPP 4.2. Subprinciple. The general approach to withdrawals from the SWF and spending on behalf of the government should be publicly disclosed.
- GAPP 5. Principle. The relevant statistical data pertaining to the SWF should be reported on a timely basis to the owner, or as otherwise required, for inclusion where appropriate in macroeconomic data sets.
- GAPP 6. Principle. The governance framework for the SWF should be sound and establish a clear and effective division of roles and responsibilities in order to facilitate accountability and operational independence in the management of the SWF to pursue its objectives.
- GAPP 7. Principle. The owner should set the objectives of the SWF, appoint the members of its governing body(ies) in accordance with clearly defined procedures, and exercise oversight over the SWF's operations.
- GAPP 8. Principle. The governing body(ies) should act in the best interests of the SWF and have a clear mandate and adequate authority and competency to carry out its functions.
- GAPP 9. Principle. The operational management of the SWF should implement the SWF's strategies in an independent manner and in accordance with clearly defined responsibilities.
- GAPP 10. Principle. The accountability framework for the SWF's operations should be clearly defined in the relevant legislation, charter, other constitutive documents, or management agreement.

- GAPP 11. Principle. An annual report and accompanying financial statements on the SWF's operations and performance should be prepared in a timely fashion and in accordance with recognized international or national accounting standards in a consistent manner.
- GAPP 12. Principle. The SWF's operations and financial statements should be audited annually in accordance with recognized international or national auditing standards in a consistent manner.
- GAPP 13. Principle. Professional and ethical standards should be clearly defined and made known to the members of the SWF's governing body (ies), management, and staff.
- GAPP 14. Principle. Dealing with third parties for the purpose of the SWF's operational management should be based on economic and financial grounds and follow clear rules and procedures.
- GAPP 15. Principle. SWF operations and activities in host countries should be conducted in compliance with all applicable regulatory and disclosure requirements of the countries in which they operate.
- GAPP 16. Principle. The governance framework and objectives, as well as the manner in which the SWF's management is operationally independent from the owner, should be publicly disclosed.
- GAPP 17. Principle. Relevant financial information regarding the SWF should be publicly disclosed to demonstrate its economic and financial orientation, to contribute to stability in international financial markets and enhance trust in recipient countries.
- GAPP 18. Principle. The SWF's investment policy should be clear and consistent with its defined objectives, risk tolerance, and investment strategy, as set by the owner or the governing body(ies) and be based on sound portfolio management principles.
    - GAPP 18.1. Subprinciple. The investment policy should guide the SWF's financial risk exposures and the possible use of leverage.
    - GAPP 18.2. Subprinciple. The investment policy should address the extent to which internal and/or external investment managers are used, the range of their activities and authority, and the process by which they are selected, and their performance monitored.
    - GAPP 18.3. Subprinciple. A description of the investment policy of the SWF should be publicly disclosed.
- GAPP 19. Principle. The SWF's investment decisions should aim to maximize risk-adjusted financial returns in a manner consistent with its investment policy and based on economic and financial grounds.
    - GAPP 19.1. Subprinciple. If investment decisions are subject to other than economic and financial considerations, these should be clearly set out in the investment policy and be publicly disclosed.
    - GAPP 19.2. Subprinciple. The management of an SWF's assets should be consistent with what is generally accepted as sound asset management principles.

- GAPP 20. Principle. The SWF should not seek or take advantage of privileged information or inappropriate influence by the broader government in competing with private entities.
- GAPP 21. Principle. SWFs view shareholder ownership rights as a fundamental element of their equity investments' value. If an SWF chooses to exercise its ownership rights, it should do so in a manner that is consistent with its investment policy and protects the financial value of its investments. The SWF should publicly disclose its general approach to voting securities of listed entities, including the key factors guiding its exercise of ownership rights.
- GAPP 22. Principle. The SWF should have a framework that identifies, assesses, and manages the risks of its operations.
  - GAPP 22.1. Subprinciple. The risk management framework should include reliable information and timely reporting systems, which should enable the adequate monitoring and management of relevant risks within acceptable parameters and levels, control, and incentive mechanisms, codes of conduct, business continuity planning, and an independent audit function.
  - GAPP 22.2. Subprinciple. The general approach to the SWF's risk management framework should be publicly disclosed.
- GAPP 23. Principle. The assets and investment performance (absolute and relative to benchmarks, if any) of the SWF should be measured and reported to the owner according to clearly defined principles or standards.
- GAPP 24. Principle. A process of regular review of the implementation of the GAPP should be engaged in by or on behalf of the SWF.

Linaburg–Maduell Transparency Index

In order to assess the level of transparency of a SWF, a global benchmark, the Linaburg–Maduell Transparency Index, was developed at the Sovereign Wealth Fund Institute by Carl Linaburg and Michael Maduell. The index (Fig. 12.2) is a summary of the fund's score on 10 principles:

The index provides a score of 1 to 10 with 10 representing maximum transparency and 8 considered a minimum acceptable level. Only three of the 10 largest SWFs have ratings of 8 or above: Government Pension Fund-Global in Norway, Temasek, and Hong Kong Monetary Authority Investment Portfolio. China Investment Corporation and GIC Private Limited have index ratings of 7, and the remaining SWFs in the top 10 are rated 6 and lower. Clearly, aside from a small group using best practices, SWFs need to continue to make strides to improve transparency.

ESG investing by SWFs

What is interesting from the perspective of ESG investing is that a high percentage of these funds are from countries which themselves would score low

Point	Principles of Linaburg-Maduell Transparency Index
+1	Fund provides history including reason for creation, origins of wealth, and government ownership structure
+1	Fund provides up-to-date independently audited annual reports
+1	Fund provides ownership percentage of company holdings, and geographic locations of holdings
+1	Fund provides total portfolio market value, returns, and management compensation
+1	Fund provides guidelines in reference to ethical standards, investment policies, and enforcer of guidelines
+1	Fund provides clear strategies and objectives
+1	If applicable, the fund clearly identifies subsidiaries and contact information
+1	If applicable, the fund identifies external managers
+1	Fund manages its own web site
+1	Fund provides main office location address and contact information such as telephone and fax

Developed by Carl Linaburg and Michael Maduell

FIGURE 12.2   Principles of Linaburg-Maduell Transparency Index.

on many of the individual ESG issues. Many of these funds originate in the Middle East and Asia where ESG investing, and corporate disclosure of ESG issues, has lagged other regions, especially Europe. Many of these countries are producers and exporters of hydrocarbons and are countries where social and cultural factors have not developed the highest standards of treatment of women and minorities and where institutional governance greatly lags best practices. However, at least for the oil exporters, investing in an increasingly lower carbon world can provide a hedge against falling future income if revenue from oil sales declines. And the long-term focus of these funds makes them more receptive to the long-term opportunities and risk mitigation potential of some ESG investments. With this in mind, it may be less surprising, then, that to address climate change issues and to contribute to long-term value creation, in 2017 SWFs from Abu Dhabi, Kuwait, New Zealand, Norway, Saudi Arabia, and Qatar came together to announce a new One Planet SWF Working Group. The Group committed to develop an ESG Framework to address climate change issues, including the development of methods and indicators that can inform investors' priorities as shareholders and participants in financial markets. The Framework is designed to accelerate the integration of climate change analysis into the management of these large, long-term, and diversified asset pools.

To improve the resilience and sustainable growth of these pools, the Framework aims to help SWFs to:

- foster a shared understanding of key principles, methodologies, and indicators related to climate change;
- identify climate-related risks and opportunities in their investments; and
- enhance their investment decision-making frameworks to better inform their priorities as investors and participants in financial markets.

The Framework has three Principles—Alignment, Ownership, and Integration—and several Subprinciples:

- Principle 1: Alignment

  SWFs build climate change considerations, which are aligned with the SWFs' investment horizons, into decision-making.
    - Principle 1.1. SWFs recognize that climate change will have an impact on financial markets.
    - Principle 1.2. Due to their long-term investment horizon and diverse investment portfolios, SWFs recognize that climate change presents financial risks and opportunities which should be incorporated into the investment framework.
    - Principle 1.3. In accordance with their respective mandates, SWFs should report on their approach to climate change.
- Principle 2: Ownership

  SWFs encourage companies to address material climate change issues in their governance, business strategy and planning, risk management, and public reporting to promote value creation.
    - Principle 2.1. SWFs expect company boards to understand the consequences of their business practices for climate emissions and to set clear priorities for the company to address relevant climate change issues.
    - Principle 2.2. SWFs expect companies to plan for relevant climate scenarios and incorporate material climate risks in their strategic planning, risk management, and reporting.
    - Principle 2.3. SWFs encourage public disclosure by companies to understand how climate change may affect their future performance, and what actions they are taking.
    - Principle 2.4. SWFs should encourage the development and adoption of agreed standards and methods that promote the disclosure of material climate-related data.
- Principle 3: Integration

  SWFs should integrate the consideration of climate change related risks and opportunities into investment management to improve the resilience of long-term investment portfolios.

- Principle 3.1. SWFs should identify, assess, and manage portfolio risks generated by the expected transition to a low-emissions economy and from the potential physical impacts of climate change.
- Principle 3.2. SWFs can draw on, and develop, analytical tools to inform portfolio allocation and investment decisions.
- Principle 3.3. SWFs should consider investment opportunities that arise from the global effort to address climate change.
- Principle 3.4. SWFs should consider approaches to reducing portfolio exposure to climate-related risks.
- Principle 3.5. SWFs can promote research on issues related to the financial implications of climate change.

ESG investing policy in selected sovereign wealth funds

As with other types of investor, SWFs have different levels of commitment and different motivations for incorporating ESG issues in their investment decision-making. Some are concerned about the financial risks entailed by investing in companies with poor performance on environmental and governance issues. Some are motivated by the fund's mission or greater purpose to go beyond just financial gain in providing for the country's population. And some are more concerned with the long view and the impact ESG factors will have on future generations.

Let's now look at what several individual SWFs are doing in term of ESG investing.

Norway's Government Pension Fund-Global

Norway's Government Pension Fund-Global was established in 1990 to manage revenues from Norway's North Sea oil sales. In 2019 its AUM was roughly $1 trillion, and it is the largest of the world's SWF (although Saudi Arabia has announced plans to increase their Public Investment Fund to $2 trillion in coming years). This fund is sometimes called the "Oil Fund" to distinguish it from another, older Government Pension Fund. It is managed by Norges Bank Investment Management (NBIM) on behalf of the Ministry of Finance which owns the fund for the benefit of the Norwegian people. Roughly 65% of the fund is invested in public equities, with the remainder in fixed income and real estate. The fund owns roughly 1.4% of all global public equities, in over 9000 companies in 73 countries. The fund was established to allow the Norwegian government sufficient revenue to adapt to a world of lower oil prices or to ride out an economic recession. It also has a role in easing any impacts from an ageing population. It has two purposes: provide for oil revenues to be available for future generations, and to provide the government flexibility in fiscal policy. Large increases in revenue could have an inflationary impact if they were to flood into a relatively small regional economy. The fund provides a buffer so these impacts can be dampened and, conversely, it can support fiscal stimulus in weaker times. It invests for the long term. The fund's objective is to achieve a long-term real rate of return in excess of the rate of growth of the world's economy. It is a globally diversified, long term investor contributing to a sustainable economy and stable business climate. And at the same time, it encourages businesses to improve social and environmental standards.

The fund's approach to ESG is in the context of risk. It seeks to earn the highest possible return with moderate risk, and it recognizes that an investee company's impact on society and the environment can affect that company's profitability and the fund's return on investment. As a long-term investor the fund depends on sustainable growth, well-functioning markets, and good corporate governance. It is a signatory of the UN Principles for Responsible Investment (PRI) and contributes to the further development of these and other international standards. It engages regularly with international organizations, regulators and standards setters, industry partners, and academics. It sets its own priorities for and expectations of companies, seeing good corporate governance as a premise for responsible business practices. It has developed comprehensive expectation positions for investee companies on: children's rights; climate change; water management; human rights; tax and transparency; anticorruption; and ocean sustainability. The major categories of expectations on ocean sustainability, for example, are that companies will:

- Integrate ocean sustainability into strategy
- Integrate material ocean-related risks into risk management
- Disclose material priorities and report associated metrics and targets
- Act responsibly and transparently on ocean-related governance

Despite the potential for lower returns and questionable effectiveness, the fund has divested or chosen not to invest in several areas. It has developed criteria for companies in specific sectors and countries that it chooses not to invest in. The Ministry of Finance provides guidelines for observation or exclusion of companies which:

- produce weapons that under normal use violate basic humanitarian principles
- produce tobacco
- sell weapons or military material to certain excluded states
- mining companies and power producers that receive 30% or more of their revenue from thermal coal, or base 30% or more of their business on thermal coal (with some qualifications)
- Observation or exclusion can be decided for companies where there is an unacceptable risk of the company contributing to or being responsible for:
  - gross or systematic human rights violations such as murder, torture, deprivation of liberty, forced labor, and the worst forms of child labor

* serious violations of individuals' rights in war or conflict situations
* environmental damage
* actions or omissions that, at an aggregate company level, to an unacceptable degree lead to greenhouse gas emissions
* gross corruption
* other particularly gross violations of basic ethical standards

The fund, through NBIM its manager, has had a complicated, nuanced approach to oil and gas investments. The source of the fund's wealth, of course, is Norway's sale of oil from the North Sea. It, therefore, depends on the successful operation of the exploration and production companies operating there, as well as downstream shipping, refining, and distribution systems. On the other hand, investing in assets with less correlation to oil and gas would help diversify the fund, although it should be noted that oil price changes have historically accounted for a small part of the risk in energy share prices. Also, support for divesting fossil fuels has been made on environmental grounds.

The Ministry of Finance's assessment of energy stocks in the fund's portfolio is weighted by the following considerations (Meld, 2019):

* The Norwegian economy is vulnerable to oil price risk.
* The oil price risk has been significantly reduced over time, and the capacity to absorb such risk is now high.
* An exclusion of the energy stocks in the GPFG will serve to further reduce the oil price risk, but the effect appears to be limited.
* Sector level classifications of companies are inaccurate for reducing oil price risk.
* To exclude exploration and production companies from the GPFG appears to be a more accurate means to reduce oil price risk.
* Climate risk is an important financial risk factor for the GPFG. (The Ministry goes on to note that climate risk must be assessed and managed at the company level. NBIM currently has a broad set of tools for managing climate risk, including corporate governance initiatives and risk-based divestment and a conduct-based climate criterion has also been established in the guidelines for observation and exclusion.)
* Broad support for the financial objective of the GPFG is important but cannot be taken for granted. If the energy sector is omitted from the GPFG on the grounds that this will promote climate policy objectives, it may undermine the financial objective of the Fund and impair its contributions to future welfare.

It was also recognized that some of the largest integrated oil companies are also some of the largest investors in renewable energy, and that continued investment in these companies can be important to the future of renewables. In order to reduce its concentration and exposure to a potential drop in oil prices, it was announced in March 2019 that the fund plans to gradually sell the bulk of its holdings in oil and gas exploration and production companies. This is a long list of 134 companies accounting for more than 1% of the fund's trillion-dollar holdings. But it announced it would retain shares of companies with investments in renewable fuels. This included BP, Exxon Mobil, and Shell among others. While the move was clearly justified as an effort to hedge the country's wealth against a substantive drop in hydrocarbon prices, there is a strong element of environmentalism in it as well. It should be noted that many press reports inaccurately stated that Norway would be divesting its holdings of fossil fuel companies, but even a casual reading of NBIM and the Ministry of Finance statements show this is not the case.

The French Pension Reserve Fund

The French Pension Reserve Fund (Fond De Reserve Pour Les Retraits or FRR) has a mission "to invest and optimize returns on the monies entrusted to it by the public authorities on behalf of the community with the aim of financing the pension system." Since 2003, FRR has been required to show a firm commitment in the area of responsible investment. It believes that ESG factors need to be integrated into its decisions because these criteria can have a material impact on company valuations and the returns to the fund. A second reason for ESG considerations is the concern about externalities these factors generate for an industry or the economy as a whole. An earlier approach to ESG investing by the fund was a "best in class" approach which promoted best practices of social and environmental responsibility among large European listed companies. More recently, the fund has identified four priorities:

- Priority 1: Integrating ESG factors into asset management. The aim is to broadcast FRR's values by defining a limited number of objective and measurable ESG criteria.
- Priority 2: Conducting social responsibility. FRR extends its monitoring activities beyond equities and bonds of the largest companies, to emerging markets and small- and mid-cap companies. It also will restrict its investment in tax havens.
- Priority 3: Exercise of the FRR's voting rights. FRR's socially responsible investment strategy entails an active policy of proxy voting.
- Priority 4: Contribution to research on Responsible Investment and support for international initiatives. FRR is an active participant in the UN PRI, the Carbon Disclosure Project (CDP), CDP Water, Extractive Industries Transparency Initiative (EITI), and International Corporate Governance Network (ICGN).

FRR also has continued a policy of exclusion of companies in certain industries. Recognizing the adverse health impacts of tobacco, and believing that dialogue will be ineffective, FRR has decided to exclude the tobacco industry from its portfolio. It also has implemented an ambitious project to limit its portfolio's greenhouse gas emissions by excluding companies who have more than 20% of their revenue attributable to thermal coal or which generate more than 20% of their electricity, steam, or heat production from coal.

Temasek Holdings Private Limited

Temasek was founded in 1974. Its sole shareholder is the Ministry of Finance of the Government of Singapore. It has headquarters in Singapore and offices around the globe. Singapore became an independent country in 1965 and the Singapore Government became the owner of several important companies such as Singapore Airlines, Singapore Telecommunications, and others. Temasek was created to hold and manage these assets on a commercial basis and to contribute to Singapore's economic development, industrialization, and financial diversification. Temasek has the distinction of having a woman, Ho Ching, as its CEO. (She carries additional influence being married to Singapore's Prime Minister.) In 2019 Temasek had AUM of approximately $375 billion. It is now an important global investor, and its investment strategy has four themes:

- Transforming Economies
    Tapping the potential of transforming economies like China, India, South East Asia, Latin America, and Africa through investments in sectors such as financial services, infrastructure, and logistics.
- Growing Middle Income Populations
    Leveraging growing consumer demands through investments in sectors such as telecommunications, media and technology, and consumer and real estate.
- Deepening Comparative Advantages
    Seeking out economies, businesses, and companies with distinctive intellectual property and other competitive advantages.
- Emerging Champions
    Investing in companies with a strong home base, as well as companies at inflection points, with the potential to be regional or global champions.

Temasek's ESG strategy begins with the following statement from Chairman Lim Boon Heng: "To succeed as an investor is not an end in itself. Ultimately, that success must be translated into a better and more sustainable world, with more opportunities and a kinder place for people and communities." Temasek is a signatory of the UN's Sustainable Development Goals, and is working toward an "ABC" world of:

- Active economy:
  - Productive jobs
  - Sustainable cities
  - Fulfilling lives
- Beautiful society
  - Resilient individuals
  - Inclusive communities
  - Just societies
- Clean earth
  - Fresh air
  - Clean water
  - Cool world

Temasek believes that effective management of ESG factors will lead to superior long-term results. It considers how sustainability will affect company performance when analyzing investments, engages in sustainability discussions with investee companies and participates in international discussions on ESG investing best practices. Here are some specific ESG related actions:

- The fifth Ecosperity conference, exploring the topics of food, education, and healthcare, was held on June 5, 2018.
- Temasek partnered in Unleash, an innovation lab for 1000 young people to co-create solutions for the Sustainable Development Goals.
- Partnered Singtel to raise awareness for electronic waste.
- Supported EcoBank to collect used toys, clothing, books and homeware for charity.
- Temasek is also involved in substantial development of solar energy through investments in Sembcorp Industries and the wholly owned SP Group.
- Temasek is an investor in NIO, a China based startup active in the Electrical Vehicle market in China.
- The company has six foundations supporting various community causes and needs.

China Investment Corporation

In 2007 the China Investment Company (CIC) was established to manage the People's Republic of China's massive and rapidly growing foreign reserves. CIC has three subsidiaries, CIC International Co., Ltd. (CIC International), CIC Capital Corporation (CIC Capital), and Central Huijin Investment Ltd. (Central Huijin). To fulfill its mandate, CIC seeks to maximize the return of long-term investments; to explore ways to forge a platform for diversified investment of China's foreign exchange; to achieve higher long-term returns within acceptable risk tolerance through a balanced allocation of public-market instruments and long-term assets; to preserve and increase the value of state-owned financial assets, by constantly exploring ways to engage in the management of key state-owned financial institutions as a shareholder; and *to review, inherit, and develop values and rules to facilitate sustainable development.* (Emphasis added.) It is committed to observing the Santiago Principles and its code of conduct framework. Its investment portfolio in 2017 consisted of Public Equity (43.6%), Alternative assets (39.3%), Fixed income (19.9%), and Cash and others (1.2%).

ESG investing in China, as in Asia as a whole, has been gaining ground, but lags other regions, especially Europe. Investor focus is still on more traditional short-term financial gain. ESG reporting by companies has increased but seems to have plateaued. Social and governance issues are infrequently considered. But at least some environmental issues have garnered attention. In 2016 the Global Carbon Project ranked China as the top carbon dioxide emitter in the world, releasing 10,151 metric tons of carbon dioxide in that year. (In comparison, the US came in second at 5312 metric tons of carbon dioxide, while India took third place with 2431 metric tons of carbon dioxide.) It's estimated that air pollution causes about 1.6 million deaths annually in China. Recognizing the severity of the problem, in 2018, the National People's Congress agreed to a massive spending outlay to cut pollution and aggressively increase renewables. Expansion of green finance, electric vehicles, and sustainable agricultural practices are all expected to contribute to environmental improvements and are attracting investment interest.

There does not appear to be a strategic integration of ESG issues in CIC's investment policy. However, there are several projects that can be seen to further ESG goals. CIC has expressed a commitment to improve governance and transparency, and one important effort of CIC is poverty alleviation within China. The approach involves four steps: first, projects are selected based on the availability of local resources. Poverty alleviation is having its greatest effect where local resources that can give an area an advantage are used to develop unique industries, which in turn translates into economic advantage. Second, a competent and professional team dedicated to project management conducts on-site inspections and supervision. Third, fund deployment is strictly supervised to ensure funds are used for their intended purposes. Fourth, strict bidding procedures for engineering projects are followed and there is an inspection system to ensure project quality.

With growing recognition of the importance of ESG factors to long-term investments, it seems likely that CIC's investment policy will evolve to more fully incorporate ESG analysis and CIC will become an important investor in ESG-favorable assets.

New Zealand Superannuation Fund

The New Zealand Superannuation Fund was created in 2001 to manage retirement and pension benefits to the population aged 65 and over. It is a long-term, growth-oriented, global investment fund. Its mandate is to manage and administer the fund in a manner consistent with:

- best practice portfolio management;
- maximizing return without undue risk to the Fund as a whole; and
- avoiding prejudice to New Zealand's reputation as a responsible member of the world community.

The fund believes that ESG factors are material to long-term investment returns and to New Zealand's reputation in the world community. ESG factors are therefore integrated into the fund's investment decisions and monitoring of external mangers. Its investment policies are closely aligned with the UN's PRI. In 2016 the fund launched a comprehensive climate change strategy which has four parts:

- Reduce the fund's exposure to fossil fuel reserves and carbon emissions.
- Analyze climate change implications in investment research and allocations.
- Engage with companies and investment managers on relevant proxy voting.
- Search for new investment opportunities in alternative energy, energy efficiency, and transformational infrastructure.

While the fund prefers engagement, companies that are directly involved in the following activities are excluded from the Fund:

- the manufacture of cluster munitions,
- the manufacture or testing of nuclear explosive devices,
- the manufacture of antipersonnel mines,
- the manufacture of tobacco,
- the processing of whale meat,
- recreational cannabis, and
- the manufacture of civilian automatic and semiautomatic firearms, magazines or parts.

Future Fund, Australia's Sovereign Wealth Fund

The Future Fund was established in 2006 to invest for the benefit of future generations of Australians and now manages a total of six public asset funds. The fund believes that effective management of ESG risks and opportunities supports its requirement to maximize returns. It notes that relevant ESG factors vary by industry and across asset classes but can include any of the following: occupational safety, human and labor rights, climate change, sustainable supply chain, corruption, and bribery. It integrates ESG factors in researching investments and in appointing investment managers. It considers ESG issues in its proxy voting decisions, and also engages with investee companies either directly or with investment managers. Finally, it excludes companies which manufacture tobacco products or military weapons related to Conventions or Treaties ratified by Australia.

Middle East Sovereign Wealth Funds

Twenty of the eighty largest SWFs are located in the oil producing countries of the Middle East. The largest of them are:

- Abu Dhabi Investment Authority
- Saudi Arabian Monetary Authority (SAMA)
- Kuwait Investment Authority
- Qatar Investment Authority
- Investment Corporation of Dubai
- Public Investment Fund (Saudi Arabia)
- Abu Dhabi Investment Council
- International Petroleum Investment Company (Abu Dhabi)
- Mubadala Investment Company (Abu Dhabi)
- National Development Fund of Iran

These funds have similarities but also some differences. The source of their funding has been the escalation in oil prices and growth in oil export revenues. The funds' purposes include recycling oil payments into the world's economy, providing for future generations and attempts at diversifying away from the host country's narrow reliance on hydrocarbons. But there are also differences in focus and needs, based on the different sizes of these economies, needs of their populations and consequent budgetary requirements.

As mentioned earlier, four of these funds, the Abu Dhabi Investment Authority, the Kuwait Investment Authority, the Public Investment Fund of the Kingdom of Saudi Arabia, and the Qatar Investment Authority, have joined the New Zealand Superannuation Fund and Norges Bank Investment Management (NBIM) in forming the One Planet Sovereign Wealth Fund Working Group. But others of these Middle Eastern SWFs also have significant ESG investments. We next look at the specifics of some of these funds.

Mubadala Investment Company (Abu Dhabi)

Mubadala Investment Company PJSC was established in January 2017 with the merger of the Mubadala Development Company and the International Petroleum Investment Company. It is wholly owned by the government of Abu Dhabi. Its mandate is to facilitate the diversification of the Abu Dhabi economy, managing long term, capital-intensive investments designed to deliver financial and social benefits to the citizenry. Mubadala is one of the largest investors in renewable energy. It is the 100% owner of Masdar, a global leader in renewable energy and sustainable urban development. Through Masdar, Mubadala is a 20% owner of the London Array which is a 175 turbine 630-Megawatt offshore wind farm located 20 km off the Kent coast in the outer Thames Estuary in the United Kingdom. It is the second largest offshore wind farm on Earth. Other projects include Masdar City, a planned community designed to be a hub for clean-tech companies and home of the International Renewable Energy Agency. In total Masdar has invested over $2.7 billion in renewable energy projects in the UAE, Jordan, Mauritania, Egypt, Morocco, the UK, Serbia, and Spain. Here are some other Masdar investments:

- Shams 1. Masdar has an 80% interest in Shams 1, one of the world's largest Concentrated Solar Power (CSP) plants and the first of its kind in the Middle East and North Africa region.
- CCUS (Abu Dhabi). The Carbon Capture, Usage and Storage (CCUS) project captures up to 800,000 tons of Carbon Dioxide (CO_2) per annum from current emissions. The CO_2 is transported via a pipeline network and injected into reservoirs for enhanced oil recovery. The injected CO_2 will remain geologically stored in the reservoirs.
- Mohammed Bin Rashid Al Maktoum Solar Park in Dubai (under development). In June 2016, a Masdar-led consortium was selected to develop the 800 MW third phase of the Mohammed Bin Rashid Al Maktoum Solar Park in Dubai.

Public Investment Fund of Saudi Arabia

The Public Investment Fund of Saudi Arabia (PIF) was established in 1971 to provide financing support for projects of strategic significance to the national economy. Ownership of Saudi Aramco is expected to be transferred to PIF. Although its public equity offering was delayed in 2018, the transferred Saudi Aramco stake would make PIF the world's largest SWF with over $2 billion in AUM.

PIF has four stated objectives:

- Grow the assets of the Fund
- Unlock new sectors
- Build strategic economic partnerships
- Localize cutting-edge technology and knowledge

PIF has provided significant funding for industries within the Kingdom and more recently has been an active investor globally, both directly and through participation in other funds. Some significant, high profile investments:

- Stakes in UBER, Tesla, Magic Leap, and Noon
- Investments in General Electric, Lockheed Group, and Blackstone

- Thirty-eight percent stake in South Korea's Posco Engineering & Construction Co.
- Stake in AccorInvest
- An announced plan to invest $45 billion in Softbank's Vision Fund focused on tech
- Plan to invest $40 billion in US infrastructure
- Russian Direct Investment Fund
- Saudi-Jordanian Investment Company Initiative
- French Private Equity Fund
- NEOM, a $500 billion planned city fueled by renewables to be built in the far north west of Saudi Arabia
- The Red Sea tourist development project
- Plan to establish the Saudi Recycling Company
- National Energy Efficiency Services Company, promoting efficient energy use in the Kingdom

PIF is one of the six founding members of the One Planet SWF Group and has launched a number of initiatives which support long-term investment to address climate change. This includes the launch of a 200 GW solar energy plan for Saudi Arabia, and investment in renewables and utilities, recycling, and energy efficiency services companies. PIF program objectives for 2018−20 in the Utilities Sector include:

- Realize operational excellence at the portfolio assets level, leading to enhanced fuel consumption efficiency, and reduced capital costs.
- Invest in solar power and renewables to localize the sector across the value chain and lead the Kingdom to become a global player in the industry.
- Invest in energy modernization, including the use of smart systems, and bidirectional infrastructure to integrate renewable energy sources.

In the Food and Agriculture sector, the Kingdom plans to implement highly efficient sustainable production technologies for factories, livestock farms, and fisheries, in addition to more efficient use of natural and renewable water resources in agricultural areas.

Other sovereign wealth fund activities

In addition to the SWFs highlighted in the foregoing pages, many other SWFs are incorporating ESG factors in their investment decisions, with different levels of commitment. For example, PGGM is the manager of the second biggest pension fund in the Netherlands, with €220 billion of assets under management. PGGM considers responsible investment to be an integral part of its investment approach. It consciously takes into account ESG factors in its investment processes. There are seven areas of focus in which it believes it can have an impact:

- Climate change, pollution, and emissions
- Water scarcity
- Food security
- Healthcare
- Human rights
- Stable financial system
- Corporate governance

The fund has moved from exclusionary investing to what it calls "investing in solutions." It now seeks areas where as a long-term investor it can create sustainable financial value while also using capital to contribute to solutions to large social issues, such as climate change.

The Nigeria Sovereign Investment Authority (NSIA) was established in 2011. It has three separate mandates:

- Stabilization fund (20%) provides financial support to government in times of economic stress.
- Future Generation fund (40%) invests in a diversified portfolio of growth investments to provide funds to future generations of Nigerians when hydrocarbon reserves are exhausted.
- Infrastructure fund (40%) enhances the development of infrastructure through investment in domestic projects.

NSIA thus has a triple mission: develop domestic infrastructure, stabilize government budgets, and save for future generations. In early 2019 NSIA backed a 15-year green bond issue, the first green bond in the Nigerian market. NSIA has also begun to focus on sustainable agriculture in Nigeria. It has backed the financing of FAFIN, a 10-year fund with a commitment to sustainability. NSIA also has formed a joint venture with Old Mutual to set up an additional $200 million fund focused on integrated commercial farming and agricultural food processing projects in Nigeria. These projects are expected to be commercially competitive but provide added benefits such as food security and import substitution.

We will briefly mention one more fund, Ithmar Capital, owned by Moroccan government entities. In 2019 Obaid Amrane was appointed CEO of Ithmar Capital Fund. Significantly, in addition to other important executive roles, Mr. Amrane had been a member of the Executive Board of the Moroccan Agency for Sustainable Energy (MASEN) since its creation in 2010. Ithmar Capital has undertaken several interesting ESG projects. With the World Bank it has created the Green Growth Infrastructure Fund, the first green infrastructure fund dedicated to the African continent. The main goal of this fund is to direct the flow of private capital to responsible infrastructure investments primarily in clean energy and water projects. It has also entered into partnerships with Ghana and Senegal to explore coinvestment opportunities including the development of large-scale solar projects and sharing expertise in renewable energy.

Chapter 13

ESG in managing family foundations and family offices

Chapter Outline

The family office	248	The Rockefeller Foundation	261
Chan Zuckerberg Initiative	250	Bloomberg Family Foundation	
The Giving Pledge	253	(Bloomberg Philanthropies)	262
Bill & Melinda Gates Foundation	253	The Ford Foundation	265
Lilly Endowment Inc	257	Carnegie Corporation of New York	267
Day One Fund	257	**Providing Services to the Foundation**	
Open Society Foundations	258	**Community**	**269**
The Robert Wood Johnson		Council on Foundations	269
Foundation	260	The Foundation Center	270

"The rich are different from you and me," said F. Scott Fitzgerald. And Ernest Hemingway replied, "Yes, they have more money!" We can add that the very rich also are different in that they sometimes take large amounts of that money and put it into financial vehicles which are also different. Different in many ways but of special interest here is that they are different in their ability to make an impact on environmental, social, and governance (ESG) issues with their investment practices. Institutional investors such as pension funds, university endowments, and sovereign wealth funds can also have a significant impact, but they usually have diverse stakeholders with diverse interests that can make it difficult to gain a consensus on ESG investments. The institutional investors also have more elaborate reporting requirements and they often have financial return needs that can make their ESG investment choices more limited. Private investors however can be freed from many of these constraints by creating family foundations, with the largest also making use of a form of administration and management called the family office. Although there are differences and overlap, we will use the two terms, family foundation and family office, interchangeably here.

A key advantage of the individual or family foundation, versus diverse investment pools is that it will usually not have to please many different opinions. Secondly, there are some reporting requirements but far fewer than that required of institutional investors. And the family foundation can decide

Environmental, Social, and Governance (ESG) Investing. DOI: https://doi.org/10.1016/B978-0-12-818692-3.00013-X

to accept below market, or even zero financial return if it so chooses. So, what is a family foundation? A family foundation is a type of private foundation set up by an individual or related individuals and funded by their assets. (Other private foundations, such as those established by corporations are subject to the same rules.) The foundation is set up to pursue philanthropic goals and enjoys some tax advantages. As with all private foundations, family foundations must spend 5% of their assets each year and must make its grants available for public viewing. Also, the foundation's investment income is taxable at a rate of 1% or 2%. Assets contributed to the foundation can include cash, life insurance and annuities, public and private securities, real estate, Individual Retirement Account (IRA) assets, and other holdings. An attractive feature is that these contributions can be made from pretax income and they can be deducted from the donor's adjusted gross income, up to certain limits. Foundations may be either operating foundations which are directly involved in running a charitable project, or they can be nonoperating foundations which primarily make financial grants to charities. They may be managed by the founding family or by independent, professional managers. The foundation can operate indefinitely, surviving the death of the founder, or it can be dissolved or transformed, for example, into a donor-advised fund. An interesting development is the desire for modern day extremely wealthy individuals to want to use their wealth for charitable purposes during their lifetime as opposed to bequeathing their fortunes to charity upon their death. They want to be involved in impacting the issues facing this generation and don't see the necessity of postponing their participation. Some of the great names in philanthropy are Rockefeller, Carnegie, Frick, Vanderbilt, Stanford, and Duke. These names are known now for their charitable activities not for the companies which provided the resources for their giving. Generations to come may similarly know Gates, Buffet, Bloomberg, and Zuckerberg not for their business successes but for their charities.

The family office

As the wealth of ultrahigh net worth individuals has soared, their foundation management requirements have gone beyond what can be provided by the typical accountant, broker, or estate attorney. These private investors' needs are similar to those of the large institutional investors and so the services required sometimes go beyond even the private client/wealth management departments of banks and brokerage houses. They may also desire a greater level of privacy and confidentiality in their affairs and can do so by bringing their investment process "in house," forming a "family office." There are no specific licensing or registration requirements of a family office, except for modest restrictions on the relationship of the principals with the founding antecedent. The family office provides a suite of services to one client, the family, although that client may consist of several, related individuals. One rule of thumb is that a family office is appropriate to manage assets of $100 million and probably necessary to manage assets of $250 million and over.

There are three generic types of family office: The Single-Family Office (SFO) is the starting point and most common. As a family grows and spreads to subsequent generations, the SFO might expand to be a Multi-Family Office (MFO), accommodating several different branches of the original family. If the family has a family business with business assets closely intertwined, then there might evolve an Embedded Family Office (EFO). Some employees, for example, the Chief Financial Officer, might do double duty in overseeing the financial affairs of the business as well as playing a key role in the family office.

The services provided by the family office can encompass all the requirements for managing the family's financial affairs, as well as providing legal services and even social services. For example, these services can include:

- investment management
- estate and wealth transfer planning
- philanthropic activities
- real estate transactions
- insurance
- risk management
- other legal services
- social and personal assistance
- security
- bill paying

The full range of services can be seen in Fig. 13.1.

Whether organized in a family office or more simply in a family foundation, this form of charitable organization has grown to massive proportions. In 2017 total private giving from individuals, foundations, and corporations added up to over $400 billion. Leading this torrent of charitable largesse are the 20 largest US foundations, listed in Fig. 13.2.

The focus of these family foundations is sometimes sweeping: improving the human condition or solving world poverty. But the charitable scope of other foundations, especially the newer ones, is often narrow, sometimes on only a single cause. In this way, the investment can have more impact than if funding were spread over a wider group of projects. Also, the foundation may not have the resources, financial, or administrative to understand and impact more than one or a few areas. Fig. 13.3 lists some of the larger family foundations and their areas of focus.

Their size, independence, and low levels of transparency and accountability have led to criticism of these foundations that they sometimes prefer direct action to collaboration with government agencies and other nonprofits. This has occasionally led to foundations setting their own global health

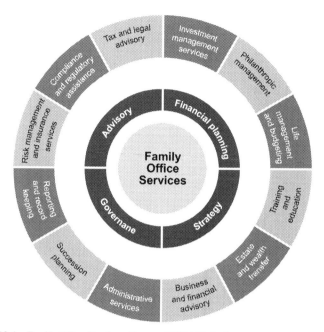

FIGURE 13.1 Family Office Services. *Source: EYGM Limited.*

agenda which may not always be in synch with other agencies or even what developing countries see as their top priorities. Some foundations also have been perceived as pursing political agendas as well. Those that focus on groups which face discrimination and poverty are often at odds with the governments in countries where they operate. Despite these criticisms, family foundations have devoted immense amounts of money and the efforts of extremely talented individuals to addressing society's most pressing problems.

Next, we will look at some of the largest foundations in detail.

Chan Zuckerberg Initiative

"Disrupting" the traditional model of the federal tax exempt, nonprofit charitable foundation, Mark Zuckerberg and his wife Priscilla Chan created their own vehicle for charitable pursuits, the "Chan Zuckerberg Initiative" (CZI). CZI was established in 2015 as a limited liability company, owned by Zuckerberg and Chan. Unlike a charitable trust or private foundation, CZI can invest in for-profit companies, make a profit itself although that is not its goal, engage in lobbying activities, and it can make political donations. The founders believe the ability to undertake these activities gives them more options to make a meaningful impact in their areas of philanthropic focus.

Rank	Foundation	Investment assets	ASSET ALLOCATIONS			
			Corporate stocks	U.S. and state government obligations	Corporate bonds	Other investments
1	Bill & Melinda Gates Foundation	$39,910.7	$27,647.4	$5,325.0	$712.5	$6,225.9
2	Ford Foundation	$11,950.0	$214.3	$789.2	$83.7	$10,862.7
3	Lilly Endowment	$10,241.1	$9,236.1	$0.0	$0.0	$1,005.0
4	Foundation to Promote Open Society	$10,126.3	$0.0	$0.0	$0.0	$10,126.3
5	Robert Wood Johnson Foundation	$9,644.6	$1,741.0	$287.1	$0.0	$7,616.4
6	William and Flora Hewlett Foundation	$8,857.1	$2,916.9	$475.5	$413.9	$5,050.8
7	Bloomberg Family Foundation	$7,817.7	$0.0	$0.0	$0.0	$7,817.7
8	W. K. Kellogg Foundation	$7,663.3	$4,844.1	$170.6	$0.9	$2,647.6
9	J. Paul Getty Trust	$6,812.7	$349.2	$0.2	$18.6	$6,446.7
10	David and Lucile Packard Foundation	$6,678.1	$0.0	$533.8	$0.0	$6,144.3
11	Andrew W. Mellon Foundation	$6,081.4	$332.8	$258.3	$135.4	$5,354.9
12	Gordon and Betty Moore Foundation	$6,055.6	$237.1	$729.9	$0.0	$5,088.6
13	Leona M. and Harry B. Helmsley Charitable Trust	$5,379.8	$469.1	$0.0	$0.0	$4,910.7
14	John D. and Catherine T. MacArthur Foundation	$5,259.9	$2,980.5	$105.1	$33.4	$2,140.9
15	Rockefeller Foundation	$3,856.3	$361.1	$25.9	$0.0	$3,469.2
16	Walton Family Foundation	$3,651.9	$0.0	$0.0	$0.0	$3,651.9
17	Kresge Foundation	$3,524.2	$1,174.3	$37.4	$166.0	$2,146.5
18	California Endowment	$3,465.0	$1,287.1	$48.0	$203.7	$1,926.2
19	Open Society Institute	$3,411.1	$0.0	$0.0	$0.0	$3,411.1
20	JPB Foundation	$3,393.2	$1,982.1	$467.3	$0.0	$943.8

FIGURE 13.2   Largest U.S. foundations. *Source:* Pensions&Investments, from IRS tax filings. Data are in millions, as of Dec 31, 2016 except: 1 as of Aug. 31, 2017; 2 as of June 30, 2017; 3 as of March 31, 2017.

NAME	FOCUS
Bill & Melinda Gates Foundation	Poverty, Health, Education
Howard G. Buffett Foundation	Food Security, Conflict Mitigation, Public Safety
Ford Foundation	Poverty, Injustice, Democratic Values, International Cooperation, Advancing Human Achievement
Lilly Endowment	Community Development, Education and Youth, Religion
Foundation to Promote Open Society	Democratic Practice, Education, Economic Governance and Advancement, Equality and Antidiscrimination, Health and Rights, Human Rights Movements and Institutions, Information and Digital Rights, Journalism, Justice Reform and the Rule of Law
Robert Wood Johnson	Health
William and Flora Hewlett Foundation	Education, Environment, Global Development and Population, Performing Arts, Cyber
Bloomberg Family Foundation	Environment, Public Health, Arts, Government Innovation, Education, Women's Economic Development, Science
W.K. Kellogg Foundation	Children, Families, Communities
J. Paul Getty Trust	Art
The Andrew W. Mellon Foundation	Humanities, Arts, Higher Education
Ford Foundation	Poverty, Injustice, Democratic Values, International Cooperation, Advancing Human Achievement

FIGURE 13.3   ESG focus of selected family foundations.

Grants are awarded from three funding entities: the Chan Zuckerberg Foundation, the Chan Zuckerberg Initiative Donor-Advised Fund, and Chan Zuckerberg Advocacy. CZI was funded in its first few years by annual contributions of roughly $1 billion of Facebook stock. Subsequently, however, the founders pledged to ultimately contribute 99% of their Facebook shares which at the time of the pledge had a market value of roughly $45 billion (more about the Giving Pledge below.) CZI sees its mission as finding new ways to combine technology with community-driven solutions and collaboration in the areas of science, education, justice, and opportunity. As of mid-2019, CZI had provided grants to over 88 entities in education, 123 in science, 86 in justice and opportunity, 128 in community, and 3 in an "other" category. It is not modest in its goals. In healthcare, it hopes to "cure all diseases in our children's lifetime." To that end it announced that it would invest $3 billion over a 10-year period beginning in 2016. While this is a significant sum of money, it is a small fraction of total global spending on medical research.

The Giving Pledge

The Giving Pledge is a campaign to encourage wealthy people to give the bulk of their fortunes to charity. It was begun by Bill Gates and Warren Buffett in 2010 with forty wealthy Americans committing to giving away at least half their wealth. As of early 2019 there were over 200 signatories, almost all billionaires, with cumulative wealth in excess of $1 trillion. These people now come from more than 23 different countries. The most famous signatory is Warren Buffet who pledged to give 99% of his wealth to philanthropy during his lifetime or at his death. The Pledge is more of a moral commitment than a binding legal contract. Beyond asking the wealthy to pledge at least 50% of their wealth to charity, it doesn't specify an exact amount or percentage of wealth to donate, doesn't specify the timing of donations nor what charities or causes are to be the beneficiaries. The group founding the Pledge hoped that their coming forward to be explicit about their intentions for giving away the majority of their wealth would help inspire conversations, discussions, and action about how much to give, for what purposes and to what end. They also hoped that the Pledge could bring together those committed to this kind of giving in order to exchange knowledge on how to do it in the best possible way.

Bill & Melinda Gates Foundation

The Bill & Melinda Gates Foundation (BMGF) grew out of an earlier incarnation as the 1994 William H. Gates Foundation. Its founder was the former head of the Microsoft Corporation and he has regularly been named the richest person in the world, surpassed more recently by Amazon's Jeff Bezos, about whom more later. BMGF believes in focusing on a few big goals and working with partners on innovative solutions. BMGF assets in 2018 totaled over $50 billion. Grant payments from inception were $45.5 billion, with annual direct grantee support of $4.6 billion in 2016 and $4.7 billion in 2017. To manage its operations and grant making it has over 1500 employees. It supports grantees in 49 states, the District of Columbia and more than 130 countries. While the Gates contributed more than $35.8 billion to fund BMGF, the high quality of the foundation's work has been widely recognized and Warren Buffett, chairman of Berkshire Hathaway, has donated roughly $24.5 billion more to BMGF between 2006 and 2018.

Its areas of focus are extreme poverty and poor health in developing countries and the failures of America's education system. It identifies several grant making areas:

- Global Development Program—developing country projects on family health, vaccine delivery, emergency relief, and access to computers and the Internet.
  - Emergency Response
  - Family Planning
  - Global Libraries
  - Integrated Delivery
  - Maternal, Newborn & Child Health
  - Nutrition
  - Polio
  - Vaccine Delivery
- Global Growth & Opportunity Program—projects on sustainable transformative change in the face of inequities and market failures, to realize the potential of untapped markets, and to improve inclusiveness of economic and social benefits.
  - Agricultural Development
  - Financial Services for the Poor
  - Gender Equality
  - Water, Sanitation, and Hygiene
- Global Health Program—seeks innovative, ambitious, and scalable solutions to address health problems that have a major impact in developing countries.
  - Discovery & Translational Sciences
  - Enteric and Diarrheal Diseases
  - HIV
  - Malaria
  - Maternal, Newborn & Child Health Discovery & Tools
  - Neglected Tropical Diseases
  - Pneumonia
  - Tuberculosis
  - Vaccine Development and Surveillance
- Global Policy & Advocacy—seeks to build strategic relationships with governments, private philanthropists, media organizations, public policy experts, and other key partners that are critical to the success of the foundation's mission.
  - Tobacco Control
  - Development Policy and Finance
  - Global Education Program

- United States Program—education, libraries and access to the Internet, and emergency relief in the United States as well as community grants and local efforts in the Pacific Northwest.
  - ⁂ K−12 Education
  - ⁂ Economic Mobility and Opportunity
  - ⁂ Postsecondary Success
  - ⁂ Washington State programs
- Charitable Sector Support—resources providing assistance and support to charitable entities.

The foundation believes that climate change is an important major issue but does not fund efforts specifically aimed at reducing carbon emissions. Instead, it believes that many of its global health and development grants directly address problems that climate change creates or exacerbates.

We can look in more detail at one example, its activity in Agricultural Development where its goal is to support country-led inclusive agricultural transformation across sub-Saharan Africa and South Asia. This initiative has four strategic goals: increase agricultural productivity for smallholder farmers; increase smallholder farmer household income; increase equitable consumption of a safe, affordable, nutritious diet year-round; and increase women's empowerment in agriculture. The foundation sees the challenge arising from a combination of low productivity, low profitability, systems, and policies that fail to meet the needs of the many smallholder farmers, and a lack of opportunity and resources for women and food systems that do not provide adequate nutrition. Its strategy is to invest in three main ways: global public goods in the form of new products, tools, technologies, systems, and approaches to advance inclusive agricultural transformation; country systems to support country agricultural strategies and help drive systems innovation through country, private sector, and other in-country partnerships to enable more effective delivery of products, tools, technologies, and services; and farmer impact in either public or private sector platforms that provide multiples services to smallholder farmers.

The foundation pursues a dual-track approach to assist countries in sub-Saharan Africa and South Asia. It supports both regional and in-country efforts, partnering with both public and private sectors as well as with donors and other development partners in support of government national agriculture strategies. It has significant projects underway in Ethiopia, Nigeria, Tanzania, and India.

BMGF's Agricultural Development strategy is organized around the following 10 programmatic portfolios:

- Enabling Country Systems: Africa
- Seed Systems and Varietal Improvement
- Crop Discovery and Translational Sciences
- Livestock

- Nutritious Food Systems
- Global Policy and Advocacy
- Policy and Data
- Digital Farmer Services
- Women's Empowerment

Another top priority for BMGF is fighting malaria. An estimated 219 million people suffered from the disease in 2017 and about 435,000 died. More than 90% of the deaths were in Africa, and over 60% were among children under five. BMGF has committed more than $2.9 billion in grants to combat malaria and $2 billion to the Global Fund to Fight AIDS, Tuberculosis, and Malaria. The foundation's malaria strategy was updated in 2018 and can be summarized in a series of pivots:

- The High Burden to High Impact initiative was launched in November 2018 with the leadership of WHO and the RBM Partnership to End Malaria. It focuses on work in high-burden countries to rapidly reduce deaths.
- Deepen partnerships and collaboration with other leading donors and agencies to produce more coordinated support in service of affected country governments.
- Establish platforms to support next-generation surveillance and data use, with an emphasis on scaling genetic epidemiology to inform decision-making at every level and to determine how to get more out of tools and limited resources.
- Optimize coverage of chemoprevention through existing channels to save lives now.
- Test models that can scale access to, and quality of, care and medicines across public and private sector channels.
- Accelerate the number and pace of R&D for transformational endgame tools.

There are three strategy goals:

- Drive down the burden—Many of the tools needed to fight malaria already exist, yet cases continue to rise in many high-burden countries. Finding ways to do more with the tools currently available can save lives and bring us closer to ending malaria.
- Shorten the Endgame—by investing in next-generation surveillance systems, elimination in regions where drug-resistant malaria has emerged, and accelerating endgame research and development efforts today.
- Get Ahead of Resistance—Mitigate the emergence of drug and insecticide resistance by eliminating falciparum malaria in the Greater Mekong Subregion, developing a robust pipeline of active ingredients and analyzing entomological and genetic epidemiological data to quickly respond to threats.

Since the early 2000s, diagnosis, treatment, and prevention helped reduce malaria cases by more than 40% and reduce deaths by more than 60% worldwide. But gains have plateaued. With commitment and collaboration from global partners and affected countries, eradication of the parasite is feasible and is the only sustainable approach to addressing malaria.

Lilly Endowment Inc

The Lilly Endowment was founded by the Lilly family in 1937. It was initially funded with shares of the pharmaceutical company Eli Lilly. In the 80 years up to 2017, it distributed grants totaling almost $10 billion to roughly 10,000 charitable organizations. Its mission is the "promotion and support of religious, educational, or charitable purposes." It has three areas of emphasis:

- Community Development
- Education and Youth
- Religion

Its approach is to identify experienced organizations active in areas of interest, then provide funding, consulting, technical assistance, research, evaluation support, and connections to other organizations with similar interests. This approach contrasts with that of some other foundations which seek new paths to effectiveness, rather than working primarily through existing entities. Some examples of programs that Lilly has supported:

- Education Grant to the Hispanic Scholarship Fund. In 2018 the Lilly Endowment provided a $30.7 million grant to support Hispanic students' college graduation.
- Religion. In 2012 and 2013, Lilly Endowment made grants to 67 theological schools to eliminate or reduce student indebtedness. In 2016 it provided a $1.2 million grant to The Association of Theological Schools in Pittsburgh, for the coordination of efforts to address economic challenges facing future ministers.
- Community Development Grant. The Lilly Endowment has been a regular supporter of organizations in Indiana and especially Indianapolis. For example, in 2017 it provided a $300,000 community development grant for general operating support to the Arts Council of Indianapolis.

Day One Fund

In 2018 Jeff Bezos established the Day One Fund, a $2 billion fund to focus his philanthropic activities. Bezos, the richest person in the world depending on the price of Amazon stock, had asked his Twitter followers for their thoughts on what charities he should support. Ultimately, he settled on funding existing nonprofits that help the homeless and creating a network of new nonprofit tier-one preschools in low-income communities. In late 2018 the fund's Day 1 Families Fund gave $97.5 million in grants to 24 existing organizations working with the homeless. Each organization received either $2.5 million or $5 million. The Day 1 Academies Fund plans to build and operate a network of high-quality, full-scholarship Montessori-inspired preschools in underserved communities.

Open Society Foundations

The Open Society Foundations constitute an international network of philanthropic organizations founded by George Soros and operating in 37 countries. It traces its roots back to philanthropic activities begun in 1979. From inception to 2018 it has disbursed more than $15 billion in grants to many nongovernmental organizations, in more than 120 countries. Its mission is founded in the belief that the world's challenges require the free exchange of ideas and thought, and that everyone should have a voice in shaping policies that affect them. It works to build inclusive societies, grounded in respect for human rights and the rule of law, with government accountability and the participation of all people. It supports a diverse array of independent voices and independent organizations around the world and has a focus on supporting those who face discrimination purely for who they are and for those who find themselves pushed to the margins of mainstream society. The Open Society Foundations support a broader network of entities and programs operating in more than 120 countries. It often supports activities with strong political positions and has consequently been subject to criticism by opponents. This criticism has also led to the foundation having to close certain in-country offices.

The Open Society Foundations' work is organized into the following thematic, geographic, and advocacy programs:

- The Africa Regional Office works at the pan-African level to build a free and democratic Africa, where leaders respect human rights, work to improve citizens' lives, and are held to account for their actions.
- The Asia Pacific Regional Office aims to promote and bolster human rights and expand inclusive democracy.
- The Documentary Photography Project supports photography and other visual media in the belief that images can empower, shift public perception, and drive social change.
- The Early Childhood Program promotes the well-being of young children through a rights-based approach, emphasizing parent and community engagement, professional development, and government accountability.
- The Open Society Foundations Economic Justice Program was launched in 2019, combining the Economic Advancement Program and the Fiscal

Governance Program, and is focused on promoting equity, openness, and accountability in fiscal and economic systems around the world.

- The Education Support Program seeks to promote quality education for all.
- The Eurasia Program works to strengthen civil society, uphold human rights, and maintain space for independent debate and discussion in Central Asia, Eastern Europe, the South Caucasus, and Turkey. (In November 2018 the Open Society Foundations was forced to close their offices in Turkey due to governmental backlash to its activities.)
- The Global Drug Policy Program promotes drug policies rooted in human rights, sustainable development, social justice, and public health.
- The Higher Education Support Program works to promote open society values by supporting universities that nurture critical minds, defend pluralism, and foster active citizenship.
- The Human Rights Initiative seeks to ensure that people can exercise their rights around the world.
- The Information Program supports those who seek new methods to understand and respond to the technological changes that affect people's basic rights.
- The International Migration Initiative works to improve protections for refugees and vulnerable migrants, to stop the exploitation of migrant workers, and to build stronger ties between host communities and newcomers.
- The Latin America Program addresses rights and governance issues in Latin America and the Caribbean through grant making, network building, and collaboration with partners.
- The Middle East and North Africa Program supports a diverse group of civil society organizations, research centers, universities, and media organizations across the region.
- The Open Society European Policy Institute works to emphasize human rights both inside and outside the European Union.
- The Open Society Fellowship was founded in 2008 to support individuals pursuing innovative and unconventional approaches to fundamental open society challenges.
- The Open Society Initiative for Europe supports organizations that promote active participation in democracy and uphold open society values— particularly in places where civil and political rights are at risk.
- The Open Society Justice Initiative's team of human rights lawyers and staff pursue strategic litigation and other legal work that supports the mission and values of the Open Society Foundations.
- Open Society-US supports efforts to advance equality, fairness, and justice, with a focus on the most marginalized communities and the most significant threats to open society in the United States.
- The Open Society Program on Independent Journalism supports journalism that verifies, exposes, and explains reality.

- The Public Health Program works to build open societies in which all people's health and human rights are valued.
- The Roma Initiatives Office works with activists and communities across Europe to achieve long-term change for Roma.
- The Scholarship Programs work in politically constrained places to support students and scholars who want to freely pursue the academic studies and professional skills they need to lead positive social change in their home communities.
- The Women's Rights Program invests in social movements that advance the power of women, LGBTQI, and gender nonconforming people to have voice and agency in all aspects of their lives.

The Robert Wood Johnson Foundation

The Robert Wood Johnson Foundation was established by Robert Wood Johnson II the founder of health products maker Johnson and Johnson, at his death in 1968. As the United States' largest philanthropy focusing on public health, it awards roughly $500 million per year in grants for organizations addressing health issues, in the following categories:

- Health Systems
  - Health Care Coverage and Access
  - Health Care Quality and Value
  - Public and Community Health
- Healthy Communities
  - Built Environment and Health
  - Disease Prevention and Health Promotion
  - Health Disparities
  - Social Determinants of Health
- Healthy Children and Families
  - Child and Family Well-Being
  - Childhood Obesity
  - Early Childhood
- Leadership for Better Health
  - Health Leadership Development
  - Nurses and Nursing

In carrying out its work, the Foundation is guided by the following principles:

- Seek bold and lasting change rooted in the best available evidence, analysis, and science, openly debated.
- Treat everyone with fairness and respect.
- Act as good stewards of private resources, using them to advance the public's interest with a focus on helping the most vulnerable.

- Cultivate diversity, inclusion, and collaboration.
- Speak out as leaders.

The Rockefeller Foundation

The Rockefeller Foundation was founded in 1913 by John D. Rockefeller, the scion of Standard Oil. Its total giving has been estimated at over $14 billion. Its mission is a rather sweeping "promoting the well-being of humanity throughout the world." The Foundation advances new frontiers of science, data, policy, and innovation while building collaborative relationships with partners and grantees. Its areas of focus are:

- Health—Some of the Rockefeller Foundation's historical health projects are: eradicating hookworm in the American South, launching the field of public health, and seeding the development of the life-saving yellow fever vaccine. It believes that by using data science to create actionable insights for communities, it can continue that legacy, and catalyze equitable and quality health for all.
- Food—Its work on food is currently implemented through YieldWise Food Loss, launched in 2016, which aims at halving food loss and waste. YieldWise Food Waste focused on food waste in the United States and through the Alliance for Green Revolution, launched in 2006, which is focused on doubling yield and incomes for African farmers.
- Power—The Rockefeller Foundation is working with governments, the private sector, technologists, and other advocates to accelerate electrification in environmentally and economically sustainable ways. Its Smart Power for Rural Development initiative aims to spark long-term economic growth and power opportunities to those living in poverty and with limited access to electricity.
- Jobs—Through Impact Hiring, the Foundation helps young people access stable employment and career-building jobs, and helps employers address critical talent challenges. It is also advancing gender inclusivity in the workplace through the 100×25 campaign, which aims to bring more women to the C-suite by 2025.
- Resilient Cities—The Adrienne Arsht-Rockefeller Foundation Resilience Center at the Atlantic Council is the leading institution working to make communities around the globe more resilient to climate change, economic shifts, migration flows, or security challenges.
- Innovation—Early innovations from the Rockefeller Foundation ranged from funding the scientists who developed the vaccine for yellow fever to catalyzing the field of impact investing. Its current innovation initiatives are in the areas of:
  - Innovative Finance
  - Impact Investment Management

* Data Science for Social Impact
* Data and Technology
* Co-Impact—The Rockefeller Foundation believes that the biggest problems require big partnerships. To deliver large-scale, sustainable change to underserved populations across the developing world in the critical areas of health, education, and economic opportunity, it has joined in Co-Impact, along with other leading philanthropists, to create a new model for collaborative philanthropy and social change at scale.

Bloomberg Family Foundation (Bloomberg Philanthropies)

The Bloomberg Family Foundation was created in 2006 by Mike Bloomberg, founder of the global data, software and media company Bloomberg, L.P. He has signed the Giving Pledge, committing to leave the majority of his wealth to charity. Bloomberg Philanthropies includes the Bloomberg Family Foundation, corporate and personal philanthropy, and Bloomberg Associates, a pro bono consultancy that works with mayors in cities around the world. Through 2018, Bloomberg has given over $8 billion to charity, and in 2018 Bloomberg Philanthropies invested $767 million in 510 cities in 129 different countries. Its areas of focus are:

* Environment
    * Beyond Carbon: moving the United States toward a 100% clean energy economy.
    * America's Pledge: bringing together private and public sector leaders to ensure the United States remains a global leader in reducing emissions and delivering the country's ambitious climate goals of the Paris Agreement.
    * American Cities Climate Challenge: an opportunity for 20 ambitious cities to significantly deepen and accelerate their efforts to tackle climate change and promote a sustainable future for their residents.
    * The Global Coal and Air Pollution program supports international efforts to rapidly transition beyond coal power.
    * Sustainable Cities: The C40 Cities Climate Leadership Group is a network of more than 90 of the world's largest cities taking action to address climate change.
    * Vibrant Oceans Initiative works in key areas around the world to restore fish populations.
* Public Health
    * Drowning is the third leading cause of unintentional death worldwide. Bloomberg Philanthropies is investing in a pilot program to identify potential solutions to reduce drowning and supporting drowning prevention interventions in high-risk areas.

* Maternal and Reproductive Health: Bloomberg Philanthropies has committed $62 million since 2006 to reproductive health programs in Africa, Asia, and South America.
* Bloomberg Philanthropies has committed more than $250 million over 12 years (2007–19) to work in low- and middle-income countries and large cities that have a high burden of road-related fatalities. The Bloomberg Philanthropies Initiative for Global Road Safety focuses on implementing key interventions proven to reduce road traffic deaths and injuries and advocating for stronger road safety legislation.
* Since 2016, Mike Bloomberg has been the World Health Organization Global Ambassador for Noncommunicable Diseases (NCD) and Injuries. In this role, he is increasing global awareness of NCDs and injuries, and engaging political, economic, and health leaders to address these challenges through the Partnership for Healthy Cities and the Task Force on Fiscal Policy for Health.
* The Obesity Prevention Program is addressing the global obesity epidemic by raising public awareness of the problem and supporting policies to prevent the rise of obesity in Mexico, Colombia, Brazil, South Africa, and the United States.
* Tobacco Control: The Bloomberg Initiative to Reduce Tobacco Use is working to implement proven tobacco control policies around the world.
* Combatting Opioids: Bloomberg Philanthropies is addressing the opioid public health epidemic and saving lives by supporting high-impact, state-based interventions that can be replicated by other states and localities.
* Data for Health: The Data for Health Initiative is a 4-year, $100 million effort cofunded with the Australian Department of Foreign Affairs and Trade that will work directly with 20 developing countries to strengthen birth and death records as well as improve mechanisms for collecting risk factor data.
* The Resolve to Save Lives Cardiovascular Health Initiative aims to reduce the number of people dying from heart disease and stroke in low- and middle-income countries.
* Government Innovation
  * The What Works Cities program helps cities improve the way they use data to identify and respond effectively to their residents' needs.
  * The Mayors Challenge is a competition for city leaders that identifies and elevates next-generation solutions that have the potential to transform the way city halls work and improve the lives of citizens.
  * Autonomous Vehicles in Cities: A yearlong collaboration between Bloomberg Philanthropies and the Aspen Institute helped ensure that

the needs of people are prioritized as we enter what many are calling a "second automobile revolution."

* Innovation teams: helping mayors generate and implement bolder ideas.
* The Bloomberg Harvard City Leadership Initiative provides mayors and senior staff free enrollment in a program blending the best of Harvard Kennedy School's public administration expertise with Harvard Business School's management expertise.
* CityLab is an annual global conference hosted in partnership with Bloomberg Philanthropies, the Aspen Institute, and The Atlantic where more than 500 participants including mayors, city innovators, artists, funders, academics, and urbanists gather to explore how to improve cities and spread urban strategies that work.
* The Cities of Service coalition is a network of municipal governments that leverage impact volunteering by citizens.
* The Financial Empowerment Center model offers a new way for mayors and local governments to increase the quality and consistency of local financial services to residents.

- Arts
  * Bloomberg Connects: Bloomberg Philanthropies is funding the development of digital programs at leading cultural institutions around the world to increase access and visitor engagement.
  * Public Art Challenge: The foundation's first Public Art Challenge, announced in the fall of 2014, supported creative projects in four cities, catalyzing $13 million for local economies, 10 million views, 245 partnerships, and 490 public programs. In 2018 five cities were selected to receive up to $1 million in funding for temporary public art projects that address an important civic issue.
  * The Arts Innovation and Management program provides $30 million in unrestricted general operating support over 2 years to more than 260 small and midsized nonprofit arts organizations in six US cities.
  * ArtPlace is a nationwide public–private partnership to drive revitalization in cities by putting arts at the center of community development.
  * Bloomberg Arts Internship supports a summer internship program in Baltimore, New York City, and Philadelphia that gives young residents the tools they need to excel in high school, college, and beyond.
- Education
  * Policy: Bloomberg Philanthropies is working to strengthen America's educational system by supporting effective policies aimed at improving student outcomes.
  * College Access and Success: Bloomberg Philanthropies' college access and success initiatives aim to directly help students apply to,

enroll in, and graduate from top institutions by providing support and guidance.
* Career and Technical Education: Innovative apprenticeship pilot programs to help students obtain credentials or certifications and work experience during high school.
- Founder's Projects
  * American Cities Initiative: helping city leaders address climate change, combat obesity and gun violence, and catalyze new opportunities for artists and volunteers.
  * Johns Hopkins University: the largest gift to an American University, Mike Bloomberg has donated $1.5 billion.
  * US Virgin Islands Hurricane Relief.
  * Women's Economic Development initiative has enrolled more than 195,500 women in training, more than 105,000 children in school in sub-Saharan Africa.

The Ford Foundation

The Ford Foundation was founded in 1936 by the family behind the Ford Motor Company. For much of its existence, it was the largest and most influential foundation in the world. In 2017 it paid out over $550 million in grants. In 2015 its mission evolved "to reduce poverty and injustice, strengthen democratic values, promote international cooperation, and advance human achievement." Its approach is to build upon the three areas of individual leadership, strong institutions, and innovative, often high-risk ideas.

It has identified the underlying drivers of inequality to be:

- Entrenched cultural narratives that undermine fairness, tolerance, and inclusion.
- Failure to invest in and protect vital public goods such as education and natural resources.
- Unfair rules of the economy that magnify unequal opportunity and outcomes.
- Unequal access to government decision-making and resources.
- Persistent prejudice and discrimination against women, people with disabilities, and racial, ethnic, and caste minorities.

To address these drivers of inequality, the Foundation makes grants in the following interconnected areas:

- Civic Engagement and Government
  * The Foundation works to engage diverse communities, and develop innovative ways to inform, engage, and mobilize people. It supports

research, advocacy, and networking aimed at protecting and expanding civic space, and reversing global trends toward destabilization and constraint. It also works to ensure better and more effective protections and protocols to address problems like the harassment, intimidation, and violence too often aimed at activists, journalists, and defenders. It is active in Brazil, Eastern Africa, India, Nepal, Sri Lanka, Mexico, Central America, Middle East, North Africa, and the United States.

⁕ In the United States, it supports efforts to help young activists and other emerging leaders channel their efforts into meaningful policy reform on issues relevant to injustice and inequality in their own communities. It supports strategic litigation and legal advocacy to eliminate voter suppression and safeguard the right to vote. It also supports efforts to make sure the 2020 census is fair and accurate, and it supports groups and networks as they build grassroots constituencies and develop strategies to make government more responsive and accountable.

- Creativity and Free Expression
  ⁕ The Foundation supports stories told through literary, visual, and performing arts; documentary and emerging media; and investigative journalism. It seeks voices that have been marginalized, distorted, ignored, or silenced.
- Future of Work(ers)
  ⁕ Strengthening Connections—It supports efforts to bring together technologists, workers, researchers, policy experts, private sector leaders, and social justice advocates to leverage existing collaborations and create new ones.
  ⁕ Shaping solutions in policy and practice—It supports efforts to develop, test, and implement innovative labor and social protection policies, as well as private sector practices and models.
  ⁕ Strengthening worker organization, voice and power—It invests in building the capacity of workers and worker-centered organizations to engage in and shape the debate about work today and in the future.
- Gender, Racial, and Ethnic Justice
  ⁕ The Foundation supports the building of research and evidence on the scope of the problem, and interventions that can influence policy and practice. It also seeks to cultivate philanthropy and bilateral donors to ensure increased and more coordinated funding for the field. It is active in India, Nepal, Sri Lanka, Southern, and Western Africa and the United States.
- Just Cities and Regions
  ⁕ The Foundation has a 4-year initiative (2018–21) on affordable housing which leverages grants and catalytic impact investments—in the form of program-related investments and mission-related investments.

- Natural Resources and Climate Change
  - ⊛ The Foundation works to ensure that oil, gas, and mineral producers respect the rights of communities—and that the benefits and costs related to mining, oil, and gas are distributed more equitably. It also supports efforts to promote climate change policies and investments that benefit rural and indigenous communities and it aims to strengthen the capacities of organizations working on issues of land tenure, extractives, natural resource-related tax justice, and climate change, and to cultivate philanthropy and other funders to amplify and sustain these efforts.
- Technology and Society
  - ⊛ The Foundation supports an emerging field of organizations with specialized expertise in technology systems, law, and policy that seek to establish norms, regulations, technical standards, and enforcement of rules for technology that protect the public in the digital landscape. It also invests in the technical skills, intelligence, and capacity of civil society groups working in established social justice fields like human rights, government accountability, and civic engagement.

Carnegie Corporation of New York

The Carnegie Corporation of New York was established as a charitable entity by Andrew Carnegie in 1911. In its day it was the largest single charitable trust in existence. And it was only one of several previously established Carnegie charitable organizations. The original Deed of Gift specified that the foundation should carry out its work in perpetuity. To maintain its spending capacity, it targets a yearly spending rate of 5.5%. For the 10-year period ending in 2014, it awarded 5012 grants totaling $1.188 billion. For 2017, it had Grant Appropriations of $157 million. Grants were initially focused on the construction of public libraries, church organs, and universities, colleges, schools, and general educational agencies. Notably, however, in his original letter of gift, Carnegie recognized that as times change priorities for grant making should too and left it to the Trustees to change policies when they felt it necessary or desirable. So, here are the Corporation's current programs and focus areas:

- Education
  - ⊛ Leadership and Teaching to Advance Learning—improving systems of preparing, recruiting, and developing teachers and education leaders.
  - ⊛ New Designs to Advance Learning—developing whole school models that provide more effective learning environments for diverse learners.
  - ⊛ Public Understanding—supporting research on strategies that can drive parent and family engagement in education.

- Pathways to Postsecondary Success—improving alignment in student learning expectations between K−12 and postsecondary education.
- Integration, Learning, and Innovation—advancing integrated approaches that enable greater collaboration, coherence, and dynamism.
- Democracy
  - Field Building—support for state and local groups aiding immigrant communities.
  - Strategic Communications—informing the immigration reform debate and providing messaging for communities.
  - Policy Development—improving federal and state policies regarding immigration and civic integration.
  - Nonpartisan Civic Engagement—encouraging legal residents to become American citizens and informed voters.
- International Peace and Security
  - Nuclear Security—reduce nuclear risks resulting from geopolitical and technological change, gaps in nuclear governance, and regional challenges with a nuclear dimension in North Korea and Iran.
  - Global Dynamics—reduce the risk of global instability by promoting deeper understanding of domestic and foreign policy developments in the Euro-Atlantic and Asia regions and their implications for US and global security, with particular attention to Russia and China.
  - Transnational Movements and the Arab Region—improve conditions in the Arab region by empowering Arab social scientists to address political, economic, and social drivers underlying conflict, and advance new approaches to transnational trends including political violence.
  - Peacebuilding in Africa—strengthen the field of peacebuilding on the continent by promoting scholarship within Africa, connecting African experts with international peacebuilding communities, and drawing applicable lessons from other regions of the world.
  - Cross-Cutting Challenges and Special Initiatives—bring nongovernmental expertise to bear on international security issues by strengthening independent scholarship, bridging the gap between academia and policy, deepening congressional knowledge of international affairs, and responding to special challenges and opportunities affecting international security.
- Higher Education and Research in Africa
  - Postdoctoral Support—increase the ranks of advanced African academics by offering postdoctoral opportunities, including through new models designed by African educators.
  - Diaspora Linkages—strengthen training and research on the continent by bridging African academic diaspora with African universities.

- Higher Education Policy and Research—advance higher education policies and practice by generating and disseminating data-driven research and publications on Africa's higher education sector and building capacity for research management.
- Special Projects
  - Academic Leadership Award—recognizing individuals who demonstrate vision and an outstanding commitment to excellence and equity in undergraduate education.
  - Andrew Carnegie Fellows—a competitive fellowship program in the social sciences and humanities.
  - Carnegie Medal of Philanthropy—recognizing individuals and families with exceptional and sustained records of philanthropic giving.
  - Nunn-Lugar Award for Promoting Nuclear Security—recognizing individuals and institutions whose work is helping to prevent the proliferation of nuclear weapons and to reduce the risk of their use.

Providing Services to the Foundation Community

The largest bank and brokerage firms, as well as specialized niche firms, all provide investment and other services to foundations. In addition, there are other services provided to the foundation community by organizations such as the Council on Foundations and the Foundation Center.

Council on Foundations

The Council on Foundations sees its mission as providing "opportunity, leadership and tools needed by philanthropic organizations to expand, enhance, and sustain their ability to advance the common good." Some of its activities and services are:

- The Philanthropy Exchange is a private social network allowing Council members to discuss topics of common interest, share resources, and develop relationships. There is an opportunity to connect with peers involved in similar issues or roles around the globe; search an online library of best practices, resources, and events; and seek and give candid advice in a private community of their peers.
- The Council promotes public policy to allow philanthropic activity to remain vibrant, inclusive, innovative, and effective. This is undertaken in several ways:
  - Engagement with members, policymakers, and their staff.
  - Education: The Council operates The Community Foundations National Standards program, maintains a full-time legal staff, analyzes and communicates implications and impact of proposed policy

changes, performs and commissions research, and works to educate Members of Congress on potential impacts of policies and regulations.

⚬ Facilitation: The Council maintains relationships with the Executive branch of government and facilitates discussion of issues of interest.

- Council Events: The Council sponsors webinars, learning forums, summits, conferences, online discussions, and professional events in Washington, other physical locations around the country, and online.
- Programs and Initiatives: Some of the Councils programs and initiatives are:

⚬ Bridging divides—facilitate conversations, encourage unlikely collaborations, develop shared policy agendas, and grapple with difficult questions that bring people together across perspectives and position.

⚬ HUD Secretary's Award for Public-Philanthropic Partnerships—presented by the US Department of Housing and Urban Development, in partnership with the Council.

⚬ Inclusive Economic Prosperity.

⚬ Opportunity Zones.

⚬ Supporting Veterans and Military Families.

⚬ Global Philanthropy.

⚬ Leading Corporate Philanthropy.

⚬ Sustainable Goals and Philanthropy. The Council partners with other organizations to help engage foundations in the context of the Sustainable Development Goals for global development. It hosts meetings and webinars on relevant topics and organizes resources in depth knowledge resources.

⚬ Impact Investing—The Council provides educational resources on impact investing and acts to facilitate dialogue among foundations, investors, and policymakers. Some activities are:

- Engaging policymakers to promote a supporting regulatory environment. One such initiative is the IRS Guidance on Mission-Related Investments.
- Organizing provocative conversation among foundations and other partners such as community development financial institutions and investment firms.
- Aggregating resources to demystify the process of impact investing.
- Building relationships with thought leaders and intermediaries.

The Foundation Center

The Foundation Center traces its roots to the mid-1950s and has a mission "to strengthen the social sector by advancing knowledge about philanthropy in the United States and around the world." It believes accountability and transparency into foundation activities is the best policy, and that foundations should therefore have "glass pockets." In addition to its online presence it has four regional hubs and a broad network of 400 information centers on funding activity. It is the leading source of information about philanthropic activity globally and provides data, analysis, and training. It provides knowledge, transparency, and guidance to fundraisers and grantmakers. One interesting analytical tool is their "Foundation Landscapes," which combines multiple resources including data visualization tools and original resources to provide focus and perspective on individual issues. For example, the "Funding The Ocean" landscape acts as a knowledge hub to provide the philanthropy community with centralized access to data, resources, and tools relevant to ocean conservation issues.

Chapter 14

Faith-based investing

Chapter Outline

Common features	273	LKCM Aquinas Catholic Equity		
Christian Values Investing	274	Fund		291
GuideStone	275	Catholic Values ETF		291
New Covenant Funds	275	Islamic values investing		291
The Interfaith Center on Corporate		Green Sukuk Bonds		293
Responsibility	276	Islamic Values Indexes, Mutual		
Christian Super	277	Funds, and ETFs		294
Timothy Plan Funds	281	MSCI Islamic Index Series		296
Eventide Funds	282	FTSE Shariah Indexes		296
Catholic Values Investing: Socially		Amana Mutual Funds		297
Responsible Investment Guidelines	284	The Iman Fund		298
USCCB Investment Policies	287	Shariah Compliant ETFs		299
Catholic Values Mutual Funds	289	Jewish Values Investing		299
Ave Maria Mutual Funds	289	Jewish Values Indexes, Mutual		
		Funds, and ETFs		300

Faith-based or religious values investing refers to investment activity designed specifically to be consistent with the moral and social teachings of that religion while providing financial returns to assure the continuing financial stability of the organization. It may not necessarily earn market or above market financial returns and may recognize that it can be difficult or even impossible to find investments that perfectly align with moral or social values.

Common features

There are differences in beliefs both between religions and within any one religion so it should not be surprising that there is no one size fits all for faith-based investing. But there are some features which to varying degrees are common across the investing styles of each of the major faiths. Religious investing can take many forms: investments in targeted mutual funds and ETFs, as well as focused investments in public and private equity, bespoke as well as generic bonds, real estate, and other alternatives. One frequent

Environmental, Social, and Governance (ESG) Investing. DOI: https://doi.org/10.1016/B978-0-12-818692-3.00014-1

attribute of faith-based investing is negative screening, where the individual or organization screens out companies which are active in "sin" industries such as alcohol, tobacco, gambling, and pornography. Faith-based investors will also use positive screens to invest in companies and assets which are consistent with their beliefs and often find themselves in a middle ground, where assets or companies may be otherwise attractive but not necessarily ideal from a social or moral point of view. In this case, active engagement as shareholders is seen as a tool to influence investee companies to tilt toward favored activities.

Every major religion has some guidelines for investing in ways that are consistent with its beliefs. In the following sections, we look in more detail at some of these practices. It is important to note that the objective of this chapter is not to provide an in-depth discussion of each religion per se. Instead, our goal is to understand the financial products which are used to further the investment goals of those who follow the teachings of each of these faiths.

Christian values investing

The "Protestant Work Ethic" often expressed as the Calvinist or Puritan ethic emphasizes hard work, frugality, saving, and investment in the future, as well as a rejection of sinful activities. As with other religions, Protestant denominations range widely from liberal to conservative. The Church of England's Ethical Investment Advisory Group (EIAG) provides investment guidance consistent with the Church's beliefs. It advises and supports the Church's three National Investment Bodies (NIBs) which invest on behalf of many beneficiaries and invest in a manner which forms an integral part of the Church's witness and mission. Stewardship, active engagement, and investment exclusions are all important aspects of this investment policy. The EIAG advises on assets, sectors, and markets which are not appropriate for investment. It also advises on engagement and proxy voting, relationships with investment managers and other investors, and on investment policy issues. The NIBs recognize a fiduciary duty to their beneficiaries, within a Christian context. They are signatories of the UN PRI and pledge to incorporate environmental, social, and governance (ESG) factors into their investment decisions. They explicitly recognize climate change as an ethical investment issue. Their ethical restriction policy applies to holdings in the following industries: indiscriminate weaponry, conventional weaponry and nonmilitary firearms, pornography, tobacco, gambling, high-interest-rate lending, human embryonic cloning, extraction of thermal coal, and production of oil from oil sands, all subject to revenue thresholds. EIAG also provides the NIBs with advice on investing implications of the Church's teaching and values on a range of issues, including climate change, supply chain ethics, and extractive industries.

GuideStone

In the United States, GuideStone is the largest provider of focused Christian values mutual funds. It was founded in 1918 to provide investment services for the retirement needs of Southern Baptist Convention ministers, widows, and workers. In 2001 it registered its first mutual fund. Its successful investment performance, combined with its values approach, led it to open its fund to the public in 2014. In 2012 and again in 2019 it was recognized by Lipper as the best overall small fund family. As of March 2019, it offered 24 mutual funds across most major asset classes and had $13.3 billion in AUM. GuideStone believes that it is not necessary to sacrifice performance for religious values (or vice versa). Companies are excluded from their portfolios if they are "publicly recognized" as being in the following industries: alcohol, tobacco, gambling, pornography, and abortion. More generally, their funds will not invest in any company whose products, services, or activities are "publicly recognized as being incompatible with the moral and ethical posture of GuideStone Financial Resources." GuideStone also engages in shareholder advocacy to advance their values. Its list of restricted companies ranges between 3% and 5% of the S&P 500, 6% and 8% of the MSCI EAFE Index, and 1% and 2% of the Bloomberg Barclays US Aggregate Bond Index. The restricted list is not made public and based on their funds' positive performance there would seem to be a nuanced application of exclusionary criteria. The company notes that while their underlying investment portfolio strongly aligns with Christian principles and values, companies, like people, are not perfect and that it is virtually impossible to invest in absolutely "pure" companies.

New Covenant Funds

New Covenant Funds make investment decisions consistent with the social-witness principles adopted by the Presbyterian Church, which believes that church investment is "an instrument of mission and includes theological, social, and economic considerations." Three tools are used: screening, shareholder advocacy, and community investing. Positive screens are used to seek out companies based on their approach to environmental responsibility, fair-hiring practices, and efforts to support international human rights. Negative screens may exclude alcohol, tobacco, gambling, and the production of war materials, among others. Beyond negative screening, there is an approach called Mission Responsibility Through Investment (MRTI). MRTI implements policies on faith-based investing by engaging investee corporations through correspondence, dialogue, voting shareholder proxies and recommending similar action to others, and occasionally filing shareholder resolutions. Specific concerns that MRTI promotes are the pursuit of peace; racial, social, and economic justice; environmental responsibility; and securing women's rights.

New Covenant's community investing provides financial capital for economic development in communities that are often overlooked or excluded by traditional financial structures. Community banks, credit unions, and loan funds, along with other community-based businesses build opportunity by helping to provide market-based jobs, housing, and local services. In an effort to create conditions supporting peace in Israel-Palestine, the Presbyterian Foundation has made a series of investments there including construction loans, microfinance, and direct investment.

New Covenant offers a family of funds including Balanced Growth, Growth, Balanced Income, and Income. The best performing fund, New Covenant Growth Fund, had a stellar 10-year annualized return of 12.5% as of June 2019. In May 2019 it transitioned from being actively managed to a passive fund while continuing to maintain its ESG tilt. The fund investment policy follows values established by the General Assembly of the Presbyterian Church (United States). The fund uses both positive and negative screens. It overweights companies with favorable ESG scores while screening out companies in alcohol, tobacco, weapons, gambling, for-profit prisons, and human rights violators.

The Interfaith Center on Corporate Responsibility

The Interfaith Center on Corporate Responsibility (ICCR), founded in 1971, is an organization of over 300 global institutional investors representing more than $400 billion in AUM. Its members represent faith-based organizations, socially responsible asset management companies, unions, foundations, and other responsible investors along with a global network of nongovernmental organizations (NGO) and business partners. ICCR was one of the first organizations to promote ESG investing, initially focusing on using its collective investment weight in response to human rights abuses in South Africa. Over time, the organization has broadened the range of issues with which it is engaged. In 2018 ICCR launched the Investor Alliance for Human Rights, a global investor network driving corporate and investor human rights due diligence in alignment with the UN Guiding Principles on Business and Human Rights. The Alliance consists of 137 institutions from 14 countries representing assets of $3.5 trillion. ICCR works through corporate dialogues, filing shareholder resolutions and roundtable discussions among companies, investors, and other stakeholders including NGOs, community groups and industry trade associations. Some important recent initiatives include: calling for increased due diligence to eliminate forced labor risks in global supply chains, curbing greenhouse gases (GHG), pressing for more sustainable food systems, improved corporate water stewardship policies, and more affordable and accessible health care and financial services. ICCR's current priority issues are:

- Corporate governance: board independence and diversity, executive compensation, lobbying, and political spending.
- Health: drug pricing, health-care policy, and global health-care challenges.
- Climate Change: GHG reduction, methane emissions, and electric utilities.
- Financial Services: risk management and responsible lending.
- Food: antibiotics in meat production, food waste, and labor.
- Human Rights: human trafficking and slavery, the "no (employment) fees" initiative, fair chance hiring, and improved garment worker conditions to avoid a repeat of events such as the 2013 deaths of 1134 workers in Bangladesh.
- Water: human right to water and corporate water impacts.

Christian Super

Christian Super, an Australian fund manager, manages retirement resources for 27,000 members and has $1.5 billion in AUM. Since 1984 it has invested these funds ethically in line with Christian values. The core values are:

- Display integrity through high standards of behavior, ethical processes, and ethical dealings with all, including members, employers, the broader industry and each other.
- Be relational with a "people over process" focus.
- Products, people, and processes are professional.
- Be intentional and prudent in all activities.
- Be innovative as an organization and as individuals.

The Fund's Ethical Investment Positions cover a wide range of issues with probably the most detailed and thorough descriptions of its exclusions:

- Alcohol: The Fund will avoid investments in any company that derives more than 5% of its revenue from alcoholic beverage production or 20% of its revenue from their distribution. Companies that are involved in responsible marketing of alcohol will not be excluded. The Fund will also avoid investment in companies that have irresponsible sales practices.
- Animal testing: The Fund will screen out companies involved in farming practices of overcrowding or factory farming and exclude on a case-by-case basis companies that do not allow animals time outside or space to walk. It will also consider any cases of the live exportation of animals that involve poor planning or management resulting in unnecessary animal suffering. It will also exclude companies that continue to conduct

animal testing unnecessarily without consideration to the "3Rs" of replacement, reduction, and refinement of animal testing procedures.
- Bribery and corruption: The Fund will exclude companies where:
  - there is proof of, or research indicates, a high likelihood of involvement in bribery or corruption; and
  - denial of wrongdoing is continuing and/or tangible commitments to taking appropriate preventative action is minimal.

  To be considered for reinclusion, a company must demonstrate a commitment to the development of appropriate policies and practices to prevent future occurrences of corruption. This may include an admission of guilt, removal of involved personnel, improvement of policy, and cooperation with law enforcement authorities. The Fund will attempt to engage with companies where improvements could be made.
- Cannabis: The Fund excludes any company who derives more than 5% of their revenue from the production or 20% of their revenue from distribution of cannabis and its related products for recreational use. Companies involved in production and distribution for medicinal use and research will not be excluded from the investible universe.
- Christian values: Where inappropriate business activities arise, the Fund will exclude the company on a case-by-case basis. These behaviors include the deliberate or indiscriminate destruction of human life, the abuse of human dignity and freedoms, the damaging of health and well-being, the wanton destruction of creation in pursuit of short-term profit and reaping reward from unjust behavior.
- Climate change: The Fund will favor the best performers within each sector and seek out investments which mitigate climate change. Companies with poor climate change policies and practices will receive a lower internal rating and in extreme cases will be excluded.
- Consumer debt: The Fund will avoid companies where there is involvement in predatory lending practices and who deliberately and unconscionably exploit the poor and those who are unable to repay loans. Companies that are involved in other unethical credit practices (e.g., misleading/misinforming borrowers on contract details and hidden costs, targeting youth with credit cards, regular offers of increased credit limits, etc.) will be under-weighted in the portfolio or excluded in extreme cases. It will give special consideration in the case of companies focused on socially aware impact investing, such as in microfinance.
- Food industry: The Fund reviews major food (including fast food) producers to assess their overall commitment to nutrition and health through their product range, marketing practices, and promotion of active lifestyle, with a view of excluding those companies that consistently perform below industry standards.
- Fossil fuel: The Fund will exclude companies deriving more than 15% of their revenue from the following activities:

* Mining thermal coal
* Exploration and development of oil sands
* Liquefaction of coal
* Exploration and development of oil shale (not to be confused with shale oil or shale gas)
* Brown coal (or lignite) fired power generation

  When global electricity generation from renewable energy sources surpasses generation from coal, the 15% revenue tolerance will be reduced to 10%. For companies in the oil and gas sectors those that consistently display a worst-in-sector approach through a lack of readiness to adapt will be excluded from the portfolio. Further consideration of exclusion for companies deriving the majority of their revenue from oil will be made once electric vehicles represent a viable alternative to existing vehicles, which shall be considered to be when they reach either 5% of new motor vehicles sold or 2% of total motor vehicle stock. For domestic equities, a more nuanced range of additional factors (such as climate change preparedness and transition to renewable energy) may be considered in the analysis of whether exclusion is warranted. The Fund will continue to monitor and revise this position to ensure that the types of activities and fossil fuels covered by the summary position keep pace with technological and environmental developments. When cleaner fuel sources and methods of energy production emerge and become more widely used, the position will be adjusted accordingly.
* Gambling: Christian Super will avoid investing in companies involved in gambling-related products and services. This includes, but is not limited to:
  * Operation or ownership of gambling establishments, for example, casinos, online gambling sites, and racetracks.
  * Production of gambling machines, for example, slot machines and video lottery terminals.
  * Production of gambling software

    It recognizes that to an extent gambling falls under individual choice and thus it will apply a 5% of revenue tolerance level.
* Genetic engineering: The Fund excludes companies on a case-by-case basis where they:
  * Fail to be transparent about their genetic engineering activities,
  * Have no or inadequate systems in place to address moral risk,
  * Cause undue harm, particularly by causing disadvantage to those in need, or
  * Create undue dependence on their products (e.g., agricultural terminator genes).
* Human rights and responsibilities: The Fund excludes any company where human rights violations result as a direct consequence of that company's actions or inactions. The Fund will use its discretion in the

application of human rights, acknowledging that in some instances human rights will come into conflict with themselves and also need to be subordinate to Christian truths in their importance.

- Labor issues: Christian Super engages with, and in the most systemic and egregious cases excludes, companies who fail to uphold appropriate standards in relation to workplace safety, freedom of association, forced labor, child labor, discrimination, harassment, and other similar practices. It also recognizes the responsibility companies have to ensure appropriate labor standards within their supply chains. It also seeks to invest in companies that have demonstrated strong labor practices, including commitment to a good work/life balance, excellent safety records, employment programs for marginalized groups, and family-friendly policies.
- Marketing: The Fund excludes from investment any company consistently involved in a material level of improper marketing practices, including:
  - Marketing that deliberately lies and deceives.
  - Marketing of products to the vulnerable (including children) that damages their health and/or overall well-being.
  - Marketing agencies where the majority of their business promotes products or services that we have excluded on ethical grounds.
  - Highly sexualized or violent advertising.
- Ocean stewardship: Christian Super will seek to promote good ocean stewardship by avoiding investment in companies and technologies that negatively affect the ocean, whether through pollution, promoting climate change, or over-fishing, and by positive investment in companies that show initiative in these areas or promote positive technologies.
- Sanctity of life: Christian Super excludes companies involved in the direct service of abortion or drugs intended to induce abortion. It seeks to invest in health care and/or hospitals, particularly where it involves the development of new facilities and services in previously underserved areas. It will not invest in health care and hospitals where objectionable activities form a material component of services provided, or where revenue from such services is material and it may consider engagement where more efforts are possible.
- Sex industry: It excludes from investment any company found to be involved in the production or development of inappropriate adult products or adult entertainment.
- Stem Cells: Christian Super will exclude any company involved in stem cell research that involves the destruction of human embryos.
- Tobacco: Applying a revenue tolerance of 2% for production and 10% for distribution, the Fund excludes investments in any company that manufactures or distributes consumable tobacco products.
- Uranium: The Fund excludes companies involved in uranium mining if they are found to be exporting uranium to states that are not in

compliance with the International Atomic Energy Agency safeguards. Further, it will carefully watch owners and operators of nuclear power plants and exclude on a case-by-case basis where such companies lack appropriate policies and safety procedures or are involved in questionable activities.

- Violent entertainment: Christian Super excludes on a case-by-case basis any company that is involved in the promotion of inappropriately violent real-life activities for entertainment.
- Waste stewardship: The Fund excludes companies that flagrantly ignore their responsibilities to appropriately address waste stewardship practices in their own operations and supply chains; and that do not demonstrate a tangible commitment to taking appropriate action to manage waste.
- Water stewardship: Christian Super seeks to exclude companies found harshly monopolizing water resources to the exclusion of others and destroying people's ability to access water for their own use. It will also seek investment in technologies, and overweight companies involved in technologies, promoting the fair, affordably priced, and sustainable availability of water.
- Weapons
  - Military weapons and firearms: The Fund avoids companies that derive more than 5% of revenues from the manufacture of military weapons and small firearms. In addition, companies that derive more than 10% of revenues from the distribution of small firearms are excluded as well.
  - Firearms: This also covers companies deriving more than 5% of revenues from the manufacture or more than 10% of revenues from distribution of firearms of pistols, handguns, rifles, shotguns, and handheld automatic or semiautomatic weapons and ammunition for such weapons.
  - Controversial weapons (absolute): Controversial weapons are weapons which are indiscriminate in targeting and disproportionate in impact, on civilian populations; the effects of which may continue long after initial deployment. These include atomic, biological, or chemical weapons, as well as antipersonnel landmines and cluster munitions. Christian Super applies an absolute exclusion to any company involved in the production or distribution of controversial weapons. This includes the production of key components that are specifically designed for and are directly linked to the lethality of these weapons.

Timothy Plan Funds

Timothy Plan Funds practice what it calls "Biblically Responsible Investing," in contrast to sustainable investing. In 1992 a search for funds to support the retirement needs of pastors of independent churches turned up several socially screened funds, but those funds screened only for a few social issues such as alcohol and tobacco. There were none that screened for other moral issues such as abortion and pornography. Thus in 1994 the Timothy family of funds were formed to initially focus on five major factors: abortion, pornography, alcohol, tobacco, and casino gambling. Years later, screens for antifamily entertainment and alternative lifestyles were added to the mix. Now, the funds exclude securities issued by any company that is involved in the production or wholesale distribution of alcohol, tobacco, or gambling equipment, gambling enterprises, or which is involved, either directly or indirectly, in abortion or pornography, or promoting antifamily entertainment or alternative lifestyles. And it is noted that because the funds do not invest in excluded securities and will divest securities that are subsequently discovered to be ineligible, investing in these funds may be riskier than other funds that invest in a broader array of securities.

Timothy Plan now offers a wide range of funds:

- Small Cap Value
- Large/Mid Cap Value
- Large/Mid Cap Growth
- Aggressive Growth
- Growth & Income
- Fixed Income
- High Yield Bond
- International
- Emerging Markets
- Israel Common Values
- Defensive Strategies
- Strategic Growth
- Conservative Growth

There are also two Timothy Plan ETFs. The US Large Cap Core ETF tracks the performance of the NASDAQ Victory US Large Cap Volatility Weighted BRI Index, which includes Timothy Plans biblical screens. The High Dividend Stock ETF tracks the performance of the NASDAQ Victory US Large Cap High Dividend Volatility Weighted BRI Index, which also includes Timothy Plan's traditional biblical screens.

Eventide Funds

Eventide Funds pursues "investing that makes the world rejoice." Its vision is to serve individuals, financial advisors, and institutions by providing high-performance investments that create compelling value for the global common good. As of mid-2019 it had more than $3.8 billion in AUM. Its investment philosophy is based on the belief that high-quality companies that excel at creating value for others and trade at a discount to intrinsic value offer superior long-term risk-adjusted returns. At the same time, it believes in investing in companies that create compelling value for the global common good. Here are some of its mutual fund offerings:

- Eventide Gilead Fund is a diversified equity mutual fund representing Eventide's best ideas. It seeks long-term capital appreciation and has a historical emphasis on health care and information technology.
- Eventide Healthcare & Life Sciences Fund has a diversified focus on health care and life sciences. Investments are concentrated in drug-related industries and the fund may be invested in illiquid securities.
- Eventide Multi-Asset Income Fund is a diversified mutual fund representing the best ideas for income. It seeks attractive current income, plus capital appreciation. As a multiasset fund it will have up to 40% of nontraditional sources of income.
- Eventide Global Dividend Opportunities Fund represents best ideas in dividend-paying stocks. It seeks attractive dividend income plus capital appreciation. A secondary objective is dividend growth.
- Eventide Limited-Term Bond Fund invests in limited duration bonds representing a best ideas approach to fixed-income investing. It seeks attractive limited duration bond income.

All of these Eventide funds also focus on identifying and investing in companies capable of sustaining profitability and growth by serving well the needs of customers, employees, suppliers, communities, the environment, and society broadly. The funds seek to invest in companies that reflect the following values:

- Respecting the value and freedom of all people, the right to life at all stages and freedom from addictive behaviors caused by gambling, pornography, tobacco, and alcohol.
- Demonstrating a concern for justice and peace through fair and ethical relationships with customers, suppliers, and business partners and through avoidance of products and services that promote weapons production and proliferation.
- Promoting family and community by protecting children from violent forms of entertainment and serving low-income communities.
- Exhibiting responsible management practices, including fair dealing with employees, communities, competitors, suppliers, and customers.
- Practicing environmental stewardship: This includes practices considered more sustainable than those of industry peers, reduction in environmental impact when compared to previous periods, and/or the use of more efficient and cleaner energy sources.

The company notes that its ethical values screens can cause underperformance.

Catholic values investing: socially responsible investment guidelines

As with the other religions, Catholic values investors come in many forms: individuals, family offices, health care, and other service organizations as well as Catholic nonprofits, Catholic educational institutions, parishes, and dioceses. Investment strategies may be combinations of negative screening, positive selection based on ESG criteria and shareholder engagement and proxy voting. In 2003 the United States Conference of Catholic Bishops (USCCB) established guidelines for investing in a manner consistent with the values of the Catholic religion. An underlying principle is that financial resources should be managed with faithful, competent, and socially responsible stewardship. There is a recognition that a reasonable return is necessary in order for the church to function effectively and to carry out its mission. The combination of religious mandate and fiscal responsibility motivated the USCCB to develop a clear and comprehensive set of policies to guide investments and other activities related to corporate responsibility. Three basic themes provide background for these guidelines:

- Church as shareholder and investor: Individuals as well as those responsible within church institutions must invest funds responsibly. It is a moral and legal fiduciary responsibility to ensure an adequate return on investment for the support of the work of the church, and there are broader moral concerns. As part-owners, investors must cooperate in shaping the policies of those companies through dialogue with management, through votes at corporate meetings, through the introduction of resolutions and through participation in investment decisions. Policies such as those which support enterprises that promote economic development in depressed communities, and which help the church respond to local and regional needs are praiseworthy. When the decision to divest seems unavoidable, it should be done after prudent examination and with a clear explanation of the motives.
- Shareholder responsibility: Shareholders can and should vote on the selection of corporate directors and on investment questions and other policy matters, but the question of how to relate the rights and responsibilities of shareholders to those of other people and communities affected by corporate decisions is complex and insufficiently understood. Serious, long-term research and experimentation in this area is encouraged and more effective ways of dealing with these questions are essential to enable firms to serve the common good.
- Church as economic actor: Members of the Church play an economic role united together as the Church. It employs many people; it has investments; it has extensive properties for worship and mission. All the moral principles that govern the just operation of any economic endeavor apply

to the Church and its agencies and institutions; indeed, the Church should be exemplary. Historically, the Conference corporate responsibility policies have consisted primarily of exclusions, choosing not to invest in companies that comprise about 10% of the S&P 500. Through these current guidelines, the Conference seeks to put in place policies that are broader, more explicit, active, flexible, and effective in applying the teaching of the Church to the realities of the market.

With these three background themes, USCCB socially responsible investment guidelines are based on the two fundamental and interdependent principles of responsible financial stewardship and ethical and moral investing:

- Principle 1: The Conference should exercise responsible financial stewardship over its economic resources. In practical terms, this means obtaining a reasonable rate of return on its investments. For example, the Conference now expects its managers to perform at least at the level of the market.
- Principle 2: In its investment policy the Conference should exercise ethical and social stewardship based on Catholic moral principles. These investment strategies recognize the reality that socially beneficial activities and socially undesirable or even immoral activities are often inextricably linked in the products produced and the policies followed by individual corporations. Given the realities of mergers, buyouts, and conglomeration, it is increasingly likely that investments will be in companies whose policies or products make the holding of their stock a "mixed investment" from a moral and social point of view. Nevertheless, by prudently applying traditional Catholic moral teaching, and employing traditional principles on cooperation and tolerance, as well as the duty to avoid scandal, the Conference can reflect moral and social teaching in investments.

These two principles help identify investment opportunities that meet both the financial needs and social criteria of the Conference. The principles are carried out through the following types of strategies:

- Do no harm (avoid evil): This strategy involves two possible courses of action: (1) refusal to invest in companies whose products and/or policies are counter to the values of Catholic moral teaching or statements adopted by the Conference of bishops; and (2) divesting from such companies. The decision to divest, or to refuse to invest, would be based on the principle of cooperation and the avoidance of scandal. It would have to be done prudently, with care taken to minimize the financial impact and possible other negative consequences. In some cases, Conference policy may not absolutely require divestment, but significant Conference investments in these areas might cause confusion or scandal (e.g., heavy investment in conventional military weapons producers, gambling stocks, etc.). In these cases, prudence would be the guiding principle.

- Active corporate participation: Under this approach, the Conference should vote its proxies and use its opportunities as a shareholder to support policies in accord with its values and oppose those in conflict with them. This strategy involves actively using the Conference's position as shareholder to influence the corporate culture and to shape corporate policies and decisions. These activities could include dialogue with corporate leadership, initiating or supporting shareholder resolutions, and working with various religious and other groups who are working for corporate responsibility, writing letters to corporate executives and board members to advocate specific steps or to support or raise objections to a corporation's activities or policies. This approach could also enable the Conference to deal effectively with the reality of "mixed investments." One way to be a socially responsible investor is to set limits for corporations engaged in questionable or objectionable activities, to hold a minimal position in those companies that fall under the threshold, and then to use one's position as shareholder to work actively to influence or redirect the activities or policies of the corporation toward activities and policies which are socially beneficial and serve the common good. Investments of this type may be tolerated, after careful application of the principle of cooperation and the duty to avoid scandal, so long as the Conference engages in active participation and there is a reasonable hope of success for corporate change.
- Positive strategies ("promote the common good"): These strategies involve at least two possible courses of action: (1) supporting policies and initiatives in companies owned by the Conference that promote the values of Catholic moral and social teaching or positions advocated by Conference statements while earning a reasonable rate of return; (2) investments that promote community development, which, in some cases, may result in a lower rate of return, but which nevertheless are chosen because they give expression to the Church's preferential option for the poor or produce some truly significant social good. In the first case, the Conference can support companies and financial institutions which, in addition to their fiscal merits and investment advantages, have strong records in such areas as labor relations, affirmative action, affordable housing (e.g., market-rate certificates of deposit in institutions with special programs for low cost housing, or common stocks of companies that produce socially superior products and perform well in the market, etc.). In the second case, the Conference has positive experience with community development investments through the Catholic Campaign for Human Development.

USCCB investment policies

Based on the foregoing, USCCB developed investment policy recommendations covering the following areas:

- Protecting human life:
    - Abortion investment policy of the USCCB is absolute exclusion of investment in companies whose activities include direct participation in or support of abortion. Direct participation in abortion may include, but not be limited to, companies involved in the manufacture of abortifacients and publicly held health-care companies that perform abortions when not absolutely required by federal or state law. The Conference will consider supporting shareholder resolutions on abortion-related issues when deemed appropriate.
    - Contraceptives: The USCCB will not invest in companies that manufacture contraceptives or derive a significant portion of its revenues from the sale of contraceptives, even if they do not manufacture them.
    - Embryonic stem cell/human cloning: The USCCB will not invest in companies that engage in scientific research on human fetuses or embryos that (1) results in the end of prenatal human life; (2) makes use of tissue derived from abortions or other life-ending activities; or (3) violates the dignity of a developing person. Specific activities covered by the policy will include:
        - Embryonic stem cell research
        - Fetal tissue research or stem cell research derived from embryos
        - Human cloning
- Promoting human dignity
    - Human rights: USCCB will actively promote and support shareholder resolutions directed toward protecting and promoting human rights. For example, USCCB could join efforts to influence corporations that are engaged in extractive industries or are operating in countries with significant human rights concerns. USCCB will use selected shareholder resolutions and other means to encourage companies to provide sufficient wages, working conditions, and other social benefits that enable their employees and families to meet basic human needs. USCCB will seek means to encourage efforts by companies to promote a respect for fundamental human rights, especially in those countries in which these companies operate that have documented practices that deny or violate the human rights of their citizens.
    - Racial discrimination: USCCB will divest from those companies whose policies are found to be discriminatory against people of varied ethnic and racial backgrounds that have been historically disadvantaged. USCCB will actively promote and support shareholder

resolutions directed toward equal opportunities for minorities. USCCB as a shareholder will actively work for the inclusion of minorities on corporate boards.

- Gender discrimination: The USCCB will direct its investment advisors to invest in companies that actively promote corporate policies on equal pay and promotion opportunities for women, and accommodation of legitimate family needs. The USCCB will exercise its responsibility as shareholder to promote the active participation of women in the life of the company, particularly in terms of policy and decision-making, and inclusion in corporate leadership positions.
- Access to pharmaceuticals (e.g., HIV/AIDS): USCCB will encourage companies to undertake or participate in programs designed to make life-sustaining drugs available to those in low-income communities and countries at reduced, affordable prices, consistent with Catholic values. USCCB will actively encourage and support shareholder resolutions directed toward making life-sustaining drugs more available and affordable to low-income communities and nations.
- Curbing pornography: The USCCB will not invest in a company whose purpose is to appeal to a prurient interest in sex or to incite sexual excitement. The USCCB will promote and support initiatives, including in some cases, shareholder resolutions, to promote responsible and family-oriented program content development by media companies.
- Reducing arms production
  - Production and sale of weapons: The Conference will avoid investment in firms primarily engaged in military weapons production or the development of weapons inconsistent with Catholic teaching on war (e.g., biological and chemical weapons, arms designed or regarded as first-strike nuclear weapons, indiscriminate weapons of mass destruction, etc.) The Conference will support shareholder actions to limit weapons production, to limit foreign sales of weapons, and to convert corporate capacity to nonmilitary uses.
  - Antipersonnel landmines: USCCB will not invest in companies that are directly involved in the manufacture, sale, or use of antipersonnel landmines.
- Pursuing economic justice
  - Labor standards/sweatshops: USCCB will actively promote and support shareholder resolutions directed toward avoiding the use of sweatshops in the manufacture of goods. USCCB will promote and support shareholder resolutions to promote generous wage and benefit policies and adequate worker safety guidelines.
  - Affordable housing/banking: The Conference will not deposit funds in a financial institution that receives less than a "satisfactory" rating from federal regulatory agencies under the Community Reinvestment

Act. It will encourage the financial institutions where it deposits its resources to undertake programs and implement policies to secure an "outstanding" rating under the act.

- Protecting the environment: USCCB investment policy will actively promote and support shareholder resolutions which encourage corporations to act "to preserve the planet's ecological heritage, addressing the rampant poverty in the poorest nations, redirecting development in terms of quality rather than quantity in the industrial world, and creating environmentally sensitive technologies. USCCB investment policy will encourage policies and businesses that undertake reasonable and effective initiatives for energy conservation and the development of alternate renewable and clean energy resources and offering incentives to corporations to reduce greenhouse gas emissions and assistance to workers affected by those policies."
- Encouraging corporate responsibility: USCCB will encourage companies to report on social, environmental, as well as financial performance. USCCB will actively promote and support shareholder resolutions directed toward adoption of corporate social responsibility guidelines within companies.

Catholic values mutual funds

Catholic values investors have several choices of investment vehicles to meet their requirements. Some investment firms offer bespoke faith-based portfolio services through their investment advisory programs. These services offer a broad range of investment choices which can be tailored to the individual or institutional needs of the investor. There are also standardized pooled investment options. One of the more popular choices in mutual funds is the Ave Maria Mutual Fund family of funds.

Ave Maria Mutual Funds

Ave Maria Mutual Funds have roughly $2 billion invested in companies that align financial goals with Catholic moral beliefs. Proprietary criteria are utilized to screen out companies that promote or support activities contrary to the core moral teachings of the Catholic Church, but equal emphasis is also placed on investment performance. All investments are screened to eliminate any company engaged in abortion, pornography, embryonic stem cell research, or those that make corporate contributions to Planned Parenthood. The strategy is termed Morally Responsible Investing and is different from socially responsible investing in that it screens out companies engaged in activities that are not pro-life or pro-family. The screens used are established by Ave Maria's Catholic Advisory Board which provides guidance and meets regularly to review the Funds' religious standards and criteria.

Fund name	Assets	Focus	Five-year return annualized	Ten-year return annualized
Rising Dividend Fund	864.4	Dividend paying common stocks	7.74	13.52
Growth Fund	695.2	Mid-cap and larger companies with potential for above ave growth	12.89	15.29
Value Fund	238.8	Companies believed to be undervalued	3.94	10.52
S&P 500 Index			10.71	9.71
World Equity Fund	62.1	Companies of all capitalization from around the world	5.11	
MSCI World Index			6.60	8.85
Bond Fund	353.4	Primarily domestic gov and corp investment grade debt. May be up to 20% equities	3.11	4.50
Bloomberg Barclays Intermediate Gov/Credit Index			2.39	3.24

FIGURE 14.1   Performance of selected Ave Maria Funds and benchmarks. Data from *Ave Maria Mutual Funds web site. Assets in $ Millions, returns are annualized percentage. All data as of June 30, 2019.*

Fig. 14.1 shows 5- and 10-year performance data for the Ave Maria Mutual Funds, along with benchmarks.

The Ave Maria Bond Fund received the 2019 Lipper Fund Award as the best of 42 A-rated corporate bond funds, based on performance for the 3-year period ended November 30, 2018. While some Ave Maria funds were above benchmarks and some below, depending on choice of time period, in general, it is likely that most Catholic values investors were satisfied that the financial performance of these funds was reasonable and that they were suitable investments to achieve both financial and social/moral objectives.

LKCM Aquinas Catholic Equity Fund

Another fund, the LKCM Aquinas Catholic Equity Fund seeks to maximize long-term capital appreciation, while incorporating Catholic values investing principles in the investment process. The adviser's strategy in managing the Fund is to identify high-quality companies that exhibit certain characteristics, including high profitability levels, strong balance sheet, competitive advantages, ability to generate excess cash flows, meaningful management ownership stakes, attractive reinvestment opportunities, and/or strong market share positions.

The Fund practices socially responsible investing within the framework provided by the USCCB's Socially Responsible Investment Guidelines with respect to companies that engage in, participate in, or otherwise support activities related to, among other things, abortion, contraceptives, embryonic stem cells, human cloning, human rights, weapons production, and pornography. The Fund's investment approach incorporates these Guidelines through a combination of screening portfolio companies, dialogue with companies whose policies and practices conflict with the Catholic Guidelines, and/or potentially excluding from the Fund's portfolio the securities of those companies that are unwilling to alter their policies and practices over a reasonable period of time. If the Fund invests in a company whose policies and practices are inconsistent with the Catholic Guidelines, the Adviser may attempt to influence the company or sell the company's securities or otherwise exclude future investments in such company. For the period ending March 31, 2019, the Fund's annualized return trailed that of the S&P 500 Index, for the 5-year period (6.76% vs 10.91%) and the 10-year period (13.52% vs 15.92%).

Catholic values ETF

While mutual funds focused on Catholic Values Investors have seen significant uptake, ETF growth has been slower, despite several advantages to the ETF structure versus mutual funds. One relatively new ETF is the Global X S&P 500 Catholic Values ETF which began trading in 2016. Its performance tracks that of companies within the S&P 500 whose business practices adhere to the Socially Responsible Investment Guidelines as outlined by USCCB and excludes those that do not. As of mid-2019 it had AUM of $270 million. Its annualized annual return up to mid-2019 for the 1- and 3-year periods was 9.45% and 14.13%, respectively.

Islamic values investing

Total assets in global Islamic finance were estimated to be between $2.5 and $3 trillion in 2019. Islamic investing is governed by Shariah laws. In general,

Islamic finance is equity-based, asset-backed, ethical, sustainable, environmentally, and socially responsible. It entails risk-sharing amongst the parties and is grounded in "real" (physical) assets. It seeks to promote financial inclusion and social welfare. Noncompliance with Shariah law of conventional financial products and services has led to the exclusion of large populations of Muslims from financial markets. These populations are among the poorest in the world and most in need of access to banking and finance. The development of Shariah-compliant products is helping to improve their life circumstances.

A starting point for Islamic investing is recognizing that some industries and companies are deemed inconsistent with Islamic principles and are therefore excluded from candidacy for investment. Another well-known feature of Islamic investing is that interest is considered to be exploitive of the borrower and is therefore not permitted. Many conventional financial services and products are consequently not consistent with these principles. Practices which are prohibited under Shariah law include the following:

- Interest is prohibited as being exploitive.
- Uncertainty and risk: some derivatives and short selling can have excessive risk (Although in a portfolio context, these may actually be risk-reducing strategies.)
- Speculation and gambling are prohibited.
- Materiality: each transaction must be related to a real, underlying economic asset or transaction.
- Profit and loss sharing or "skin in the game." Contract participants should all share in the risk/returns of the transactions.
- Forbidden activities, companies, and industries include alcohol, tobacco, arms, pornography, and gambling.

These provisions entail taking on less risk exposure and consequently allowed investors following Islamic principles to more successfully weather the Global Financial Crisis of 2008.

There are several financing arrangements which are compliant with Shariah rules:

- Profit and loss partnerships ("mudarabah") where Party A provides capital and Party B manages the project, with both sharing in profits.
- Profit and loss joint venture ("musharakah") where Party A and Party B each provide capital and each share, in a predetermined formula, in the profit and loss of the undertaking.
- Leasing: Party A owns the property, and Party B pays a periodic rental fee and either purchases the property at the end of the term, or Party A reclaims it.

Western-style interest-paying bonds, options, and other derivatives are typically excluded from consideration under Shariah law. But other asset classes are available, particularly public and private equity and a special form of Shariah-compliant bond called "sukuk." There are a variety of forms of sukuk. One is the "sukuk al-ijara." In this lease-like structure, an asset is transferred to an owner and leased back, with the user paying rent. This is the structure used by the UK government in issuing the first Shariah-compliant bond outside of the Islamic world. Issued in 2014, the bond was secured by three UK government properties. The bond provided £200 million for a 5-year term with rent of 2.036%.

Green sukuk bonds

From an ESG investing perspective, an interesting convergence is the growth in the green bond movement combined with sustainability interests of Islamic investors. This has culminated in the issuance of "Green Sukuk" Bonds. Sukuk and green bonds have many similarities including:

- Funds are raised for a specific project or purpose
- They are asset-based
- They are both focused on consistent social or environmental values
- Environmental stewardship is central to their motivation

With early assistance and guidance from the World Bank, Malaysia has issued several bonds targeted to renewable energy projects. These bonds are structured to be consistent with Shariah principles. The Securities Commission of Malaysia issued Socially Responsible Sukuk Guidelines which incorporated the requirements for the issuance of sustainable and responsible investment (SRI) sukuk. The guidelines were accompanied by the following incentives to attract green investors:

- Financing incentives providing government guarantees of up to 60%
- Tax incentives for green tech
- Tax deductions for 5 years
- Outright grants to green SRI sukuk issuers to finance external project reviews

These efforts resulted in several new sukuk issues, financing a projected total of 7200 MW of renewal energy by 2020. Beginning in July 2017, funded projects include:

- Tadau Energy Sdn. Bhd. The first green energy sukuk provided $59 million equivalent to finance a 50 MW solar plant in Sabah, Malaysia.
- Quantum Solar issue of about $240 million.
- PND Merdeku financing for construction of an 83 story building the first triple green-rated building in Malaysia.

- Sinar Kamiri: proceeds from the sukuk will be solely used for the design, construction, ownership, operation, and maintenance of a 49 MW Solar Photovoltaic facility at Sungai Siput, Perak in Malaysia.
- UiTM Solar: financing supporting one of two large-scale solar (LSS) photovoltaic power purchase agreements (PPAs), which Tenaga Nasional Bhd (TNB) inked in March 2017.

Islamic values indexes, mutual funds, and ETFs

In order to meet the needs of Islamic values investors, several equity indexes have been created. The indexes can be used as performance benchmarks for Shariah-compliant portfolios and as the basis for passive as well as actively managed portfolios. Mutual funds and ETFs based on these indexes offer those investors convenient, inexpensive instruments to achieve financial goals while respecting their religious values. These Shariah-compliant funds have been around since the 1960s but have gained increased interest more recently with the growth in wealth in Islamic countries and the maturation of their financial institutions. The indexes are designed to be subsets of conventional benchmarks that pass rules-based screens for Shariah compliance. The resulting indexes tend to be highly correlated to their conventional counterparts and provide Shariah-compliant versions of a wide variety of these popular conventional benchmarks. A supervisory board of Islamic scholars is responsible for defining and maintaining the rules governing the Shariah screening process. For the S&P Dow Jones Indices, the company retains oversight on all other index methodology issues, including rules for company selection in the benchmark index, weighting, and index maintenance. Shariah screening is performed at two primary levels: business activity and financial ratios. At the first level, the business activities of each company are evaluated. Companies with significant involvement in certain noncompliant business activities such as conventional financial services, alcohol, tobacco, gaming, pork, pornography, and most conventional media organizations are excluded. At the second level, the remaining companies are examined for compliance with board-approved financial ratios such as degree of leverage, cash holdings, and the percentage of revenue derived from noncompliant activities. There are some differences in screening criteria in alternative indexes, reflecting a lack of consensus on all aspects of required exclusions. Fig. 14.2 shows sector coverage of the S&P 500 Shariah Index compared to the conventional S&P 500 Index.

Because nearly all firms involved in conventional financial services are not Shariah-compliant, the S&P 500 Shariah Index and funds based on it have very low sector coverage of financials. Consumer-related sectors are somewhat underrepresented as well, due to the exclusion of media and gaming firms, along with companies involved in the production or sale of alcohol, tobacco, and pork products. Finally, utilities and telecommunication

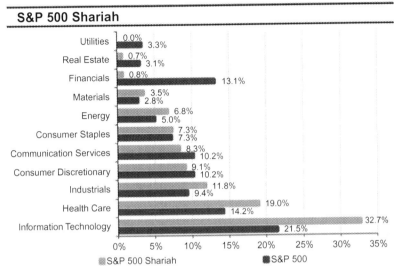

FIGURE 14.2   Sector composition comparison of the S&P 500 Shariah Index. *Source: S&P Dow Jones Indices LLC. Data as of June 28, 2019. Charts are provided for illustrative purposes.*

services are subject to exclusion because these firms typically have relatively high leverage ratios. Overall, the performance of these Shariah-compliant indexes and funds has been roughly comparable to the corresponding conventional indexes. Differences can be attributed to the differential sector weightings. In periods where the financial sector, in particular, has outperformed, conventional portfolios have done better, and conversely, when financials have been weak, these indexes have done better

There are many Shariah-compliant indexes covering a wide range of market segments: developed, emerging and frontier markets, at the regional and country level. There are also indexes covering specific strategies and property, infrastructure, and health-care sectors. Here are some details for a few of these indexes.

- The S&P 500 Shariah Index was created in 2006. As of mid-2019 it had 235 constituents, with a mean market cap for each of about $60 million. Its 10-year annualized return was 14.43% versus 14.81% for the conventional S&P 500.
- S&P Global 1200 Shariah has 602 constituents with a total market cap of about $45 billion. The largest sector is Information Technology (27.5%), followed by Health Care (18.9%), and Industrials (13.9%). Notably, Financials account for only 0.6%. Geographically, US companies account for 69% of the total. Ten-year annualized return was 12.3% versus a benchmark of 11.29%.

- S&P Global Healthcare Shariah Index has 88 constituents with a total market cap of about $46 billion. Forty-four of the companies are US-based, 26 are Japanese, and the remainder are scattered about Europe. Ten-year annualized return was 13.1% versus a benchmark of 14.01%.
- S&P Global Infrastructure Shariah has 34 constituents, with no more than four in any one country. Total market cap is about $9 billion. Ten-year annualized return was 6.46% versus a benchmark of 9.33%.

MSCI Islamic index series

MSCI has developed a series of indexes which follow Shariah investment principles and are based on one or more conventional MSCI Equity Indexes. The company has a Shariah advisory committee of Shariah scholars who certify its Islamic Index Methodology which consists of two steps. First businesses are screened to determine if their activities are consistent with Shariah principles. Excluded industries include alcohol, tobacco, pork, conventional financial services, gambling, music, hotels, cinema, and adult entertainment. Secondly, companies are screened out based on excessive leverage as reflected in three financial ratios. In calculating these ratios, the denominator can be either total assets or average market capitalization. Two separate series of Islamic Indexes are developed based on which of these denominators is used. The MSCI Islamic Index Series uses total assets, while the MSCI Islamic M-Series uses average market capitalization. Fig. 14.3 lists the MSCI Islamic Indexes and MSCI Islamic M-Series Indexes.

The MSCI World Islamic Index has 513 constituents from the large and mid-cap segments of 23 developed markets countries. Its 10-year performance trailed the conventional MSCI World index 9.7% versus 11.33%.

FTSE Shariah indexes

FTSE also offers an extensive list of Shariah Indexes. This series of indexes is certified as Shariah compliant by Yasaar Ltd., an impartial consultancy and leading authority on Shariah. Here is a brief list of these indexes:

Islamic Index Series	Islamic Index M-Series
MSCI World Islamic Index	MSCI ACWI Islamic M-Series Index
MSCI Asia Pacific Small Cap Islamic Index	MSCI EM (Emerging Market) Islamic M-Series Index
MSCI Emerging Market Islamic Index	MSCI Europe Islamic M-Series Index
MSCI Emerging Market Islamic Small Cap Index	Pacific Islamic M-Series Index
MSCI Frontier Market Index	MSCI North America Islamic M-Series
MSCI GCC International Index	
MSCI GCC International Small Cap Index	
MSCI GCC Domestic Index	
MSCI GCC Domestic Small Cap Index	

FIGURE 14.3   MSCI Islamic Indexes and MSCI Islamic M-Series Indexes. *Based on data from MSCI website.*

- FTSE Shariah Global Equity Index Series is based on the large and mid-cap stocks in the conventional FTSE Global Equity Index Series universe.
- FTSE NASDAQ Dubai Shariah Index Series. The index series is designed to represent the performance of the largest and most liquid Shariah-compliant companies from UAE, Kuwait, and Qatar.
- FTSE Bursa Malaysia Hirjah Shariah and EMAS Shariah Indexes. The indexes are designed to measure the performance of the major capital segments of the Malaysian market, dividing it into large cap, mid cap, small cap, fledgling, and Shariah-compliant market segments.
- FTSE SET Shariah Indexes. This index series covers all segments of the Thai capital market, divided into large, mid, small, and fledgling according to market capitalization. There is also a range of sector indexes segmented according to industry classification benchmark (ICB) and provides 10 industry, 19 super sector, and 39 sector indexes
- FTSE TWSE Taiwan Shariah Indexes. This is a series of indexes providing focused exposure to Shariah-compliant Taiwanese markets.
- FTSE/JSE Africa Shariah indices are designed to represent the performance of South African compliant companies.
- FTSE SGX Shariah Index Series. This index reflects the stock performance of companies in the Asia Pacific region whose business activities comply with Islamic Shariah Law. Constituents are screened for business activity and financial ratio compliance.
- FTSE Shariah Developed Minimum Variance Index. This index delivers reduced index volatility by overweighting stocks that reduce index volatility and underweighting stocks that increase index volatility.

These indexes provide benchmarks for mutual funds and ETFs offered by many different financial firms. The following section describes some of these pooled funds.

Amana Mutual Funds

Saturna Capital manages a series of mutual funds for Islamic investors:

- Amana Developing World. This fund has an objective of long-term capital growth, consistent with Islamic principles. As of mid-2019 it had AUM of $33 million. The Fund diversifies its investments across the companies, industries, and countries of the developing world, and principally follows a large-cap value investment style. The Fund seeks companies demonstrating both Islamic and sustainable characteristics. The Fund's adviser employs a sustainable rating system based on its own, as well as third-party, data to identify issuers believed to present low risks in ESG. Negative screening is used to exclude companies engaged in alcohol, tobacco, pornography, weapons, gambling, and fossil fuel extraction. This fund outperformed the MSCI Emerging Markets benchmark for the 1-year comparison period but trailed for the 3- and 5-year periods.

- Amana Growth Fund. This fund follows a large-cap value investment style, favoring companies expected to grow earnings and stock prices faster than the economy as a whole. It seeks companies demonstrating both Islamic and sustainable characteristics. As of mid-2019 it had AUM of $2.15 billion. Compared to the S&P 500, this fund outperformed for 1 year (20.01% vs 10.42%), 3 years (18.38% vs 14.22%), and 5 years (13.03%), but slightly underperformed for the 10-year period (13.94% vs 14.70%).
- Amana Income Fund. This fund seeks current income as its primary target, while also having objectives of preserving capital and observing Islamic principles. Because Islamic principles rule out receiving interest, this fund makes diversified investments in dividend paying mostly large-cap stocks. In mid-2019 it had AUM of $1.35 billion. This fund outperformed the S&P 500 for the 1-year comparison but trailed for longer time periods.
- Amana Participation Fund. Under normal conditions, this fund invests at least 80% of its total net assets in short and intermediate-term Islamic income-producing investments. Its objectives are capital preservation and current income, consistent with Islamic principles. It invests primarily in notes and certificates issued for payment by foreign governments, their agencies, and financial institutions in transactions structured to be in accordance with Islamic principles. It had $83 million in AUM in mid-2019. Its performance trailed that of the FTSE Sukuk benchmark for 1- and 3-year comparison periods.

The Iman Fund

The Iman Fund is a registered mutual fund which seeks to match the total return of the Dow Jones Islamic Market USA Index. As of mid-2019 AUM totaled $124 million. The fund invests in US common stocks that meet Islamic principles. It excludes investments in certain industries such as alcohol, tobacco, defense, and weapons companies, providers of conventional financial services (banking, insurance, etc.) and providers of entertainment services (hotels, casinos/gambling, cinema, pornography, music, etc.). It also excludes interest-bearing debt obligations. Its top holdings at year-end 2018 were Amazon, Apple, Microsoft, Alphabet, Procter and Gamble, salesforce, United Health, Colgate-Palmolive, Merck, and Johnson & Johnson. None of these equities accounted for more than 4.27% of total assets. The Fund is governed by its Board of Trustees which consists of nationally and internationally known Muslim scholars and community workers. The Board engaged Allied Asset Advisors, Inc. as the Fund's investment advisor. For most time periods it has outperformed its benchmarks, the Dow Jones Islamic Market US and World Indexes. Ten-year annualized return for the period ending mid-2019 was 13.97 for the Iman Fund, versus 13.59% for the Dow Jones Islamic Market US Index, and 11.58% for the Dow Jones Islamic Market World Index.

Shariah compliant ETFs

Islamic or Shariah ETFs are similar to other ETFs in that the ETF tracks a benchmark index. In this case, the index is one of those that track assets which are Shariah compliant, whereas a conventional ETF would track a benchmark index that includes some companies which would be excluded due to their noncompliance with Shariah principles. ETFs are collective investment vehicles and are similar to mutual funds, but they have several advantages: they can be bought and sold like stocks at any time during the trading day; theoretical prices can be determined intraday; tax treatment is often more favorable; and expenses are usually lower than those of mutual funds. Several investment firms offer Islamic or Shariah ETFs based on the Shariah-compliant indexes discussed earlier in this chapter. Here are a few examples of these ETFs:

- iShares MSCI World Islamic UCITS ETF is an exchange-traded fund that aims to track the performance of the MSCI World Islamic Index as closely as possible. It is managed by BlackRock. The fund size as of mid-2019 was $119 million.
- Wahed's FTSE USA Shariah ETF offering represents an interesting convergence of a robo-advisor with Islamic values investing. Wahed is a NY based company where investors can quickly open an online account and funds will be automatically invested based on individual risk preferences. Investment choices involve Wahed's FTSE USA Shariah ETF, Sukuk investments, and a gold ETF. The Wahed FTSE USA Shariah ETF is based on the FTSE USA Shariah Index and was expected to be listed on NASDAQ as of 2019.

Jewish values investing

Consideration of Jewish values in investing involves the integration of purpose and meaning in the investing process. While there are important differences among the Orthodox, Reform, and Conservative branches, Jewish values, traditions, and motifs can be used to guide investment decisions. The strengths and benefits of the Jewish community can be integrated in different ways into the investment process, according to the different types of investors, asset classes, and investor preferences. The Reform Pension Board (RPB), for example, established a Jewish Values Investment Policy based on the Jewish values of tikkun olam (repair of the world) and tzedek (justice), along with the fundamental beliefs articulated in the resolutions of the Central Conference of American Rabbis, the Union for Reform Judaism, and the Commission on Social Action of Reform Judaism. RPB's investment policy maintains a primary focus on fiduciary responsibility of a retirement plan but integrates Jewish values in consideration of ESG practices, and support for Israel.

Jewish values investing covers a broad range. Some investors choose to focus on Israel, either macroeconomic impacts or specific themes, sectors, or projects. Often, investors target startups involved in global efforts in education, health care, poverty alleviation, and the environment. Other investors support shareholder voting campaigns for various ESG causes. Still others support causes that are not specifically identified as Jewish, but are aligned with Jewish values such as investing in social causes in local neighborhoods, or environmental assets such as green bonds.

There can also be a recognition of the benefits of communal investing structures including:

- Explicit framing of motivations and intentions. The community allows dialogue and reflection that is hard to achieve in isolation.
- Sharing of best practices and the opportunity for communal learning.
- Multiplying the impact of investments through the synergy of a communal effort.

Judaism encourages consideration of values throughout business dealings and the Bible makes a point of referring to the other party in business dealings as a brother. Investment decisions are moral decisions and counterparts should be treated with respect.

Investment choices consistent with Jewish values run the full range of ESG favorable assets including public and private equity, bonds, and alternatives especially those that address issues such as education, health care, poverty, and the environment. In addition, many Jewish investors seek out these types of investments with specific focus on Jewish communities and Israel.

Jewish values indexes, mutual funds, and ETFs

Pooled investment vehicles for those interested in Jewish values primarily focus on Israel-based companies. The MSCI Israel Index is designed to measure the performance of the large and mid-cap segments of the Israeli equity market. It has 12 constituents and covers approximately 85% of the float-adjusted market capitalization in Israel. It is heavily weighted to information technology (41.94%) and financials (33.39%). Total market cap for the index companies was $81 billion in mid-2019.

S&P has several indexes covering Israel. Among them:

- The Dow Jones Israel Select Consumer Index measures the performance of a select portion of equity securities trading on the Tel Aviv Stock Exchange in the consumer goods and services sectors. There are 33 Israel-based constituent companies in this index.
- The S&P/Harel Energy Index is comprised of eligible companies classified as energy sector and gas utilities and independent power producers and energy traders. Fourteen of the companies are based in Israel and one in the United States.
- The S&P/Harel Communications Index is based on nine Israeli companies classified as communications services, communications equipment, and cable and satellite.
- The S&P/Harel Consumer Goods Index covers 15 Israeli companies classified in food and staples retailing; food, beverage, and tobacco; apparel, accessories and luxury goods; specialty stores; and automotive retail.
- The S&P/Harel Materials Index is comprised of 10 companies classified in the materials or textiles subindustries. Nine of the companies are located in Israel, one in the United States.
- The S&P/Harel Health Care Index consists of 20 companies classified within the health-care sector. Seventeen of the companies are located in Israel and three in the United States.

And while there are not any broad-based Jewish values ETFs at the moment, there are several Israel-focused funds. Among the largest are BlackRock's iShares' EIS, BlueStar's technology-focused ITEQ, and VanEck Vectors' ISRA.

- EIS—iShares MSCI Israel ETF: The iShares MSCI Israel ETF tracks the investment results of a broad-based index composed of equities in Israeli information technology, financials, and health-care companies. Among those equities are TEVA Pharmaceuticals, Check Point Software Technologies, Bank Hapoalim, and Bank Leumi Le Israel. Net assets in the ETF as of mid-2019 was $138 million. Its 10-year average annual return was 5.08%, close to its benchmark's 5.49%.
- The BlueStar Israel Technology ETF: This fund tracks the investment results of the BlueStar Israel Technology Index, an index of more than 58 technology companies listed on the Tel Aviv, NASDAQ, NYSE, London Stock Exchange, and Singapore Exchange. The investment goal of the fund is to provide investors with diversified exposure to the dynamic Israeli technology sector. The basic requirement for a company to be included is one of the following: at least 20% of the company's employees are located in Israel, 20% of long-lived assets located in Israel, or have a major R&D center in Israel. Other considerations include tax status, incorporation, or management domiciled within Israel. With the application of these criteria, 73% of the companies are in the United States, 22% in Israel, and 4% in the United Kingdom. By industrial

sector, the highest percentage of companies are in software and IT services (52%) and semiconductors (12%).

- VanEck Vectors Israel ETF seeks to match the price and yield performance of the BlueStar Global Index. Seventy-three percent of the index component countries are located in Israel and 23% are in the US Companies in the information technology sector account for 43% of net assets, financials are 20%, health care 11%, and real estate 7%.

Chapter 15

ESG investing-organizations having direct impact

Chapter Outline

Women's Sports Foundation   305
USA for UNHCR   308
Michael J. Fox Foundation for Parkinson's Research   309
Elton John AIDS Foundation   310
Water.org   310
Ocean Conservancy   312
Project AWARE   313
Sea Shepherd Conservation Society   313
UNICEF and UNESCO   315
    UNICEF   315
    UNESCO   317
Red Cross and Red Crescent Societies   319
The Salvation Army   322
Meals on Wheels   327
Habitat for Humanity   327

The previous chapters looked at several different sources of environmental, social, and governance (ESG) investing. In this chapter we consider some examples of charities, organizations which are the recipients of those investments. They are the "tip of the spear" in "making a difference." These are enterprises that generate direct social or environmental benefits and can have the most focused impact on ESG issues. Donations or other gifts to these organizations are made with the intention of generating positive, measurable social and environmental impact. Generating a financial return, if any, is a secondary objective at best. These charities often compete for funds with other nonprofits such as academic institutions, religious charities, donor-advised funds, and private foundations. The enterprises here are also recipients of public and private donor funds and put them to work to accomplish a variety of goals, primarily in the areas of sustainable agriculture, renewable energy, conservation, microfinance, and basic human services such as clean water, housing, nutrition, healthcare, and education. Some of these organizations are relatively young and have celebrity connections helping to publicize their activities. For example, Water.org is a favored cause of the actor Matt Damon, a co-founder. Some are called NGOs, nongovernmental organizations, a term covering a broad range of organizations. They often function like government agencies, but are independent of governments, although they may have some government funding. Others like the Red Cross and the Salvation Army have a long history of service. There are thousands of

Environmental, Social, and Governance (ESG) Investing. DOI: https://doi.org/10.1016/B978-0-12-818692-3.00015-3
303

registered charities in the United States alone and tens of thousands around the globe. In this chapter, we will look in some detail at several of these charities, but first some general observations.

Noting that our focus is primarily the United States, charitable giving by the American people is consistently impressive and not widely publicized. Overall charitable giving by US individuals, foundations, and corporations to US charities in 2017 was estimated at $410 billion, an increase of 5.2% over the 2016 level. Fig. 15.1 lists the 20 charities with the greatest amount of donations, based on data compiled by Forbes magazine.

One concern often expressed by donors is what percentage of contributions actually goes to charitable purposes as opposed to overhead or fundraising expense. For the list of charities in Fig. 15.1, Forbes calculated three financial efficiency ratios:

- Charitable commitment (sometimes called program support or program expense). This is the percentage of total expenditures which went to charitable purpose, as opposed to rent, salaries, fundraising, etc. This ratio averages in the 86%−87% range. New charities with high startup costs can have low ratios and charities receiving food, medicine, or other gifts in kind can have high ratios. Of the organizations listed, several had charitable commitment ratios of 99−100: Feeding America, Americares, Task Force for Global Health, Direct Relief, and Step Up for Students.

Name	Private support	Total revenue
United Way Worldwide	3.47	3.92
Feeding America	2.65	2.72
Americares Foundation	2.38	2.38
Task Force for Global Health	2.16	2.2
Salvation Army	2.03	4.3
St. Jude Children's Research Hospital	1.51	2.09
Direct Relief	1.22	1.24
Habitat for Humanity International	1.1	1.99
Boys & Girls Clubs of America	0.99	2.04
YMCA of the USA	0.97	7.4
Food for the Poor	0.94	0.95
Compassion International	0.89	0.89
Catholic Charities USA	0.86	3.74
Goodwill Industries International	0.80	5.87
Samaritan's Purse	0.76	0.80
Lutheran Services in America	0.73	22.06
American Cancer Society	0.73	0.86
World Vision	0.73	1.04
Step Up for Students	0.71	0.71
Nature Conservancy	0.69	1.14

FIGURE 15.1 Largest US charities. *Forbes. Amounts in $ billion.*

On the lower end, this ratio was 67% for Nature Conservancy, 71% for St. Jude, and 79% for the American Cancer Society.
- Donor dependency. This is the ratio of expenses to revenue. A ratio over 100 means the charity spends more than it takes in and is therefore more dependent on ongoing donor support. A charity with a ratio of 80 would spend only 80% of what it raised in that year. In years when financial markets do well, the ratio tends to be lower, as revenues increase relative to expenses. In down years, expenses tend to be higher relative to revenue. Most of the charities in Fig. 15.1 have donor dependency ratios of 90%–100%. Some run an annual surplus based on fee-based services and other revenue sources.
- Fundraising efficiency. Charities depend on donations, and a significant flow of donations in order to pursue their activities. It costs money to find these donors and to process their contributions. If a charity has few large donors, or receives gifts in kind, it may have very low fund-raising costs. The average fundraising efficiency for the biggest charities is 91%, meaning that fundraising costs are 9%. A ratio below the 65%–70% range is generally considered to be very inefficient. Most of the top 20 charities have fundraising efficiencies in the 90%–100% range. Those in the 80%–85% range are: YMCA, St. Jude, American Cancer Society, and Nature Conservancy.

On this last issue of fundraising expense, several services provide an assessment of individual charity's performance on this and other operating issues. Charity Navigator, for example, is an independent evaluator of charity organizations' financial health, accountability, and transparency. It is the largest such evaluator and assesses over 9000 US-based charities. It's organized as a nonprofit and accepts no advertising or donations from the entities it evaluates. One caveat of using this type of evaluation alone is that it does not look at an organization's program effectiveness. It only looks at its organizational structure. However, it would seem that efficiency ratings are useful especially when looking at extreme values. Charity Navigator has listed the ten charities spending more than 50% of their budget on professional fundraising fees and as little as 4.7% on program activities (Charity Navigator, 2019). The list of these most inefficient fundraisers is given in Fig. 15.2.

While there are many established charities doing important work without an affiliation with a media star, celebrities are increasingly lending their support and fund-raising influence to favored causes. Fig. 15.3 lists several of these charities.

Let's look at the details of some of these celebrity-related charities.

Women's Sports Foundation

The Women's Sports Foundation was founded in 1974 by the tennis legend, Billie Jean King. It is dedicated to creating leaders by ensuring girls' access

Name	Program expenses (%)	Professional fundraising fees (%)
Disabled Police and Sheriff's Foundation	4.7	90.3
Cancer Survivors' Fund	8.3	88.6
The Committee for Missing Children	6.4	87.9
Autism Spectrum Disorder Foundation	18.1	76.5
HonorBound Foundation	20.3	67.0
Kids Wish Network	19.7	61.0
Children's Leukemia Research Association	23.8	60.4
California Police Activities League	32.2	56.6
Find the Children	27.6	52.6
Law Enforcement Education Program	8.2	51.9

FIGURE 15.2   10 Charities overpaying their for-profit fundraisers. *Based on data from Charity Navigator.*

Name	Celebrity
The Children's Health Fund	Paul Simon
Christopher & Dana Reeve Foundation	Christopher Reeve
Elton John AIDS Foundation	Elton John
Michael J. Fox Foundation for Parkinson's Research	Michael J. Fox
National Constitution Center	George H.W. Bush, Bill Clinton, Slade Gorton, Dikembe Mutombo, Sandra Day O'Connor, Marc E. Platt, Edward G. Rendell, Ben Sherwood, Joseph Torsella
New York Restoration Project	Michael Kors, Bette Midler
People for the Ethical Treatment of Animals	Pink, Pamela Anderson, Alec Baldwin, Woody Harrelson, Alicia Silverstone
Tony La Russa's Animal Rescue Foundation	Tony La Russa
USA for UNHCR	Angelina Jolie
Women's Sports Foundation	Chris Evert, Mia Hamm, Holly Hunter, Billie Jean King, Martina Navratilova

FIGURE 15.3 Some celebrity-related charities. *Based on data from Charity Navigator.*

to sports and is considered to be the voice of women's sports. Its Program Services include Participation, Education, Advocacy, Research, and Leadership. Some of its activities:

- The Foundation distributes upwards of $10,000 per week to provide opportunities for socioeconomically underprivileged and inactive girls to participate in sports and physical activity.
- Its advocacy efforts have directly affected the amount of scholarship dollars supporting educational opportunities for female student-athletes in the United States.
- It advocates for equal playing fields for professional and Olympic athletes.
- Over the past 41 years, the Foundation has awarded more than $80 million in programming to advance participation, research, and leadership in sports and physical activity for girls and women.
- Major grant programs:
  - Getting over 1 million girls active in physical activity (GoGirlGo)
  - Providing grass-roots sports opportunities to over 6000 girls of color aged 11–18 (Sports 4 Life)
  - Over 1300 grants to aspiring champion athletes and teams to help defray the expensive travel, training, and equipment expenses required for them to reach their championship potential (Travel & Training).
- Over the past 30 years, the Foundation has produced more than 40 national, evidence-based research studies that provide a data driven approach to gender equity.
- The Foundation advocates for Title IX of the Education Amendments of 1972 by working with the NCAA leadership, the Office of Civil Rights, coaching organizations, parents, and the media to provide education and guidance to achieve compliance with the law.
- The Foundation's support of national laws prohibiting sex discrimination has resulted in an increase in high school girls' varsity sports participation from 1 in 27 in 1972 to 2 in 5 girls in 2016.
- The Foundation worked with the USOC to develop a comprehensive plan for their new independent agency, which will oversee sexual abuse investigations in club and Olympic sport.
- In the 2014 Winter Olympic and Paralympic Games (Sochi): Twelve recipients of the Travel & Training Fund competed in Sochi, with two women earning medals for Team USA—one silver and one bronze.
- In the 2012 Olympic and Paralympic Games (London): Thirty-one Travel & Training Fund recipients traveled to London, with one team and four individual recipients earning seven medals—five gold, one silver, and one bronze.

USA for UNHCR

USA for UNHCR, the United Nations Refugee Agency has a relatively high fundraising expense ratio of 28.2 % but scores favorably on ratings of accountability and transparency. For 2017 it spent over $36 million on its Refugee Programs and Awareness Activities and it has the actress Angelina Jolie as one of its very visible supporters. It has several different programs to improve the circumstances of refugees and displaced persons around the world:

- Emergency relief efforts respond when violence erupts, or war breaks out. UNHCR actions include the following:
  - Rapid response. UNHCR is able to deploy within 72 hours of a large-scale emergency, and jumpstart relief and protection assistance.
  - Together with its partners, USA for UNHCR helps ensure refugees have what they need to survive—shelter, medical care, food, water, and special protection and care for vulnerable children and women, including prevention and response to sexual violence.
  - Survival needs. UNHCR is able to provide refugee families with essential lifesaving aid for weeks, months, or years. They provide refugees with shelter. This can mean setting up tented camps for tens of thousands of people, supplying materials for housing, or providing cash assistance to refugees living in apartments or abandoned buildings in towns and cities.
       They also supply the basics like blankets, sleeping mats, and other supplies like clothing, shoes, soap, kitchen sets, heaters, solar lamps, and mosquito nets.
  - Health and nutrition. UNHCR works closely with partner organizations to supply clean water and nutritious food, set up sanitation programs, and ensure refugees have access to emergency and basic health care services.
  - Safety net. In time of war, governments are often not able to provide for the security and human rights of their citizens. The protection of millions of refugees and displaced persons is the core mandate of UNHCR. Both before and after emergencies, they work to ensure refugees' rights are respected and that refugees are not forced to return to countries where they are in danger. UNHCR offers legal and protection assistance to minimize threats of violence, including sexual assault, a risk even in countries of asylum.
- Cash assistance. Eighty-five percent of refugees do not live in camps and need to pay for ordinary living expenses. UNHCR interviews refugees to establish eligibility, and when approved, provides access to existing banking systems and access to ATMs.
- Education. Half of all refugees are under the age of 18 and 40% of these children have no access to elementary education. In 2016 UNHCR helped 984,000 refugee children enroll in primary school through its partnership

with the Educate a Child program, including more than 250,000 children who were previously not in school. Another 42,000 refugees participated in accelerated learning programs. More than 4000 refugee students received an Albert Einstein German Academic Refugee Initiative scholarship to study at universities in 38 countries and an additional 1500 refugee students enrolled in "connected learning" programs that combine face-to-face learning with online classes.

- Innovation. USA for UNHCR supports innovative programming that includes refugees' needs for mobile connectivity and renewable energy technology into refugee camps.
- Building livelihoods. After emergency aid, refugees require opportunities for employment, the ability to learn a new trade or a chance to start a business. USA for UNHCR supports livelihood programming that advances economic empowerment opportunities for refugees, supports vocational and skills training and facilitates access to microfinancing and loans.
- Resettlement in the United States. USA for UNHCR does not resettle refugees, but supports programming that helps make the United States a more welcoming place by amplifying the voices of resettled refugees, connecting people to resettled refugee families to provide meaningful help and assistance in their transition into their new communities, and helping address unmet needs, such as providing free legal services.

Michael J. Fox Foundation for Parkinson's Research

The Michael J. Fox Foundation for Parkinson's Research was created in 2000 by the actor, who was diagnosed with the disease himself in 1992 at the age of 31. The Foundation is dedicated to finding a cure for Parkinson's disease through an aggressively funded research agenda and to ensuring the development of improved therapies for those living with Parkinson's today. Its 2019 agenda set the following areas of focus:

- Leverage improved knowledge of diseases of the brain to advance precision medicine approaches that can support the development of disease-modifying treatments.
- Use an integrated "roadmap" approach to understand Parkinson's disease, drug development, and the measurement of therapeutic activity/outcome in order to translate complex disease understanding into new treatments faster.
- Facilitate late-stage development and approvals of therapies by advancing patients' role in research and addressing policy, regulator, and payer considerations related to new therapies.
- Continue investment in developing, participating, and/or leading multistakeholder collaborations and consortia to increase knowledge-sharing, learning, and impact.

- Engage the patient community regionally/nationally, online, at community events and in all relevant settings to educate and inform them of their vital role in helping to achieve its mission by participating in clinical trials and advocacy and grassroots activities.

Elton John AIDS Foundation

The Elton John AIDS Foundation (EJAF) was founded by Sir Elton in 1992 in the United States and in the United Kingdom in 1993. Its ratings on financial efficiency, accountability, and transparency are among the highest for all charities. The US foundation focuses its efforts on programs in the United States, the Americas, and the Caribbean, while the U.K. foundation funds HIV-related work in Europe, Asia, and Africa. Together, they are among the world's leading organizations supporting innovative HIV prevention programs, efforts to eliminate stigma and discrimination associated with HIV/AIDS, and direct care and support services for people living with HIV/AIDS. Since its founding, EJAF has raised over $150 million for programs across the US and in 55 countries around the globe. Direct services include HIV/AIDS-related medical and mental health treatment, testing and counseling, food distribution, assisted living, social service coordination, and legal aid. EJAF's US organization regularly evaluates its grant-making priorities and targets its grant awards where they will make the greatest impact. EJAF has expanded not only the amount of money given but also strategically targeted key regions and populations that are poorly served by current prevention efforts and most at risk of infection including: critically under-funded communities of the Southern United States, the Caribbean, and Latin America; highly marginalized populations such as injection drug users, men who have sex with men, incarcerated individuals, sex workers, and migrants/immigrants; and under-served populations such as Black Americans, Latinos, women, and young people. EJAF focuses on supporting community-based prevention programs, harm reduction programs, public education to reduce the stigma of HIV/AIDS, advocacy to improve AIDS-related public policies and address the civil rights of racial, sexual, ethnic, and gender minorities, and direct services to persons living with HIV/AIDS, especially populations with special needs. Direct services include HIV/AIDS-related medical and mental health treatment, testing and counseling, food distribution, assisted living, social service coordination, and legal aid.

Water.org

Water.org evolved from the merger of H2O Africa (co-founded by the actor Matt Damon) and Water Partners. Its programs have resulted in providing over 20 million people with access to safe water and sanitation, over 6 million in 2018 alone. In 2018 its WaterCredit program provided 1.4 million loans of an average size of $362. While other water focused charities empha-size providing water and building wells, Water.org takes the approach of pro-viding access to affordable financing. It has four solutions:

- WaterCredit addresses one of the barriers to safe water and sanitation: lack of affordable financing. WaterCredit brings small, easily repayable loans to those who need access to affordable financing and expert resources to make household water and toilet solutions a reality. It has 113 global partners and has raised a total of $1.7 billion to support small loans. Each $1 is estimated to have $57 of impact. Eighty-seven percent of borrowers are women, and to date, 99% of loans have been repaid.
- New Ventures serves as the principal source of funding to research, develop, and explore new approaches to solving the water crisis. Twenty-five initiatives in nine countries were piloted through New Ventures funding.
- WaterEquity is an impact investment manager which raised $50 million in its initial fund from investors including Bank of America, the Overseas Private Investment Corporation (OPIC), Ceniarth LLC, Niagara Bottling, and the Conrad N. Hilton, Skoll, and Osprey Foundations. Proceeds go to support microfinance institutions, micro-utilities, toilet manufacturers, and water purification kiosks throughout India, Indonesia, Cambodia, and the Philippines. The fund targets a 3.5% return and projects reaching 4.6 million people with safe water and/or sanitation over its 7-year term. The fund has a blended capital structure including a $5 million first loss guar-antee that covers both investment returns and principal.
- Global engagement. Water.org shares lessons learned and best practices among local partners, government stakeholders, bi-and multilateral donor agencies, and large advocacy organizations. It believes that over time these efforts will lead to a global finance market in which financial insti-tutions and practitioners will use finance as a tool to increase access, leaving aid dollars for others in need. Its engagement partners include:
  - End Water Poverty
  - Government of India Ministry of Drinking Water and Sanitation
  - India Post Payments Bank
  - India Sanitation Coalition
  - IRC-WASH
  - Sanitation and Water for All (SWA)
  - Skoll
  - Sustainable Sanitation Alliance (SuSanA)
  - UNICEF
  - UN-Water
  - USAID
  - WaterAID India
  - World Bank Group

- World Economic Forum
- World Health Organization

Water.org is just one of several charities working to improve the globe's water supplies. Many are focused on drinking water and sanitation. Several others are concerned with the oceans and the health of aquatic life. A few of these latter charities are Ocean Conservancy, Project AWARE, and Sea Shepherd Conservation Society. Each of these organizations has a different approach to ocean conservation and it's interesting to compare them.

Ocean Conservancy

Ocean Conservancy (OC) is a nonprofit environmental advocacy group, and another charity receiving very high marks from Charity Navigator. It was founded in 1972 to encourage healthy and diverse ocean ecosystems and now has over 120,000 members. Ocean Conservancy utilizes research, education, and science to inform, inspire, and empower people to speak and act on behalf of the oceans. It strives to be the world's foremost advocate for the oceans and has four strategic priorities: restoring sustainable American fisheries, protecting wildlife from human impacts, conserving special ocean places, and reforming government for better ocean stewardship. Here are some of its programs:

- Confronting ocean acidification. OC utilizes science, policy, and communication to protect local communities and wildlife from the acidification of the ocean.
- Government relations. Headquartered in Washington DC, OC works to ensure funding for ocean programs.
- Ocean climate. OC's Ocean Futures Initiative works to understand the effects of climate change and acidification of the oceans.
- Protecting Florida. OC recognizes the need for immediate action to tackle problems with Florida's ocean and coasts.
- Protecting the Arctic. OC works with indigenous communities, legislators, scientists, and the public for science-based solutions to protecting the Arctic.
- Restoring the Gulf of Mexico. OC is working to ensure both a successful restoration and a more resilient Gulf.
- Smart ocean planning. OC helps coastal communities to develop strong, sustainable local economies alongside healthy ocean ecosystems and wildlife.
- Sustainable fisheries. OC's fish team works to reduce overfishing, thereby rebuilding vulnerable fish populations and preserving fish populations.
- Trash free seas. It is working on innovative solutions to reduce the amount of trash ending up in our oceans.

Project AWARE

Project AWARE is a California-based nonprofit dedicated to staying in the forefront of ocean issues. It had its origins in 1989 as an outgrowth of the Professional Association of Diving Instructors (PADI), a recreational diving membership and training organization. Its mission is to connect the passion for ocean adventure with the purposes of marine conservation. Its two critical focus areas are community and policy. Each year it develops actions under its Clean Ocean and Healthy Ocean programs. In 2019 for example, it supported the community and advanced policies on Plastic Debris and Sharks & Rays. Some of its recent campaigns are:

- #LoveTheUnloved Photo Contest. Some marine species are less photogenic and charismatic than others. This program seeks to increase awareness and protection for sea cucumbers.
- #NextMillion2020. This program sets a goal of collecting one million pieces of marine trash.
- #NoExcuseforSingleUse seeks to raise awareness of the millions of tons of plastic which end up in our oceans.
- #MakeTime4Makos. Recognizing the reclassification of Mako sharks as endangered, this program seeks to influence governments to extend protections and reduce fishing pressures.
- #Adopt a Dive Site. This program urges scuba diving leaders to engage in ongoing local protection and monitoring of underwater sites. Participants commit to carrying out monthly Dive Against Debris surveys. They are supported by a full suite of survey tools, a yearly report on the state of the local dive site and recognition tools for dive centers, resorts, and leaders.
- Pledge to follow Project AWARE's 10 Tips for Divers to Protect the Ocean Planet. A code of conduct for divers with 10 points:
  - Take Action
  - Give Back
  - Be an Eco-tourist
  - Shrink Your Carbon Footprint
  - Be a Buoyancy Expert
  - Be a Role Model
  - Take Only Photos-Leave Only Bubbles
  - Protect Underwater Life
  - Become a Debris Activist
  - Make Responsible Seafood Choices

Sea Shepherd Conservation Society

The Sea Shepherd Conservation Society (SSCS) is a nonprofit, marine conservation organization based in Washington State. It's extremely aggressive tactics in confronting illegal whaling, especially by Japanese entities, have led to criticism by some other conservation groups and legal action against some members of the society. But whether one approves of their tactics or not, there is no debating that they have raised awareness of whaling activities by countries such as Japan and Norway and seal-hunting by Canadians and Namibians, among others. The founder, Paul Watson was originally a member of GreenPeace but left to start SSCS in 1977 when his direct-action form of activism was at odds with Greenpeace's more pacifist approach. SSCS's mission is to end the destruction of habitat and slaughter of wildlife in the world's oceans to ensure their survival for future generations. As mentioned, it uses direct-action tactics to investigate, document, and act when necessary to expose and confront illegal activities on the high seas. Some of its programs are:

- For Salmon Farm Research: Operation Virus Hunter. SSCS is sending its research vessel, the R/V Martin Sheen, for the fourth year to British Columbia to continue scientific research into the critical decline of Pacific Northwest wild salmon due to diseases and parasites.
- For the Sea Turtles: Operation Jairo. SSCS conducts programs to protect sea turtle hatchings from poaching in Costa Rica, Honduras, Florida, Antigua, Barbuda and Nicaragua.
- For the Vaquita Porpoise: Operation Milagro V. SSCS ships, the M/V Farley Mowat and the M/V White Holly, patrol and protect the vaquita porpoise and other critically endangered marine mammal and other species that inhabit the Upper Gulf of California.
- For Ending Illegal, Unreported and Unregulated Fishing: IUU Fishing. There are three IUU issues of special concern for Africa: unlicensed foreign industrial vessels; fishing in prohibited areas using illegal nets; and unreported catch and by-catch by legal operators. It is the single greatest threat to cetaceans, with over 300,000 whales and dolphins killed through entanglement annually.
- For Anti-Poaching & Research: Operation Treasured Islands. SSCS is working with Mexican authorities to patrol and defend the protected marine reserve of Revillagigedo Archipelago and with scientists to research several of the diverse marine species native to the area including whale sharks, scalloped hammerheads, and false killer whales.
- For Ending Cetacean Captivity: Operation 404. SSCS has undercover teams investigating dolphinariums worldwide.
- For Ocean Cleanup: Operation Clean Waves. SSCS is working with local communities in Kirabati to determine how to best alleviate the pressures currently weighing on Fanning Island's ecosystem and people. There are three main objectives: Plastic Management System, Reef Assessment, and Clean Water Solutions.
- For Ending Illegal Fishing: Operation Mamacocha. This SSCS campaign addresses Illegal, Unreported, Unregulated (IUU) fishing in the Eastern

Tropical Pacific Marine Corridor encompassing the waters, coasts, and islands off the shores of Costa Rica, Panama, Colombia, Ecuador, and Peru. It includes the Galápagos Islands and Marine Reserve, Cocos Island, Malpelo Island, and Coiba National Park, all of which are UNESCO World Heritage Sites.

- For Beaked Whale Research: Operation Divina Guadalupe. A group of Mexican and US scientists aided by SSCS study the habitat and behavior of the rare Cuvier beaked whale, the most extreme mammal divers in the world.

The foregoing charities have focused programs addressing specific areas of concern. Next we look at some organizations which have a broader scope.

UNICEF and UNESCO

UNICEF and UNESCO are both United Nations agencies engaged in charitable acts. They receive substantial support from celebrities as well as other donors. UNICEF is focused on protecting and caring for children and UNESCO seeks to build peace through international cooperation in Education, the Sciences, and Culture.

UNICEF

UNICEF works with partners around the world to promote policies and expand access to services that protect all children. Its child protection and inclusion initiatives are:

- Adolescent development. UNICEF invests in programs that improve adolescents' education, critical thinking, and emotional and physical wellbeing, as well as encouraging adolescents' positive engagement with the world around them. Keeping students in school is one of UNICEF's main goals, and it is committed to enhancing quality education with an emphasis on measurable learning outcomes. UNICEF also supports programs that offer alternative educational pathways for disadvantaged and excluded adolescents, including in emergencies and postconflict settings. Improving the health and nutrition of pregnant women and providing quality reproductive health services is another priority. UNICEF supports countries as they advocate for and implement high-impact HIV prevention, treatment, and care for adolescents.
- Children uprooted. UNICEF works around the world to help make sure migrant and refugee children are protected and that their rights are respected. It provides lifesaving humanitarian supplies in refugee camps. It runs child-friendly spaces—safe places where migrant and refugee children can play, where mothers can rest and feed their babies in private, and where separated families can reunite. It supports national and local

governments to put in place laws, policies, systems, and public services that are inclusive of refugee and migrant children, address their specific needs, and help them thrive. It collects, analyzes, and disseminates data. It helps keep families together and provide support to family-based solutions that are alternatives to the detention of migrant and displaced children. It works with governments, the private sector, and civil society. It has also developed a six factor Agenda for Action:

- Press for action on the causes that uproot children from their homes
- Help uprooted children to stay in school and stay healthy
- Keep families together and give children legal status
- End the detention of refugee and migrant children by creating practical alternatives
- Combat xenophobia and discrimination
- Protect uprooted children from exploitation and violence

- Communication for development. UNICEF has a strong track record of amplifying the voices of children and communities by harnessing the power of communication to promote child survival, development, protection, and participation. Successful case studies include polio immunization, curbing maternal mortality, and delaying child marriage for girls.
- Gender equality. UNICEF is accelerating gender equality by addressing gender-specific discrimination and disadvantages and has developed a Gender Action Plan as a road map to help level the playing field.
- Child protection from violence and abuse. UNICEF promotes the strengthening of all components of child protection systems—human resources, finances, laws, standards, governance, monitoring, and services. UNICEF and its partners support the mapping and assessment of child protection systems. It also engages in advocacy and awareness raising and supports discussions, education programs, and communication for development strategies at community and national levels, within villages, across professional and religious groups, and within diaspora communities. It supports children's caregivers and arranges for safe spaces for children to play, learn, and receive support for their psychological and mental well-being; identifies, reunites, and cares for children separated from their families and caregivers; supports holistic assistance for children and adults who have suffered gender-based violence; actively works to release children associated with armed forces or armed groups and supports their community reintegration; promotes integrated case management of vulnerable children; helps to coordinate humanitarian actors working on child protection, gender-based violence and mental health and psychosocial support of children; monitors, reports on and responds to grave child rights violations; and actively works to put in place measures that reduce the risks of and prevent children from being harmed. UNICEF also supports research, data collection, and analysis to broaden the evidence base on child protection.

- Children with disabilities. UNICEF has a long history of fighting for the rights of disabled children. Its vision is to build a world where every child can grow up healthy, protected from harm and educated, so they can reach their full potential. It has identified three disability goals:
  - Be an inclusive organization for all
  - To develop leadership on the rights of children with disabilities and build capacity among our staff and our partners
  - Mainstream disability across all of our policies and programs, both in development and humanitarian action
- Environment and climate change. Environmental sustainability provides major opportunities to deliver better results for children. UNICEF is strengthening its engagement at both global and local level together with its partners. Some recent priorities were:
  - Strengthen UNICEF policy and guidance on environmental sustainability as a cross-cutting issue.
  - Strengthen the inclusion of environmental sustainability in UNICEF programs.
  - Advocate for full recognition and inclusion of children in the policy discourse on environmental sustainability.
  - Strengthen opportunities for children's development and well-being to benefit from environmental sustainability related public and private finance.
  - Incorporating environmental sustainability management in the organization.
- Social inclusion, policy, and budgeting. Working with other UN agencies, UNICEF collaborates with partners to stimulate dialogue around macrolevel policies that guide national frameworks, legislative reform and budgetary allocations affecting children and families. This work is centered around:
  - Global economic crisis and recovery
  - Child poverty and social protection
  - Public finance and local governance
  - Migration
  - Child-sensitive social protection

Other UNICEF programs focus on child survival, education, and reaching children in humanitarian emergencies.

UNESCO

The United Nations Educational, Scientific and Cultural Organization (UNESCO) is based in Paris and is a UN agency which seeks to build peace through international cooperation in Education, the Sciences, and Culture. UNESCO's programs also contribute to the achievement of the Sustainable

Development Goals. To address global challenges, it works with a wide range of partners: institutions, individuals, and entities of many kinds—governments, the wider UN family, other intergovernmental organizations, NGOs, Private Sector companies, corporate and philanthropic foundations, media organizations, parliamentarians, Goodwill Ambassadors and many other specialized networks in UNESCO's field of activities such as the Category 2 Institutes and Centers, Clubs for UNESCO, UNESCO Associated Schools, and UNESCO Chairs. It has five major programs: education, culture, natural sciences, social and human sciences, culture and communication, and information.

- Education. UNESCO is the only United Nations agency with a mandate to cover all aspects of education. It leads the Global Education 2030 Agenda through Sustainable Development Goal 4. It provides global and regional leadership in education, strengthens education systems worldwide and responds to contemporary global challenges through education with gender equality an underlying principle. Themes include global citizenship and sustainable development, human rights and gender equality, health, and HIV and AIDS, as well as technical and vocational skills development.
- Culture. UNESCO has a three-pronged approach: it spearheads worldwide advocacy for culture and development, while engaging with the international community to set clear policies and legal frameworks and working on the ground to support governments and local stakeholders to safeguard heritage, strengthen creative industries and encourage cultural pluralism.
- Natural sciences: Science for a Sustainable Future. UNESCO works to assist countries to invest in science, technology, and innovation (STI) to develop national science policies, to reform their science systems, and to build capacity to monitor and evaluate performance through STI indicators and statistics taking into account the broad range of country-specific contexts. UNESCO also works with its member States to foster informed decisions about the use of science and technology, in particular in the field of bioethics.
- Social and human sciences. UNESCO with its Member States and all its partners works to better understand and address the challenges of diversified societies, particularly through its intergovernmental Programme for Management of Social Transformations, its Youth Programme as well the Culture of Peace and Non-Violence Programme which include initiatives for democracy and global citizenship, intercultural dialogue, and peacebuilding. UNESCO also seeks to promote the development and the practice of sporting activities to foster social integration in different cultural and political contexts. It also continues to build and reinforce linkages among ethicists, scientists, policymakers, judges, journalists, and civil

society to assist Member States in enacting sound and reasoned policies on ethical issues in science and technology.
- Communication and information. UNESCO strives to foster freedom of expression, media development, and access to information and knowledge and directly contributes to many of the UN's Sustainable Development Goals. It also advances freedom of expression and the safety of journalists online and off-line. It combats online hate speech, as well as disinformation and misinformation through awareness raising initiatives, steady monitoring, capacity-building activities, and technical support to Member States. UNESCO also supports universal access to information and knowledge through promoting Open Solutions, including Open Educational Resources, access for marginalized people, and multilingualism in the cyberspace. The Organization develops media and information literacy curricula, furthers gender equality in media operations and content, and encourages pertinent media coverage of crisis and emergency situations. UNESCO contributes to media diversity and pluralism by fostering diversity of content, audience, sources, and systems. In addition, the Communication and Information Sector also coordinates UNESCO's inter-sectoral work on Artificial Intelligence.

Red Cross and Red Crescent Societies

The charitable organization probably best known to Americans is the Red Cross. Its visibility and impact are a direct result of the size of its program expenditures, which totaled over $2.8 billion for its 2018 fiscal year. The American Red Cross is just one of 191 National Red Cross and Red Crescent Societies around the globe. Many figures in US history had connections with the Red Cross. The US branch was founded by Clara Barton in 1881. John D. Rockefeller was one of the founding donors and the abolitionist Frederick Douglass was involved in its early days. The International Red Cross and Red Crescent Movement is a global humanitarian network of 80 million people that helps those facing disaster, conflict, and health and social problems. Looking at the American Red Cross mission statement, it seeks to "prevent and alleviate human suffering in the face of emergencies by mobilizing the power of volunteers and the generosity of donors." It aspires to act so that:

- all people affected by disaster across the country and around the world receive care, shelter, and hope;
- our communities are ready and prepared for disasters;
- everyone in the country has access to safe, lifesaving blood and blood products;
- all members of the armed services and their families find support and comfort whenever needed; and

- in an emergency, there are always trained individuals nearby, ready to use their Red Cross skills to save lives.

The Global Red Cross Network shares seven Fundamental Principles:

- Humanity. The Red Cross endeavors to prevent and alleviate human suffering wherever it may be found. Its purpose is to protect life and health and to ensure respect for the human being. It promotes mutual understanding, friendship, cooperation, and lasting peace amongst all peoples.
- Impartiality. It makes no discrimination as to nationality, race, religious beliefs, class, or political opinions. It endeavors to relieve the suffering of individuals, being guided solely by their needs, and to give priority to the most urgent cases of distress.
- Neutrality. Red Cross may not take sides in hostilities or engage at any time in controversies of a political, racial, religious, or ideological nature.
- Independence. The Red Cross is independent. The national societies, while auxiliaries in the humanitarian services of their governments and subject to the laws of their respective countries, must always maintain their autonomy so that they may be able at all times to act in accordance with Red Cross principles.
- Voluntary service. The Red Cross is a voluntary nonprofit relief movement.
- Unity. There can be only one Red Cross society in any one country. It must be open to all.
- Universality. The Red Cross is a worldwide institution in which all societies have equal status and share equal responsibilities and duties in helping each other.

The American Red Cross (ARC) is active in the following areas:

- Disaster relief. ARC responds to an average of 62,000 disasters each year. Ninety-five percent of its disaster relief workers are volunteers and, somewhat surprisingly, 90% of disasters responded to are home fires.
  - Home fire relief. Since 2014, 610 lives have been saved, 1,817,262 smoke alarms installed, 752,393 households made safer, and 1,436,732 youth reached through campaigns.
  - Hurricane relief. The Red Cross provides shelter, food, and comfort to families affected by hurricanes and tropical storms. It pre-positions supplies for faster response, opens evacuation shelters to keep people safe during the storm, provides food and shelter until families can return home, distributes water, food and relief supplies to impacted communities, helps those who need first aid or medical care, and generally gives hope, help, and comfort. One example of its hurricane relief efforts is its response to 2017's Hurricane Harvey which had a major impact in Louisiana and Texas. In responding to this hurricane alone, ARC together with its partners, served over 4.5 million meals,

provided almost 415,000 overnight stays in shelters, distributed over 1.6 million items such as diapers and cleaning supplies, and provided immediate financial assistance to more than 575,000 households.

- Wildfire relief. ARC annually provides aid to victims of wildfires. In response to the 2018 California Camp Fire, Hill Fire and Woolsey Fire, ARC, and its partners, as of May 2019, had served over 380,000 meals, provided over 61,000 overnight shelter stays, distributed 81,000 relief items, provided recovery financial assistance to over 10,000 households, and made almost 67,000 health, mental health, and spiritual care contacts.
- Flood relief. ARC aids flood victims by providing safe, dry shelters, serving water and water meals, enriching children's lives, aiding the special needs of people with disabilities, providing first aid, giving comfort and emotional support, distributing clean up supplies, assessing damage, and helping families to prepare recovery plans.
- Earthquake relief. ARC conducts search and rescue efforts, provides medical care, serves food and water, distributes relief supplies, builds emergency shelters, restores water supplies, helps restore communications, and rebuilds communities. It also teaches disaster preparedness techniques. In responding to the 2010 earthquake in Haiti (a response that is still in progress) ARC has provided food, water, medical care, emergency shelter, cash grants, and other essentials to millions of people. Donors have given $488 million to ARC for this effort, coordinated with more than 50 partners.
- Winter storm relief. ARC provides meals and snacks, cleaning and relief supplies, overnight shelter stays, and one-on-one counseling assistance to those adversely affected by severe winter weather.

- Blood supply. The Red Cross provides about 40% of the nation's blood and blood components, all from generous volunteer donors. Each year, an estimated 6.8 million people in the United States donate blood. 13.6 million whole blood and red blood cells are collected in the United States in a year.
- Health and safety training and education. For health care providers, first responders, lifeguards, and others, ARC provides a wide range of education and training in: First Aid, CPR, Automated External Defibrillator (AED), babysitting and care giving, swimming, Certified Nurse Assistant (CAN), and Basic Life Support (BLS).
- Military and veteran families. ARC helps members of the military, veterans, and their families prepare for, cope with, and respond to, the challenges of military service. Volunteers provide home comforts and critical services on bases and in military hospitals around the world. They support military families during deployments and emergencies and continue serving veterans after their service ends. Over a recent 1-year period, the Red Cross provided services to 162,200 military and veteran families and

provided over 65,000 emergency communications to 117,580 military members and their families.

- International services. The Red Cross's mission spans the globe. There are over 17 million volunteers worldwide and 191 countries with a Red Cross or Red Crescent society. It has provided for the vaccination of over 2 billion children since 2001 and has provided international assistance to 185 million people. In addition, more than 9,000 families have been reconnected and assistance to 29 million people has been impacted through the Missing Maps project, which is an open, collaborative effort to map areas where humanitarian organizations are trying to meet the needs of vulnerable people.

The Salvation Army

Established first in London in 1865, the Salvation Army states that it exists to meet human need wherever, whenever, and however it can. It is a registered charity that operates in 130 countries worldwide, assists 25 million Americans annually, runs charity shops, shelters for the homeless, and coordinates disaster relief and humanitarian aid to developing countries. As an outgrowth of the Christian Church a review of the Salvation Army could also be included in Chapter 14's discussion of faith-based organizations. The other charities covered in this chapter do not have religious affiliations, but because it provides its services without regard to the religious affiliations of recipients it seems appropriate to include the Salvation Army here. Its services include the following:

- Help disaster survivors through:
  - Emergency preparedness. It educates other first responders and the public about how to prepare for and respond to natural disasters and aids in the development of emergency disaster plans.
  - Long-term disaster recovery. The Salvation Army aids victims of natural disasters throughout the recovery process. It collaborates with local, state, and federal governments to develop and execute a long-term disaster relief and recovery plan, including restoration and rebuilding initiatives, meeting basic needs, covering medical expenses, cutting funeral costs, and distributing in-kind donations to help victims rebuild their lives.
  - Immediate emergency response. It gathers donations, resources, and volunteers in a predetermined staging area. Its disaster assistance includes providing food, water, and shelter to victims, lending a hand with cleanup, and putting people in touch with their loved ones.
  - Spiritual and emotional care. It helps treat the emotional stress and trauma of disaster victims and first responders with emotional support and spiritual comfort.

- Brighten the holidays. Bringing Christmas cheer to families living in poverty by:
  - Angel tree program. Anonymous donors adopt 1 million children to receive new clothes and gifts.
  - Bill-pay assistance. The Salvation Army helps struggling households pay their utility bills, offsetting the added financial burdens that come with Christmas expenses.
  - Grocery and food assistance. The Salvation Army hosts sit-down Christmas dinners, delivers meals, and stocks food pantries for low-income families, struggling seniors, and those without a home.
  - Holiday events. It gives hope and relief to low-income families, shut-ins, children of prisoners, and those without a home through traditions such as hospital visits, nursing home events, meal delivery, bell ringing, gifting programs, and clothing and Christmas toy donations.
- Provide shelter to 30,000 homeless Americans through:
  - Emergency shelters. Each Salvation Army homeless shelter features a safe place to eat, sleep, and shower at no cost.
  - Group homes and transitional living centers provide food, shelter, educational support, counseling services, and vocational direction.
  - Family service programs help parents and children of all ages stay together. In addition to providing temporary homeless shelters, it provides families with meal-planning, utility, and long-term housing assistance.
- Cure hunger. It provides over 56 million meals each year through:
  - Food pantries. Salvation Army offers access to free fresh produce and canned goods, providing valuable meal supplementation while helping those in need maintain their independence and dignity.
  - Meal programs. It provides a range from sit-down programs that provide nutritious, hot meals, and valuable human interaction, to mobile meals that deliver sustenance to those who cannot reach a food distribution center, to feeding programs across hundreds of shelters and residential facilities.
  - Community gardens provide a no-cost, renewable source of produce, as well as vital work structure for those involved in the cultivation and care of the food.
- Meet the greatest need. The Salvation Army seeks to serve those most desperate for physical, emotional, and spiritual assistance. It recognizes that human need differs from state to state, city to city, and even person to person, and looks for solutions to each unique situation. It can provide everything from feeding programs and emergency shelters to domestic abuse asylum and disaster relief services.
- Overcome poverty through:
  - Shelter. It provides 10.8 million nights per year of both short- and long-term housing assistance to families and individuals who've been displaced.

- Pathway of hope. This initiative provides individualized services to families with children to break the cycle of crisis and vulnerability that repeats generation after generation. By helping families overcome challenges like unemployment, unstable housing, and lack of education, it can lead families down a path toward increased stability and, ultimately, self-sufficiency.
  - Meal assistance. The Salvation Army provides over 60 million nutritious, warm meals to people in need.
  - Employment assistance. It provides services including equipping parents with educational resources, career coaching, and opportunities for job placement.
- Combat addiction programs:
  - Combat addiction. Salvation Army provides holistic work therapy, group and individual counseling sessions, spiritual direction, and life-skills development.
  - Regain health and stability. Salvation Army member beliefs encourage developing a personal relationship with God as provided by Jesus Christ, as many residents learn to depend on God, rather than drugs or alcohol, for hope and relief.
  - Build work and social skills. The program equips members to provide for themselves and others as they set and maintain sustainable employment goals.
  - Restore families. Many who have been rehabilitated are reunited with their families and are able to resume healthy daily routines.
- Share God's love. Without doubt many disaster survivors seek solace in religion: in times of disaster 59% of people prefer support from a religious counselor or clergy member.
- Assist the unemployed through:
  - Skill-set evaluations identify the strengths and abilities of the individual for a better job match.
  - Placement assistance gives those in need résumé, interview, and job placement assistance.
  - Educational and skill supplementation helps people pursue and complete educational requirements, training, certifications, and other prerequisites for gainful employment. For those with mental health or substance-abuse issues, Salvation Army helps them find the treatment and/or medication they need.
  - Continued support goes beyond employment. Salvation Army caseworkers assist with obtaining financial planning, insurance coverage, as well as helping to ensure affordable and safe care for children while parents are working.
- Equip families through:
  - Kroc community centers offer after-school programs, recreational opportunities, and community programs dedicated to fostering healthy futures.

- At summer camps for kids, campers from low-income families learn to swim, play sports, create music, make art, and scout, as their trained counselors help them navigate the complicated emotions and struggles often associated with their lives back home.
  - After-school programs. Over 400 after-school programs nationwide provide a safe place to study, read, learn, connect with friends, play sports, and enrich the mind.
- Fight human trafficking through:
  - Awareness initiatives raise awareness of the injustices of human trafficking by partnering with local coalitions. Salvation Army also helps prevent future crimes through prevention activities and works to reduce demand for forced labor and commercial sex. It also helps rescue and restore current victims by improving the identification and prosecution of local traffickers.
  - A legacy of justice. In the 1800s, Salvation Army pioneered an undercover sex trafficking investigation, which directly shaped the Criminal Law Amendment Act of 1885. By 1900, The Salvation Army had created over 100 "rescue homes" throughout London to help those fleeing prostitution. Over a century later, it remains fully committed to abolishing the sex trade from every corner of the world.
  - Comprehensive care management. It provides ongoing care to those escaping human trafficking. Along with the immediate needs of shelter, transportation, food, and clothing, it addresses physical and psychological trauma through a variety of services.
- Serve veterans by providing:
  - Shelters which give veterans a place to rest their head, a hot meal, help finding employment, and a fresh start.
  - Adult rehabilitation centers for those battling PTSD and drug and alcohol addiction after returning home.
  - Community to offset the loneliness and depression often seen years after returning home.
- Love the elderly. Seniors and the elderly are served through:
  - Community centers serve each local senior citizen community in unique ways to meet specific needs.
  - Residences: Salvation Army offers housing assistance and living quarters for the elderly.
  - Activities: The Salvation Army works to stimulate the minds and bodies of older adults via educational opportunities, low-impact exercise, dances, lunches, fellowship, and countless other "young at heart" activities.
  - Adult day care centers are offered to older adults unable to independently care for themselves.
- Serve the LGBTQ community.

- Shelter: The Salvation Army created a dorm in Las Vegas to offer safety and shelter to transgender people, which is a group statistically more vulnerable to assault.
- Job training. Unique programs help LGBTQ individuals cultivate vital life skills needed for successful and stable careers.
- Help with substance abuse: The Salvation Army recognizes the need for all people, regardless of income, to have access to rehabilitation programs. LGBTQ-friendly programs provide housing, food, counseling, community, and employment along with work to treat the symptoms, and ultimately the root causes, of prolonged alcohol and drug dependence.
- Food insecurity: More than a quarter of LGBTQ Americans are food insecure and rely on the Supplemental Nutrition Assistance Program. As one of the nation's largest providers of social services, Salvation Army understands the importance of helping people maintain their dignity when looking for nutritious food.
- Teenage suicide. LGBTQ youth contemplate suicide at almost three times the rate of heterosexual youth. With a presence in every zip code in the nation, Salvation Army is committed to providing spiritual and emotional care to those in need regardless of race, gender, ethnicity, sexual orientation, or gender identity.
- Stop domestic abuse services:
  - The Cascade Women's and Children's Center provides immediate assistance to victims of domestic violence at this 24-hour shelter. The center provides everything from health referrals, counseling, and transportation to GED certification programs, parenting classes, employment assistance, and permanent housing placement.
  - The Phoenix Elim House offers a safe haven to families of up to eight and children 17 and under, harboring over 1 million women each year.
  - Northwest Division Center provides confidential emergency and transitional shelters, helping victims of domestic abuse take steps toward recovery and living independently.
- Teach kids through:
  - Homework assistance and counseling. The Salvation Army provides one-on-one after-school assistance with homework and school assignments, as well as the teaching and advancement of literacy and study skills.
  - Dance, art, and music programs enable children to experience music and art education in positive no-cost or low-cost environments. Classes focuses on everything from choir, band, and dancing to drawing, writing, and acting.
  - Sports, clubs, and extracurricular activities are provided in no-fee and low-cost after-school programs which give children from low-income

neighborhoods a chance to play sports, learn athletic skills, and cultivate healthy, safe relationships with friends.

* Parental involvement coaching equips parents with the skills needed to support and sustain their children's educational needs.

Meals on Wheels

Meals on Wheels was founded in the United Kingdom during World War II to provide meals first to service men and women and later to a needy population at large. It has since spread throughout the U.K. and to the United States, Ireland, Canada, and Australia. Depending on the country and local circumstances meals are delivered by a variety of conveyances and to recipients of varying ages and varying limitations on their own physical and financial condition. In the United States there are approximately 5000 community-based programs supported by Meals on Wheels America, the national leadership organization. The local programs provide meals to individuals who would otherwise have difficulty providing for themselves, or would need to resort to alternative, higher-cost services like hospitals or nursing homes. In New York City, CityMeals on Wheels has delivered 60 million meals since its founding in 1981, with over 2 million delivered in 2018 to over 18,000 recipients with an average age of 85 years. In addition to nutrition, the programs support seniors' well-being by providing companionship and increasing their sense of independence and well-being by reducing the need for institutionalization. But the benefits of this care and compassion go beyond delivering meals. Staff and volunteers are the "eyes and ears" in the homes of the most at-risk members. They can observe first-hand any changes in their physical or mental conditions.

Habitat for Humanity

Habitat for Humanity (HFH) is a well-known nonprofit providing housing services in 70 countries and in all 50 US states. It states its mission as: "Seeking to put God's love into action, Habitat for Humanity brings people together to build homes, communities and hope." It is a Christian organization but has a clearly stated policy against proselytizing. It will not offer assistance on the expressed or implied condition that people must adhere to or convert to a particular faith or listen and respond to messaging designed to induce conversion to a particular faith. An important celebrity supporter is President Jimmy Carter. Since its founding in 1976, HFH has helped more than 22 million people build or improve their home. In 2018 alone, it helped more than 8.7 million people, and an additional 2.2 million gained the potential to improve their living conditions through training and advocacy. A key feature of HFH is the use of volunteer labor and HFH makes no profit on housing sales. In addition to home construction, HFH provides services in neighborhood revitalization, disaster response financial education, and innovative shelter solutions through the Terwilliger Center.

The previous section of this chapter looks at the activities of several well-known charities. There are, however, literally thousands more that are equally worthy of donor consideration. Several services are available for donors to sift through these organizations. The aforementioned Charity Navigator is a popular source. Others are CharityWatch and the Better Business Bureau's Wise Giving Alliance.

Chapter 16

What's next for ESG investing?

Chapter Outline

Empirical studies of environmental, social, and governance investment performance 331

The future of environmental, social, and governance investing 332

Environmental, social, and governance investment concerns to be addressed 333

Over the last decade, the amount of assets being invested in socially responsible investment products has increased dramatically, and with the growing importance of the Millennial generation and the emergence of Generation Z, this trend is likely to accelerate. Roughly one quarter of all global assets under management (AUM) are now being invested with a consideration of environmental, social, and governance (ESG) factors. It's estimated that ESG AUM global totals are over $23 trillion. In the United States, ESG-focused AUM were estimated to be $12 trillion at the start of 2018. This is about 26% of total assets under professional management. As impressive as these totals are, interest in ESG seems even more widespread. One large Wall Street firm found that 75% of individual investors sought to include ESG considerations into their investment choices. Modern Portfolio Theory has given us the twin concepts of risk and return in evaluating investment portfolios. The advent of ESG investing adds a third leg. An efficient portfolio frontier can now be conceived as a three-dimensional surface, optimizing risk, financial return, and now ESG impact.

In Chapter 2, ESG, SRI, and impact investing, we compared several different types of ESG investing including divestment, impact and mission investing, and integrating ESG considerations in a more sophisticated portfolio approach. These alternative styles are illustrated in Fig. 16.1, reproduced from Chapter 2, ESG, SRI, and impact investing.

This figure is a conceptual summary of the various social investment styles. It compares these styles with reference to financial return on the vertical axis and ESG returns on the horizontal access. Conventional investment portfolios, with no consideration of ESG factors, will have a distribution of financial returns centered around a median market rate of return. ESG returns to these conventional portfolios would be minimal. As we have seen in

Environmental, Social, and Governance (ESG) Investing. DOI: https://doi.org/10.1016/B978-0-12-818692-3.00016-5

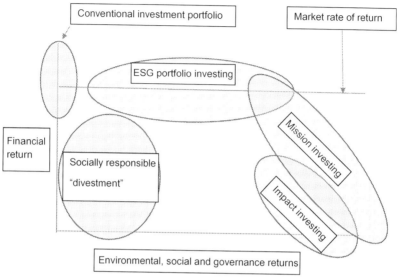

FIGURE 16.1 Financial return versus environmental, social, and governance returns for various investment styles.

Chapter 9, Defining and measuring ESG performance, a portfolio designed to reflect ESG factors can be structured to have similar financial returns to conventional portfolios and also have a range of ESG returns superior to the conventional portfolio. The historical financial performance of divestment portfolios, on the other hand, has been relatively poor, with few exceptions. Fig. 16.1 represents this latter investment style as having subpar financial performance, and some, albeit weak social and environmental influence as well. Mission investing and impact investing are shown as overlapping strategies. Both are more targeted than ESG investing. Some mission investing portfolios have been shown to yield market rates of return when designed to do so. In general, many mission investing strategies require a rate of return at least adequate to support the continuing operation of the organizational structure. Impact investing, however, includes at least some organizations which are comfortable with submarket and negligible financial returns. But it is assumed that their close focus will allow them to yield greater social and environmental benefits from their investments.

Aside from divestment, mission, and impact investing, an ESG portfolio investment strategy must have a financial return that is not too far below a "market" rate of return if it is to continue to attract funds for any length of time. Investors undertaking divestment, mission, and impact strategies may be comfortable sacrificing return, but for ESG investing to grow, the resulting portfolio will need to have risk parameters and earn financial returns in the range expected from competing conventional investments.

Empirical studies of environmental, social, and governance investment performance

What does the data tell us? While there are many individual studies showing conflicting results, several meta-studies support the conclusion that companies with strong ESG performance also score highly on traditional financial metrics. Here we summarize some of these reviews presented in Chapter 9, Defining and measuring ESG performance.

One analysis surveyed over 200 sources and concludes that:

- 90% of the studies show that sound sustainability standards lower the cost of capital;
- 88% of reviewed sources find that companies with robust sustainability practices demonstrate better operational performance, which ultimately translates into cash flows; and
- 80% of the reviewed studies support the conclusion that companies with strong ESG performance also score highly on traditional financial metrics.

Another paper reviewed more than 100 academic studies, 56 research papers, 2 literature reviews, and 4 meta-studies. Their key finding: "The evidence is compelling: Sustainable Investing can be a clear win for investors, and for companies. However, many SRI fund managers, who have tended to use exclusionary screens, have historically struggled to capture this. We believe that ESG analysis should be built into the investment processes of every serious investor, and into the corporate strategy of every company that cares about shareholder value. ESG best-in-class focused funds should be able to capture superior risk-adjusted returns if well executed."

Some results of this review:

- 100% of the academic studies agree that companies with high ESG ratings have a lower cost of capital in terms of debt and equity.
- 89% of the studies show that companies with high ESG ratings exhibit market-based outperformance, while 85% of the studies show these companies exhibit accounting-based outperformance.
- The most important factor is Governance.
- 88% of studies of actual fund returns show neutral or mixed results, with the complication that most of these funds are using negative screens. Fund managers have struggled to capture outperformance in the broad socially responsible investment category of strategies, but "they have, at least, not lost money in the attempt."

Yet another review of dozens of studies of the financial performance of impact investing concluded that returns for market rate seeking impact investments were comparable to those of conventional investment portfolios.

A 2015 paper examined approximately 2200 academic studies that had looked at the relationship between ESG and financial performance.

This study appears to be the most complete and exhaustive overview of academic research on the topic to that date. The results of the study support the business case for ESG investing; 90% of the studies reviewed find a nonnegative relation between ESG and financial performance and the large majority of studies find a positive relationship. Of the three categories of factors, Governance displays the strongest correlation with positive financial performance. It's also noted that in addition to positively impacting fund performance, ESG can uncover nonfinancial risks that may become costly for companies in the future.

Finally, BlackRock compared traditional and ESG-focused equity benchmarks for the period 2012–18. Based on their analysis, one could conclude that ESG portfolios offer some protection against ESG-related risks as well as having historical performance comparable to that of conventional portfolios.

It's important to repeat these results, covered in Chapter 9, Defining and measuring ESG performance, because there is often confusion in the financial press about the financial performance of ESG investing, much of it due to the subpar performance of divestment strategies. In summary, *the case for ESG investing having comparable financial performance appears to be empirically well founded.*

The future of environmental, social, and governance investing

Some generalized conclusions about the future of ESG investing:

- The investing public will increasingly be interested in understanding the ESG characteristics of its investments.
- More companies will provide corporate responsibility reports and the quality and depth of that reporting will improve.
- Companies will continue to expend corporate resources on ESG issues at the expense of short-term financial return to investors. Some of this expenditure will be motivated by a desire for the company to be a good corporate citizen, some will be brand positioning, and some might be a result of personal interests by senior executives and board members.
- Institutional investors will increase their level of engagement with investee companies. Divestment and even "hands off" investment strategies will lose favor.
- Financial service providers will continue to innovate new ESG products.
- ESG data will improve.
- The historic underperformance of divestment strategies is unlikely to change, but divestment will continue to be popular where investment performance is either less important or less scrutinized.

- While ESG is growing, it is still the focus of a minority of investors; 75% of US investing is in conventional portfolios and 80% of university and college endowments similarly follow conventional investing prescriptions. There is consequently an opportunity to convert some of these investors to an ESG focus, but there are also objections to be overcome.
- FinTech will have an impact on ESG as it is impacting all areas of finance. Big Data, Artificial Intelligence (AI), and increasing use of robo-advisors will all have some impact of effectiveness and volume of investments with a social purpose.

Environmental, social, and governance investment concerns to be addressed

Although ESG investment in total is likely to increase, there are some issues that will need to be addressed:

- Definitions and usage of the terms associated with ESG or socially responsible investing are unclear, used interchangeably, and often confusing and even misleading.
- ESG covers a broad range of sometimes conflicting issues. How should an investor assess the importance of carbon emissions versus racial and gender discrimination? For example, some funds and portfolios that are classified as ESG compliant have a high weighting of tech companies which score favorably on environmental issues. But these same tech companies have poor records in hiring and promoting women and minorities. One solution is for investors to use customizing tools of financial services firms to construct an ESG portfolio which matches their specific interests. These bespoke services are available but there are information and transaction costs associated with them.
- For pooled funds, achieving consensus on ESG issues will continue to be challenging. It may be that Governance issues are easier to gain agreement on than some of the most pressing environmental and social issues and it's interesting to note that several empirical studies found that positive Governance scores were correlated positively with financial performance.
- Many retirement funds are underfunded. An aging population will result in more retirees and current historically low yields will put pressure on investment returns. In that environment an investment strategy that sacrifices even some return will be called into question. Divestment strategies that are currently used may be difficult to sustain if they have subpar financial performance.
- Few ESG-oriented exchange-traded funds (ETFs) have sufficient liquidity. The most active traditional ETFs have median daily dollar volumes in excess of $400 million. While volumes may build over time, the

largest ESG funds trade a median of barely $2—4 million dollars per day. ETFs are low cost pooled investments but entering and exiting ETF positions where there is thin liquidity can result in unreasonably high execution expense or "slippage." This can threaten the viability of the investment strategy.

- Data issues must be addressed. While we expect ESG data to improve, it will take time and effort. Some companies disclose ESG data, some don't. And disclosed data may be inconsistent. Currently, most data are self-reported by companies, with often questionable consistency and metrics. Vendor ESG ratings are often inconsistent. Also, two widely used classification systems are the Global Industry Classification Benchmarks (GICS) and the Industry Classification Benchmarks (ICB). GICS is an industry classification taxonomy developed by MSCI and S&P. It comprises 10 sectors, 24 industry groups, 68 industries, and 154 subindustries into which all major public companies are categorized. ICB is a taxonomy, developed by Dow Jones and FTSE, which is used to segregate markets into sectors. It uses a system of 10 industries, divided into 20 super-sectors further segregated into 41 sectors, which then contain 114 subsectors. These classification systems are commonly used to filter stocks on the basis of their lines of business. The problem with these classification systems is that their categorization is one dimensional and based only on the core business activity of the company. It does not take into account the other noncore businesses that the company may be engaged in and that may be material to the investor's ESG interests.

  Some other data issues are as follows:

- Materiality—are the factors being measured or reported important or fundamental to the company's efforts.
- Coverage—less than 5% of the world's publicly listed companies report their emissions. The percentage reporting on other issues is even lower.
- Outcomes versus inputs—where measures of outcomes are not available, such as actual amount of emissions, resort is often made to measuring inputs such as budget or staffing which can be identified as addressing emissions. But the efficacy of inputs can be highly variable: a company devoting significant inputs to pollution issues may yet have higher emissions than a company with half that level of inputs.

None of these issues are insurmountable, and all are likely to see improvement given the continued interest in ESG investing.

A confirmation of American business leaders' embrace of ESG goals came in August 2019 when 181 CEO members of the Business Roundtable signed a new Statement on the Purpose of a Corporation. This Statement is reproduced here:

Business Roundtable Redefines the Purpose of a Corporation to Promote 'An Economy That Serves All Americans'

"Americans deserve an economy that allows each person to succeed through hard work and creativity and to lead a life of meaning and dignity. We believe the free-market system is the best means of generating good jobs, a strong and sustainable economy, innovation, a healthy environment, and economic opportunity for all.

Businesses play a vital role in the economy by creating jobs, fostering innovation, and providing essential goods and services. Businesses make and sell consumer products; manufacture equipment and vehicles; support the national defense; grow and produce food; provide health care; generate and deliver energy; and offer financial, communications, and other services that underpin economic growth.

While each of our individual companies serves its own corporate purpose, we share a fundamental commitment to all of our stakeholders. We commit to:

Delivering value to our customers. We will further the tradition of American companies leading the way in meeting or exceeding customer expectations.

Investing in our employees. This starts with compensating them fairly and providing important benefits. It also includes supporting them through training and education that help develop new skills for a rapidly changing world. We foster diversity and inclusion, dignity, and respect.

Dealing fairly and ethically with our suppliers. We are dedicated to serving as good partners to the other companies, large and small, that help us meet our missions.

Supporting the communities in which we work. We respect the people in our communities and protect the environment by embracing sustainable practices across our businesses.

Generating long-term value for shareholders, who provide the capital that allows companies to invest, grow, and innovate. We are committed to transparency and effective engagement with shareholders.

Each of our stakeholders is essential. We commit to deliver value to all of them, for the future success of our companies, our communities and our country" (Business Roundtable, 2019).

With this kind of support from America's corporate leaders, there will be no turning back from a future where the goal is "doing well while doing good."

References

ACSRI, 2017. Report to the community. Advisory Committee on Socially Responsible Investing. Columbia University. Available at: https://finance.columbia.edu/files/gateway/content/ACSRI/ACSCRI%20Report.%20Feb%202017.%20Final.%20022217.pdf (accessed 29.05.19.).

AIMA, 2018. From niche to mainstream: responsible investment and hedge funds. Alternative Investment Management Association. Available at: https://www.aima.org/article/press-release-responsible-investment-by-hedge-funds.html (accessed 15.02.19.).

Barclays, 2018. The case for sustainable bond investing strategies. Barclays Impact Series. Available at: https://www.investmentbank.barclays.com/content/dam/barclaysmicrosites/ibpublic/documents/our-insights/ESG2/BarclaysIB-ImpactSeries4-ESG-in-credit-5MB.pdf (accessed 03.01.19.).

Broadridge, 2018. 2018 proxy season review. Broadridge and PWC. Available at: https://www.broadridge.com/_assets/pdf/gated/broadridge-2018-proxy-season-review.pdf (accessed 12.11.18.).

Business Roundtable, 2019. Business roundtable redefines the purpose of a corporation to promote "an economy that serves all Americans". Available at: https://www.businessroundtable.org/business-roundtable-redefines-the-purpose-of-a-corporation-to-promote-an-economy-that-serves-all-americans (accessed 19.08.19.).

CFA, 2018. DUAL-CLASS SHARES:THE GOOD, THE BAD, AND THE UGLY. CFA Institute. Available at: https://www.cfainstitute.org/-/media/documents/survey/apac-dual-class-shares-survey-report.ashx. (accessed: 20.5.2019).

CalPERS, 2018. Governance & sustainability principles. CalPERS. Available at: https://www.calpers.ca.gov/docs/forms-publications/governance-and-sustainability-principles.pdf (accessed 8.11.18.).

Carney, M., 2018. A transition in thinking. Bank of England. Available at: https://www.bankofengland.co.uk/-/media/boe/files/speech/2018/a-transition-in-thinking-and-action-speech-by-mark-carney.pdf (accessed 19.11.18.).

Ceres, 2017. Engage the chain. Available at: https://www.ceres.org/annual-report/2017/progress/ceres-tools-inspire-sustainable-solutions (accessed 10.06.18.).

Charity Navigator, 2019. 10 Charities overpaying their for-profit fundraisers. Available at: https://www.charitynavigator.org/index.cfm?bay = topten.detail&listid = 28 (accessed 07.08.19.).

Clark, G.L., Feiner, A., Viehs, M., 2014. From the Stockholder to the Stakeholder: Oxford University and Arabesque Partners Study. Oxford University Press, Oxford. Available at: http://papers.ssrn.com/sol3/papers.cfm?abstract_id = 2508281 (accessed 08.11.16.).

DOL, 2018. Field assistance bulletin no. 2018-01. Available at: https://www.dol.gov/agencies/ebsa/employers-and-advisers/guidance/field-assistance-bulletins/2018-01 (accessed 08.12.18.).

Easterby, S., 2018. Climate activists are lousy salesmen. WSJ April 25, 2018.

Edelman, P.H., Jiang, W., Thomas, R.S., 2018. Will tenure voting give corporate managers lifetime tenure? *Vanderbilt Law Research Paper No. 18-04*. Available at: https://papers.ssrn.com/sol3/papers.cfm?abstract_id = 3107225 (accessed 27.11.18.).

Esty, D., Cort, T. (Eds.), 2017. State of ESG Data and Metrics. The Journal of Environmental Investing 8 (1), . Available at: http://www.thejei.com/wp-content/uploads/2017/11/Journal-of-Environmental-Investing-8-No.-1.rev_-1.pdf. (accessed: 10.1.2018).

ETF Managers Trust, 2017. 2017 Investment Company Factbook, 2017. Investment Company Institute, 2017. Available at: https://www.ici.org/pdf/2017_factbook.pdf. (accessed: 21.3.2019).

ERISA, 2017. Meeting your fiduciary responsibilities. U.S. Department of Labor, Employee Benefits Security Administration. Available at: https://www.dol.gov/sites/default/files/ebsa/about-ebsa/our-activities/resource-center/publications/meeting-your-fiduciary-responsibilities.pdf (accessed 19.10.18.).

FDIC, 2007. Trust examination manual. Appendix C: fiduciary law. FDIC. Available at: https://www.fdic.gov/regulations/examinations/trustmanual/appendix_c/appendix_c.html (accessed 21.11.18.).

FSB, 2017. Implementing the Recommendations of the Task Force on Climate-related Financial Disclosures. FSB. Available at: https://www.fsb.org/wp-content/uploads/Annex.pdf. (accessed: 19.6.2018).

Fink, L., 2018. Larry Fink's annual letter to CEOS: a sense of purpose. Blackrock. Available at: https://www.blackrock.com/corporate/investor-relations/larry-fink-ceo-letter (accessed 08.11.18.).

Freshfields Bruckhaus Deringer, 2005. A legal framework for the integration of environmental, social and governance issues into institutional investment. UNEP FI. Available at: http://www.unepfi.org/fileadmin/documents/freshfields_legal_resp_20051123.pdf (accessed 20.11.18.).

Friede, G., Busch, T., Bassen, A., 2015. ESG and financial performance: aggregated evidence from more than 2000 empirical studies. J. Sustain. Fin. Invest. 5 (4), 210−233. Available at: https://ideas.repec.org/a/taf/jsustf/v5y2015i4p210-233.html (accessed 03.04.19.).

Friedman, M., 1970. The social responsibility of business is to increase its profits. The New York Times Magazine. Available at: http://umich.edu/~thecore/doc/Friedman.pdf (accessed 16.07.18.).

Fulton, M., Kahn, B.M., Sharples, C., 2012. Sustainable investing: establishing long-term value and performance. Deutsche Bank. Available at: https://www.db.com/cr/en/docs/Sustainable_Investing_2012.pdf (accessed 07.11.18.).

Goldman Sachs, 2015. Measuring the immeasurable: scoring ESG factors. GSAM Perspectives. Available at: https://www.gsam.com/content/dam/gsam/pdfs/common/en/public/articles/perspectives/2015/MeasuringImmeasurable.pdf?sa = n&rd = n (accessed 08.06.18.).

Gond, J.-P., O'Sullivan, N., Slager, R., Homanen, M., Viehs, M., Mosony, S., 2018. How ESG engagement creates value for investors and companies. United Nations, Principles for Responsible Investing. Available at: https://www.unpri.org/academic-research/how-esg-engagement-creates-value-for-investors-and-companies/3054.article (accessed 07.03.19.).

Gramm, P., Solon, M., 2018. Keep Politics Out of the Boardroom. Wall Street Journal (accessed: 19.7.2018).

GSIA, 2017. Global sustainable investment review. Available at: http://www.gsi-alliance.org/members-resources/trends-report-2016/ (accessed 13.07.18.).

Hart, O., Zingales, L., 2017. Companies should maximize shareholder welfare not market value. J. Law Fin. Account (2), 247−274. Available: https://scholar.harvard.edu/files/hart/files/108.00000022-hart-vol2no2-jlfa-0022_002.pdf (accessed 04.12.18.).

International Monetary Fund (IMF), 2008. Sovereign wealth funds: a work agenda. IMF. Available at: https://www.imf.org/external/np/pp/eng/2008/022908.pdf (accessed 19.04.19.).

International Working Group of Sovereign Wealth Funds (IWGSWF), 2017. Santiago principles: generally accepted principles and practices. Available at: http://www.ifswf.org/santiago-principles-landing/ santiago-principles (accessed 14.04.19.).

Jensen, M.C., Meckling, W.H., 1976. The theory of the firm: managerial behavior, agency costs and ownership structure. J. Fin. Econ. 305. Available at: https://www.sfu.ca/~wainwrig/Econ400/jensen-meckling.pdf (accessed 12.10.18.).

JUST, 2018. Redefining Impact Investing with the Wisdom of the Crowd, August 1, 2018. Available at: https://justcapital.com/news/redefining-impact-investing-with-the-wisdom-of-the-crowd/. (accessed: 7.7.2019).

KPMG, 2017. The Road Ahead: The KPMG Survey of Corporate Responsibility Reporting 2017. KPMG, 2017. Available at: https://home.kpmg/xx/en/home/insights/2017/10/the-kpmg-survey-of-corporate-responsibility-reporting-2017.html. (accessed: 12.1.2018).

Kaissar, N., 2018. Yale champions social investing (whatever that is). Bloomberg Opinion, October 19, 2018.

Kleeman, D., Sargis, M., 2018. How does sustainability affect investor decisions. Morningstar Quantitative Analytics Quarterly. Available at: https://www.morningstar.com/content/dam/marketing/shared/pdfs/sustainability/QAQ8152018.pdf?cid = EMQ_ (accessed 24.10.18.).

Krosinsky, C., Purdom, S. (Eds.), 2017. Sustainable Investing. Routledge, Oxon and New York.

Levine, M., 2018. Shareholder value could be worse. Bloomberg Opinion. Available at: https://www.bloomberg.com/view/articles/2018-09-27/shareholder-value-could-be-worse?srnd = opinion-finance (accessed 27.09.18.).

Lovelace, B., Jr., 2018. Billionaire Sam Zell: BlackRock's Larry Fink is 'extraordinarily hypocritical' to push social responsibility. Available at: https://www.cnbc.com/2018/01/16/sam-zell-blackrock-ceo-fink-is-hypocritical-to-push-social-responsibility.html (accessed 05.12.18.).

Malkiel, B.G., 1973. A Random Walk Down Wall Street. W.W.Norton, New York.

Matthews, J., 2014. Secrets in Plain Sight: Business & Investing Secrets of Warren Buffett. eBooks on Investing (accessed:21.5.2014).

Meld. St. 14, 2019. Energy stocks in the government pension fund global. Report to the Storting, Royal Ministry of Finance. Available at: https://www.regjeringen.no/contentassets/c8cd5eea5a2b499388462ffcc70e4339/en-gb/pdfs/stm201820190014000engpdfs.pdf (accessed 19.04.19.).

Monheit, B.M., Debney, J., 2018. Letter to Black Rock. American Outdoor Brands Corportion. Available at: http://ir.aob.com/phoenix.zhtml?c = 90977&p = irol-investorHome (accessed 17.11.18.).

Morningstar, 2018. Sustainable funds U.S. landscape report. Morningstar Research. Available at: https://www.morningstar.com/company/esg-investing (accessed 02.01.19.).

Mudaliar, A., Bass, R., 2017. Evidence on the financial performance of impact investments. Global Impact Investing Network (GIIN). Available at: https://thegiin.org/assets/2017_GIIN_FinancialPerformanceImpactInvestments_Web.pdf (accessed 28.01.19.).

Munnell, A.H., Chen, A., 2016. New developments in social investing by public pensions. Center for Retirement Research at Boston College. Available at: http://crr.bc.edu/wp-content/uploads/2016/11/slp_53.pdf (accessed 24.12.18.).

NYCCO, 2018. Pension/investment management. City of New York. Available at: https://comptroller.nyc.gov/services/financial-matters/pension/corporate-governance/proxy-voting-dashboard/ (accessed 10.11.18.).

OECD, 2017. Investment governance and the integration of environmental, social and governance factors. OECD. Available at: https://www.oecd.org/finance/Investment-Governance-Integration-ESG-Factors.pdf (accessed 07.12.18.).

PEW, 2018. The state pension funding gap: 2016. The PEW Charitable Trusts. Available at: https://www.pewtrusts.org/en/research-and-analysis/issue-briefs/2018/04/the-state-pension-funding-gap-2016 (accessed 30.12.18.).

PIMCO, 2017. 10 reasons ESG investing is growing. Available at: https://www.pimco.co.uk/en-gb/insights/blog/10-reasons-esg-investing-is-growing/ (accessed 06.12.18.).

PRA, 2018. Transition in thinking: the impact of climate change on the UK banking sector. Bank of England, Prudential Regulatory Authority. Available at: https://www.bankofengland.co.uk/prudential-regulation/publication/2018/transition-in-thinking-the-impact-of-climate-change-on-the-uk-banking-sector (accessed 02.11.18.).

Richardson, B.J., 2007. Do the fiduciary duties of pension funds hinder socially responsible investing? Banking and Finance Law Review. Available at: https://papers.ssrn.com/sol3/papers.cfm?abstract_id = 970236 (accessed 18.09.18.).

SEC, 2016. Fiscal Year 2016 Agency Financial Report. SEC, 2016. Available at: https://www.sec.gov/reportspubs/annual-reports/about-secafr2016shtml.html. (accessed: 3.5. 2018).

Serafeim, G., Seesel, A., 2018. Does sustainable investing lead to lower returns? Barron's. Available at: https://www.barrons.com/articles/does-sustainable-investing-lead-to-lower-returns-1529712000 (accessed 17.11.18.).

Shier, S.L., 2017. Responsible investing for the modern fiduciary. Northern Trust. Available at: https://www.northerntrust.com/documents/line-of-sight/wealth-management/responsible-investing-modern-fiduciary.pdf (accessed 17.11.18.).

Stout, L., 2013. The Shareholder Value Myth. Cornell Law Faculty Publications. Available at: https://scholarship.law.cornell.edu/cgi/viewcontent.cgi?article = 2311&context = facpub. (accessed: 10.6.2019).

The Global Compact, 2004. Who cares wins: connecting financial markets to a changing world. United Nations. Available at: https://www.unglobalcompact.org/docs/issues_doc/Financial_markets/who_cares_who_wins.pdf (accessed 06.02.19.).

UNEP FI, 2009. Fiduciary responsibility: legal and practical aspects of integrating environmental, social and governance issues into institutional investment. UNEP FI. Avaialble at: http://www.unepfi.org/fileadmin/documents/fiduciaryII.pdf (accessed 20.09.18.).

UNGC, 2017, The SDG investment case. Available at: https://www.calpers.ca.gov/docs/board-agendas/201801/full/day1/04-pri-blueprint-background.pdf (accessed 03.09.18.).

UNGC, 2018. The ten principles of the UN global compact. Available at: https://www.unglobalcompact.org/what-is-gc/mission/principles (accessed 11.06.18.).

UPMIFA, 2006. Uniform Prudent Management of Institutional Funds Act. National Conference of Commissioners on Uniform State Laws. Available at: http://www.uniformlaws.org/shared/docs/prudent%20mgt%20of%20institutional%20funds/upmifa_final_06.pdf.m (accessed 26.11.18.).

USSIF, 2018. The report on US sustainable, responsible and impact investing trends 2018. Forum for Sustainable and Responsible Investment (USSIF). Available at: https://www.ussif.org/files/Trends/Trends%202018%20executive%20summary%20FINAL.pdf (accessed 11.05.19.).

Warren, E.B., 2016. Shareholder Letter. Berkshire Hathaway, Inc. Available at: https://www.berkshirehathaway.com/letters/2016ltr.pdf. (accessed: 4.2.2018).

Westcott, S., 2018. 2018 proxy season brings some surprises. The Advisor, Alliance Advisors. Available at: https://allianceadvisors.com/wp-content/uploads/2018/06/Alliance-Advisors-Newsletter-Jun.-2018-2018-Proxy-Season-Brings-Some-Surprises-1.pdf (accessed 13.11.18.).

Index

Note: Page numbers followed by "*f*" and "*t*" refer to figures and tables, respectively.

A

Abortion investment policy of USCCB, 287
Abu Dhabi Investment Authority, 243
ACCRIP. *See* Advisory Committee on
    Corporate Responsibility in Investment
    Policies (ACCRIP)
ACH. *See* Automatic Clearing House (ACH)
ACIR. *See* Advisory Committee on Investor
    Responsibility (ACIR)
ACSR. *See* Advisory Committee on
    Shareholder Responsibility (ACSR)
ACSRI. *See* Advisory Committee on Socially
    Responsible Investing (ACSRI)
Active corporate participation, 286
Active engagement, 274
Active ownership, 219–220
ACWI. *See* All Country World Index (ACWI)
Adolescent development, 315
Adrienne Arsht-Rockefeller Foundation
    Resilience Center, 261
Adverse selection, 60–62
Advisory Committee on Corporate
    Responsibility in Investment Policies
    (ACCRIP), 215–216
Advisory Committee on Investor
    Responsibility (ACIR), 212
Advisory Committee on Shareholder
    Responsibility (ACSR), 219
Advisory Committee on Socially Responsible
    Investing (ACSRI), 220
Advocacy, 305–308
AED. *See* Automated External Defibrillator
    (AED)
Agency Problem, 46–47
Agency securities, 129
    federal debt, 130*f*, 131*f*
    money market mutual funds, 128*f*
"Agency-principal" perspective, 31
AGM. *See* Annual General Meeting (AGM)

AI. *See* Artificial intelligence (AI)
AIDS, 256
Alcohol, 277
Alignment, 234
All Country World Index (ACWI), 111
Alternative trading systems (ATS), 103
Amana Developing World, 297–298
Amana Growth Fund, 298
Amana Income Fund, 298
Amana Mutual Funds, 297–298
Amana Participation Fund, 298
American Outdoor Brands Corporation, 30
American Red Cross (ARC), 320–322
Animal testing, 277–278
Annual General Meeting (AGM), 148–149
Annuities, 79
Anti-corruption, 175
Anti-Poaching & Research, 314
Antipersonnel landmines, 288
Apartheid era South Africa, 14
Arabesque, 200–201
ARC. *See* American Red Cross (ARC)
Arms production, 288
Arnold Ventures, 23
Artificial intelligence (AI), 167–168, 333
ArtPlace, 264
Asset
    managers, 92–94, 93*f*
    securitization, 70–71
Assets under management (AUM), 1–2,
    92–93, 106, 115–116, 156, 185, 228,
    329
Assets Under Supervision (AUS), 198–199
Atlantic Council, 261
ATS. *See* Alternative trading systems (ATS)
AUM. *See* Assets under management (AUM)
AUS. *See* Assets Under Supervision (AUS)
Australia's Sovereign Wealth Fund, 242–243
Auto insurance, 79

Automated External Defibrillator (AED), 321
Automatic Clearing House (ACH), 73
Ave Maria Mutual Funds, 289–290

B

Babysitting, 321
Bank lending, 62
Bank of England (BoE), 75
Bank of Japan (BOJ), 75
Bank Rate, 75
Banker's Acceptances, 127
Banking, 17–18
Banking Act (1933), 66
Banking system, 59–60
Basic Life Support (BLS), 321
Beaked Whale Research, 315
Benchmark indexes, 185–186
Berkshire Hathaway, 106–107, 253–254
"Best in class" approach, 200, 238–239
"Beta" Stocks, 100
Better Business Bureau's Wise Giving
    Alliance, 328
Betterment, 115–116, 201–203
BGRN. *See* iShares Global Green Bond ETF
    (BGRN)
Biblically Responsible Investing, 281–282
Big Data, 333
Bill & Melinda Gates Foundation (BMGF),
    253–257
BIO. *See* Brown Investment Office (BIO)
Black Swans, 99
BlackRock, 151, 156–157, 162–163, 182,
    188–193
BlackRock Impact Bond Fund, 193
BlackRock Impact US Equity Fund, 192–193
Blood supply, 321
Bloomberg Connects, 264
Bloomberg Philanthropies, 262–265
BLS. *See* Basic Life Support (BLS)
Blue bonds, 141
Blue sky laws, 105
BlueStar Israel Technology ETF, 301–302
BMGF. *See* Bill & Melinda Gates Foundation
    (BMGF)
Board Chair and/or Nominations Committee
    Chair, 165
BoE. *See* Bank of England (BoE)
BOJ. *See* Bank of Japan (BOJ)
Bonds, 10, 117
    agency securities, 129
    corporate bonds, 129–132

credit instruments, 121–122
ESG bond funds, 136–139
fidelity, 140–141
Fisher's law, 122
fixed income indexes and funds, 136–143
fixed income trading, 133–136
FV and PV, 118–120
green bonds, 141–143
    indexes and ETFs, 142–143
IRR, 120–121
managers, 139–141
money market instruments, 124–127
municipal securities, 132–133
PIMCO, 139–140
sovereign debt, 133
term structure and yield curve, 122–124
    Moody's Seasoned Aaa Corporate Bond
        Yield, 125f
US Treasury securities, 127–129
Breaking buck, 127
Bribery, 278
Brown Investment Office (BIO), 215
Brown University, ESG in, 217–220
Brown University Sustainable Investment
    Fund (BUSIF), 216
"Bulge Bracket", 67
BUSIF. *See* Brown University Sustainable
    Investment Fund (BUSIF)
Business, 335
    partners, 276–277
    roundtable, 9, 334–335
    social responsibility of, 29–32
Business Involvement Screen, 196
"Buy and Manage" investment approach,
    84–85

C

California Public Employees' Retirement
    System (CalPERS), 90–91, 91f, 152,
    157–158, 161
CAMELS. *See* Capital adequacy, Asset
    quality, Management, Earnings,
    Liquidity, and Sensitivity (CAMELS)
CAN. *See* Certified Nurse Assistant (CAN)
Cannabis, 278
Capacity building, 223
Capital, 94
Capital adequacy, Asset quality, Management,
    Earnings, Liquidity, and Sensitivity
    (CAMELS), 73
Capital asset pricing model (CAPM), 100

CAPM. *See* Capital asset pricing model (CAPM)
Captive insurance, 80
Carbon Capture, Usage and Storage (CCUS), 244
Carbon dioxide (CO_2), 244
Carbon Disclosure Project (CDP), 198, 218, 238
Care giving, 321
Carnegie Corporation of New York, 267–269
Cascade Women's and Children's Center, 326
Casualty insurance, 79
Catalytic portfolio, 84
Catastrophe insurance, 80
Catholic Guidelines, 291
Catholic values ETF, 291
Catholic values investing, 284–291
Catholic values mutual funds, 289
CBI green designation. *See* Climate bond initiative green designation (CBI green designation)
CCIR. *See* Corporation Committee on Investor Responsibility (CCIR)
CCSR. *See* Corporation Committee on Shareholder Responsibility (CCSR)
CCUS. *See* Carbon Capture, Usage and Storage (CCUS)
CDP. *See* Carbon Disclosure Project (CDP)
CDP Water, 238
Celebrity-related charities, 305, 306*f*
Central banks, 71–76
Central credit unions, 64–65
Central Huijin Investment Ltd. (Central Huijin), 240–241
Ceres, 178–179
Certified Nurse Assistant (CAN), 321
Cetacean Captivity, 314
CFA-PRI survey, 137
Chan Zuckerberg Initiative (CZI), 19, 250–253
Charitable commitment, 304–305
Charities, 304, 306*f*
  celebrity-related charities, 305, 306*f*
  US charities, 304*f*
Charity Navigator, 305
CharityWatch, 328
Child protection from violence and abuse, 316
Children uprooted, 315–316
Children with disabilities, 317
China Investment Company (CIC), 240–241
China National Offshore Oil Corporation (CNOOC), 229

Christian Super, 277–281
Christian values, 278
  investing, 274–283
Church
  as economic actor, 284–285
  as shareholder and investor, 284
CIC. *See* China Investment Company (CIC)
CIC Capital. *See* CIC Capital Corporation (CIC Capital)
CIC Capital Corporation (CIC Capital), 240–241
CIC International. *See* CIC International Co., Ltd. (CIC International)
CIC International Co., Ltd. (CIC International), 240–241
CityLab, 264
Clawbacks, 155–156
Clean Air Act, 168–169
"Clean diesel" technology, 168–169
Climate bond initiative green designation (CBI green designation), 142
Climate change, 2, 5, 234–235, 255, 278
Climate risk, 237
CNOOC. *See* China National Offshore Oil Corporation (CNOOC)
Coal, 216
Collateralized bond obligations, 70
Collateralized debt obligations, 70
College and university endowment management, ESG in
  Brown University, 215–217
  Columbia University, 220–221
  Commonfund, 222
  ESG investing in schools, 221
  Hampshire College, 209–221
  Harvard's endowment, 217–220
  IEN, 222–223
  NACUBO, 223–224
  organizations providing analysis, support, consulting, and investing services, 222–225
  UC, 214–215
  US SIF, 224–225
  Yale University, 212–214
Columbia University, ESG in, 220–221
COMET. *See* Company Engagement Tool (COMET)
Commercial banks, 62*f*, 63–64, 66
Commercial paper (CP), 126
Commonfund, 222
Communication for development, 316

Community and Affordable Housing Investments, 85

Community development, 286

Community investing, 275–276

Community Reinvestment Act, 288–289

Company Engagement Tool (COMET), 196

Company's profit-making activities, 33

Compounding of interest, 118–119

Comprehensive insurance, 79

Concentrated Solar Power (CSP), 244

Conference corporate responsibility policies, 284–285

Conflict Risk Network (CRN), 216

"Connected learning" programs, 308–309

Constructive engagement, 15

Consumer debt, 278

Consumer Finance Protection Board, 72

Consumer Protection Act, 61

Contingent pension reserve funds, 229

Contraceptives, 287

Controversial weapons, 281

Convening key stakeholders, 223

Conventional investment portfolios, 25–26, 329–330

Conventional monetary tools, 73–74

Corporate
  activism, 29–30
  bonds, 129–132
  credit unions, 64–65
  documents, 36
  ESG
    reporting, 176–177
    services providing assessment, 177–179
  governance, 150–152
  profits, 35–36
  raiders, 71
  responsibility, 289

Corporation Committee on Investor Responsibility (CCIR), 212

Corporation Committee on Shareholder Responsibility (CCSR), 219

Corruption, 278

Cost savings, 62

Council Events, 270

Council on Foundations, 269–270

Coupon payments plus (CP plus), 121–122

CP. *See* Commercial paper (CP)

CP plus. *See* Coupon payments plus (CP plus)

CPR, 321

Credit
  instruments, 121–122
  risk, 63
  unions, 64–66
  to credit unions, 64–65

Criminal Law Amendment Act, 325

CRN. *See* Conflict Risk Network (CRN)

"Crowd out" private contributions, 29–30

CSP. *See* Concentrated Solar Power (CSP)

Cumulative preferred stock, 98

Curbing pornography, 288

Customers, taxing, 29–30

CZI. *See* Chan Zuckerberg Initiative (CZI)

D

Dark pools, 103–104

Day One Fund, 257–258

Defined Benefit Plans, 86–87

Defined Contribution Plans, 86

Democracy, 268

Demographics, 3

Department of Labor (DOL), 52–53

Depository Institutions Deregulation and Monetary Control Act (1980), 65–66

Development funds, 229

Direct economic value generated and distributed report (EVG&D report), 171

Disaster Recovery (DR), 64

Disaster relief, 320–321

Discount Bonds, 121

Discount rate, 74

Dive Site, 313

Diversification, 61, 98–100

Divestment, 221
  portfolios, 329–330
  strategies, 14–15, 333
    historic underperformance, 332
    sin stocks, 15–18
    South Africa, 14–15

"Do no harm" strategy, 285–286

Dodd-Frank Act, 69, 72

Dodd-Frank Wall Street Reform, 61

DOL. *See* Department of Labor (DOL)

Donor dependency, 305

Donor intent, 207

Dow Jones Islamic Market USA Index, 298–299

Dow Jones Israel Select Consumer Index, 301

DR. *See* Disaster Recovery (DR)

Dual-stock voting structure, 36–37

E

Earthquake relief, 321

ECAs. *See* Export Credit Agencies (ECAs)

ECB. *See* European Central Bank (ECB)

ECNs. *See* Electronic communications
  networks (ECNs)
Economic justice, 288–289
Economies of Scale and Scope, 62
Education, 305–308
Efficient market hypothesis (EMH), 101
Efficient portfolios, 98–99
EFO. *See* Embedded Family Office (EFO)
EIAG. *See* Ethical Investment Advisory
  Group (EIAG)
EIS, 301
EITI. *See* Extractive Industries Transparency
  Initiative (EITI)
EJAF. *See* Elton John AIDS Foundation
  (EJAF)
Electronic communications networks (ECNs),
  103
Elton John AIDS Foundation (EJAF), 310
EMAS Shariah Indexes, 297
Embedded Family Office (EFO), 249
Embryonic stem cell/human cloning, 287
EMH. *See* Efficient market hypothesis (EMH)
Employee Retirement Income Security Act
  (ERISA), 48
  rules, 87–89
Employment risk, 207
Endowment, 215
Endowment Model, 208
Energy stocks assessment, 237
Environment, 175, 289
Environment and climate change, 317
Environmental, social, and governance (ESG),
  23, 97, 111, 117, 145, 157–158, 205,
  216, 247, 274, 329
  bond funds, 136–139
    low-ESG portfolios in Euro and US IG
      markets, 138*f*
    Morningstar categories, 138*f*
  empirical studies, 331–332
  fiduciary duty, 57–58
  financial return *vs.*, 330*f*
  future, 332–333
  goals, 146
  indexes, 109–114
  integration, 200, 219
  investors, 167
  issues into their investment analysis, 137*f*
  mutual funds and ETFs rate ESG
    performance of portfolio companies
    conceptual critiques of ESG investing,
      180–181
    empirical studies, 181–183

    ESG investing require lower returns, 180
    Morningstar, 180
  oriented mutual funds, 186–188
  performance
    Ceres, 178–179
    corporate ESG reporting, 176–177
    global reporting initiative, 169–172
    JUST Capital, 179
    MSCI, 177–178
    quality issues in ESG reporting,
      175–176
    RepRisk ESG Business Intelligence, 178
    SASB, 173–174
    services providing assessment of
      corporate ESG, 177–179
    standards for companies to report ESG
      impacts, 168–175
    Sustainalytics, 177
  portfolio construction, 167–168
  portfolio investment strategy, 330
  practices, 1–3
    climate change, 5
    defining and measuring ESG
      performance, 10
    faith-based investing, 11
    fiduciary duty in investment
      management, 9
    financial institutions, 9
    financial markets, 10
    future, 12
    investing, 2–3, 7
    investing-organizations, 12
    in managing college and university
      endowments, 11
    in managing family foundations and
      family offices, 11
    in managing institutional investor funds,
      11
    in managing sovereign wealth and
      government sponsored funds, 11
    perception, 4–5
    portfolios, 2
    PRI, 5–6
    shareholder engagement, 10
    theories of firm, 7–9
  SRI, and impact investing, 8
Environmental returns, 25–26, 26*f*
Environmental Standards, 170
Equities, 10, 97
  CAPM, 100
  collective investment vehicles, 107–108
  EMH, 101

Equities (*Continued*)
 ESG indexes, 109–114
 FTSE Russell, 111–112
 indexes, 108–109
 investing in equities, 106–107
 Morningstar, 113–114
 MSCI, 110–111
 random walk, 101
 regulation, 105–106
 risk, return, and diversification, 98–100
 robo-advisors, 115–116
 trading venues, 103–105
 types of orders, 101–103
ERISA. *See* Employee Retirement Income
  Security Act (ERISA)
ESG. *See* Environmental, social, and
  governance (ESG)
ESG ANALYTICS, 195
ESG COMET, 196
ESG investing, 13–14, 29, 59–60, 185,
  227–228, 329, 333–335. *See also*
  Faith-based investing
 in China, 241
 ESG investing-organizations, 303–304
  EJAF, 310
  HFH, 327–328
  Meals on Wheels, 327
  Michael J. Fox Foundation for
   Parkinson's Research, 309–310
  OC, 312
  Project AWARE, 313
  Red Cross and Red Crescent Societies,
   319–322
  Salvation Army, 322–327
  SSCS, 313–315
  UNESCO, 317–319
  UNICEF, 315–317
  USA for UNHCR, 308–309
  Water.org, 310–312
  Women's Sports Foundation, 305–307
 policy in selected SWFs, 235–246
 by SWFs, 232–235
ESG METRO, 196
ESGQ tool, 200–201
ETFs. *See* Exchange-traded funds (ETFs)
Ethical business practices, 1–2
Ethical Investment Advisory Group (EIAG),
  274
EUR-denominated bond, 141–142
Eurasia Program works, 259
European Central Bank (ECB), 75
Eventide Funds, 282–283

Eventide Gilead Fund, 283
Eventide Global Dividend Opportunities Fund,
  283
Eventide Healthcare & Life Sciences Fund,
  283
Eventide Limited-Term Bond Fund, 283
Eventide Multi-Asset Income Fund, 283
EVG&D report. *See* Direct economic value
  generated and distributed report
  (EVG&D report)
Exchange-traded funds (ETFs), 76–77, 97,
  159–161, 186–188, 190, 294–296,
  300–302, 333–334
 rate ESG performance of portfolio
  companies, 180
 screening tools, 141
 trading, 168
Exchange-traded funds, 107–108
Export Credit Agencies (ECAs), 172
Extractive Industries Transparency Initiative
  (EITI), 238

F
Faith-based investing, 11, 22, 273. *See also*
  ESG investing
 Amana Mutual Funds, 297–298
 Ave Maria Mutual Funds, 289–290
 Catholic values ETF, 291
 Catholic values investing, 284–291
 Catholic values mutual funds, 289
 Christian Super, 277–281
 Christian values investing, 274–283
 Eventide Funds, 282–283
 features, 273–274
 FTSE Shariah indexes, 296–297
 Green Sukuk bonds, 293–294
 GuideStone, 275
 ICCR, 276–277
 Iman Fund, 298–299
 Islamic values indexes, mutual funds, and
  ETFs, 294–296
 Islamic values investing, 291–299
 Jewish values indexes, mutual funds, and
  ETFs, 300–302
 Jewish values investing, 299–302
 LKCM Aquinas Catholic Equity Fund, 291
 MSCI Islamic index series, 296
 New Covenant Funds, 275–276
 Shariah compliant ETFs, 299
 Timothy Plan Funds, 281–282
 USCCB investment policies, 287–289

Family foundations, 247, 249
  Bloomberg, 262–265
  BMGF, 253–257
  Carnegie Corporation of New York,
    267–269
  Council on Foundations, 269–270
  CZI, 250–253
  Day One Fund, 257–258
  Ford Foundation, 265–267
  Foundation Center, 270–271
  Giving Pledge, 253
  Lilly Endowment Inc., 257
  Open Society Foundations, 258–260
  providing services to foundation
    community, 269–271
  Robert Wood Johnson Foundation,
    260–261
  Rockefeller Foundation, 261–262
Family offices, 247–269
Fannie Mae Green MBS, 142
FASB. *See* Financial Accounting Standards
    Board (FASB)
Fat tails, 99
Favored assets, 80
FD. *See* Full disclosure (FD)
FDIC. *See* Federal Depositors Insurance
    Corporation (FDIC)
Fed. *See* Federal Reserve System (FRS)
Fed funds rate, 124–126
Federal Depositors Insurance Corporation
    (FDIC), 64
Federal funds rate, 74
Federal health insurance programs, 78
Federal Home Loan Bank Act, 65–66
Federal Home Loan Bank Board (FHLBB),
    65–66
Federal National Mortgage Association
    supports, 129
Federal Reserve System (FRS), 71–72
FedWire Funds Transfer Service, 73
FHLBB. *See* Federal Home Loan Bank Board
    (FHLBB)
Fidelity, 140–141
  PIMCO's three-step approach, 140*f*
Fidelity International Sustainability Index
    Fund, 194
Fidelity Investments Inc., 193–194
Fidelity Select Environment & Alternative
    Energy Portfolio
    (FSLEX), 194
Fidelity Sustainability Bond Index Fund
    (FNDSX), 194

Fidelity US Sustainability Index Fund,
    193–194
Fidelity Women's Leadership Fund, 194
Fiduciary, 45–47
  agency problem, 46–47
  duty, 48
  fiduciary II, 56–57
  Freshfields Report, 54–56
  obligations, 48–49
  OECD, 58
  Prudent Man rule, 49–51
  rule, 54
  United Nations PRI, 57–58
  UPIA, 51–53
  UPMIFA, 53–54
Fiduciary duty, 16, 48, 207
  in investment management, 9
Financial Accounting Standards Board
    (FASB), 165, 173
Financial capital, 90
Financial efficiency ratios, 304–305
Financial Industry Regulatory Authority
    (FINRA), 105, 129–132
Financial infrastructure, 75
Financial institutions, 9, 13, 61
  asset managers, 92–94
  asset securitization, 70–71
  CalPERS, 90–91
  central banks, 71–76
  commercial banks, 62*f*, 63–64
  conventional monetary tools, 73–74
  credit unions, 64–66
  Florida SBA, 91–92
  hedge funds, 94
  information asymmetries, moral hazard, and
    adverse selection, 60–62
  insurance companies, 78–86
  insurance types, 78–83
  investment banks, 66–71
  largest pension funds, 87–90, 88*f*
  mergers and acquisitions, 71
  MetLife Inc., 84–85
  pension funds, 86–92
  prime brokerage, 71
  private equity, 94–95
  Prudential Financial Inc., 84
  shadow banking, 76–78
  trading and research, 68–70
  unconventional monetary policy, 74–75
  Zurich Insurance Group, 85–86
Financial intermediaries, 76–78
Financial markets

Financial markets (*Continued*)
  bonds, 10
  equities, 10
Financial returns, 25–26, 26*f*
Financial risks, 235
Financial services, 77
  providers, 332
Financial Services Modernization Act
  (FSMA), 66
Financial Stability Board (FSB), 77
FINRA. *See* Financial Industry Regulatory
  Authority (FINRA)
FinTech, 333
Firearms, 281
Firm, 29, 35–36
First Aid, 321
Fisher's law, 122
Five Senators, 65–66
"5-5-5" program, 85–86
Fixed income, 117
  indexes and funds, 136–143
  investment, 2–3, 197
  markets, 10
  products, 196
  trading, 133–136
    external sovereign defaults, 134*f*
Flood relief, 321
Florida State Board of Administration (SBA),
  91–92
FNDSX. *See* Fidelity Sustainability Bond
  Index Fund (FNDSX)
Fond De Reserve Pour Les Retraits.
  See French Pension Reserve Fund
  (FRR)
Food industry, 278
Ford Foundation, 265–267
Forest Stewardship Council (FSC), 219
Forum for Sustainable and Responsible
  Investment (USSIF), 185, 224–225
Fossil fuel, 278–279
Foundation Center, 270–271
Fraternal life insurance, 80
Free-market system, 335
French Pension Reserve Fund (FRR),
  238–239
Freshfields Report, 54–56
Friedman's theory, 32–33
FRR. *See* French Pension Reserve Fund
  (FRR)
FRS. *See* Federal Reserve System (FRS)
FSB. *See* Financial Stability Board (FSB)
FSC. *See* Forest Stewardship Council (FSC)

FSLEX. *See* Fidelity Select Environment &
  Alternative Energy Portfolio (FSLEX)
FSMA. *See* Financial Services Modernization
  Act (FSMA)
FTSE All World Tobacco Index, 17
FTSE Bursa Malaysia Hirjah Shariah, 297
FTSE NASDAQ Dubai Shariah Index Series,
  297
FTSE Russell, 111–112
FTSE SET Shariah Indexes, 297
FTSE SGX Shariah Index Series, 297
FTSE Shariah Global Equity Index Series,
  297
FTSE Shariah indexes, 296–297
FTSE TWSE Taiwan Shariah Indexes, 297
FTSE USA Shariah ETF, 299
FTSE/JSE Africa Shariah indices, 297
FTSE's Green Revenues data model, 111
Full disclosure (FD), 69
Funding Agreement, 127
Fundraising efficiency, 305
Funds, 74, 242
  approach to ESG, 236
  Ethical Investment Positions, 277–281
  of funds, 106
  managers, 331
Future Fund, 242–243
Future Generation fund, 246
Future value (FV), 118–120

G

Gadflies, 148–149
Gambling, 279
Gen Xers, 2–3
Gender discrimination, 288
Gender equality, 316
General Motors (GM), 15
"General partner", 94
Generation Z, 1–2, 329
Genetic engineering, 279
Genetically modified organisms (GMOs), 110,
  192
George Soros, 258
Germain Depository Institutions Act (1982),
  65–66
GHG. *See* Greenhouse gases (GHG)
GICS. *See* Global Industry Classification
  Benchmarks (GICS)
Giving Pledge, 253
Glass Lewis, 150
Glass-Steagall Act. *See* Banking Act (1933)

Global banking services, 63
Global Drug Policy Program, 259
Global engagement, 311–312
Global Financial Crisis, 61, 74, 126, 208
Global Industry Classification Benchmarks
    (GICS), 334
Global Philanthropy, 270
Global Red Cross Network, 320
Global Reporting Initiative (GRI), 168–172
Global sustainable investment, 26–27
Global X S&P 500 Catholic Values ETF, 291
GM. *See* General Motors (GM)
GMOs. *See* Genetically modified organisms
    (GMOs)
Goldman Sachs Asset Management (GSAM),
    198–199
Governance, 331–332
Government Pension Fund-Global in Norway,
    232
Great Depression, 65–66
Great Financial Crisis, 64–65
Green bonds, 10, 117, 141–143
    ETF, 143
    market, 3
Green Growth Infrastructure Fund, 246
Green Investments, 85
Green Mortgage Backed Securities facility
    (MBS facility), 142
Green Sukuk bonds, 293–294
Greenhouse gases (GHG), 276–277
"Greenwash", 32
GRI. *See* Global Reporting Initiative (GRI)
GRNB. *See* VanEck Vectors Green Bond
    Fund (GRNB)
GSAM. *See* Goldman Sachs Asset
    Management (GSAM)
GuideStone, 275

H

Habitat for Humanity (HFH), 327–328
Hampshire College, ESG in, 209–221
Hart and Zingales theory, 32–33
Harvard Management Company (HMC),
    218–219
Harvard's endowment, ESG in, 217–220
Health and safety training and education, 321
Health insurance, 78–79
Health Maintenance Organization (HMO), 79
Hedge funds, 76–77, 94
HFH. *See* Habitat for Humanity (HFH)
HFT. *See* High frequency traders (HFT)

High Dividend Stock ETF, 282
High frequency traders (HFT), 102–103
High Yield (HY), 129–132
HMC. *See* Harvard Management Company
    (HMC)
HMO. *See* Health Maintenance Organization
    (HMO)
Home fire relief, 320
Homeowners insurance, 79
Hong Kong Monetary Authority Investment
    Portfolio, 232
Housing/banking, 288–289
Human capital, 90
Human dignity protection, 287–288
Human life protection, 287
Human rights, 174, 287
    and responsibilities, 279–280
Humanity, 320
Hurricane relief, 320–321
HY. *See* High Yield (HY)

I

ICB. *See* Industry Classification Benchmarks
    (ICB)
ICCR. *See* Interfaith Center on Corporate
    Responsibility (ICCR)
ICE. *See* InterContinental Exchange (ICE)
ICGN. *See* International Corporate
    Governance Network (ICGN)
ICMA. *See* International Capital Market
    Association (ICMA)
IEN. *See* Intentional Endowments Network
    (IEN)
IFSWF. *See* International Forum of Sovereign
    Wealth Funds (IFSWF)
IG. *See* Investment Grade (IG)
Illegal, Unreported and Unregulated Fishing
    (IUU Fishing), 314–315
ILO Tripartite Declaration. *See* International
    Labour Organization Tripartite
    Declaration (ILO Tripartite
    Declaration)
Iman Fund, 298–299
IMC. *See* Investment Management Company
    (IMC)
IMM. *See* Impact multiple of money (IMM)
Impact investing, 8, 18–21, 25–26, 329–330
    Rise Fund, 18–21
        largest US community foundations, 21*f*
        largest US foundations, 20*f*
        largest US university endowments, 22*f*

Impact investing (*Continued*)
spectrum, 198–199
studies of financial performance, 331
Impact managed portfolio, 84
Impact multiple of money (IMM), 19–21
Impartiality, 320
Independence, 320
Individual Retirement Accounts (IRA), 86
Individual investors, 1–2
Industry Classification Benchmarks
(ICB), 334
Inertia, 207
Information and contracting efficiencies, 61
Information asymmetries, 60–62
Infrastructure fund, 246
Infrastructure Investments, 85
Initial public offering (IPO), 38–39, 68
Institutional investor fund management,
ESG in
betterment, 201–203
BlackRock, 188–193
Fidelity Investments Inc., 193–194
GSAM, 198–199
JPMAM, 200–201
JUST Capital, 203–204
PIMCO, 194–198
sustainable investment
choices, 188–193
Institutional investors, 1–2, 161–165, 332
Institutional Shareholder Services (ISS), 149
Insurance
companies, 78–86
profitability, 80
types, 78–83
largest US life insurance companies in
2017, 83f
total US insurance industry cash and
invested assets, 81f, 82f
Integrated "roadmap" approach, 309
Integration, 234–235
Intentional Endowments Network (IEN),
222–223
InterContinental Exchange (ICE), 103
Interest rate risk, 64
Interfaith Center on Corporate Responsibility
(ICCR), 276–277
Intermediation, 61
Internal rate of return (IRR), 120–121
International Capital Market Association
(ICMA), 143
International Corporate Governance Network
(ICGN), 238

International Forum of Sovereign Wealth
Funds (IFSWF), 229
International Labour Organization Tripartite
Declaration (ILO Tripartite
Declaration), 169
International Organization for Standardization
(ISO), 169
International Red Cross and Red Crescent
Movement, 319–320
International services, 322
International Working Group (IWG), 229
Investability, 206
Investing/investment, 23. *See also* ESG
investing; Faith-based investing
advice fiduciary, 54
banks, 66–71
Global IB Bank revenue, 67f
conservatism, 227–228
decision-making process, 200
in equities, 106–107
exclusions, 274
funds, 11
offerings, 186–188
policy, 231
portfolios, 23
Investment Grade (IG), 129–132
Investment management, 215
Fiduciary duty in, 9
Investment Management Company (IMC),
220
Investor Alliance for Human
Rights, 276–277
Investor Stewardship Group (ISG), 163
Investors, 181, 185
IPO. *See* Initial public offering (IPO)
IRA. *See* Individual Retirement Accounts
(IRA)
IRR. *See* Internal rate of return (IRR)
ISG. *See* Investor Stewardship Group (ISG)
iShares, 189–190
ESG MSCI EAFE ETF, 191
ESG MSCI EM ETF, 191
ESG MSCI USA ETF, 191
ESG MSCI USA Small-Cap ETF, 192
ESG US Aggregate Bond ETF, 192
ESG USD Corporate Bond ETF, 191
Global Clean Energy Index ETF, 190–191
MSCI Global Impact ETF, 193
MSCI Israel ETF, 301
MSCI KLD 400 Social Index ETF, 192
MSCI USA ESG Select ETF, 192
MSCI World Islamic UCITS ETF, 299

iShares Global Green Bond ETF (BGRN), 143
Islamic values indexes, 294—296
Islamic values investing, 291—299
ISO. *See* International Organization for Standardization (ISO)
ISS. *See* Institutional Shareholder Services (ISS)
Ithmar Capital, 246
IUU Fishing. *See* Illegal, Unreported and Unregulated Fishing (IUU Fishing)
IWG. *See* International Working Group (IWG)

J

J.P. Morgan Asset Management (JPMAM), 200—201
Jensen and Meckling theory, 31
Jewish values indexes, 300—302
Jewish values investing, 299—302
Junk bonds, 123—124
JUST Capital, 179, 203—204
JUST US Large Cap Diversified Index (JULCD), 179, 204

K

Keating Five. *See* Five Senators
Knowledge exchange, 223
Kuwait Investment Authority, 243

L

Labor/labour, 175
  issues, 280
  standards/sweatshops, 288
Large-scale solar (LSS), 294
Largest pension funds, 87—90
Leadership, 305—308
Leading Corporate Philanthropy, 270
LGBTQ individuals, 326
LGBTQI, 260
Liability insurance, 79
LIBOR. *See* London InterBank Offered Rate (LIBOR)
Life insurance, 78
Lilly Endowment Inc., 257
Limited liability company (LLC), 19, 250—253
"Limited partners", 94
Linaburg—Maduell Transparency Index, 232
Liquidity gap, 101

Lit pools, 103
LKCM Aquinas Catholic Equity Fund, 291
LLC. *See* Limited liability company (LLC)
London InterBank Offered Rate (LIBOR), 124—126
London Whale scandal, 155—156
LoveTheUnloved Photo Contest, 313
LSS. *See* Large-scale solar (LSS)

M

MakeTime4Makos, 313
Marketing, 280
Markowitz efficient portfolios, 98—99
MASEN. *See* Moroccan Agency for Sustainable Energy (MASEN)
Materiality, 175
Materiality Map, 174
Mayors Challenge, 263
MBS facility. *See* Green Mortgage Backed Securities facility (MBS facility)
Meals on Wheels, 327
Medicaid, 78
Medium Term Note (MTN), 132
MetLife Inc., 84—85
MFO. *See* Multi-Family Office (MFO)
Michael J. Fox Foundation for Parkinson's Research, 309—310
Middle East Sovereign Wealth Funds, 243
Military and veteran families, 321—322
Military weapons, 281
Millennial generation, 1—2, 329
Millennials, 2—3
Milton Friedman theory, 29
Minimum Variance Index, 297
Ministry of Finance, 236—237
Missing Maps project, 322
Mission investing, 22—23, 25—26, 329—330. *See also* Impact investing
Mission Responsibility Through Investment (MRTI), 275—276
Mixed investment, 285—286
Modern Portfolio Theory (MPT), 5, 98—99, 329
Money center banks, 63
Money Market Funds, 127
Money market instruments, 124—127
  bond yields for variety of issues and maturities, 126f
Moral hazard, 60—62
Moral Obligation bonds, 132
Morally Responsible Investing, 289—290

Morgan Stanley Capital International (MSCI), 110–111, 177–178
  ACWI, 111
    Low Carbon Target Index, 188–190
    Sustainable Impact Index, 185–186
    Islamic index series, 296, 296*f*
    Islamic M-Series Indexes, 296, 296*f*
    World Index, 109
    World Islamic Index, 296
Morningstar, 113–114, 180
  Sustainability Rating, 4–5, 180
Moroccan Agency for Sustainable Energy (MASEN), 246
Mortgage-backed security, 70–71
MRTI. *See* Mission Responsibility Through Investment (MRTI)
MSCI. *See* Morgan Stanley Capital International (MSCI)
MTN. *See* Medium Term Note (MTN)
Mubadala Investment Company, 243–244
Multi-Family Office (MFO), 249
Multiinvestor funds, 11
Municipal Bonds, 85
Municipal securities, 132–133
Mutual funds, 76–77, 107–108, 294–296, 300–302
  rate ESG performance of portfolio companies, 180
Mutual savings banks, 65–66

N

NACUBO. *See* National Association of College and University Business Officers (NACUBO)
NASDAQ, 103
  Clean Edge Green Energy Index, 185–186
  Victory US Large Cap Volatility Weighted BRI Index, 282
National Association of College and University Business Officers (NACUBO), 223–224
National Credit Union Administration (NCUA), 64–65
National Investment Bodies (NIBs), 274
Natural gas, 2
Natural resources assessment indicators, 197
NBIM. *See* Norges Bank Investment Management (NBIM)
NCUA. *See* National Credit Union Administration (NCUA)
Negative screening, 180–181, 273–274

Negative screens, 275–276
Network effect, 104, 135
Neutrality, 320
New Covenant Funds, 275–276
New Ventures, 311
New York City Comptroller's Office (NYCCO), 159
New Zealand Superannuation Fund, 241–243
New York Stock Exchange, 36–37
NextMillion2020, 313
NGO. *See* Nongovernmental organizations (NGO)
NIBs. *See* National Investment Bodies (NIBs)
Nigeria Sovereign Investment Authority (NSIA), 246
NoExcuseforSingleUse, 313
Nongovernmental organizations (NGO), 276–277, 303–304
Nonseparable antisocial corporate activities, 33
Norges Bank Investment Management (NBIM), 235–236, 243
Normalization, 176
Northwest Division Center, 326
Norway's Government Pension Fund-Global, 235–238
NSIA. *See* Nigeria Sovereign Investment Authority (NSIA)
NYCCO. *See* New York City Comptroller's Office (NYCCO)

O

OC. *See* Ocean Conservancy (OC)
Ocean Cleanup, 314
Ocean Conservancy (OC), 312
Ocean stewardship, 280
OCIO. *See* Office of Chief Investment Officer (OCIO)
OECD. *See* Organization for Economic Cooperation and Development (OECD)
Office of Chief Investment Officer (OCIO), 214
Office of Thrift Supervision (OTS), 66
"Oil Fund", 235–236
"One share, one vote" investors, 37
Open market operations, 73
Open Society Foundations, 258–260
Operation Twist, 74, 122–123
Operational risk, 64

OPIC. *See* Overseas Private Investment
    Corporation (OPIC)
Organization for Economic Cooperation and
    Development (OECD), 58
OTS. *See* Office of Thrift Supervision (OTS)
Overseas Private Investment Corporation
    (OPIC), 311
Ownership, 234

P

Pacific Investment Management Company
    LLC (PIMCO), 139–140, 194–198
PADI. *See* Professional Association of Diving
    Instructors (PADI)
PARR. *See* PIMCO Analyst Research and
    Recommendations (PARR)
Participation, 305–308
Partnerships, 223
Payments, 61
PBGC. *See* Public Benefit Guarantee
    Corporation (PBGC)
Peer networks, 223
Pension funds, 86–92
Personal injury, 79
PGGM, 245–246
Pharmaceuticals, access to, 288
Philanthropic portfolio, 84
Phoenix Elim House, 326
Physical capital, 90
PIF. *See* Public Investment Fund of Saudi
    Arabia (PIF)
PIMCO. *See* Pacific Investment Management
    Company LLC (PIMCO)
PIMCO Analyst Research and
    Recommendations (PARR), 196
PJSC (Mubadala Investment Company),
    243–244
PND Merdeku financing, 293
Poison pill, 148–149
Political value, 146
Portfolio construction, ESG factors in,
    167–168
Positive screens, 275–276
Positive strategies, 286
Power purchase agreements (PPAs), 294
PPO. *See* Preferred Provider Organization
    (PPO)
PRA. *See* Prudential Regulation Authority
    (PRA)
Preferred Provider Organization (PPO), 79
Preferred stock, 98

Presbyterian Church, 275–276
Present value (PV), 118–120
PRI. *See* Principles for responsible investment
    (PRI)
Primary Credit Rate, 74
Primary dealers, 129
Prime brokerage, 71
Principles for responsible investment (PRI),
    5–6, 158–159, 188, 236
    SDGs, 6–7
Private equity, 94–95
    funds, 19–21, 76–77, 94–95
Professional Association of Diving Instructors
    (PADI), 313
Profit maximization, 31–32
Program expense. *See* Charitable
    commitment
Program support. *See* Charitable commitment
Program trading, 102–103
Project AWARE, 313
PROMESA. *See* Puerto Rico Oversight,
    Management and Economic Stability
    Act (PROMESA)
Proprietary trading, 69
"Protestant Work Ethic", 274
Providing services to foundation community,
    269–271
Proxy, 147
    shareholder voting by, 149–150
Prudent Man rule, 49–51
Prudential Financial Inc., 84
Prudential Regulation Authority (PRA), 5,
    45–46
Public Benefit Guarantee Corporation
    (PBGC), 86
Public Investment Fund, 235–236
Public Investment Fund of Kingdom of Saudi
    Arabia, 243
Public Investment Fund of Saudi Arabia
    (PIF), 244–245
Puerto Rico Oversight, Management and
    Economic Stability Act
    (PROMESA), 132–133
PV. *See* Present value (PV)

Q

Qatar Investment Authority, 243
QE. *See* Quantitative Easing (QE)
Quality issues in ESG reporting, 175–176
Quality score, 203
Quantitative Easing (QE), 74–75

R

Racial discrimination, 287–288
Random walk, 101
Red Crescent Societies, 319–322
Red Cross, 303–304, 319–322
Reform Pension Board (RPB), 299–300
Regional banks, 63
Regulation, 105–106
Reinsurance, 80
Religious values investing. *See* Faith-based
    investing
RepRisk, 200–201
    ESG Business Intelligence, 178
Request For Quote systems (RFQ systems),
    133–134
"Required reserves", 74
Reserve investment funds, 229
Reserve requirements, 73–74
Resolution Trust Corporation (RTC), 65–66
Responsible investing, 24
Return, 98–100
Revenue Backed bonds, 132
Revenue-generating activities, 63
Reverse repo, 126
RFQ systems. *See* Request For Quote systems
    (RFQ systems)
Rise Fund, 18–21, 25
Risk, 98–100
    arbitrage, 68
    of banks, 63–64
    management framework, 232
Robert Wood Johnson Foundation, 260–261
Robert Wood Johnson II, 260
Robo-advisors, 106, 115–116, 188, 201–203,
    333
Rockefeller Foundation, 261–262
Rolling over, 126
RPB. *See* Reform Pension Board (RPB)
RTC. *See* Resolution Trust Corporation (RTC)
Rule of 72, 119–120

S

S&Ls. *See* Savings and loan associations
    (S&Ls)
S&P 500 Shariah Index, 295
S&P Global 1200 Shariah, 295
S&P Global Clean Energy Index, 185–186
S&P Global Healthcare Shariah Index, 296
S&P Global Infrastructure Shariah, 296
S&P/Harel Communications Index, 301
S&P/Harel Consumer Goods Index, 301

S&P/Harel Energy Index, 301
S&P/Harel Health Care Index, 301
S&P/Harel Materials Index, 301
Salmon Farm Research, 314
Salvation Army, 303–304, 322–327
SAMA. *See* Saudi Arabian Monetary
    Authority (SAMA)
Sanctity of life, 280
Sanitation and Water for All (SWA), 311
Santiago Principles, 229–232, 240–241
SASB. *See* Sustainability Accounting
    Standards Board (SASB)
Saturna Capital, 297–298
Saudi Arabian Monetary Authority (SAMA),
    243
Savings and loan associations (S&Ls), 65–66
Savings funds, 229
SBA. *See* Florida State Board of
    Administration (SBA)
Schools, ESG investing in, 221
Screening, 275–276
SDGs. *See* Sustainable development goals
    (SDGs)
Sea Shepherd Conservation Society (SSCS),
    313–315
Sea Turtles, 314
Securities and Exchange Commission (SEC),
    38–39, 69, 105, 149
Securitization, 70
Security, 61
Services providing assessment of corporate
    ESG, 177–179
Sex industry, 280
SFO. *See* Single-Family Office (SFO)
Shadow banking, 76–78
Shareholder engagement, 10, 156–161
    Blackrock, 156–157
    CalPERS, 157–158
    institutional investors, 161–165
    investors and companies, 146–150
    ISG, 163–164
    key corporate governance, 150–152
    NYCCO, 159
    SASB, 165
    30% Club, 164–165
    TRP, 158–159
    vanguard, 159–161
Shareholders, 29–30
    activism, 147–149
    advocacy, 275–276
    profit maximization, 34
    proposals, 152–156

responsibility, 284
rights, 36–39
value, 34–35
voting
  by proxy, 149–150
  trends, 150–152
welfare maximization, 32–34
Shariah compliant ETFs, 299
Shariah laws, 291–293
Shariah screening process, 294
Shariah-compliant indexes, 295–296
Sharpe Ratio, 208
Short-term share price, 34–35
SILT. *See* Sustainable Investment Leadership
  Team (SILT)
Sin stocks, 15–18, 89, 94
Sinar Kamiri, 294
Singapore Stewardship Principles, 198
Single-Family Office (SFO), 249
Sinovac Biotech, 148–149
"Smart Beta" service, 115–116
Snapped up, 97–98
Social bonds, 141
Social inclusion, policy, and budgeting, 317
Social investing, 89
Social media, 2–3
Social responsibility, 32
  of business, 29–32
Social returns, 25–26, 26f
Social Standards categories, 170
Socially responsible investment (SRI), 14, 48,
  89, 116, 185, 212
Socially responsible investment guidelines,
  284–291
Socially responsible mutual funds, 168
South Africa, divestment in, 14–15
Sovereign debt, 133
Sovereign wealth fund (SWF), 227–228
  activities, 245–246
  CIC, 240–241
  ESG investing by, 232–235
  FRR, 238–239
  Future Fund, 242–243
  Linaburg–Maduell Transparency Index,
    232
  Middle East Sovereign Wealth Funds, 243
  Mubadala Investment Company, 243–244
  New Zealand Superannuation Fund,
    241–242
  Norway's Government Pension Fund-
    Global, 235–238

PIF, 244–245
policy, 235–246
Temasek Holdings Private Limited,
  239–240
transparency issues and concerns, 229–232
Speculation, 69
SREP. *See* Supervisory Review and
  Evaluation Process (SREP)
SRI. *See* Socially responsible investment
  (SRI); Sustainable and responsible
  investment (SRI)
SSCS. *See* Sea Shepherd Conservation
  Society (SSCS)
Stabilization funds, 228, 246
Statistical sampling techniques, 193–194
Stem Cells, 280
Stewardship, 274
Stock exchanges, 37
Stout theory, 34
Subprime mortgage, 70–71
Sukuk, 292–293
Sukuk Al-Ijara, 292–293
Sullivan Principles, 14–15
Sunset provisions, 39
Superregional banks, 63
Supervisory Review and Evaluation Process
  (SREP), 3
SuSanA. *See* Sustainable Sanitation Alliance
  (SuSanA)
Sustainability Accounting Standards Board
  (SASB), 163, 165, 169, 173–174
Sustainable and responsible investment (SRI),
  8, 201–203, 293
Sustainable bonds, 141
Sustainable development, 214
Sustainable development goals
  (SDGs), 6–7, 25
Sustainable Impact Index, 186
Sustainable investing/investment, 182, 331
  choices, 188–193
Sustainable Investment Leadership Team
  (SILT), 200
Sustainable Investment Policy, 218–219
Sustainable Sanitation Alliance (SuSanA), 311
Sustainalytics, 177
SWA. *See* Sanitation and Water for All
  (SWA)
SWF. *See* Sovereign wealth fund (SWF)
Swimming, 321
Symbolic-speech-through-divestment, 221
Symbolism, 221

T

T. Rowe Price (TRP), 152, 158–159
Tadau Energy Sdn. Bhd, 293
"Taper tantrum", 74
"Taper" program, 74
Technology, 2
Temasek Holdings Private Limited, 239–240
Tenaga Nasional Bhd (TNB), 294
Term structure, 122–124
Theme-Based/Impact Investing, 200
Theories of firm, 7–9, 31
    analysis of securities, 39*t*
    maximize shareholder welfare, 32–34
    maximizing welfare, 34–36
    shareholder rights, 36–39
    social responsibility of business, 29–32
30% Club, 164–165
"Thrifts", 65–66
Timothy Plan Funds, 281–282
TIPS. *See* Treasury Inflation Protected
        Securities (TIPS)
TNB. *See* Tenaga Nasional Bhd (TNB)
Tobacco, 280
    smoking, 17
Trade Reporting and Compliance Engine
        (TRACE), 129–132
Trading and research, 68–70
Trading risk, 64
Traditional governance issues, 161
Transparency issues and concerns, 229–232
Treasury Bills, 122
Treasury Inflation Protected Securities (TIPS),
        129
Treasury Notes, 122
TRP. *See* T. Rowe Price (TRP)
2-degree Celsius (2DS), 152

U

UC. *See* University of California (UC)
UiTM Solar, 294
UN PRI. *See* United Nations Principles for
        Responsible Investing (UN PRI)
Unconventional monetary policy, 74–75
UNEP FI. *See* United Nations Environment
        Programme Finance Institute (UNEP
        FI)
UNESCO. *See* United Nations Educational,
        Scientific and Cultural Organization
        (UNESCO)
UNGC. *See* United Nations Global Compact
        (UNGC)

UNGP. *See* United Nations Guiding Principles
        (UNGP)
UNICEF, 315–317
Uniform Prudent Investor Act (UPIA), 51–53
Uniform Prudent Management of Institutional
        Funds Act (UPMIFA), 53–54
United Nations Educational, Scientific and
        Cultural Organization (UNESCO),
        317–319
United Nations Environment Programme
        Finance Institute (UNEP FI), 54–55
United Nations Global Compact (UNGC),
        169, 174–175
United Nations Guiding Principles (UNGP),
        175
United Nations Principles for Responsible
        Investing (UN PRI), 23–24, 57–58
United Nations Refugee Agency, 308–309
United Nations sustainable development
        goals, 25
United States (US)
    Large Cap Core ETF, 282
    for UNHCR, 308–309
    US Treasury securities, 127–129
United States Conference of Catholic Bishops
        (USCCB), 284–285
    investment policies, 287–289
Unity, 320
Universality, 320
University of California (UC), 214–215
UPIA. *See* Uniform Prudent Investor Act
        (UPIA)
UPMIFA. *See* Uniform Prudent Management
        of Institutional Funds Act (UPMIFA)
Upper-medium grade, 123–124
Uranium, 280–281
USCCB. *See* United States Conference of
        Catholic Bishops (USCCB)
USSIF. *See* Forum for Sustainable and
        Responsible Investment (USSIF)

V

Value
    chains, 3
    investors, 180–181
    value-destroying reputational risk, 24
Values/Norms-Based Screen, 200
VanEck Vectors Green Bond Fund (GRNB),
        143
Vanguard, 159–161
Vaquita Porpoise, 314

Venture capital, 94–95
Violent entertainment, 281
Virtu Electronic Trading, 103–104
Virtu Matchit, 103–104
Volker Rule, 67–69
Voluntary service, 320

W

Waste stewardship, 281
Water.org, 303–304, 310–312
WaterCredit, 311
WaterEquity, 311
Wealth Tech, 115
Wealthfront, 115–116
Weapons, 281
  production and sale of, 288
Welfare maximization, 34–36

Wildfire relief, 321
Winter storm relief, 321
Women's Sports Foundation, 305–307
World Alternative Energy Index, 185–186
Written consent, 154–155

Y

Yale University, ESG in, 212–214
Yale's Investments, 212
Yield curve, 122–124
Yield to Maturity (YTM), 121
YieldWise Food Loss, 261

Z

Zurich Insurance Group, 85–86

Printed in the United States
By Bookmasters